GPS explanation
User information for determining location via GPS:
- Please set your GPS receiver to "WGS 84" and "UTM"
- The purple grid (each section represents 15,000 m) is used for GPS navigation

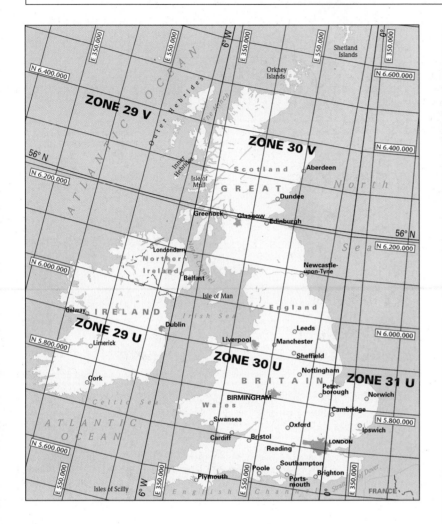

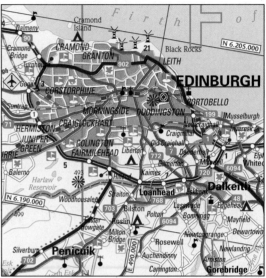

The cartography indicated in this car atlas by the colour red is represented in a scale of 1:300,000.

In this scale a span of 1 mm on the map is equivalent to 300 metres in nature.

Certain important map features, such as roads, must be featured more prominently, with the result that they are represented much wider than they are in actuality.

For example, a road that is 2 mm wide on the map is not 600 metres wide, but approximately 6 metres wide.

GPS stands for the "Global Positioning System". This system makes it possible to precisely determine your location by means of a GPS receiver that receives and interprets a number of satellite signals.

The UTM (Universal Transverse Mercator map projection) network, which is printed on the map in purple, divides the surface of the earth between 84°N and 80°S latitude into 60 zones of 6 degrees each.

Great Britain and Ireland lie in the squares 29U, 29V / 30U, 30V and 31U within the zones 29, 30 and 31.

For precise orientation within the UTM network, you will find coordinate boxes at the left, right, top and bottom margins of each map. These boxes contain coordinates called an easting (how far to the right within a zone) or a northing (how far upwards).

In addition to the familiar green grid that allows you to find places, you will also see the purple UTM grid, which is an internationally standardised system used in GPS navigation.

Page overview Great Britain, Ireland 1:301,000

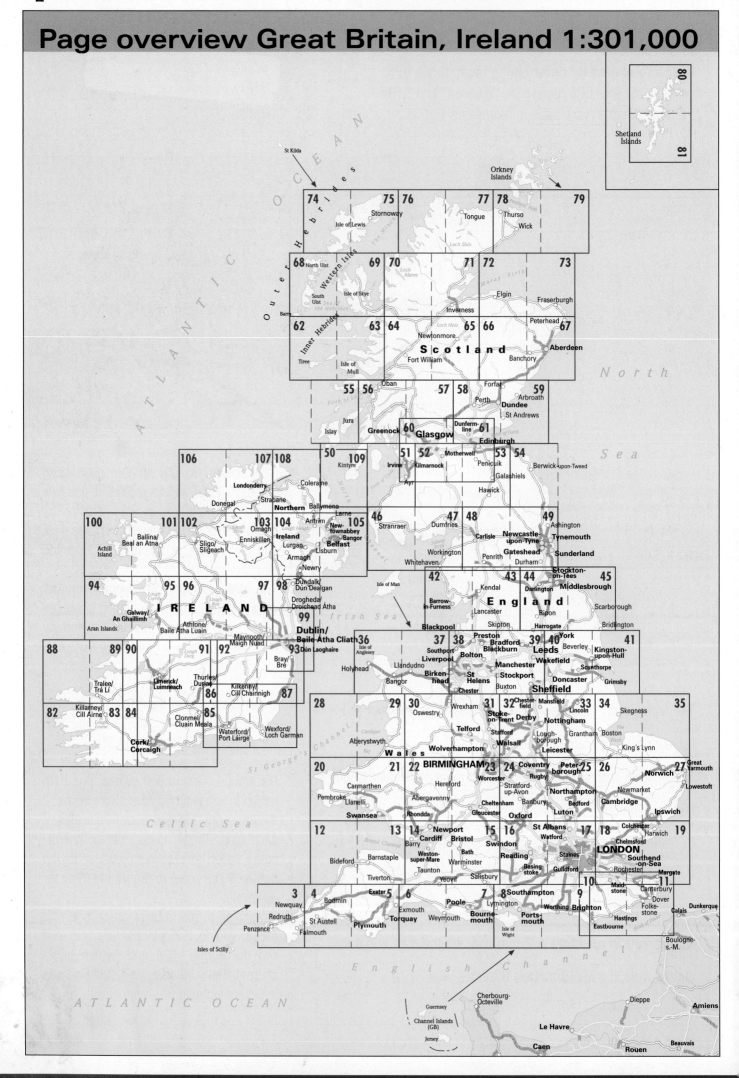

Isles of Scilly

Round Island · St Helen · Tean · White Island
King Charles' Castle · New Grimsby · St Martins
Cromwell's Castle · Bryher · Higher Town
Abbey Gardens · The Town · Tresco
Samson · Bant's Carn · Eastern Isles
Hugh Town · Maypole
Star Castle · Porth Hellick
St Mary's · Old Town
Bishop Rock · Annet · St Agnes · Gugh
Western Rocks · St Agnes

North West Passage · Broad Sound · St Mary's Sound · The Road · Crow Sound · Smith Sound

N 5.530.000 · N 5.590.000 · N 5.560.000 · N 5.530.000
E 295.000 · E 685.000 · E 700.000 · E 325.000 · E 355.000

ATLANTIC OCEAN

A · B · C · D · E · F · G · H · K · L · M

	≋	☀
V	11°	15°
VII	15°	17°
VIII	16°	19°
IX	15°	17°
X	15°	14°

Trevose Quies
Constantine
Porthcothan · Porthe
Park Head
Bedruthan Steps
Mawgan Porth
Trevarrian
Watergate Bay · Tregurrian
Towan Head · Fistral Bay · Newquay Bay · St Co Minor
Kelsey Head · Holywell Bay · Newquay
Pentire · West Pentire · Crantock
Holywell · Quir Dow
Penhale Point · Tresean
Ligger or Perran Bay · Cubert · Trencr
Bawden Rocks or Man & his man · Rejerrah · St Newlyn East · 305
Perranporth · Mount Rose · 3075 · 30
Goonhavern
St Agnes Head · Trevellas · Bolingey · Perranzabuloe · Carland Cross
St Agnes · Mithian · Penhallow · Zelah
Callestick · St Allen · Truthan · Trispen
Porthtowan · Goonbell · St Erme
Mount Hawke · Shortlanes-end · 6
Blackwater · Scorrier · Threemilestone · Truro · Tresillian
Portreath · Mawla · 30 · Chacewater · Merther
Crane Islands · 390 · Kenwyn · Merther
Navax Point · Illogan · Mount Ambrose · St Day · Baldhu · Malpas · Penkevil
Godrevy Island · Portreath · Camborne · Redruth · Carn Brea Village · Twelveheads · Kea · St Clement · Lamorr
Gwithian · Kehelland · Pool · 3047 · Carharrack · Bissoe · Old Kea · Coombe
St Ives Bay · Basewaythy · Carn Brea · Lanner · Gwennap · Carnon Downs · Peneleweey · Philleigh
The Carracks · Connor Downs · 9 · 393 · Frogpool · Perranwell · Penpol · Trelissick Gardens · Trewithian
Gurnard's Head · Trendrine Hill · St Ives · Angarrack · Barripper · Carnhell Green · Praze-an-Beeble · Penhalu-rick · Perranarworthal · Ponsa-nooth · Devoran · Carclew · Mylor Harcourt · Bridge · St Just in Roseland
Boswednack · Zennor · 587 · Helsetown · 3074 · Carbis Bay · Longstone · Phillack · Realwa · Four Lanes · Hendra · Stithians · Mabe · Trelew · Mylor Churchtown
Pendeen Watch · Porthmeor · Towednack · Cripplesease · Lelant · Gwinear · Leedstown · Wendron · Burras · Rame · Longdowns · Burnthouse · Penryn
Lower Boscaswell · Morvah · Men-An-Tol · Georgia · Nancledra · St Erth · Realwa · Crowan Moors · Halvosso · Trevarra · Budock Water · Penjerrick · Flushing
Trevellard · Higher Bojewyan · Boskednan · Chysauster · Canon's Town · St Erth Praze · Godolphin House · Trescowe · Nancegollan · Trenear · Seworgan · Penjerrick Gardens · Falmouth
Botallack · Carnyorth · Chun Castle · Great Bosullow Quoit · New Mill · Ludgvan · Crowlas · St Hilary · Goldsithney · Higher Downs · Crowntown · Constantine · Penjerrick · Pendennis
Cape Cornwall · Tregeseal · Lanyon Quoit · Trengwainton Gardens · Madron · Gulval · Marazion · Perran Downs · Rinsey · Germoe · Wendron · Mawnan Smith · Glendurgan · Pendennis Point · Bohortha
The Brisons · St Just · Bosavern · Newbridge · Carn Euny · Tremethick Cross · Chyandour · Penzance · St Michael's Mount · Perranuthnoe · Rosudgeon · Sithney · Gweek · Porth Navas · Zone Point
Ballowall Barrow · Brumbla · Sancreed · Heamoor · Goldsithney · Praa Sands · Ashton · Breage · Helston · Mawnan · Rosemullion Head
Witesand Bay · Ancient Village · Brane · Tredavoe · Newlyn · Paul · Mousehole · Cudden Point · Trewavas Head · Flambards · Helford Passage · Mawnan
Carn Towan · Croes-an-wra · Drift · Kerris · St Clement's Isle · Walloe · Porthleven · Gweek · Helford River · Helford · Flushing · St Anthony
Sennen Cove · Maen Castle · 30 · Sennen · St Buryan · Lamorna · Trewavas Head · 18 · Manaccan · St Martin · Nare Point
Longships · Land's End · Trethewey · Porthcurno · Treen · Tregiffian · Cribba Head · Mount's Bay · Mawgan · Berepper · Garras · Trelowarren · Newtown-in-St Martin · Tregidden · Gillan · Porthallow
Gwennap Head · St Levan · Logan Rock · Castallack · Gunwalloe Fishing Cove · Gunwalloe Chyanvounder · Halligaye · Cross Lanes · Traboe · St Keverne · Porthoustock
Runnel Stone · Poldhu Point · Cury · Goonhilly Downs · Trelan · Penhallick · Manacle Point · The Manacles
Isles of Scilly 2¾ hrs (Apr.–Nov.) · Mullion Cove · Mullion · 3083 · Gwenter · Ponsongath · Black Head · Coverack
Vellan Head · Mullion Island · Predannack Wollas · Ruan Major · Kuggar · Ruan Minor · Cadgwith
Kynance Cove · Church Cove · Lizard Hot Point
Lizard Point · The Lizard

	≈≈≈	☀
V	12°	15°
VII	15°	17°
VIII	15°	19°
IX	14°	17°
X	14°	14°

	〰	☀
V	12°	11°
VII	14°	14°
VIII	16°	16°
IX	17°	13°
X	16°	11°

	≈≈≈	☀
V	12°	13°
VII	14°	16°
VIII	16°	18°
IX	17°	16°
X	15°	12°

Alderney
(Aurigny)

A

B

C

Penrhyn Colom

Penrhyn Mawr

Pen-y

Llangw

Ty-hen

Porth Oer

Methlem Rhyo

Whistling Sands Capel Carmel

Braich Anelog

Castell Odo Aberdaron

Uwchmyndd

Braich y Pwll

Bodermid

Pen y Cil

Ynys Gwy fawr

■ **St Mary's Abbey**

Bardsey Island / Ynys Enlli

Bardsey Sound

E 355.000

E 385.000

N 5.830.000

D

E

F

N 5.800.000

G

H

J

K

L

M

E 355.000

E 385.000

1:301,000 · 1cm ≙ 3 km

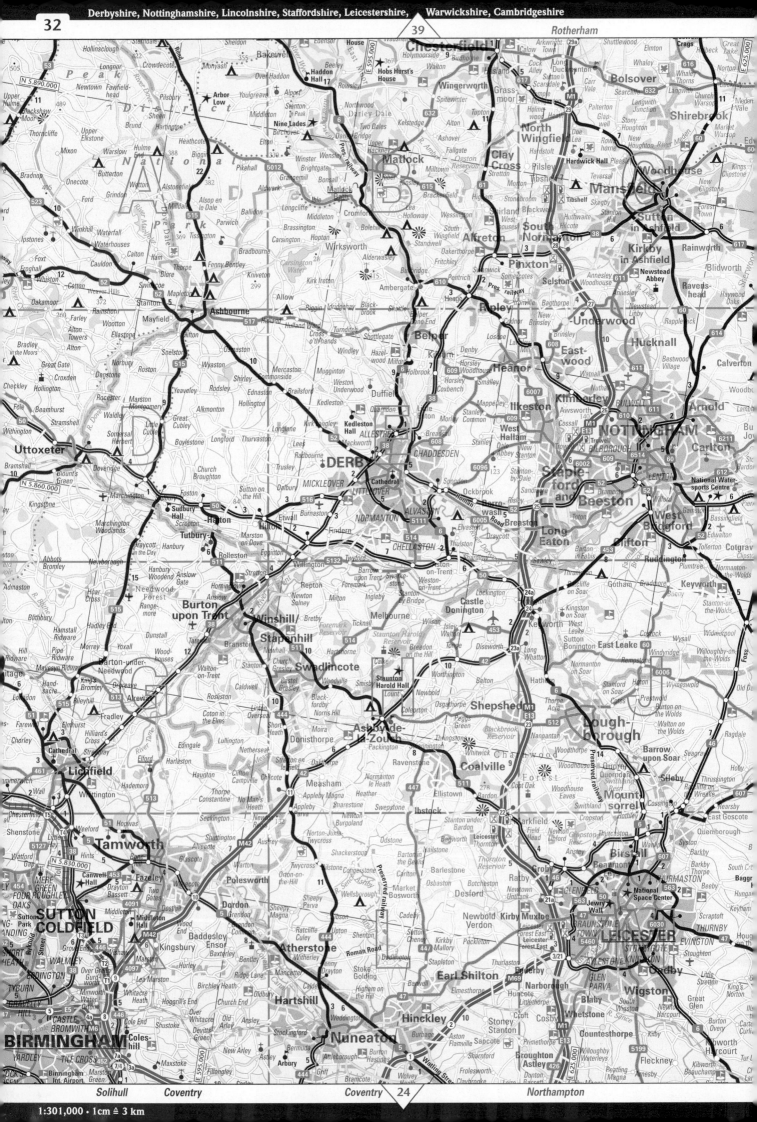

0 ____ 5 km

A | B | C

	≈≈	☀
V	10°	11°
VII	14°	15°
VIII	15°	16°
IX	14°	13°
X	14°	10°

I r i s h   S e a

N 5.920.000

The Skerries
West Mouse

Dublin 1¾ hrs/3 hrs, Dun Laoghaire 1¾ hrs
Carmel Head

D

E

F

Holyhead Bay

Church Bay

Cemlyn Cemaes Bay
Llanbadrig
Porthllechog
Bull Bay

Llanfairynghornwy
Tregele
Cemaes
Amlwch Port
Point Lynas
Pengorffwysfa

Llanfechell
Burwen
Amlwch

Rhydwyn
Mynydd Mechell
Bodewryd
Penysarn
Gadfa
Ynys Dulas

North Stack
Holyhead Mountain
Salt Island

Llanfachraeth
Llanfaethlu
Llanddeusant
Rhosbol
City Dulas
Ancient Monuments

South Stack
St Cybi
Holyhead/ Caergybi
Penrhos

Elim
Ceidio
Capel Parc
Brynrefail
Moelfre

Penrhyn Mawr
Trearddur
Newlands Park
Valley/ Valle
Caergeiliog
Llanfigael
Llantrisant
Llanerchymedd
Llandyfrydog
Mynydd Bodafon
Llanallgo

Holy Islands/ Ynys Gybi
Four Mile Bridge
Bodedern
Trefor
Carmel
Maenaddwyn
Marian-glas
Brynteg
Tynygongl
Benllech

Rhoscolyn
Bodior
Llanfairyn Nhowyn
Bryngwran
Gwalchmai
Ceint Reservoir
Llangwyllog
Rhosmeirch
Llanbedrgoch
Red Wharf Bay
Red Wharf Bay
Puffin Island

Rhoscolyn
Llanfair-neubwll
Cymyran Bay
Tywyn Trewan
Capel Gwyn
Heneglwys
Bodffordd
Llanddyfnan
Pentraeth
Llanddona
Llangoed
Penmon

Rhosneigr
Llanfaelog
Dothan
Cerrigceinwen
Mona
Llangristiolus
Penmynydd
Pen-y-garnedd
Llansadwrn
Llanfaes
Beaumaris
Beau-maris
Penmaen

4080
Bryn Du
Sir
Burial Chamber
Bethel
Pentre Berw
Gaerwen
Llanfair Pwllgwyngyll
Llandegfan
Lavan Sands/ Treath Lafan

N 5.890.000
St Cwyfan
Aberffraw
Llangadwaladr
Hermon
Trefdraeth
Môn
Llanddaniel Fab
Menai Bridge
Bangor
Llanfairf

Bodorgan
Malltraeth
Llangaffo
Castell Bryn-Gwyn
Caer Leb
Brynsiencyn
Vaynol Hall
Y Felinheli
545
Penrhyn Castle

Malltraeth Sands
Niwbwrch
Dwyran
Seion
Bethel
Llanddeiniolen
Cath
Llandegai
Abergwyngregyn

Llanddwyn Island
Malltraeth Bay
Newborough Warren
Llanfair-is-gaer
Pentir
Tregarth
Rachub
Bethesda
Drosgl

Abermenai Point
The Bar
Roman Fort
Caernarfon
Dinas Dinorwig
Penisa'r Waun
Mynydd Llandegai
Carnedd
Snowd

Llanfaglan
St Mary's Church Bontnewydd
Bryn Bras Castle
Cwm-y-glo
Clwt-y-bont
Dinorwig
Carnedd Dafydd

Caernarfon Bay (Bae Caernarfon)
Dinas
Llanwnda
Waunfawr
Llanberis
Moel Eilio
Nant Peris
Carnedd Llewelyn
Pen Ll

Dinas Dinlle
Llandwrog
Rhostryfan
Rhosgadfan
Penffridd
Moel Tryfan
Betws Garmon
Glyder Fawr
Glyder Fach

Trwyn Maen Dylan
Groeslon
Carmel
Mynydd Mawr
Llyn Cwellyn
Snowdon Yr Wyddfa
Yr Wyddfa
Carnedd Moel-siab

Clynnog-fawr
Pontllyfni
Penygroes
Talysarn
Nantlle
Pass of Llanberis
Carnedd y Cribau

Capel Uchaf
Nasareth
Nebo
Rhyd-Ddu
Yr Aran
Plas Gwynant
Beddgelert

Trwyn y Gorlech
Yr Eifl
Tai'n Lôn
National

Carreg Ddu
Trefor
Bwlch Mawr
Clynnog
Garneddgoch
Dinas Emrys
Moel Penamne

Porth Dinllaen
Tre'r Ceiri
Llanaelhaearn
Bwlch derwin
Caerau
Pant Glâs
Bryncir
Pass of Aberglaslyn
Pont Aberglaslyn
Nantmor
Cnicht
Rhiwbryfdir
Llechv Slate

Morfa Nefyn
Nefyn
Pistyll
Fron
Pen-sarn
Garndolbenmaen
Moel Hebog
Croesor
Tanygrisiau

Groesffordd
Edern
Garn Boduan
Llithfaen
Cenin
Dolbenmaen
Moel-ddu
Penmorfa
Plas Brondanw
Blaenau Ffestiniog

Porth Ysglaig
Rhos-y-llan
Llandudwen
Carn Pentyrch
Llangybi
Llannor
Rhoslan
Golan
Prenteg
Garreg
Rhyd
Coed Cymru

Tudweiliog
Dinas
Boduan
Llëyn Peninsula/ Penrhyn Llŷn
Rhosfawr
Y Ffôr
Llanarmon
Penarth Fawr
Gell
Tremadog

1:301,000 · 1cm ≙ 3 km

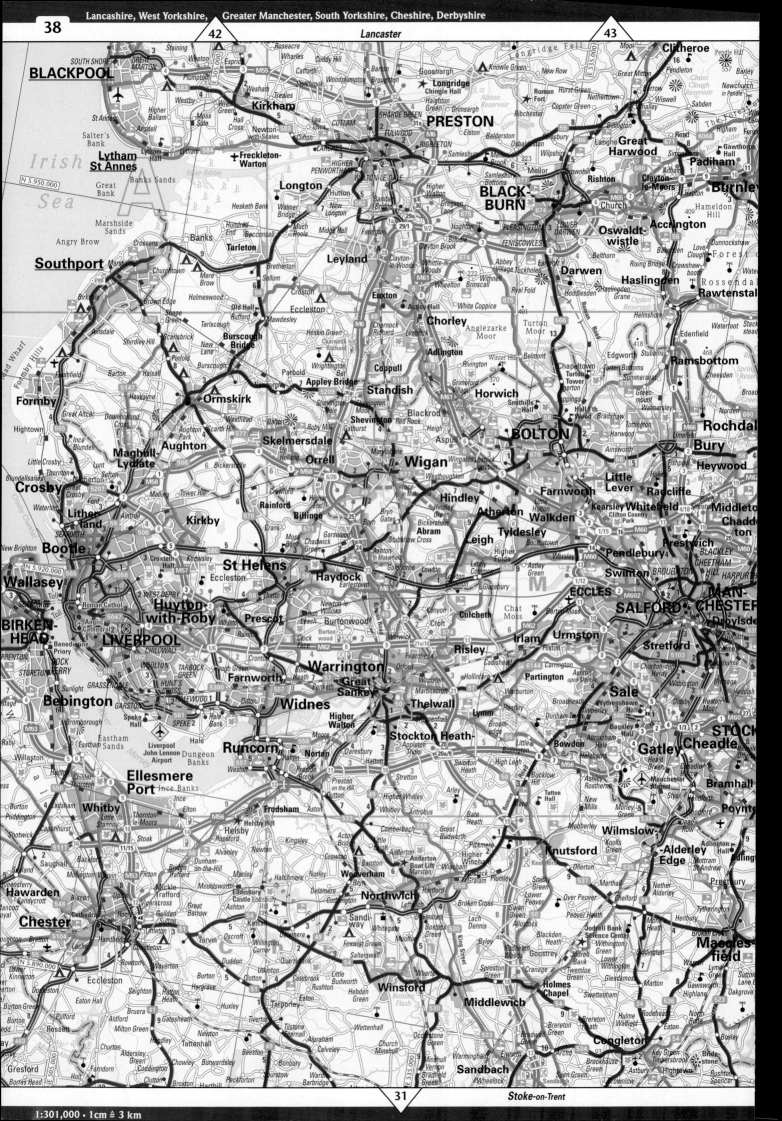

	≈≈	☀
V	10°	10°
VII	15°	15°
VIII	16°	15°
IX	15°	13°
X	15°	9°

N 6.010.000

N 5.980.000

Irish Sea

Douglas 2 hrs (Summer only) / 3 1/2 hrs

Egremont
Coulderton
Middletown
Thornhill
Netherton
Braystones
Berkermet
Calder Bridge
Ponsonby
Gosforth
Seascale
Nether Wasdale
Santon Bridge
Holmrook
Gubbergill
Drigg
Beckfoot
Preserved railway
Kokoarrah
Ravenglass
Muncaster Castle
Waberthwaite
Lane End
Hycemoor
Bootle
Annaside
Whitbeck
Silecroft
Whicham
Kirksanton
Millom
Haverigg

Cumbrian Mountains
Copeland Forest
Seatallan
Wasdale Head
Lingmell
Sca Fell
Scafell Pike
Burnmoor Tarn
Boot
Eskdale Green
Birker Fell
Stanley Force
Birker Force
Devoke Water
Woodend
Broad Oak
Dunnerdale
Ulpha Fell
Ulpha
Whitfell
Corney
Corney Fell
Prior Park
Stoneside Hill
Bootle Fell
Duddon Bridge
Swinside Fell
Broughton in Furness
Hallthwaite
Foxfield
The Green
The Hill

Pillar
Black Sail Pass
Great Gable
Great End
Stake Pass
Bow Fell
Langdale
Hardknott Pass
Wrynose Pass
Cockley Beck
Harter Fell
Furness Fells
The old man of coniston
Coniston
Torver
Broughton Mills
Hoses
Sunny Bank
Woodland Fell
Water Yeat
Blawith
Oxen Park
Rusland
Grizebeck
Lowick
Gawthwaite
Broughton Beck
Colton
Spark Bridge
Penny Bridge
Greenodd
Arrad Foot
Mansriggs

Honister Pass
Seathwaite
Glaramara
Dunmail Raise
High White Stones
Dungeon Ghyll Force
Grasmere
Chapel Stile
Elterwater Little Langdale
Clappersgate
Ambleside
Waterhead
Skelwith Bridge
Brockhole National Park
Troutbeck
Wray Castle
Outgate
Hawkshead
High Wray
Troutbeck Bridge
Grizedale
Satterthwaite
Grizedale Forest
Force Forge
Thwaite Head
Stott Park Bobbin Mill
Finsthwaite
Lakeside
Newby Bridge
Backbarrow

Powder Stone
Seatoller
Rosthwaite
Stonethwaite
Helvellyn
Patterdale
Bridgend
Hartsop
Seat Sandal
Rydale Fell
Kirkstone Pass
Windermere
Bowness-on-Windermere
Ferry
Storrs
Bowland Bridge
Crosthwaite
Winster
Mitchelland
Withers-lack
Mill Side
High Newton
Town End
Field Broughton
Lindale
Meathop
Holker
Flookburgh
Cark
Grange-Over-Sands
Kents Bank
Allithwaite
Arnside
Silverdale
Warton Sands
Carnforth
Bolton-le-Sands

Ulverston
Canal Foot
Swarthmoor
Pennington
Dalton-in-Furness
Newton
Stainton with Adgarley
Bow Bridge
Gleaston
Dendron
Leece
Newbiggin
Roosebeck
Rampside
Roa Island
Piel Island
Foulney Island
Piel Castle
Great Urswick
Urswick
Scales
Bardsea
Baycliff
Aldingham
Ravenstown

Furness Abbey
North Scale
Vickerstown
Barrow-in-Furness
Tummer Hill Scar
Biggar
Sheep Island
South End
Walney Island
Piel Bar

Humphrey Head Point
Morecambe
Cartmel Wharf
Morecambe Bay
Mort Bank
Yeoman Wharf
Lancaster Sound
Heysham Lake
Shoulder of Lune
Galson
Sunderland Point
Lower Thurnham
River Lune
Cockersand Abbey
Bernard Wharf
North Wharf
Pilling Lane
Knott End-on-Sea
Preesall
Rossall Point
Fleetwood
Thornton-Cleveleys
Bispham
Carleton
North Shore
Normoss
Blackpool Tower
BLACKPOOL
South Shore

Morecambe
Heysham
Heaton
St. Mary's
Lanca
Middleton
Stodday
Overton
Conder Green
Galgate
Thurnham
Lancaster
Cockerham
Forton
Braides
Scorton
Winmarleigh
Garstang
Nateby
Bowgreave
Calder Vale
Curchtown
Catterall
Claughton
Bilsborrow
Myerscough
Inskip
Roseacre
Great Eccleston
Little Eccleston
St Michael's on Wyre
Elswick
Wharles
Cuddy Hill
Catforth
Weeton
Esprick
Great Marton
Singleton
Staining
Hardhorn
Poulton-Le-Fylde
Out Rawcliffe
Whin Lane End
Ratten Row
Hambleton
Stalmine
Staynall
Stake Pool
Pilling

N 6.070.000

N O R T H

	≈≈	☀
V	10°	17°
VII	15°	20°
VIII	16°	21°
IX	15°	18°
X	14°	13°

S E A

N 6.040.000

N 6.010.000

Major place names: Brotton, Loftus, Easington, Whitby, Scalby, Scarborough, Eastfield, Filey, Malton, Norton-on-Derwent, Pickering, Bridlington, Flamborough Head

Brotton
Skinningrove
Loftus
Boulby
Easington
Staithes
Port Mulgrave
Hinderwell
Runswick Bay
Roxby
Borrowby
Kettleness
Ellerby
Goldsborough
Scaling
Mickleby
Lythe
West Barny
Sandsend
Roxby High Moor
Lealholm
Dunsley
Newholm
Whitby
Saltwick Bay
Aislaby
Sleights
Ruswarp
Stainsacre
Egton
Sheaton
Hawsker
Glaisdale
Egton Brigge
Ugglebarnby
Grosmont
High Bride Stones
Sneatonthorpe
Ness Point or North Cheek
Littlebeck
Raw
Beck Hole
Mallyn Spout
Goathland
Fylingthorpe
Robin Hood's Bay
Old Peak or South Cheek
Wheeldale Moor
Ravenscar
Goathland Moor
Fylingdales Moor
Staintondale
Burn Howe Rigg
Harwood Dale
Cloughton Newlands
Keldy Castle
Stape
Cloughton
Cloughton Wyke
Levisham
Bridestones
Broxa
Silpho
Burniston
CromerPoint
Newton-on-Rawcliff
Lockton
Stain Dale
Langdale End
Suffield
Hackness
Scalby Mills
Scalby
Scalby Ness Rock's
Everley
Pickering
Thornton-le-Dale
Ebberston Hall
Ayton
Black Rock's
Scarborough
Osgodby
Sawdon
Hutton Buscel
Gallows Hall
Irton
Eastfield
Cayton Bay
Snainton
Wykeham
Seamer
Allerston
Brompton
Cayton
The Wyke
Yedingham
Lebberston
Willerby
Flixton
Folkton
Gristhorpe
Low Marishes
East Knapton
East Heslerton
Ganton
Staxton
Muston
Filey
Scampston
West Knapton
West Heslerton
Sherburn
Filey Bay
Rillington
Thorpe Bassett
Wintringham
Fordon
Hunmanby
Place Newton
Foxholes
Wold Newton
Reighton Sands
Settrington
Burton Fleming
Reighton
Speeton
Helperthorpe
Weaverthorpe
Willy House
Crab Rocks
West Lutton
East Lutton
Thwing
Grindale
Bempton
Duggleby
Kirby Grindalythe
Langtoft
Dane's Dyke
Wharram le Street
Rudston
Boynton
Flamborough Head
Wharram Percy Village
Sledmere
St Mary
Flamborough
Sledmere House
Dane's Graves
Burton Agnes Hall
Sewerby
Kilham
Thornholme
Bridlington
Fimber
Wetwang
Garton-on-the-Wolds
Ruston Parva
Burton Agnes
Harpham
Hilderthorpe
Bridlington Bay
Fraisthorpe

0 ——— 5 km

NORTH

NORTH SEA

Bergen 27 hrs, Stavanger 20 ¾ hrs, Haugesund 23 hrs

Amsterdam 15 hrs

N 6.130.000

N 6.100.000

N 6.070.000

E 565.000

E 595.000

Amble · Coquet Island

Newbiggin-by-the-Sea

Ashington

HIRST

Morpeth

Guide Post

Bedlington

Blyth

COWPEN

NEWSHAM

Cramlington

Ponteland

Wide Open

Dudley

Seaton Delaval

St Mary's or Bait Island

Whitley Bay

Cullercoats

Longbenton

Tynemouth

Hexham

Corbridge

Newburn

Ryton

Prudhoe

Blaydon

NEWCASTLE UPON-TYNE

GOSFORTH

JESMOND

BLAKELAW

Wallsend

NORTH SHIELDS

South Shields

Jarrow

Hebburn

HARTON

Gateshead

WREKENTON

Whitburn

Boldon

SOUTHWICK

ROKER

MONKWEARMOUTH

SUNDERLAND

Consett

Annfield Plain

Stanley

Ouston

Washington

SOUTH HYLTON

Chester-le-Street

Houghton-le-Spring

Hetton-le-Hole

Seaham

Murton

Lanchester

Stanhope

Crawleyside

Frosterley

Wolsingham

Tow Law

Brandon

Durham

Easington

Peterlee

Crook

Willington

Spennymoor

Bishop Auckland

Shildon

Darlington

Hartlepool

0   5 km

Rubha Creagan Dubha
Cock of Arran
Newton
Lochranza
Millstone Point
443
573
359
Sannox
825
Goatfell
874
Corrie
361
Merkland Point
Brodick Castle
Brodick Bay
A' Chruach
512
Brodick
Strathwhillan
South Corriegills
503
Clauchlands Point
Lamlash
Margnaheglish
Lamlash Bay
Holy Island
458 Knockenkelly
Kingscross
Kingscross Point
Whiting Bay
Largymore
Largybeg
Largybeg Point
Dippen
Dippen Head
West Bennan
East Bennan
Shannochie
Kildonan
Bennan Head
Pladda

Isle
of
Arran

Kerrymenoch
844
Kingarth
Kilchattan Bay
Millport
Little Cumbrae Island
Gull Point
Portencross
Farland Head
Crosby
336
Ardnell Bay

Sound of Bute
Dunagoil Bay
Garroch Head
The Tàn
Fairlie Roads

Blairpark
483
North
Routdaneburn
Camphill Reservoir
760
Knockendon Reservoir
Kilbirnie
South Hourat
Glengarnock
Longbar
Beith
22
Gateside
Barrmill
Burnhouse
Dalry
Highfield
Giffordland
Gill
Drakemyre
The Den

West Kilbride
Ardrossan
Saltcoats
Irvine
Barassie
Troon
Lady Isle
Meikle Craigs

Howwood
Lochwinnoch
Millikenpark
Elderslie
Glenburn
Waterside
Gateside
Barrhead
Netherplace
Neilston
Uplawmoor
Lugton
Halket
Gabroc Hill
Windy-Yett
M77
Fullwood
Dunlop
Auchentiber
Kingsford
Stewarton
Kilwinning
Cunninghamhead
Rowallan Castle
Kilmaurs
Dean Castle
Moscow
Craufurland Castle
Kilmarnock
Crookedholm
Hurlford
Galston
Newmilns
Loudoun Castle
Springside
Knockentiber
Crosshouse
Dreghorn
Gatehead
Riccarton
Shortlees
Milrig
Sornhill
Dundonald
Earlston
Auchans
Loans
Symington
Bogend
Craigie
Mosside
Moscow

Rosemount
Adamhill
Millburn
Crosshands
Auchmillan
Monkton
Prestwick International Airport
Tarbolton
Mossgiel
15
Knowhead
PRESTWICK
Failford
Mauchline
St Quivox
Mossblown
Stair
Catrine
Ayr
SEAFIELD
WALLACETOWN
Whitletts
Annbank
Gilmilns
Doonfoot
Belston
Sundrum
Trabboch
Trabbochburn
Heads of Ayr
Greenan
Newark
Burns Cottage
Alloway
Doonholm
Ceylon
Hillhead
Ochiltree
Auchinleck
Holmend
Fisherton
Lagg
287
Culroy
Minishant
Dalrymple
Hollybush
Burnton
Sinclaiston
Skares
Cumnock
Netherthird
Dunure
Brown Carrick Hill
Sauchrie
Drumshang
Croy Brae
Knoweside
Culzean Bay
Culzean Castle
Maidenhead Bay
270
South Mains
31
77
Maybole
Grimmet
196
Dalvennan
Polnessan
Stannery Knowe
363
Patna
Dalgig
East Ayrshire
Waterhead
Littlemark
Maidens
Turnberry
Kirkoswald
Crossraguel Abbey
Kirkmichael
Cloncaird Castle
Crosshill
Cloyntie
Waterside
Preserved Railway
Benbeoch
464
Maneight
Conne
Bankglen
Dalleagle
Turnberry Bay
Brest Rocks
Matthew's Port
Downhill
252
Wallacetown
Blairquhan Castle
Loch Spallander Reservoir
307
River Doon
Pennyvenie
Clawfin
Ailsa Craig
Dipple
Ladybank
Craigfad
Straiton
Gass
Dalmellington
Enoch Hill
569
Kennedy's Pass
Dalquarran Castle
Dalmorton
Balbeg
Craig
Dalcairney
Bellsbank
Girvan
Killochan Castle
Old Dailly
Dailly
Penkill
Kilkerran
Linfairn
Big Hill of Glenmount
382
Campbells Hill
453
Carsphairn
Saugh Hill
296
Hadyard Hill
323
Loch Muck
Forest
Pinwherry Reservoir
Garleffin Fell
429
Loch Doon
Cairnsmore of Carsphairn
797
Woodland Bay
Grey Hill
297
Pinminnoch
Tormitchell
Glengennet
Dalquhairn
North Balloch
Linfern Loch
Loch Finlas
Loch Doon Castle
Lamloch
Brochloch
Carsphairn
Kennedy's Pass
77
Currarie
Pinmore
Auchensoul
Barr
South Balloch
Changue Plantation
Eldrick Hill
Craigmalloch
Dumfries and Galloway
Lendalfoot
Knockdaw Hill
260
Merkland
230
Cairn Hill
479
Carrick Forest
Cairn Avel
Carsphairn
Bennane Head
Poundland
Pinwherry
Pindonnan Craigs
335
Macaterick
498
Castlemaddy
Knockdolian
265
Colmonell
Bellamore
Kirriereoch Hill
782
695
713
Knowehead
Knockdolian
Heronsford
Cosses
230
Shiel Hill
229
Barrhill
Glentrool Forest
Ballantrae
Balkissock
Glencaird Hill
Loch Neldricken
Silver Flowe
Forest Lodge
Knocknalling
Downan Point
Glenapp Castle
Smyrton
Beneraird
439
Corwar House
Glen Trool Lodge
Loch Enoch
Loch Dungeon
Earlstoun Loch
Carlock Hill
319
Chirmorrie
195
Drumlamford Loch
Glen Trool
Loch Trool
Meikle Millyea
746
Drumbuie

0   5 km

	≋	☀
V	8°	10°
VII	13°	15°
VIII	13°	14°
IX	12°	12°
X	11°	10°

Inverquharity Memus Careston Muir Trinity Muirton of Craigo Lochnie St Cyrus Milton Ness
Shielhill Murthill Tannadice Brechin Balloch Lugie Lochside 92
northmuir Finavon Carston Cathedral & Muirton of Hillside St Cyrus
Kirriemuir Oathlaw Crosston Netherton Round Tower House Kirkhill E 535.000
Maryton Carse Aberlemno Mains Middle Preserved of Dun Kirkhill
Mosside Gray Sculptured of Melgund Drums 935 Barnhead Montrose
Padanaram Lunanhead Stones Montreathmont Forest Pitkennedy Farnell Carcary Basin
Drumgley Reswallie Turin Dubton 934 Bonnyton Maryton Montrose
Forfar Burnside Balgavies 932 Glasterlaw Bolshan Kirkton Scurdie Ness
Glamis Castle Kingsmuir Dunnichen Mildens Guthrie Boysack 92 Ferryden
Tealing Caldhame Craichie Letham Kinnell Fribckheim Inverkeilor Long Craig
Kirkton Lour Idvies Pitmuies Leysmill Chapelton Lunan Usan Boddin Point
Foffarty Inverarity Craichie Mill Tulloes Cauldcots Redcastle Lunan Bay
Gateside Whigstreet Mosston Letham Ethie Lang Craig
Angus Kirkbuddo Greystone Redford Colliston Grange Drinkendub Mains Red Head
Gallowfauld Hayhillock Carmyllie Ethie Castle Prail Castle
Carrot Bonnyton Denhead of Maxwell Auchmithie
Todhills Monikie Resr Arbirlot Marywell Meg's Craig
inveraldie Monikie Kirkton of Arbirlot St Vigeans The Deil's Heid
Burnside of Wellbank Monikie Smiddy Easter Seaton
Duntrune Craigton Muirdrum Knox **Arbroath**
Bucklerheads Newbigging Salmond's Elliot
DOUGLAS AND Kellas Carlungie Muir Elliott
ANGUS Drumsturdy Souterrain East Haven
UNDEE Mains of 92 Panbride
BALDOVIE Ardestie 930 Barry
Claypots Monifieth **Carnoustie**
Castle Barry
BROUGHTY Links
FERRY Buddon Ness
Tayport
Scotscraig **Tentsmuir**
Tay **Point**
Bridge
Tentsmuir
Forest
St Michaels
914
Leuchars
Earlshall Castle Eden Mouth
& Gardens
Guardbridge
919 St Andrews Bay
Kineaple
91
Strathkinness **St Andrews**
ocraigs Brownhills Buddo Ness
Denhead 917 Boarhills
Prior Babbet Ness
nnie Cameron Muir
Reservoir Cameron Burn Kingsbarns
915 Stavithie Cambo
Lawhead Ness
Radernie Dunino
Falfield Lathones Lochty Fife Ness
Largoward Balcomie
ester Lathallan Mill Drumrack Kirklands Craighead
wburn 184 Carnbee
arleton Kellie Crail
use Arncroach Castle West Ness
Colinsburgh Kilrenny
Abercrombie 917
917 Kilconquhar Pittenweem **Anstruther**
Elie St Monans
rlsferry St Fillan's Cave
Chapel Sauchar Point
Ness

Isle of May
Isle **Isle of May**
of May

Fidra
Craigleith
Bass Rock
Dirleton North
198 Berwick
Tantallon
Castle St. Baldred's Boat
ullane Auldhame
198
Fenton Kingston
Barns Scoughall
Mungoswells East Whitekirk
creif Drem St. Baldred's Cradle
Tyninghame Tyne Mouth

North Sea

N 6.280.000
C
E F
N 6.250.000
G H J
N 6.220.000
K L M

Forth
Firth of Forth

E 535.000 E 535.000 E 565.000

	≈	☀
V	8°	10°
VII	13°	15°
VIII	13°	14°
IX	12°	12°
X	11°	10°

0 ▬▬▬ 5 km

60

Glasgow, Edinburgh, Renfrewshire, North Ayrshire, East Ayrshire, **North Lanarkshire, South Lanarkshire, Midlothian, Scottish Borders**

0   5 km

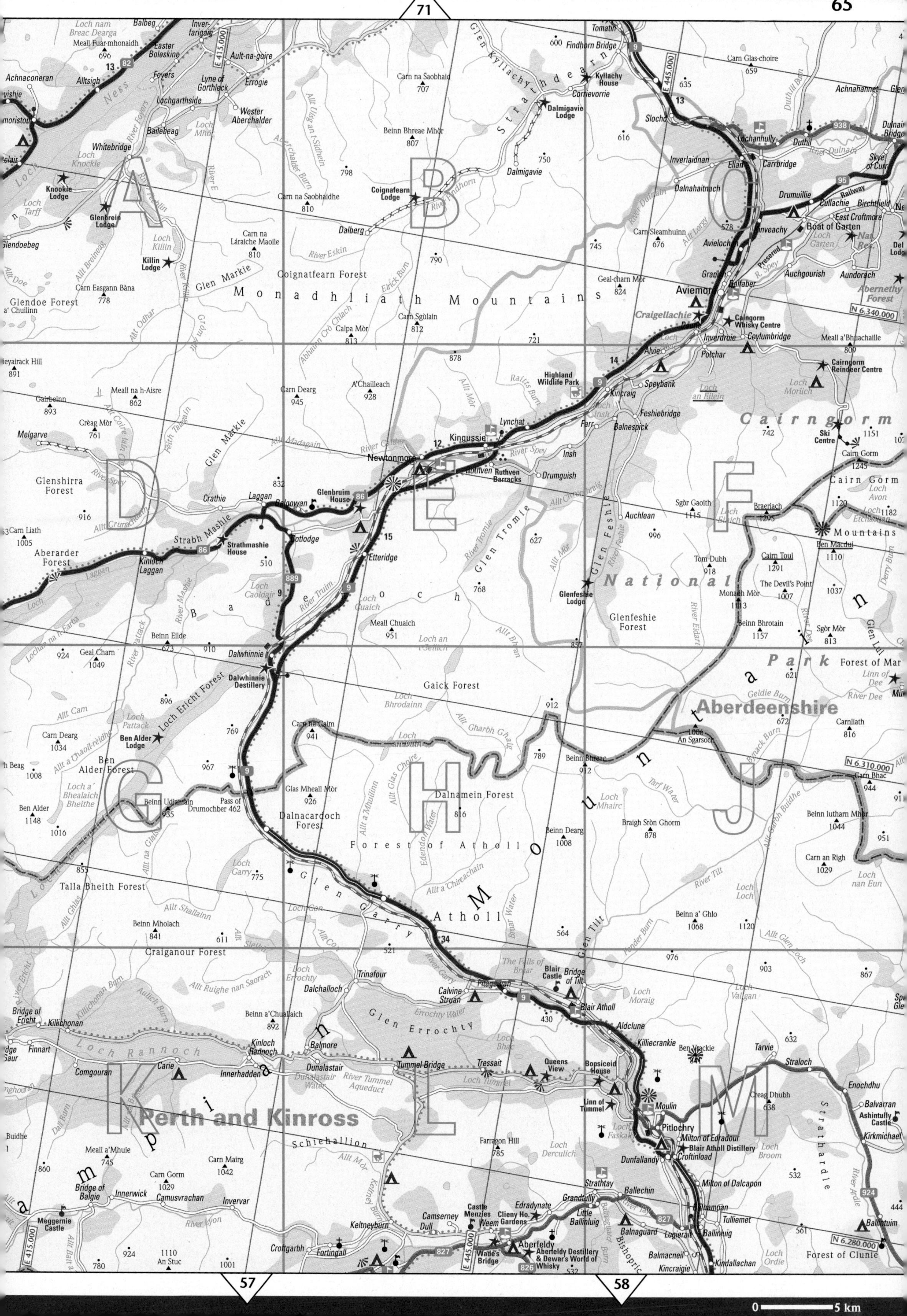

Loch nam Breac Dearga
Meall Fuar-mhonaidh 696
Balbeg
Inverfarigaig
Easter Boleskine
Foyers
Lyne of Gorthleck
Ault-na-goire
Errogie

Tomatin
600 Findhorn Bridge
Carn Glas-choire 659
Carn na Saobhaid 707
Kyllachy House
Cornevorrie
Dalmigavie Lodge
Carn Glas-choire
Achnahannet

Achnaconeran
Alltsigh
Whitebridge
Wester Aberchalder
Bailebeag
Lochgarthside

Beinn Bhreac Mhòr 807
Dalmigavie
750

13 82
Slochd
13
Lochanhully
Duthil
938
Dunain Bridge
Skye of Curr

vishie
moriston
clair
Loch Knockie
Glenbrein Lodge

Carn na Láraiche Maoile 810
Coignafearn Lodge
Dalberg
790

Inverlaidnan
Dalnahaitnach
Ellan
Carrbridge
Drumuillie
95 Railway
Cullachie
Birchfield
East Croftmore

Glendoebeg
Glendoe Forest
a' Chuilinn

Loch Tarff
Killin Lodge 778
Glen Markie
Coignatfearn Forest

Monadhliath Mountains

798
798

River Eskin

Geal-charn Mòr 824
578
Granish
Balfaber
Avielochan
Boat of Garten
Loch Garten
Nan Res
Del Lodge

Meyairack Hill 891
Gairbeinn 893
Crèag Mòr 761
Melgarve
Meall na h-Aisre 862
Carn Dearg 945
A'Chailleach 928
878
721

Highland Wildlife Park
9
Kincraig
Speybank
14
Alvie
Polchar
Inverdruie
Coylumbridge
Meall a'Bhuachaille 809

Cairngorm

Cairngorm Whisky Centre
Craigellachie
Aviemore

Cairngorm Reindeer Centre

Carn Sgùlain 812
Calpa Mòr 813
Abhainn Cró Chlach

Glenshirra Forest
Carn Liath 1005
Glen Markie
Crathie
Laggan
Balgowan
832
Glenbruim House 86
Newtonmore
Kingussie
12
Ruthven Barracks
Drumguish
Insh
Feshiebridge
Balnespick
Farr
Lynchat
Loch an Eilein
Loch Morlich
Ski Centre 742
1151
Cairn Gorm
1245

Aberarder Forest
86
Strabh Mashie
Strathmashie House
510
Catlodge
Etteridge
15
889
9
River Truim
Loch Caoldair
9
Loch Cuaich
Meall Chuaich 951
Loch an t-Seilich

Glen Feshie
Auchlean
996
Sgòr Gaoith 1115
Tom Dubh 918
Braeriach 1295
Cairn Toil 1291
The Devil's Point 1007
Ben Macdui 1110
Cairn Gorm Mountains
1182
1120
Loch Avon
Etchachan

National
Glenfeshie Lodge
Glenfeshie Forest
Monadh Mòr 1113
Beinn Bhrotain 1157
Sgòr Mòr 813
Derry

Park

Kinloch Laggan
Ben Alder Lodge
Ben Alder 1148
1016
Carn Dearg 1034
Loch Pattack
Loch a' Bhealaich Bheithe

Dalwhinnie
Dalwhinnie Destillery
910
673
Geal Charn 1049
924
896
769
967
935
Beinn Udlamain
Pass of Drumochter 462
Carn na Caim 941
Glas Mheall Mòr 926
Gaick Forest
Loch Bhrodainn
912
Dalnamein Forest
816
Beinn Bhreac 912
789
Allt Gharbh Ghaig
Tarf Water
An Sgarsoch 1006
Aberdeenshire
672
Carnliath 816
Carn Bhac 944
Forest of Mar
621
Linn of Dee
Geldie Burn

Ben Alder Forest
Beinn Eilde
Dalnacardoch Forest
Craiganour Forest
Beinn Mholach 841
611
Talla Bheith Forest
855
Loch Garry 775
Glen Garry
Forest of Atholl
Edendon Water
Allt a' Chireachain
564
Beinn Dearg 1008
Braigh Sròn Ghorm 878
Beinn a' Ghlo 1068
1120
Beinn Iutharn Mhòr 1044
951
Carn an Righ 1029
Loch nan Eun
Loch Loch
Glen Tilt
River Tilt

Bridge of Ericht
Kilichonan
Finnart
Comgouran
Carie
Innerhadden
Kinloch Rannoch
Balmore
Dunalastair
Loch Rannoch
Glen Errochty
Trinafour
Dalchalloch
Beinn a'Chuallaich 892
Calvine
Struan
9
Pitagowan
Blair Castle
Bridge of Tilt
430
Blair Atholl
Aldclune
Killiecrankie
Ben Vrackie 841
Loch Moraig
Loch Valigan
903
867
Tarvie 632
Straloch

Perth and Kinross
Schiehallion
Meall a'Mhuie 860
Carn Mairg 1042
Carn Gorm 1029
Bridge of Balgie
Innerwick
Camusvrachan
Invervar
924
1110 An Stuc
1001
Meggernie Castle

Tummel Bridge
Dunalastair Water
River Tummel Aqueduct
Tressait
Queens View
Bopsiceid House
Loch Tummel
Linn of Tummel
Moulin
Farragon Hill 785
Loch Derculich
Pitlochry
Milton of Edradour
Blair Atholl Distillery
Croftinload
Dunfallandy
Strathtay
Ballechin
Grandtully
Edradynate
Little Ballinluig
Balnaguard
Logierait
Milton of Dalcapon
827
Enochdhu
Creag Dhubh 638
Balvarran
Ashintully Castle
Kirkmichael
532
Forest of Clunie
444
Strathardle
924

Croftgarbh
Fortingall
Keltneyburn
Camserney
Dull
Castle Menzies
Weem
Clieny Ho.
Gardens
Aberfeldy
Aberfeldy Distillery & Dewar's World of Whisky
Wade's Bridge
827
826
Kindallachan
Ballinluig
Tulliemet
Balnacneil
Balmacneil
Kincraigie

0 5 km

	≈≈≈	☀
V	9°	9°
VII	12°	13°
VIII	13°	13°
IX	12°	11°
X	11°	9°

0   5 km

1:301,000 · 1cm ≙ 3 km

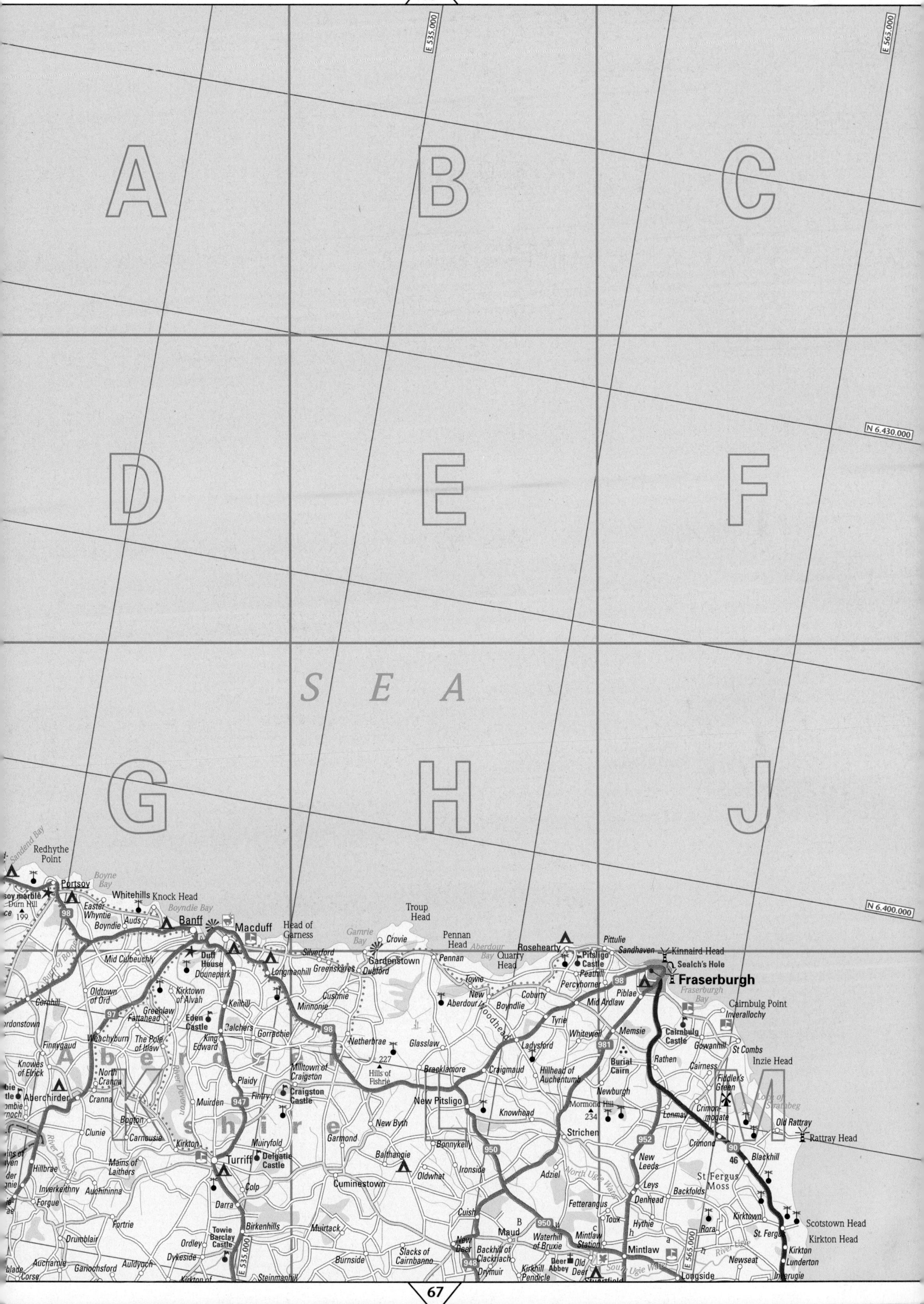

E 535.000

E 565.000

N 6.430.000

A

B

C

D

E

F

S E A

G

H

J

N 6.400.000

Sandend Bay

Redhythe Point

Boyne Bay

Portsoy

soy marble

Durn Hill

199

Whitehills Knock Head

Easter Whyntie

Boyndie

Auds

Boyndie Bay

98

Banff

Macduff

Head of Garness

Troup Head

Gamrie Bay

Crovie

Pennan Head

Aberdour Bay

Rosehearty

Pittulie

Sandhaven

Kinnaird Head

Sealch's Hole

Duff House

Mid Culbeuchly

Dounepark

Silverford

Gardenstown

Dubford

Pennan

Quarry Head

Peathill

Pitsligo Castle

Percyhorner

98

Fraserburgh

Oldtown of Ord

Kirkton of Alva

Kenhill

Longmanhill

Greenskares

Towie

New Aberdour

Coburty

Boyndlie

Mid Ardlaw

Piblae

Fraserburgh Bay

Cairnbulg Point

Inverallochy

97

Greenlaw

Fattahead

Eden Castle

King Edward

Dalchers

Gorrachie

Cushnie

Minnonie

Netherbrae

98

Woodhead

Tyrie

Whitewell

Memsie

Cairnbulg Castle

Gowanhill

St Combs

Weachyburn

The Pole of Itlaw

Glaslaw

Ladysford

Hillhead of Auchentumb

Burial Cairn

Rathen

Cairness

Inzie Head

Knowes of Elrick

North Cranna

Milltown of Craigston

227

Hills of Fishrie

Bracklamore

Craigmaud

981

Newburgh

Fiddler's Green

Aberchirder

Cranna

Plaidy

Fintry

Craigston Castle

New Pitsligo

Knowhead

Mormond Hill

234

Lonmay

Crimonmogate

Old Rattray

Rattray Head

Bogton

Clunie

Carnousie

Muirden

947

New Byth

Garmond

Strichen

952

Crimond

90

Blackhill

Hillbrae

Inverkeithny

Auchininna

Mains of Laithers

Kirkton

Muiryfold

Delgatie Castle

Balthangie

Ironside

Oldwhat

Adziel

New Leeds

Leys

Denhead

St Fergus Moss

46

Forgue

Fortrie

Turriff

Colp

Birkenhills

Cuminestown

Bonnykelly

950

Fetterangus

Backfolds

Kirkton

Scotstown Head

Drumblair

Ordley

Dykeside

Towie Barclay Castle

Muirtack

Burnside

Slacks of Cairnbanno

948

Cuish

New Deer

B

Maud

950

Waterhill of Bruxie

Mintlaw Station

Toux

Hythie

Rora

Kirkton Head

Mintlaw

a

St Fergus

Kirkton

Lunderton

Aucharnie

Gariochsford

Auldyoch

Kirkton

Steinmanhill

Backhill of Clackriach

Drymuir

Kirkhill Pendicle

Deer Abbey

Old Deer

Stuartfield

South Ugie Water

River Ugie

Longside

Newseat

Inverugie

0 ▬▬▬▬ 5 km

Sula Sgeir

Lisgear Mhòr
Rona/
Rònaidh

A

B

C

H e b r i d e s

Boreray/
Boraraigh

Soay/
Soaigh   378

376

St Kilda or Hirta/
Hiort

Dun

Sule Skerry

D

Sule Stack

Flannan
Isles

Na h-Eileanan
Flannach

N 6.430.000

A T L A N T I C

O U T E R

G

H

O C E A N

Gallan Head/
An Gallan Uigeach   An Caolas
Camas Geòdhachan
an Duilisg

Geòdha Nasabhaig

Aird
Uig

Geòdha nan

Bhaltos

Cliobh

Cnip

Bàgh Fiabhaig

Sgeir Fhiabhaig Tarras

Aird Mòr
Mangurstadh

Cradhlas-
tadh

Miabhaig

Loch
Scaslabhal

Timsgearraidh

Mangurstadh

Eadar
Dha Fhadhail

Cairisiadar

Flodai

Aird Feinis

Staca Leathann

Aird Bhreinis

Islibhig

Cleite
Leathann

Loch
Suaineabhal

Einacleit

Breanais

Tarain

Loch
Gruinea
bhat

Camas a' Mhoil

Mealasta   495

Eilean
Mhealasta

Mealasta

Giosla

Beinn Mheadhanach
397

Loch
Chaolartan

Loch
Fuarai

Loch
Cro Criosdail

Loch Tamnabhaigh
Loch Tealasbhaigh

Cearstaigh Gob na h-
Airde Mòire

Loch a'
Ghlinne

Loch Beinn Iosbh

Sròn Romul   308

Braigh Mòr

Reasort

Morsgail For
Frith/Mhors

Scarp

Mànais

Loch
Crabhdail

Ulladail

Beinn a' Bho
307

Rubha Huisinis

Huisinis

An Cliseam
679

Loch a'
Ghlinne

West

Gobhaig

Horsanais

Abhainn Bhearnaraigh

Abhainn

Rubha
Leacach

Airde Mòr

Forrest of Harris/
Frith na Hearadh

Abhainn

Mhabhaig

729

Aird
Suidhe

Cliasmaol

Northharris/
Ceann a' Tuath na Hearad

An Clise

799

Camas an t-Saoidhein

Soaidh Mòr
Rubha nan
Totag

Miabhaig

Gob Aird an
Tolmachain

Bun Abhainn Eadarra

Ben Raah
267

Loch a Siar
799

Iosaigh

Sgaoth

Aird Asaig

Taransay/
Tarasaigh

Beinn Dubh

Sound of Taransay
Caolas Tharasaigh

Losgaintir

Tarbert/
Tairbeart

Urg

Rubha
Sgeirigin

Aird
Niosaboist

Frith Losgaintir

Mhead

Rubha Mas
a' Chnuic

Rubha Romaigidh

Horgabost

Seilebost

Loch
Ceann Di

Toe head/
Gob an Tobha

Sgeir
Liath

Na Buirgh

Miabhaig

Siolaigh Bheag

Siolaigh

Ceapabhal
368

Sgarasta Mhor

Sgarasta Bheag

An Colleach

Aird
Mhighe

Drinisiadar
Ceann-na-Cleithe
Greosabhagh

Caolas Shiolaigh

Rubh' an
Teampuill

Rubha
Bhreinis

Loch
Langabhat

360

Uceasto

Leac a' Li

Geocrab

Caolas Stocinis

Scada

Pabbay/
Pabaigh

Rubh' a' Bhaile
Fo Thuath

Taobh Tuath

Taigh a' Chaolais

859

Braigh-nam-bagh

Fleoideabhagh

Beacrabhaic

Cliuthar

Eilean Stocinis

N 6.400.000

K

Eilean Hasgeir

Hasgeir
Eagach

Ensay/
Easaigh

Loch
Steisebhat

Leverburgh/
An t-Ob

Aird Mhighe

Fionnsabhagh

Aird Mhànais

Manais

Cuidhtinis

Harris/
na Hearad

North Uist/

Harris and South Lewis

Boreray/
Boraraigh

Berneray/
Beàrnaraigh

Cairminis

Killegray/
Ceileagraigh

Sramda

Lingreabhagh

Rubha
Chuidhtinis

Rubha
Ghriminis

Sgeir
Oireabhal

Vallay/
Bhàlaigh

Aird a'
Ahòrain

Ruisigearraidh

Màs a'
Champair

St Clements
Church

Roghadal

Eilean
Lingreabhagh

Bhalaigh

Scolpaig

Rubha
Bheilis

Rubha
Bhoisnis

Borgh

Borgh

Bhalteam

Langaigh

Renish Point/
Rubha Reinis

Griminis

Lingeigh

Grod-
haigh

Gilsaigh

Rubha Mhànais

Rubha Dubh
Thigh a Ghearraidh

865

Baile Mhàrtainn

Tràigh
Bhalaigh

Solas

Greinetobht

Baile Mhic Phàil

Port nan
Long

Torogaigh

Aird
Thormaid

Lingeigh

E 580.000

E 610.000

1 1/4 hrs

Butt of Lewis/
Rubha Robhanais
Eòropaidh
Coig Peighinnean
Tràigh Chumail
Port Nis
Àird Dhall
Cros
Lional
Tobha Ghabhsainn
Tabost
Gabhsann bho Thuath
Dhail bho
Port Sgiogarstaigh
Gabhsann bho Dheas
Dheas
Suainebost
Nis
Sgiogarstaigh
Mealabost Bhuigh
857
Meall Geal
Coig Peighinnean Bhuirgh
Cladach Chuidhsiadairl
Rubha Bhlanisgaidh
Bail Àrd Bhuirgh
Rubha Leathann
Siadal
Beinn Dhail
Àird Bharabhais
Stone
Circle
Rubh' a' Bhiogair
Clach an
Baile an Truiseil
Rubha a t-Seileir
Truiseil
Rinn Druim Tàllig
Cladach Dhìobadail
Rubh' an Dùnain
Labost
Black House
Brù
Sguinean nan
Rubha Caol
Bragar
Arnol
Barabhas
Creagan Briste
Bàgh Dhail Beag
858
Loch
Dail Beag
Siabost
Urghag
Blackhouse
Muirneag
Village
Dàil Mòr
248
Campaigh
Na Gearrannan
Borghastan
Beinn Bhragair
Bail' Ur Tholastaidh
Càrlabhagh
201
Tolstadh bho Thuath
Ciribhig
Dun Chòrlabhaigh
Tolsta Head/Ceann or
Beag
(Carloway Broch)
Rubha Tholasta
Bostadh
Dun Chàrlabhagh
Gleann
Crothair
Tholastaidh
Port nam Bothaig
Tolastadh a' Chaolais
Port Bun a' Ghlinne
Great
Griais
Creag Fhraoch
Bernera/
Breascleit
Cnoc an
Bearnaraigh
Circebost
t-Solais
Col
Barraglom
Tobhtaral
Bac
Sgeir Leathann
Crùlabhig
Col
Buaile na h-Ochd
Uarach
Calanais
Calanais
Breibhig
Broad Bay
Standing Stones
Gearraidh na h-Aibhne
Grianan
Tunga
Gob Rubha
or
Linsiadar
Bhatasgeir
Loch a' Tuath
Loch Urabhal
Aird Thunga
Port
Tiumpan Head/
Stornoway/
nan Giuran
Rubha an
Steòrnabhagh
Sròn Ruadh
T-Sìumpain
Isle
Newmarket
Cnoc Amhlaigh
Port Mholair
Eilean
Lacasdail
Tràigh Mhealaboist
Loch a' Ghainmhich
Sulaisiadar
Bàgh Phort Bholair
Acha Mòr
Stèinis
Mealabost
Aird
858
Aignis
Garrabost
Seisiadar
Lewis Castle
866
Loch nam
Sanndabhaig
Eye Peninsula/
Rubha na Grèine
Falcag
Loch Thobhta
Raon na
an Rubha
Bridein
Crèadha
Pabail Iarach
Rubha nam Bàirneach
Mòinteach
Tolm
Beinn Phabail
Àirinis
Gob
88
Loch Airigh
Rubh' a
Shildinis
An Cnoc
na h-Àird
Bhàigh Uaine
Stac Shuardail
Rubh' Dubh
Liurbost
Chicken Head/
Loch
Gob na Creige
Orasaigh
Griomsidar
Beinn Casgro
Rubha Raerinis
Crosbost
Ranais
Ceòs
Eilean
Lacasaidh
Chaluim
Tabhaidh Mhòr
Baile
Chille
Ailein
Cromor
Eilean Orasaidh
Sildinis
Cabharstadh
Eilean Thòraidh
Tabost Cearsiadair
Ceann Tarabhaigh
Gearraidh Bhaird
Marbhig
Airidh a Bhruaich
Taobh a'Ghlinne
Rubha na
Aird an
Ceann Shiphoirt
Creige Mòire
Troim
Calbost
Sidhean
Rubha Iosal
an Airgid
Grabhair
Park/
Eisgein
Eilean
Pairc
A' Chabag
Shiphoirt
Isles
Orasaigh
Leumrabhagh
Gob na Miolaid
Srianach
Eilean
Liubhaird
Màraig
Camas Allt
nam Bearnach
Reinigeadal
Ard
Caol
Gob Rubh' Uisinis
Geòdha
Dubh
Rubha Bhrolluim
Scalpaidh
Rubh' a' Bhàird
Leac Eascadail
Carnach
Rubha Crago
Aird Riabhach
Garbh
Cadha na Gaoidhsich
Scalpay/
Eilean
Eilean Mhuire
Scalpaigh
Ceann a
Bhàigh
Sound of Shiant/
Caolas nan Eilean
Shiant Islands/
Eilean an Thaighe
Na h-Eileanan Mòra

	≈	☀
V	9°	9°
VII	12°	13°
VIII	13°	13°
IX	12°	11°
X	11°	9°

Ullapool 2 ¾ hrs

Idrigill 1 ¾ hrs

Sròn 'a Gheodha
Dhuibh
Rubha Rèidh
Camas
Mòr
Loch
an Draing

0 ▭▭ 5 km

A T L A N T I C

	≈≈	☀
V	9°	9°
VII	12°	13°
VIII	13°	13°
IX	12°	11°
X	11°	9°

A

B

C

D

E

OCEAN

The Minch

Cape Wrath
A'Chailleach
Am Bodach
163
Kearvaig
Geodha Ruadh na Fola
Bay of Keisgaig
Geodha Ruadh
Loch Keisgaig
Am Balg
Sandwood Bay
Beinn Dearg 424
Rubh' an Fhìr Lèithe
Sandwood Loch
Loch Mòr
Abhainn an t-Strathan
Strath Shinary
Sheigra
Loch na Gainimh
Balchrick
Droman
Oldshore Beg
Oldshoremore
Eilean an Ròin Mòr
Kinlochbervie
Rubha na Leacaig
Loch Clash
Badcall
Bàgh Loch an Ròin
Inshegra
Loch Inchard
Rhuvoult
Loch Dughaill
Achriesgill
Ardmore Point
Rhiconich
Rubha Ruadh
Achlyness
Ceathramh Garbh
Handa Island
Fanagmore
Loch Laxford
Skerricha
Tarbet
Foindle
Laxford Bridge
River Laxford
Foinaven 908
Loch a' Garbh-bhaid Mòr
Sound of Handa
Scourie Bay
Scourie More
Rubh' Aird an t-Sionnaich
Scourie
Gorm Loch
Arkle 786
Loch Easain
Upper Badcall
Lower Badcall
838
Strath Stack
Loch Stack
Badcall Bay
Eilean a' Bhreitheimh
Meall Mòr
Rubh' a' Mhucard
Calbha Beag
Loch Cròcach
Achfary
Reay
Lochmore Lodge Forest
Loch na Creige Duibhe
Point of Stoer
Sgeir nan Gall
Oldany Island
Calbha Mòr
Loch a' Chàim Bhàin
Eddrachillis Bay
Allt nan Ràmh
Aultan
Cìrean Geardail
Rubha nan Còsan
Drumbeg
Kylestrome
Loch an Leathaid Bhuaine
Cluas Deas
Clashnessie Bay
Nedd
Loch Nedd
Kylesku
Glendhu Forest
Achnacarnin
Clashmore
Clashnessie
Gleann
Newton
894
Gleann Dubh
Balchladich
Rienachait
Stoer
Loch Poll
Leireag
Unapool
Kinloch
Rubh' a' Mhill Dheirg
Bay of Stoer
Clachtoll
Loch an Leothaid
Quinag 809
Gleann Coul
Rubha Leumair
Loch Beannach
Loch Riencoul
Achmelvich Bay
Rhicarn
Loch Cròcach
Eas a' Chùal Aluinn (Waterfall)
Loch an Eircill
Abhainn a' Cho
Achmelvich
Brackloch
Fionn Loch Mòr
Rubha Rodha
Baddidarach
River Inver
Allt na t-Airbe
837
Ardvreck Castle
Gorm Loch Mòr
Soyea Island
Lochinver
Glencanisp Lodge
Beinn Gharbh 539
Inchnadamph
Kirkaig Point
Loch Assynt
Inchnadamph Forest
Rubha na Còigich
Loch Kirkaig
Strathan Inverkirkaig
Abhainn na Clach Airigh
Loch Fèith an Leòthaid
River Traligill
Rubha na Brèige
Loch Culag
River Inver
Ben More Assynt 998
Eilean Mòr
Enard Bay
Glencanisp Forest
Loch na Gainimh
Stronchrubie
Camas Eilean Ghlais
Fionn Loch
Suilven 731
Canisp 847
Ben More Assynt
Rubha Mòr
Camas Coille
Reiff
Rubha a' Choin
River Polly
Loch Slonascaig
Loch Awe Cam Loch
Ducha Lod
Brae of Achnahaird
Altanghu
Eilean Mullagrach
Isle Ristol
Aird of Coigach
Loch Osgaig
Loch Veyatie
Benmore Forest
Glas-leac Mòr
Polbain
Loch Bad a'-Ghaill
Inverpolly Forest
Cul Mor 849
Knockan
Elphin
Ledbeg River
Tanera Beg
Achiltibuie
Loch Bad a'-Ghaill
Drumruinie Forest
Ledmore
Summer Isles
Polglass
Cul Beag 769
Knockan Crag Visitor Centre
837
Ladentarbat Bay
Knockan
Loch Borralan
Tanera More/ Tannara Mòr
Loch Urigill
Glas-leac Beag
Horse Island
Hone Sound
Drumruinie
835
Priest Island
Eilean Dubh
Achduart
Ben Mòr Coigach 743
Coigach
River Runie
Càrn nan Sgeir
Culnacraig
Glen Oykel
Goba' Chuaille
Geodha Mòr
River Canaird
Greenstone Point/ Rubha na Lice Uaine
Leac Dhonn
Strathcanaird
Langwell Lodge
Strath Canaird
Rappach
Loch na Claise Mòire
Rubha Mòr
Mellon Udrigle
Cailleach Head
Camas Mòr
Allt a' Chraoinidh
Coire a' Chonachair
Opinan
Rubha Beag
Isle Martin
Strath nan Lòn
Lubcroy
Rubha nan Sasan
Mellon
Gruinard Island
Stattic Point
Scoraig
Annat Bay
Ardmair
Allt Beinn Dònuill
Oykel Bri
Sluggan Bay
Gruinard Bay
Carnach
Rhue
Achgarve
Badluarach
Rireavach
Rhidorroch Forest

Ullapool to Stornoway 2 3/4 hrs

N 6,490,000
N 6,460,000
N 6,430,000
E 355,000
E 385,000

70

0 —— 5 km

1:301,000 · 1cm ≙ 3 km

Orkney Islands

ATLANTIC OCEAN

NORTH SEA

	≈≈	☀
V	8°	8°
VII	11°	12°
VIII	13°	13°
IX	12°	11°
X	11°	9°

0 ———— 5 km

Shetland Islands

A

Holm of Skaw
Lamba Ness
The Noup
Muckle Flugga
Nor Wick
Norwick
Valsgarth
Cliberswick
Harold's Wick
Balta
Huney
285
Rumblings Ness
Herma Ness
200
Skaw of Haroldswick
Burrafirth
Quoys
Haroldswick
Caldback
216
Unst
Grunka Hellier
Baliasta
Orknagable
North Holms
South Holms
Westing
Uindar
Noull
968
120
Belmont
Uyeasound
Uyea
Lund

B

Mu Ness
Strandburgh Ness
Minnes Castle
Clivocast
Haaf Gruney
Wick of Gruting
Standing Stones
The Hall
Funzie
Fetlar
Vord Hill 522
Houbie
Fetlar Inter-
pretative Centre
Aith
Funzie Bay
Urie
Lingey
Daaey
Tresta
Rams Ness
Blough Lodge
Linga
Burra Ness
North Sandwick
Colgrave Sound
Sand Wick
Wick of Tresta

C

Bruray
Bruday
Grutsay
Housay
Housay
Housay
Out Skerries
Mio Ness
Muckle Skerry
Skaw Taing
1½ hrs
Skaw
Whalsay
Brough
Lunning Sound

D

ATLANTIC

Gloup Holm
Gloup Ness
Gloup
Greenbank
Cullivoe
Stonganess
Gloup Sound
Cassa Water
Sellafirth
Gutcher
Culbister
Lochs of Lumbister
Nev of Stuis
Geo of Markamouth
Whale Geo
Ler Wick
Gruney
Point of Fethaland
114
83
Shevla-breck
94
Basta
Basta Voe
Camb
Seafield
Mid Yell
Stoal
Yell
162
209
Swarister
Hascosay
Birrier
Aywick
Otterswick
Otters Wick
Gossabrough
Heoga Ness
Lumma Holm
Swinning
West Yell
Setter
Ulsta
Hamnavoe
Copister
Littlester
Old Haa
Brough
Hamna Voe
Samphrey
Fish Holm
Linga
West Swinning
90
Hamnavoe
Lunning
Vidlin
Herra
126
Laxo
Flugarth

E

Grimister
Grimster
West Sandwick
968
Brother Isle
Muckle Holm
Long Taing
Fladda
Lamba
Little Roe
Bigga
Unarey
Collafirth
Yell Sound

F

Mossbank
Fora Ness
Firth
Booth of Toft
Graven
Brough
968
Swining
Collafirth
Sullom Voe
Girth's Voe
Gluss Isle
Scatsta
Garths Voe
83
Voxter
Trondavoe
Brae
Sullom
Burravoe
Wethersta
Busta Voe
Olna Firth
Linga
Voe
Hillside

G

ATLANTIC

Uyea
Fugla Ness
Hevdadale Head
Gruna Stack
Tufts Head
107
Ronas Voe
Heylor
Heylor
Garmus Taing
Ronas Hill
450
Assater
Hellir
North Roe
Isbister
130
Sandvoe
172
Housetter
Boro's of Housetter
Burnside
Hillswick
Collafirth
Voe
Roer Water

H

ATLANTIC

Muckle Ossa
Ockran Head
South Head
Head of Stanshi
Esha Ness
Skerry of Eshaness
Hamnavoe
Ure
Braehoulland
Stenness
Isle of Stenness
Brae Tangwick
Tangwick Haa Hus
St Magnus Bay

J

North Gluss
South Gluss
Olnafirth
Eastwick
Glusy Isle
Bardister
Burraland
Nibon
Mangaster
Egilsay
Islesburgh
Standing Stones
Busta
Roesound
Muckle Roe
Little-Ayre
970
119
Punds Water
Baa Taing
Isle of Nibon
Strom Ness
Swarbacks Minn
Vementry
Cairn
Papa Little
Busta Voe

K

L

St Magnus Bay

North Ness
Papa Stour
Biggings
Bay of Garth
Melby
Sound of Papa
87
3/4 hr
Fogla Skerry

M

Lunning Sound
Swinning Voe
West Lunna Voe

1:301,000 · 1cm ≙ 3 km

Fair Isle

Dronger
Skroo
Bu Ness
Sheep Rock
217
Stony-break
George Waterston Museum
Malcom's Head
Sumburgh 2 3/4 hrs

C

Foula

Strem Ness
Walls 2 1/2 hrs
Harriet
The Snerg
The Kame
Niggards
Ham
418
South Ness
Hametoun

A

B

D

E

F

N O R T H   S E A

N.6.670.000
N.6.640.000
E.610.000
E.580.000
N.6.670.000
N.6.640.000

Bergen 12 hrs
Aberdeen 14 hrs
Tórshavn 12 hrs, Seydisfjördur 30 hrs
Stromness 7 hrs

Fort
Hunter
2 1/2 hrs

☀	8°	11°	12°
	10°		
〰	7°	10°	11°	10°	9°	8°
V	VII	VIII	IX	X

Crif Skerry
Linga
Ness
The Keen
Neap
South Nestin Bay
Laxfirth
Skellister
Brettabister
Ling Ness
Catfirth
Eswick
Brough
Gletness
South Isle of Gletness
Hoo Stack
Hawks Ness
Wadbister
Breiwick
Laxfirth
Girlsta
Bott
Freester
Cat Firth
Muss.
281
Setter
Loch of Strom
Huxter
Hellister
Veensgarth
Mus.
Nesting
m a i n l a n d
Gremista
Heogan
Gunnista
Maryfield
Setter
Charlotte
Lerwick
Clickhimin
Fort
Holmsgarth
Bressay
Kirkabister
Gardie
Gridiscol
Brough
Isle of Noss
Noss
Score Head
Yoa of Cullingsburgh
Grut Wick
Cave of the Bard
Bard Head

970
971
Gallow Hill
Walls
Vaila
173
Bixter
Twatt
Clousta
Aith
Voe
Houlland
Houlland
Effirth
Westerfield
Heglib-ister
Tresta
Sand-sound
The Firth of Weisdale
Loch of Strom
Scalloway Museum
Scalloway
Cutts
Uradale
Easter Quarff
Wester Quarff
Fladdabister
Ocraquoy
Althsettr
Greenmow
Coall Head
Burland Broch
Brindister
Wick
East Burra
Houss
Papil
West Burra
Papa
Cheynies
Oxna
Hamnavoe Craft Trail
Grunasound
Kettla Ness
South Havra
Hildasay
South View
South Havra
Flotta
North Havra
White Ness
White Ness
North Havra
Hoy
Sand-sound
Sand
Leeans
Reawick
Wester Skeld
Easter Skeld
Silwick
Skeld
Gardenhouse
133
Stanydale Temple
Stanydale
West-Houlland
Bridge of Walls
Burd-land
Broch
Culswick
Hestingsetter
Westerwick
Gliarump
Skelda Ness
Burd-land
Stropa Ness
Watts Ness
Mu Ness
Braga Ness
Mid Walls
Dale of Dale
Bay of Deepdale
Voe of Dale
Burnfirth
Uradale
Stanydale
Voe
Gruting
Sil-Gruting

m a i n l a n d

Bremire-houll
Mail
263
Cliff Hills
Punds
Sound
Brei-wick
Wick
Airth Voe
Setteebanister
Fogrigarth
Mousa Broch
Mousa
Sand-wick
Mousa Sound
Vos-wick
Cumlewick
Sandwick
Stove
Channer-wick
North-pound
Levenwick
Southpunds
Brodam
Skelberry
Bigton
Ireland
St Ninian's Isle
Colsay
Maywick
Scous-burgh
Mill
Quendale
Toab
Bay of Quendale
Ringast
Hillwell
283
Quendale
Longfield
Bordam
Shetland Craft House Museum
Esnaboe
Virkie
Toab
Grutness
Scatness
Ness of Burgi
Horse Island
Lady's Holm
Wick of Shumi
Fitful Head
Siggar Ness
Sumburgh
Sumburgh Head

G

H

K

L

M

A T L A N T I C   O C E A N

Fair Isle 2 3/4 hrs
Foula 2 hrs

0 —— 5 km

	≈≈	☀
V	11°	10°
VII	15°	15°
VIII	16°	14°
IX	15°	13°
X	14°	10°

1:301,000 · 1cm ≙ 3 km

	≋	☀
V	11°	10°
VII	15°	15°
VIII	16°	14°
IX	15°	13°
X	14°	10°

0 ——— 5 km

	≈≈≈	☀
V	11°	10°
VII	15°	15°
VIII	16°	14°
IX	15°	13°
X	14°	10°

A   B   C

A T L A N T I C

N 5.815.000

E 385.000   E 415.000

D   E   F

	≈≈	☀
V	11°	10°
VII	15°	15°
VIII	16°	14°
IX	15°	13°
X	14°	10°

N 5.785.000

G   H   J

The Seven Hogs or
or
Maghareg Islands   Illauntan

Brandon   Rough
Head   Point
Knockdeelea   Brandon   Kilshannig
310   Point   Fahamore

Masatiompan   Brandon   Caher   Brandon
762   Point   Bay

Pointagare
Ballydavid   Tiduff   950   Stradbally Strand
Head   Brandon Mountain   Ballyquin   Lough
Gill
Ballydavid   Eeohanagh   Cloghane   Kilcummin   Kiliney   Castlegregory
Sybil   Smerwick   Brandon Peak
Head   Dun   840
an Oir   Smerwick   Stradbally
Sybil   Harbour   Mureagh   Ballinloghig   Ballyduff
Point   Ballynagall   Beenoskee
Na Gorta   824   Aughacasla
Inish-   Gallarus   Kilmalkedar   Ballysiteragh
tooskert   Clogher   (Oratory)   622   Slievenagower
Clogher   Bally-   Riasc   486
Head   403   ferriter   Balynana   *Dingle   Peninsula*
Tearaght   The Blasket   Coaghmarhin   Cummeen
Island   Centre   *Dingle*   478   Knockbeg
Beginish   Dunquin   Kilducrihy   Ventry   Conair Pass   Lough   Dromavally   379   51
514   Mount Eagle   Bellymore   Anscaul   Lougher
Great Blasket   Coumeenoole   Ventry   Milltown   Dingle
Island   Fahan   Harbour   Reenboy
Inish-   Cloghans   Raheen   Ogham   Doon-   Lispole   Lougher
nabro   Slea   Dunbeg Fort   Stones   sheane   N86   374
Head   (Promontory Fort)   Boonbane   Tobernea-   Anascaul   Mall   Buckany
Inish-   Parkmore   moodane   Inch
vickillane   Point   Minard   Minard
Reenbeg   East   Red Cliff
Point   Bull's   Gubrana   Acres
Head   Minard   Point
Head   Inch

Dingle Bay   Inch Point

seasonal   Rosbehy
Creek
E 335.000   E 415.000   Reennanallagane   Knockaun-
glass

1:301,000 · 1cm ≙ 3 km

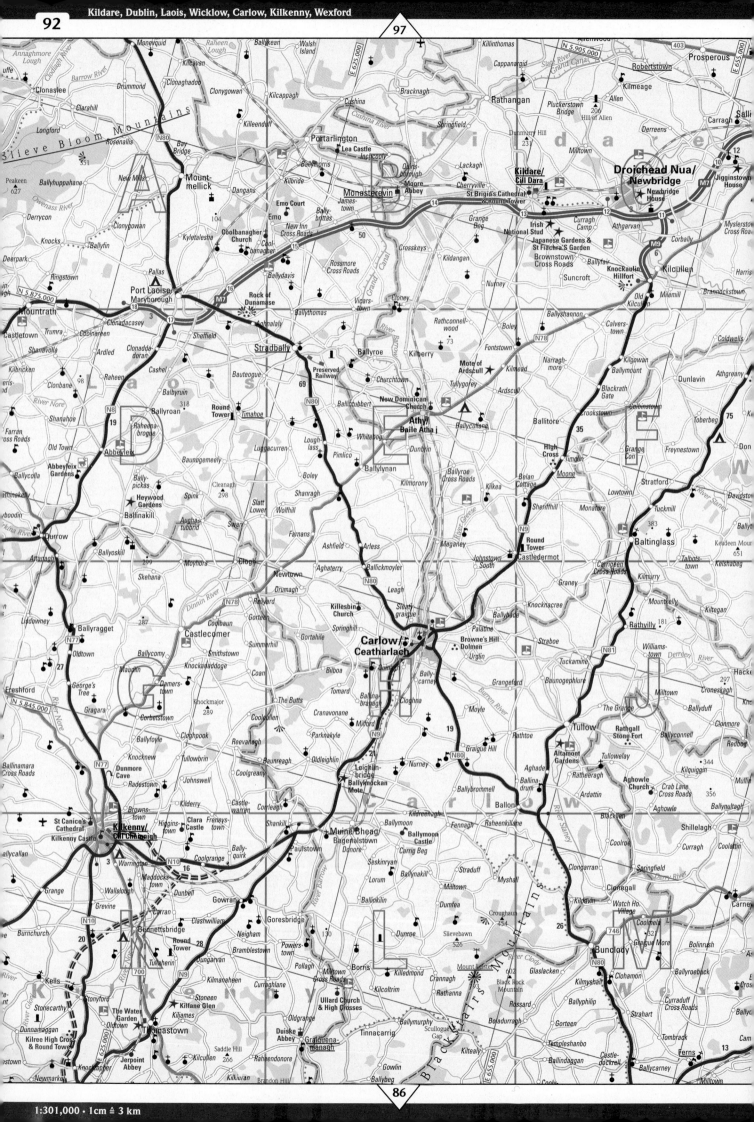

Straffan
Liffey
Hazelhatch
Henry Bridge
Newcastle
Oughterard
Rathcoole
14
N7
Saggart
Kill
Kilwarden
Johnstown
Redgap
Furness
Rathmore
Eadestown
House Roads
N81
333
Kilbride
Blessington
Reservoir
Oldcourt
ssborough House
more Place
Carrig
Lackan
Valleymount
Poulaphouca Reservoir
Ballyknockan
600
Sorrell Hill
Duff Hill
847
Moanbane
702
Mullaghcleevaun
Granabeg
416
Corragh
Table Mountain
699
Tonelagee
Wicklow Gap
Glenmacnass Waterfall
535
Lough Tay
Lugnaquillia Mountain
924
799
Round Tower
Upper Lake
Reefert Church
755
Glendalough
Cathedral
Laragh
433
Drumgoff
Clara
ga
395
Slieveboy Mountain
Aghavannagh
Croaghanmoira Mountain
662
Greenan
Rathdrum
Knocknagilky
Knockananna
Askanagap
Moyne
Cappagh
Sheenamore
400
Cushbawn
Crafield
Rathshanmore
391
Aughrim
Annacurragh
433
eland
Garryhoe
Derry Water
Killacloran
Tinahely
Moneyteige Middle
Ballykillagger
Coolroe
Curreghlawn
748
Croghan Mountain
605
Crosspatrick
Croghan
Connahill
Ballylusk
Monaseed
Pallis
white
Hollyfort
ideswell
Ballylacy
Craanford
27
Colciste
Ballygarrett
Gorey
Ballinglin
251
Tara Hill
Castletown
N11
Ballinamona
Clogh
Ballyoughter
Ashton
Ballycanew
Courtown

Milltown
Round Tower
N4
BALLYFERMOT
Kilmainham Gaol
M50
WALKINS-TOWN
9
10
4
CRUMLIN
TERENURE
N81
Marlfield
Knockannavea
393
Ballyfolan
647
Corrig Mountain
Killakee
568
Glencree
752
Kippure
Lough Bray Upper
622
Powerscourt Waterfall
724
Djouce Mountain
Sally Gap
Ballysmuttan
River Liffey
847
National Park
Kings River
Glenmalur
Avonbeg River
Avonmore River
755
Ballycullen
Ballylusk
Ballinderry
478
390
Gleneal
752
Carrick Mountain
Rathnew
Broad Lough
Glenealy
Ballinacor
Carrigmore
Kilbride
Balleese
Kilmacurragh
Avondale House
Avondale Forest Park
753
Ballinaclash
Kilmacoo
256
Redcross
23
Avoca
Woodenbridge
Shelton Abbey
747
Glenart Castle
Johnstown
Ballintombay
Coolgreany
Inch
Askintinny
Scarnagh Cross Roads
Clogga
Kilmichael Point
Killiniprin
Ballyfad

Drogheda
CONDRA
CLONTARF
National mus.
Trinity College
RINGSEND
Christ Church Cathedral
Dublin Castle
Waterways Visitor's Centre
IRISHTOWN
RATHMINES
SANDY-MOUTH
DUBLIN/
BAILE ÁTHA CLIATH
BALLES BRIDGE
RATHGAR
DUNDRUM
17
BLACKROCK
STILLORGAN
MONKS-TOWN
BALLIN-TEER
13
14
Fernhill Gardens
17
Stepaside
15
Kilternan
16
Ballybrack Megalithic Tomb
Glencullen
117
Shankill
M11
Killough
Kilmalin
Powerscourt House & Gardens
Ennis-kerry
Megalithic Tomb
Great Sugar Loaf
501
Kilmacanoge
Bray/
Bré
Killruddery House & Garden
Bray Head
Kilmurry
755
Greystones/
Na Clocha Liatha
Delgany
Carriggower
24
Kilpedder
Sragmore
Newtown
Kilcoole
Roundwood
Killadreenan
Leamore Strand
Vartry Reservoir
Diamond Hill
643
688
Newcastle
N11
Tomdarragh
Devil's Glen
344
Killiskey
Grange
Ashford
Mount Usher Gardens
Rathnew
Wicklow/
Cill Mhantáin
Wicklow Head
Ballydowling
Magherabeg
Ardmore Point
Ballywaltron
Brittas Bay
Ardanary
Mizen Head
Johnstown
Arklow/
An tInbhear Mór
Arklow Head

North Bull Island
Howth/
Binn Éadair
Baily Lighthouse
Drumleck Point
Dublin Bay
Douglas, Isle of Man 2¾ hrs
Holyhead 1¾ hrs/3 hrs, Liverpool 4 hrs/8 hrs
DUN LAOGHAIRE
James Joyce Tower
DALKEY
Dalkey Island
SALLYNOGGIN
KILLINEY
Killiney Bay
Scotsman's Bay
N 5.905.000
N 295.000

	≋	☀
V	9°	10°
VII	13°	15°
VIII	14°	15°
IX	14°	13°
X	13°	10°

St George's Channel
N 5.875.000
N 5.845.000
E 295.000

Clondalkin/
Cluain Dolcain
Tallaght/
Tamhlacht

0 ⸻ 5 km

0   5 km

	≈≈≈	☀
V	9°	10°
VII	13°	15°
VIII	14°	15°
IX	14°	13°
X	13°	10°

1:301,000 · 1cm ≙ 3 km

The Mullet (inset)

Eagle Island
The Mullet
Doonamo Fort
Aghadoon

Inset (Broad Haven area)

Stags of Broad Haven
Kid Island
Benwee Head 253
Portacloy
Knockadaff 208
Carrowteige
Pig Island
Porturlin

Main map

Eagle Island
Portaclo
Carrowteige
Kn
Aghadoon
Doonamo Fort
The Mullet
Corclogh
Broad Haven
Doon-garton
Ross
Termoncarragh Lake
Tower Hill 130
Graghil
Knocknalina
Dooncarton Stone Circle & Megalithic Tomb
Inver
Gortbrack North
Pollatomish
Inishglora
Belmullet
An Geata Mór
Cross Lough
Drumreagh
Inishkeeragh
Knocknalower
Pollagarraun Bridge
Faulagh
Bunnahowen
Glencastle Hill 229
Derreens
Carrowmore
Inishkea North
Barranagh Island
Elly Bay
Tawmore Bay
313
Knocknascollop 237
Gortmore
Lake
Glenc Low
Inishkea South 67
Dun Dohmnall
Aghleam
Termon Hill 105
Attavally
Srahmore
Carrafull 269
Black Rock
Fallmore
Ridge Point
Tristia
Bangor
Duvillaun More
Duvillaun Beg
Dooyork
Gweesalia
Doohooma
Rath Hill 61
Knocklettercuss 366
ATLANTIC OCEAN
Blacksod Bay
Tullaghan Bay
Aughness
Nephin
Saddle Head
Tullaghanbaun
Doona
Achill Head
Ridge Point
Slievemore 671
Village of Slievemore
Doogort
Valley
Snahill Lough
Slieve Alp 328
Croaghaun 665
Keem
Achill Island
Dooniver Strand
Ballycroy
Keel
River
Inishbiggle
Castlehill
Buna-curry
Bellagarvaun
Cathedral Rocks 464
Acaill
Cashel
Salia
Annagh Island
Claggan
Bellaveeny Lower
Glennamong 627
Dooega Head
Dooega
Knockmore 337
Achill
Owenduff 460
N59
62
711
Bills Rocks
Achill Sound
Belfarsad
Corraun
380
Bengorm 580
Derreen
Corraun Hill 524
540
Claggan Mountain
Mulrany
Rosturk
Kildavnet Castle
Glassilaun
Peninsula
Cushlecka
Cloghmore
Bolinglanna
Dooghbeg
Gubbaun Point
Rockfleet Castle
Achillbeg Island
Gubacarrigan
Newport Bay
Carrickfadda
Kilmeena
Glassillan-garalthagh 461
Clare Island
Maum
Kinnacorra
Drumgarv
Kinatevdilla
Lough anaphuca
Fawnglass
Grania Weal's Castle
Clew Bay
Carraholly
Roonagh Quay
Old Head
Westport Bay
Emlagh Point
Askillaun
Alcony
Louisburgh
Kilsallagh
Leckanvy
Murrisk Abbey
Westport Quay
Inishturk
Garranty
Caher Island
Granuaile Centre
Kilgeever Abbey
Mullagh
Murrisk
Killadangan
Dromore Head
Ballybeg Island
Carownisky
Formoyle
Tully Bridge
Croagh Patrick
Bunlahinch Bridge
Inishdalla
Killadoon
Srahmee Megalithic Tomb
Cregganbaun
Lough Nacorra
Knappagh
Barnabaun Point
Kinnadoohy 270
Gleoon Bridge
Liscarr
Inishshark 99
Bofin 80
Inishbofin
Davillaun
Tonakeera Point
Inishdegil More
Murrisk Peninsula
Owenmore Bridge
Carrowkennedy
Inishgort
Inishlyon
Crump Island
Doo Lough
Doo Lough Pass 761
Sheffry Hills 740
N59
Rinvyle Castle
Ardna-greevagh
Mweelrea 817
Delphi
High Island
Friar Island
Rinvyle 355
Rosroe
Cuffin
Salrock
Ben Grom 702
Aasleagh Falls
67
Aughrus More
Cleggan
Letter Beg
Tully Mountain
Tully Cross
Ardagh
Garraun 598
Kylemore Abbey
Lough Fee
Bundorragha Harbour
Cultural Centre
Glennagevlagh
Maumtrasna 673
Cruagh
Claddaghduff
Ballynew
Moyard
Dawros
Leenaun
Par

Temperature table

	≈	☀
V	11°	11°
VII	14°	16°
VIII	15°	16°
IX	15°	13°
X	14°	11°

Grid references: N 5,995,000 · N 5,965,000 · N 5,935,000 · E 415,000 · E 445,000

1:301.000 · 1cm ≙ 3 km

0 —— 5 km

A T L A N T I C

O C E A N

A B C D E G H J K L M

West T
Tory
Tory

Bloody
Foreland

Inishsirrer   Brinlack   316   Meenaclady

Gola
Island   Inish-
meane   Carrick   Gweedo

Portacurry
The Stag Rocks   Derrybeg
Owey   Middletown   Tievealehid
Island   Inishfree   431
Lower   Bunbeg
Torneady   Cruit   Quay   Krocka-   407
Point   Island   Inishfree   stoller   Dore
Bay   Rinnafarset   Gweedore
Rosses Bay   Burton-   Kincaslough   Annagary   Crolly   Lough
Aran Island   port   The Rosses   Nacung
Leabgarrow   ¼ h   Loughanure   453   Upper
Aphort   Ballinira   Grogan More   Glentornan   Du
Rutland   Lough   Crocknafarragh   Lough
Inishkeeragh   Island   Dunglow   Mfela   Ardmeen   520
Inishfree   N56   Lough   Lough   Crocknasharragh
Upper   Maghery   Craghy   Croangar   495
Maghery   316   Meenatotan
Bay   Meenacross   Commeen
Crohy   Derrydruel
Head   Doocharry   Carbat Gap

V   11°   11°
VII   14°   16°
VIII   15°   16°
IX   15°   13°
X   14°   11°

Roaninish   Donegal Coast   Derrylough   Lough   269
Trawenagh   Machugh   Ballyna-   Croagheheen   Gubbin
Gweebarra Bay   Dooey   Bay   carrick   383   D
Dunmore   Point   Derry
Head   Inishkeel   Ballincrick   176   Loughlan
Dawros   Portnoo   Lettermacaward   Forest
Head   Naran   Clooney   238   Preserved   Fintown
Inishbarnog   Rossbeg   Stone   Maas   Derkbeg Hill   railway   Lough Finn
Fort   Kilclooney   Letterilly   335   Shalogan   Lough
Tormore Island   Loughros   Glendorragha   Sandfield   House   Aghla Mountain   Muck
Point   Lough   74   Meenadeeny   568   Kno
Sturall   Loughros   Maghera   Derryness   Aderry   101   Mullanore   Graffy
Port   Beg Bay   Cloghboy   Tully More   Glenties   478
Glen   Slievetooey   Straboy   Crannogeboy   Lough   Kilrean   Tangaveane   Croveenananta
Head   Folk Village   445   Crockuna   Machugh   Meenachallow   305
Museum   Croaghagullion   Leaconnell   Ardara   Crockaslowra   Tullyhonwar   Silver Hill
Rossan   375   387   Lough   604
Point   Meenacross   Naidgraman   Common   Monargan   Binbane   Lavagh More
Glencolumkille   Kilgolly   Stravally   Aighe   Bridge   Glebe   455   672
Malin   Lergynasearhagh   353   Meenybraddan
Cloghanmore   More   Glengesh   Glengesh Pass   Neck of the   Mulmosog   Caranween   Croaghgorm or Blu
Malin Bay   Crove   Ballagh   Mountain   522
Rathlin O'Birne   Lough   Crowbane   Meentullynagarn   Lackrom
Island   Malin Beg   Inna   Crocknapeast   White Hill   Forest
Meenavean   Straleel   503   Croagh   Carraduffy   Meenataggart   Greenan
Slieve League   Mulnanaff   Drumagraa   Banagher Hill   Bridge
Carrick   595   473   Bungosteen   228   Bridge   386   Letterbarra
Bunglass Point   Derrylahan   Crownarad   Bridge   Crocknasharragh   Limestone
Teelin   494   Croagh   Brook Bridge   Lough
Carrigan   Currs   Kilcar   388   Calhame   Red Bridges   Winterhill   Eske
Head   Cashel   Largy   Milltown   Inver   Marlas Bridge   Gar
Carntullagh   Milltown   Mount
Tawny   Shalvy   Killybegs   N56   Drumnakitty   charles   Donegal
Muckros   Fintragh   Carntullagh   Drumgorman   Ballyboyle   Donegal   Finnabanes
Head   Bay   Drumoo   Dunkineely   Ballyederlan   Castle
Inishduff   Carntullagh   66   Inver Bay   Drumbar   Drummenny
Drumanoo   Head   Mountcharles   Bridge
Head   McSwyne's Bay   Doorin   Raneely   Laghy   Copany
Killultan   Ackle Back   Point   Mullanasole
St John's   Bunlin Barr   Oughtdarnid   274
Point   Donegal Historical   Bridgetown   Shannagh
Society Museum   Durnish
Donegal   Rossnowlagh   Lake   Ballintra
Lower
Bay   Coolmore   Rosscat   N15
Kildoney   Hill
Point   22   E 565,000   N15

0 —————— 5 km

Inishtrahull

A

B

C

Inishtrahull Sound

285
Umgall
247
Malin
261
Portaleen
Templemoyle
Glengad
Head
Culdaff
Dunmore
Head
Carndonagh
Tirraboy
Bocan
Stone Circle
Carrow-
menagh
Ballymagaraghy
238
Gleneely
Falmore
Ballintroohan
Balbane
Head
Magherdrumman
Leckemy
Crocknasmug
322
Inishowen
Head
Peninsula
Crockavishane
322
Stroove
Dunagree Point
Glentogher
Pensylvania
Moville
Greencastle
Magilligan
Point

Antrim Coast

344 N 6.115.000
Glencaw Hill
Magilligan Strand
Causeway Coast
Giant's
Causeway
Benbane Head
Dunseverick
Sheep
Island
Creehennan
Castlecary
Redcastle
The Skerries
Ramore Head
Dunluce
Castle
Causeway
Head
Currysheskin
Carricka
Rope Brid
Quigley's
Point
Port-
rush
Portballintrae
Ballyallaght
White Park
Bay
Ballintoy
Lagavara
Clare
Wood
Lough
Foyle
Port-
stewart
Bushmills
43
Craig
Fallgarrive
Ballinlea
Magilligan
Downhill
Mussenden
Temple
2
46
Castleroe
Artclave
29
Beardville
Billy
Ballyloughbeg
Ballinlea
Glebe
Lower
Ballyleighery
Binevenagh
Forest
Round
Knowe
Ballinteer
2
Coleraine
Blagh
Sencirl
Liscolman
Moss-Side
ichard's
Town
Londonderry
Airport
Ballymacron
Crindle
Bolea
Macosquin
29
Castleroe
Mountsandel
Fort
Bally-
nashane
Ballybogy
Derrykeighan
Cape
Castle
Carriokhugh
Rush Hall
2
Eglinton
Greysteel
Ballykelly
Letterloan
Damhead
African Game
Reserve
Garry
Wood
Dervock
Gardenvale
Balleney
Springwell
Forest
Crossgare
Seacon
Kirkhills
Stranocum
Armoy
44
Killylane
Upper
Bolie
Drum-
raighland
Leisure Park
Roe Valley
Ardmore
Ballylintagh
Ballymoney
28
Dunaghy
Ballyhoe
Bridge
Glenhead
Terrydremont
Ringsend
Cam
Forest
Mullan
Agivey
Balnamore
Milltown
Millturn
26
Bally
boylands
Kilraghts
Ballyknock
393
Loughermore
Baranour
Moys
Aghadowey
Ardreagh
Bendooragh
Phans
Loughguile
Slaghtmanus
Drumsurn
Bovevagh
Church
Killykergan
Garryduff
Knockaholet
Killagan
Bridge
Bovevagh
Ballyrogan
Caheny
Finvoy
Dunloy
Corkey
Ballyness
Garvagh
Forest
Garvagh
32
Vow
54
Slievenaghy
Clogh
Mills
Ballynagabog
Bridge
Ballymoney
40
6
Scriggan
Gortnacross
Ballytemple
Ballyna-
meen
Moneydig
McLaughlins
Corner
Glenvale
Glarryford
Newtown-
Crommelin
N 6.085.000
The Glen
Dungiven
Derrychrier
Drumsaragh
Kilrea
Rasharkin
Clogh
Feeny
Banagher
Church
Moyletra Kill
Bovedy
Harvey Hill
River Bann
Kildowney
Martins-
town
McGregor's
Corner
Fincarn
Carn
Lismoyle
Glenvale
Ballyreagh
Knockanul
Park
Dreen
Mullaghash
479
Swatragh
Moneysharvan
Tamlaght
Lisnahunshin
Gledheather
Tullynewy
Quarrytown
int Mountain
488
Sperrin Mountains
Banagher
Forest
Nat. Res.
Mullaghmore
Glenshane
554
Tirkane
Tamlaght
O'Crilly
Craigs
26
Tullymor
Sawel Moutain
678
Mullaghaneany
Glenshane Pass
Forest
Upperlands
Lisler
Teeshan
12
Killyflugh
Moydamlaght
Forest
Carna-
money
Ballyknock
Falla
loon
Culnady
Inishrush
Arthur
House
M2
Ballykeel
Sperrin
Moneyneany
Lisnamuck
Maghera
Claudy
Portglenone
Bally
backey
Ballymena
11
Goles
Forest
Carnanelly
487
Labby
Straw
Gulladuff
42
Corna-
hooklagh
Ballynease
Ahoghill
Galgorm
Gracehill
Roslin Hill
Spaltindoagh
420
Moydamlaght
Forest
Tobermore
6
Knockcloghrim
Bellaghy
54
Moravian
Settlement
10
Mullaghturk
416
Altihaskey
Curran
Luney Bridge
Newferry
Bally-
macilroy
Chesney's
Corner
Liminary
Glenhull
Mullagh
shuraren
Desertmartin
530 Slieve Gallion
Castledawson
Milltown
Whitesides
Corner
Foundry
Kidrum
Moorfields

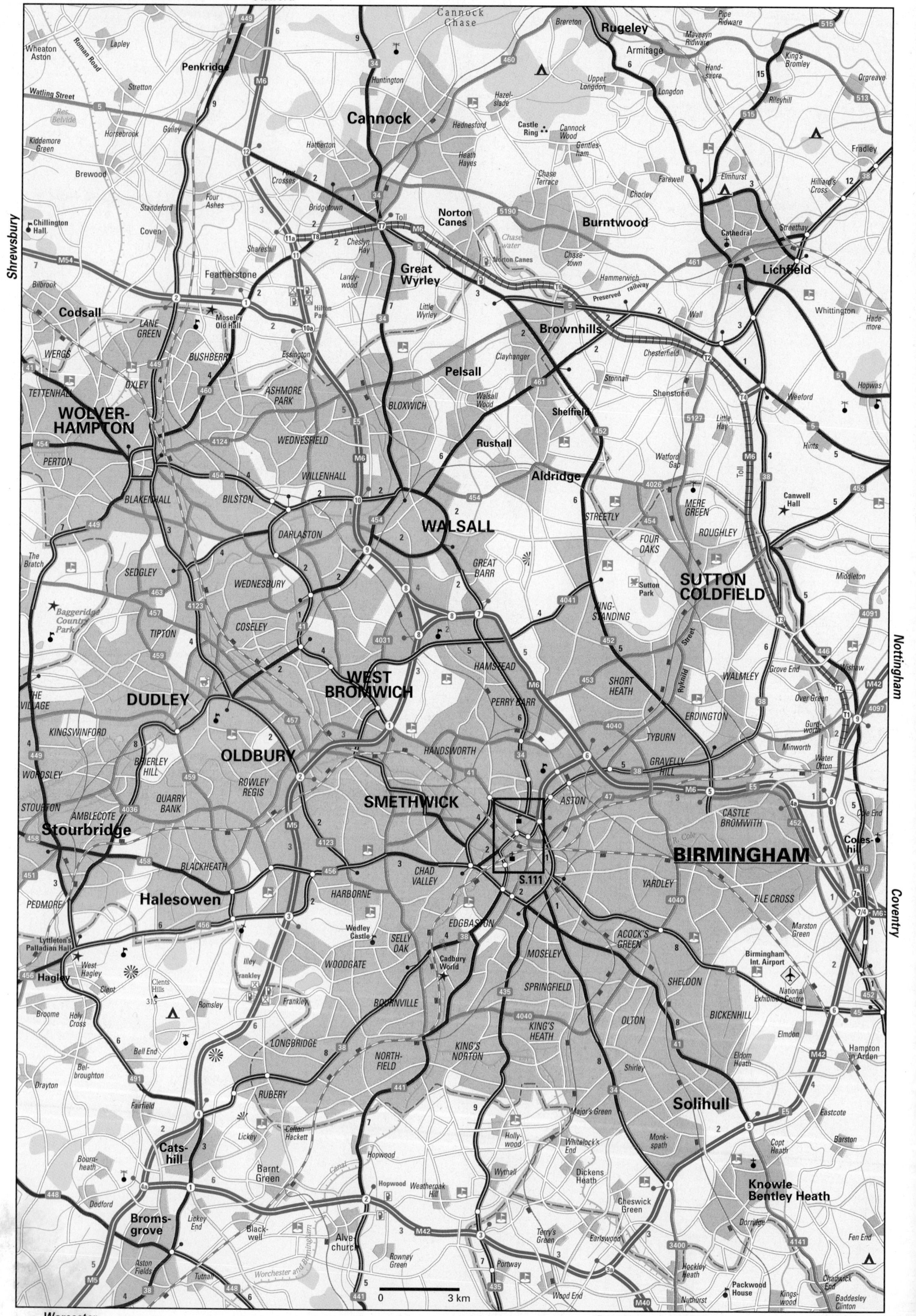
Stafford
Shrewsbury
Nottingham
Coventry
Worcester
Royal Leamington Spa
Cannock Chase
Wheaton Aston
Lapley
Roman Road
Penkridge
Stretton
Watling Street
Res. Belvide
Kiddemore Green
Horsebrook
Gailey
Brewood
Four Ashes
Standeford
Coven
Chillington Hall
Shareshill
Featherstone
Bilbrook
Codsall
Moseley Old Hall
LANE GREEN
WERGS
BUSHBERRY
OXLEY
TETTENHALL
WOLVERHAMPTON
PERTON
BLAKENHALL
The Bratch
SEDGLEY
Baggeridge Country Park
TIPTON
DUDLEY
THE VILLAGE
KINGSWINFORD
BRIERLEY HILL
WORDSLEY
STOURTON
AMBLECOTE
QUARRY BANK
Stourbridge
PEDMORE
Halesowen
BLACKHEATH
Lyttleton's Palladian Hall
West Hagley
Hagley
Clent
Clents Hills
Broome
Holy Cross
Romsley
Bell End
Belbroughton
Drayton
Fairfield
Catshill
Bournheath
Dodford
Bromsgrove
Aston Fields
Tutnall
Lickey End
Lickey
Barnt Green
Blackwell
Alvechurch
Rowney Green
Hopwood
Weatheroak Hill
Worchester and Birmingham
Cofton Hackett
RUBERY
LONGBRIDGE
NORTHFIELD
KING'S NORTON
BOURNVILLE
WOODGATE
Wedley Castle
SELLY OAK
Cadbury World
Illey
Frankley
HARBORNE
CHAD VALLEY
EDGBASTON
ROWLEY REGIS
OLDBURY
SMETHWICK
WEST BROMWICH
HANDSWORTH
HAMSTEAD
PERRY BARR
ASTON
S.111
R. Cole
BIRMINGHAM
YARDLEY
TILE CROSS
ACOCK'S GREEN
MOSELEY
SPRINGFIELD
KING'S HEATH
OLTON
SHELDON
BICKENHILL
Elmdon
Birmingham Int. Airport
National Exhibition Centre
Marston Green
Eldom Heath
Shirley
Solihull
Major's Green
Hollywood
Whitelock's End
Wythall
Dickens Heath
Cheswick Green
Monkspath
Terry's Green
Earlswood
Portway
Wood End
Hockley Heath
Nuthurst
Packwood House
Knowle
Bentley Heath
Dorridge
Copt Heath
Barston
Eastcote
Hampton in Arden
Fen End
Chadwick End
Kingswood
Baddesley Clinton
CASTLE BROMWITH
GRAVELLY HILL
TYBURN
ERDINGTON
SHORT HEATH
KINGSTANDING
Sutton Park
SUTTON COLDFIELD
FOUR OAKS
MERE GREEN
ROUGHLEY
WALMLEY
Minworth
Water Orton
Curdworth
Wishaw
Over Green
Grove End
Middleton
Coleshill
Cole End
Canwell Hall
Hints
Weeford
Hopwas
Whittington
Hademore
Lichfield
Streethay
Cathedral
Elmhurst
Hilliard's Cross
Fradley
Orgreave
King's Bromley
Rileyhill
Handsacre
Longdon
Mavesyn Ridware
Pipe Ridware
Armitage
Rugeley
Brereton
Upper Longdon
Hazelslade
Cannock Wood
Castle Ring
Gentleshaw
Chase Terrace
Chorley
Farewell
Burntwood
Chasetown
Hammerwich
Preserved railway
Wall
Chesterfield
Shenstone
Stonnall
Little Hay
Watford Gap
Brownhills
Clayhanger
Pelsall
Walsall Wood
Shelfield
Rushall
Aldridge
STREETLY
GREAT BARR
WALSALL
Hednesford
Heath Hayes
Norton Canes
Chase water
Great Wyrley
Little Wyrley
Cannock
Huntington
Hatherton
Four Crosses
Bridgetown
Cheslyn Hay
Landywood
Hilton Park
Essington
ASHMORE PARK
BLOXWICH
WEDNESFIELD
WILLENHALL
BILSTON
DARLASTON
WEDNESBURY
COSELEY
Toll
0
3 km

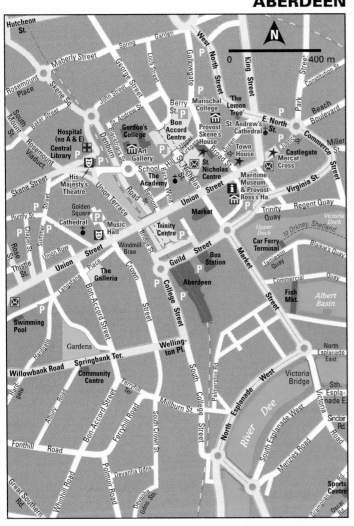

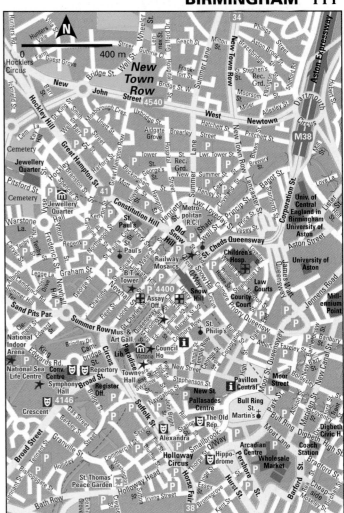

BRIGHTON AND HOVE

BRISTOL

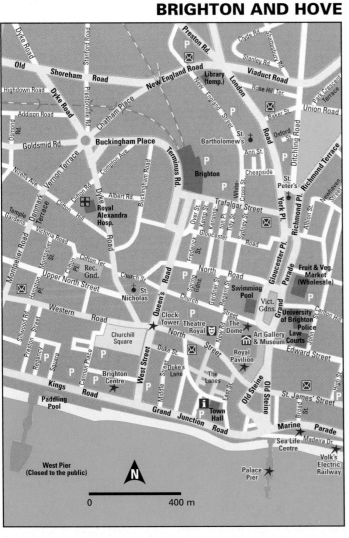

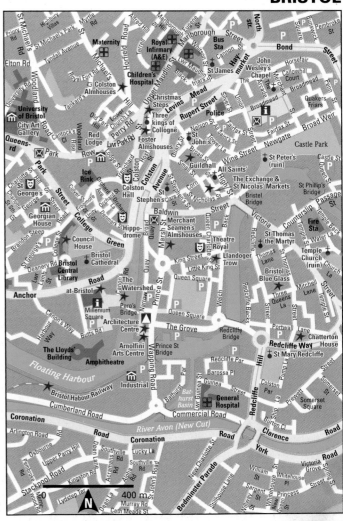

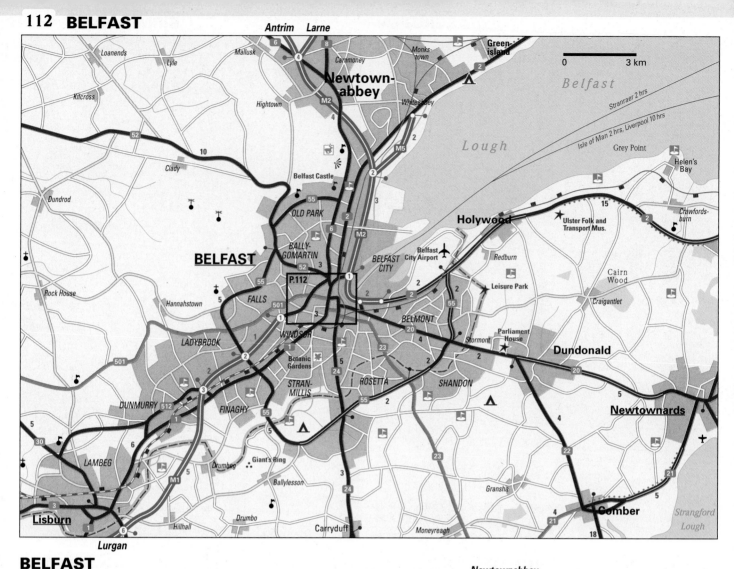

BELFAST

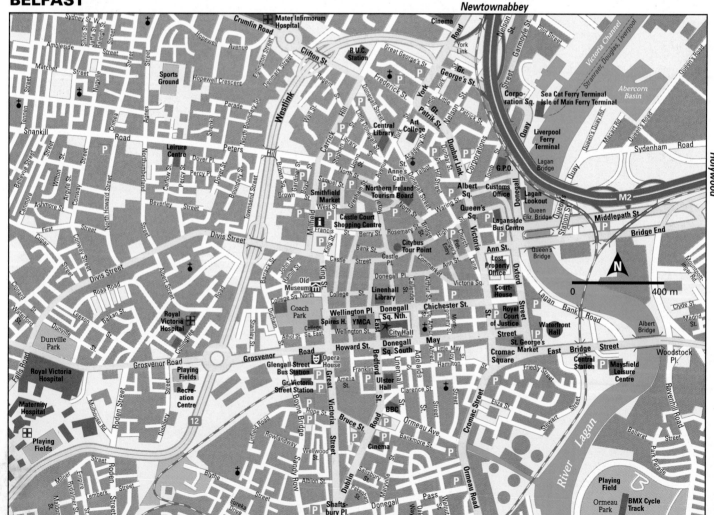

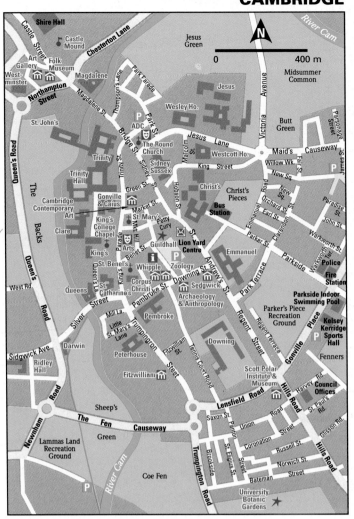

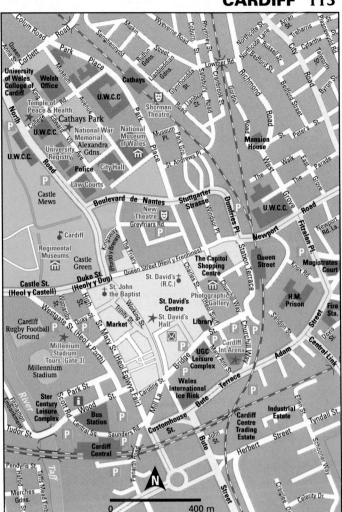

EDINBURGH

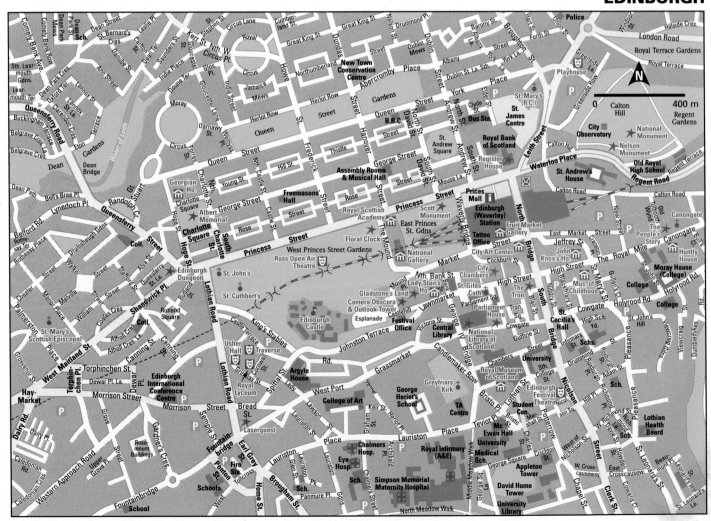

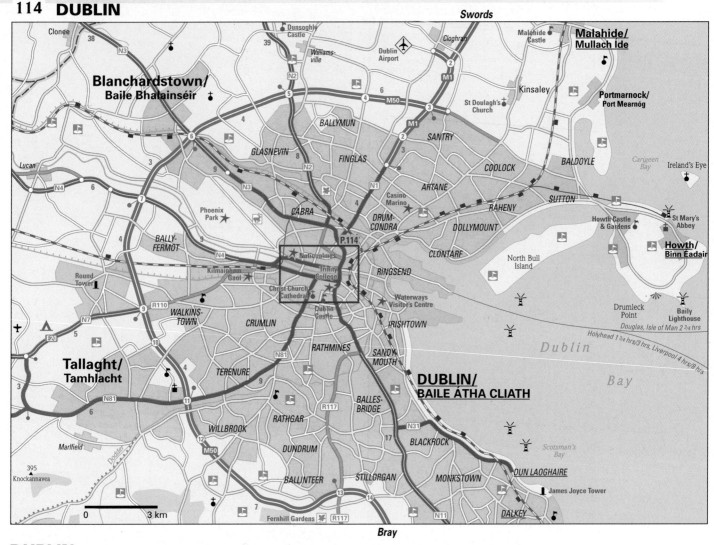

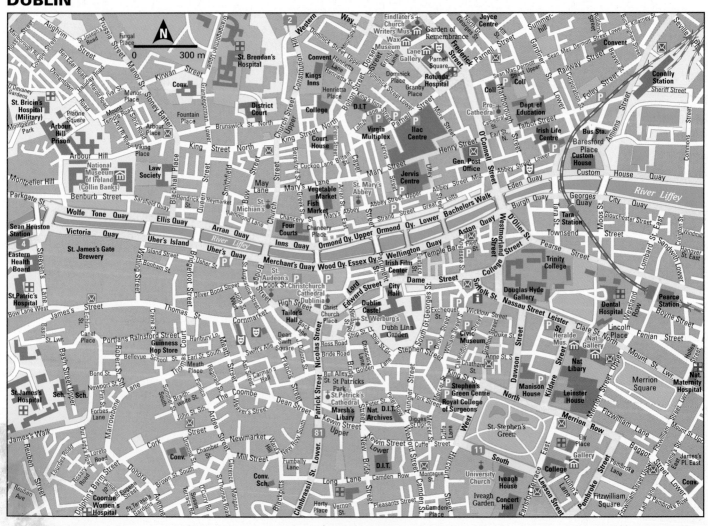

DUBLIN

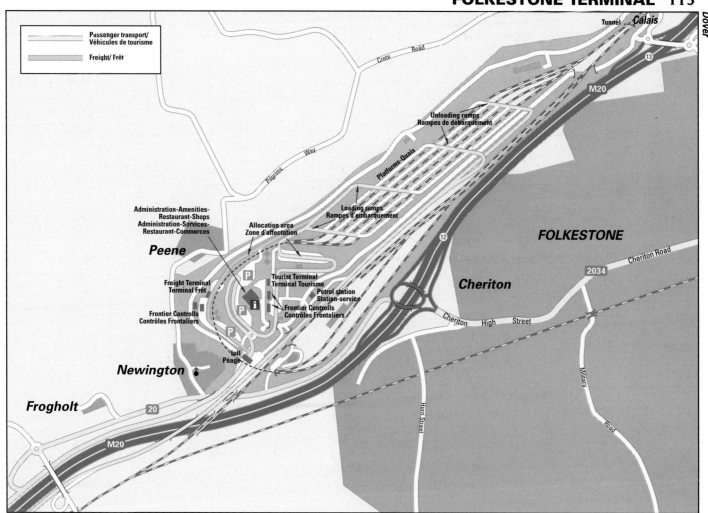

TERMINAL DE CALAIS

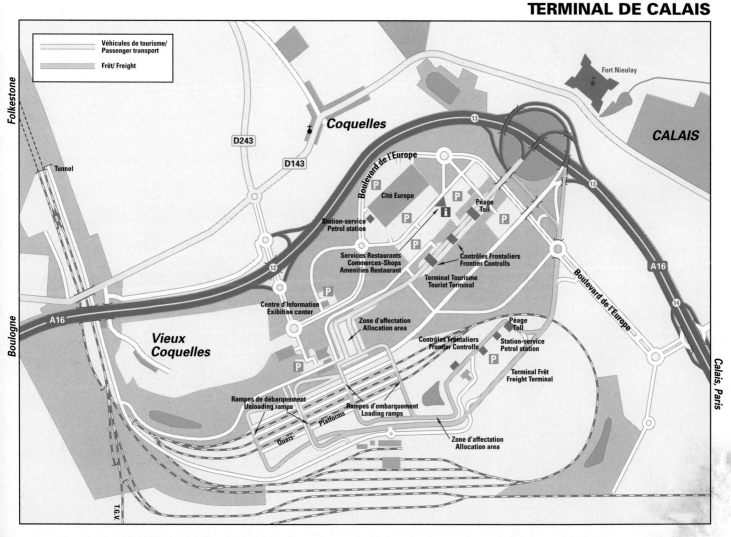

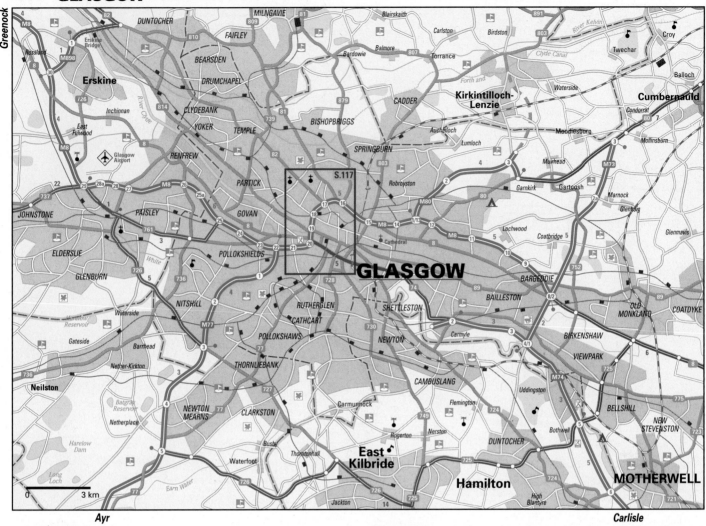

OXFORD

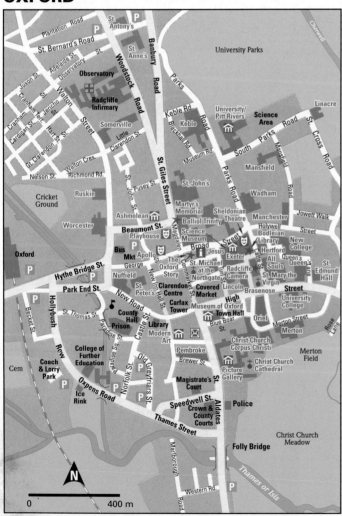

SHEFFIELD

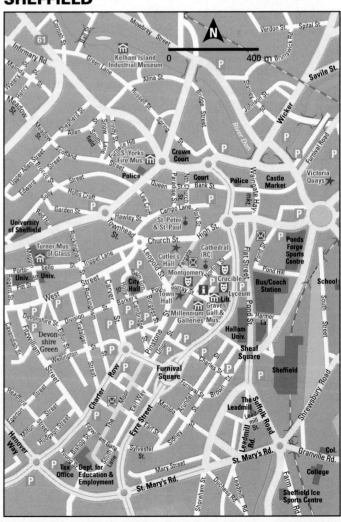

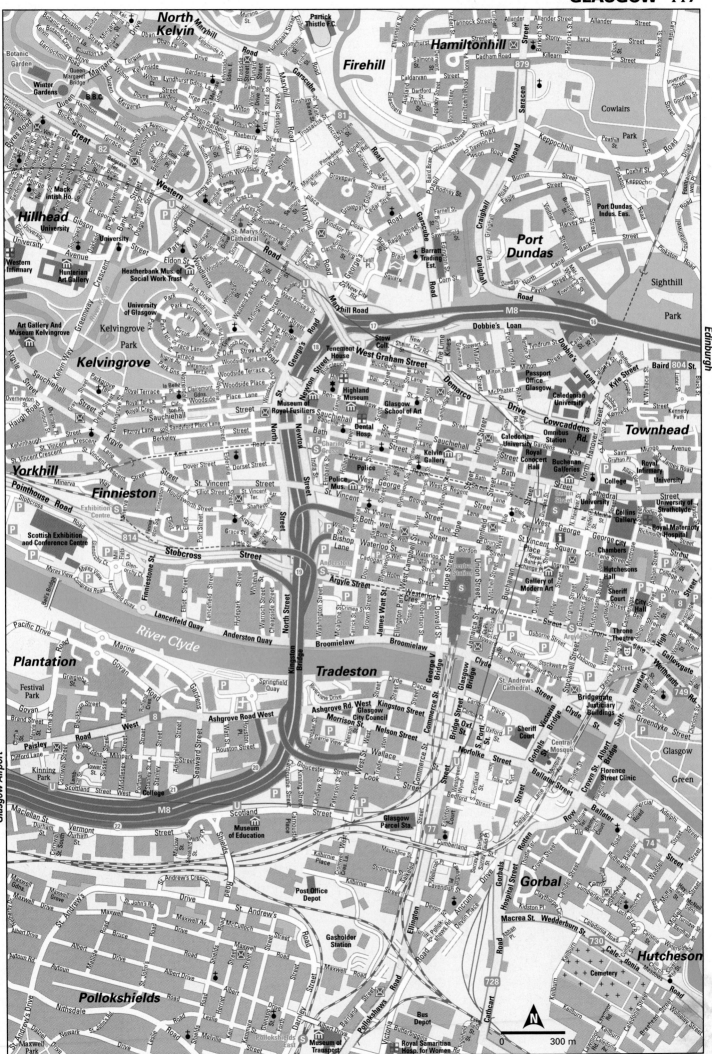

0   300 m

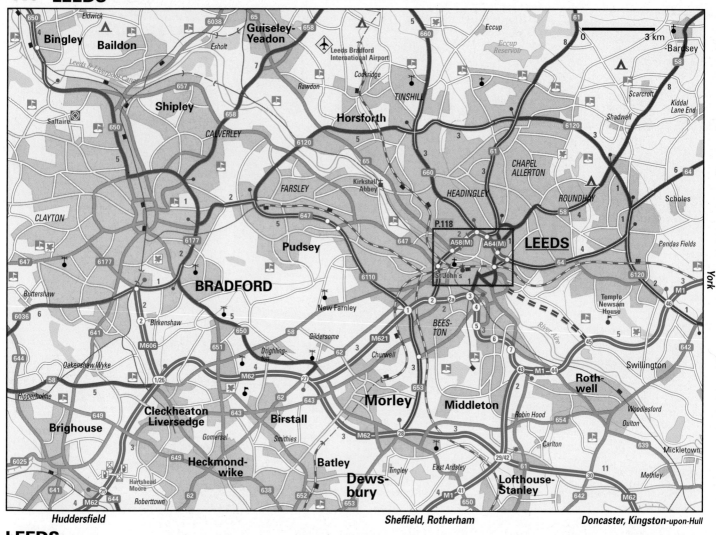

Huddersfield — Sheffield, Rotherham — Doncaster, Kingston-upon-Hull

LEEDS

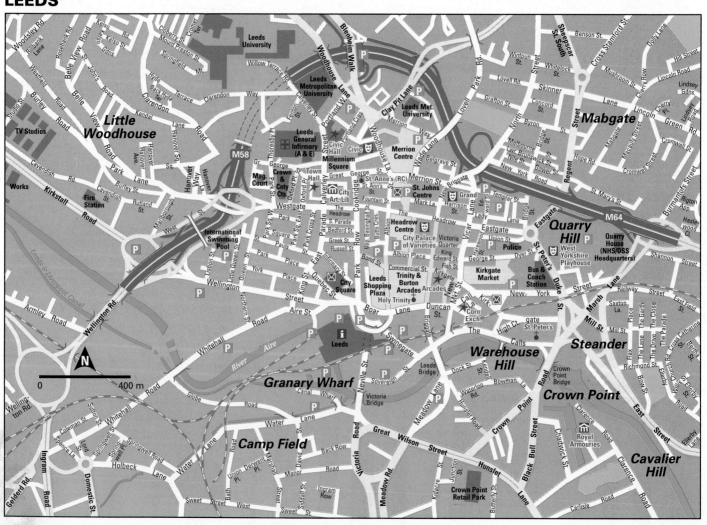

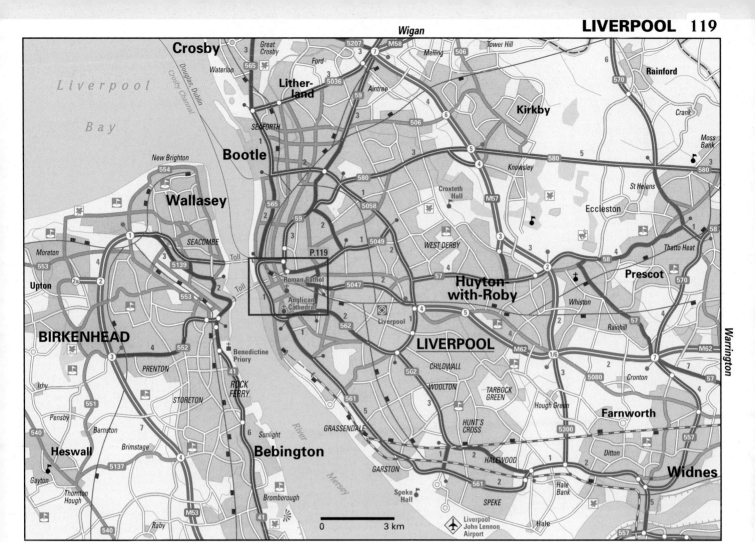

LIVERPOOL

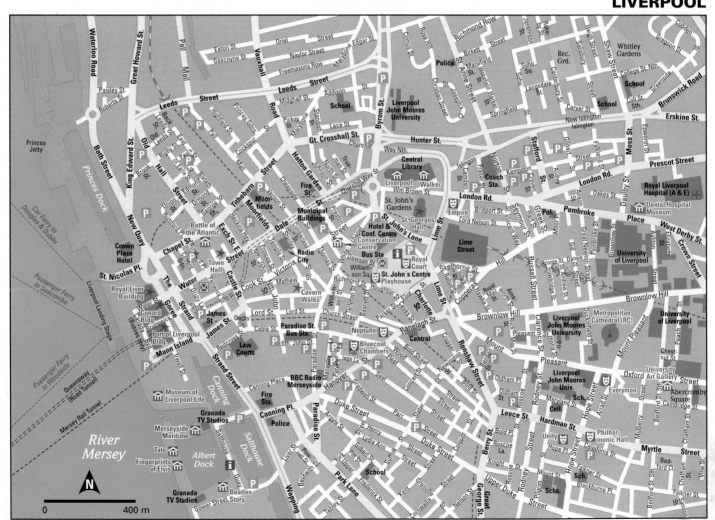

Southend-on-Sea

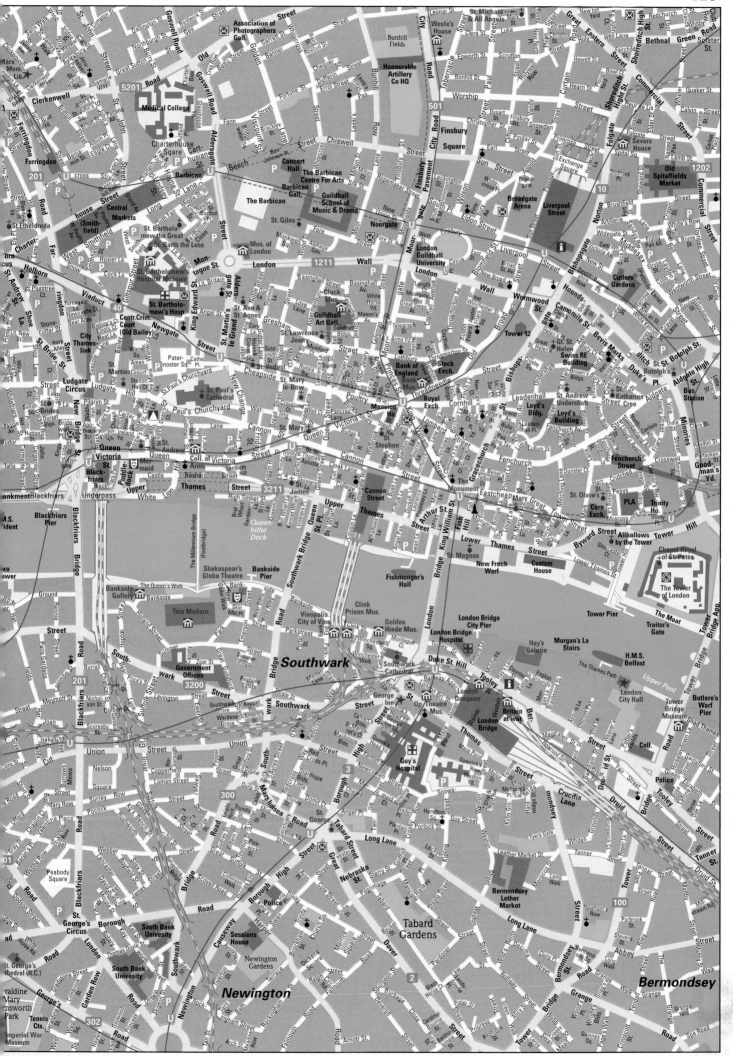

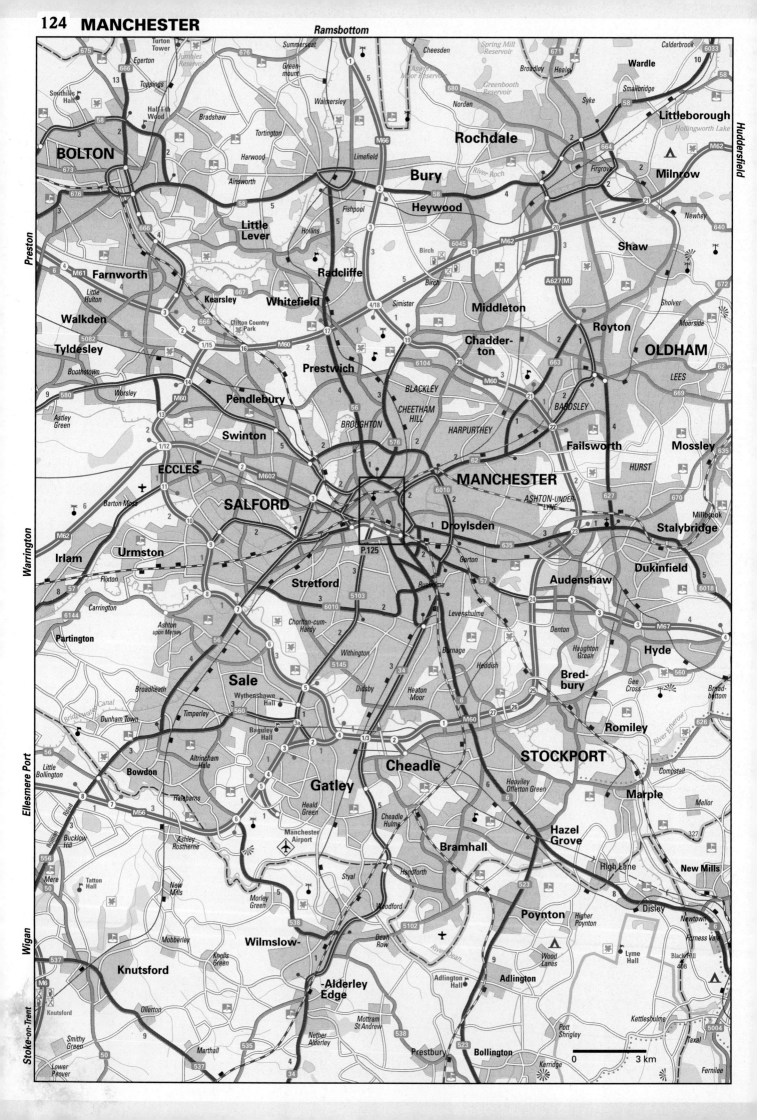

BOLTON

Rochdale

Bury

Heywood

Little Lever

Radcliffe

Whitefield

Kearsley

Farnworth

Walkden

Tyldesley

Prestwich

Middleton

Chadder-ton

Royton

OLDHAM

Shaw

Milnrow

Littleborough

Wardle

Pendlebury

SALFORD

Swinton

ECCLES

BLACKLEY

CHEETHAM HILL

BROUGHTON

HARPURTHEY

MANCHESTER

Failsworth

Mossley

ASHTON-UNDER-LYNE

Stalybridge

Dukinfield

Hyde

Irlam

Urmston

Stretford

Droylsden

Gorton

Audenshaw

Chorlton-cum-Hardy

Rusholme

Levenshulme

Denton

Haughton Green

Partington

Sale

Withington

Didsby

Burnage

Heaton Moor

Heddish

Bred-bury

Romiley

Wythenshawe Hall

Timperley

Baguley Hall

STOCKPORT

Marple

Altrincham Hale

Gatley

Heald Green

Cheadle Hulme

Heaviley Offerton Green

Marple

Bowdon

Cheadle

Hazel Grove

Manchester Airport

Styal

Handforth

Bramhall

High Lane

New Mills

Knutsford

Morley Green

Woodford

Poynton

Higher Poynton

Disley

Wilmslow

Dean Row

Alderley Edge

Wood Lanes

Lyme Hall

Adlington Hall

Adlington

Mottram St Andrew

Nether Alderley

Prestbury

Bollington

Kerridge

P.125

0   3 km

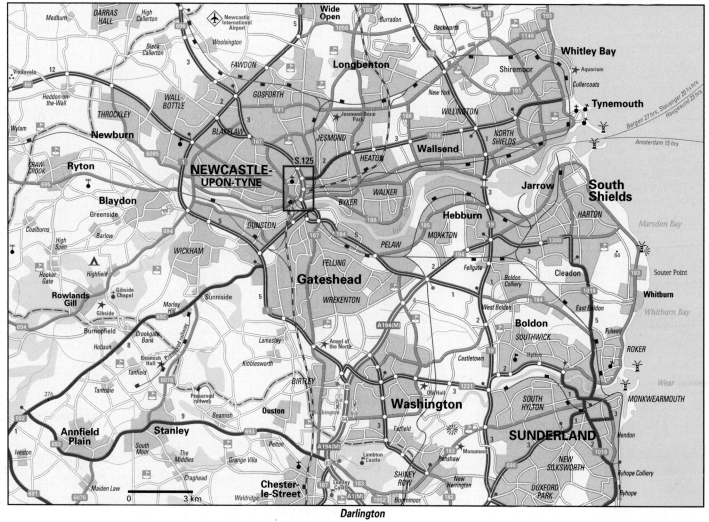

MANCHESTER

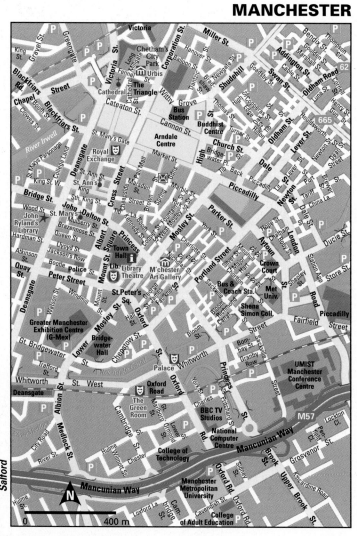

NEWCASTLE

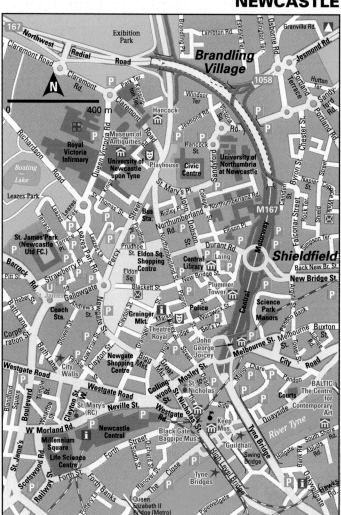

Distances within Europe (in km)	Amsterdam	Athens/Athína	Barcelona	Belgrade/Beograd	Berlin	Brussels/Bruxelles	Budapest	Bucharest/Buçuresti	Calais	Dublin	Edinburgh	Florence/Firenze	Frankfurt a. M.	Genf/Genève	Genoa/Genova	Hamburg	Helsinki	Istanbul	Copenhagen/København	Leipzig	Lisbon/Lisboa	London	Luxembourg	Lyon	Madrid	Milan/Milano	Manchester	Marseille	Moscow/Moskva	Munich/München	Naples/Napoli	Oslo	Palermo	Paris	Prague/Praha	Rom/Roma	Salzburg	Sofia/Sofija	Stockholm	Strasbourg	Turin/Torino	Venice/Venezia	Warsaw/Warszawa	Vienna/Wien	Zurich/Zürich
Amsterdam	—	3070	1590	1830	690	200	1440	2330	360	880	990	1490	460	1040	1320	500	1860	2770	810	780	2270	350	410	990	1740	1180	780	1250	2540	850	2080	1400	2770	480	960	1770	980	2220	1430	680	1260	1310	1280	1180	880
Athens/Athína	3070	—	3410	1240	2560	3030	1640	1300	3230	3930	4050	2390	2620	2700	2500	2950	3420	1210	3250	2780	4680	3400	2800	2880	4030	2300	3940	2830	3220	2110	660	3600	1580	3060	2210	1420	2090	870	3630	2610	2550	2030	2310	1900	2530
Barcelona	1590	3410	—	2170	1830	1410	2100	2890	1410	2110	2230	1160	1280	810	890	1780	3070	3110	2090	1740	1270	1580	1270	650	620	1110	1690	580	3690	1390	1630	2680	2470	1120	1680	1470	1530	2550	2710	1050	890	1390	2420	1840	1090
Belgrade/Beograd	1830	1240	2170	—	1320	1790	400	720	1990	2690	2810	1090	1380	1460	1180	1790	2180	940	2100	1460	3440	2160	1560	1570	2790	1060	2460	1590	2150	990	1600	2360	1640	1820	970	1320	850	380	2390	1370	1160	790	1070	660	1290
Berlin	690	2560	1830	1320	—	790	920	1770	990	1530	1640	1260	560	1140	1170	290	1430	2260	460	170	2890	1000	770	1260	2360	1110	1420	1490	1860	590	1760	1040	2540	1100	350	1530	730	1700	1070	780	1280	1080	590	660	850
Brussels/Bruxelles	200	3030	1410	1790	790	—	1400	2290	200	910	1020	1270	410	820	1100	660	1950	2730	970	720	2090	380	220	670	1560	960	600	1080	2650	800	1840	1560	2550	300	910	1550	940	2170	1590	440	1040	1230	1380	1130	660
Budapest	1440	1640	2100	400	920	1400	—	890	1600	2310	2420	1070	990	1300	1150	1210	1780	1340	1390	820	3240	1770	1230	1490	2710	1090	2160	1620	1960	710	1570	1960	2040	1560	580	1350	580	780	1990	1090	1140	820	680	270	1020
Bucharest/Buçuresti	2330	1300	2890	720	1770	2290	890	—	2490	3190	3300	1610	1880	2170	1700	2060	2280	730	2140	1630	4150	2660	2120	2090	3510	1780	2960	2300	1920	1700	2120	2740	2350	2450	1460	2040	1570	430	2770	2080	1680	1500	1180	1150	2010
Calais	360	3230	1410	1990	990	200	1600	2490	—	710	820	1490	610	870	1220	870	2150	2930	1170	940	2090	170	420	750	1560	1140	400	1070	2840	1000	1950	1770	2740	300	1120	1730	1140	2370	1800	640	1120	1420	1570	1340	860
Dublin	880	3930	2110	2690	1530	910	2310	3190	710	—	640	2130	1320	1570	1860	1370	2660	3630	1680	1580	2790	530	1130	1390	2260	1850	310	1780	3390	1710	2600	2280	3440	1000	1820	2440	1840	3080	2310	1340	1760	2120	2120	2040	1570
Edinburgh	990	4050	2230	2810	1640	1020	2420	3300	820	640	—	2240	1430	1680	1870	1490	1810	3750	1230	1970	2900	650	1230	1500	2370	1960	370	1890	3500	1820	2710	1270	3550	1110	1930	2550	1960	3190	1450	1460	1870	2240	2230	2150	1680
Florence/Firenze	1490	2390	1160	1090	1260	1270	1070	1610	1490	2130	2240	—	1080	880	270	1480	2590	2550	1670	1110	2430	1600	1060	790	1790	330	1880	640	2890	680	510	2280	1350	1250	1040	300	700	1510	2340	860	460	270	1610	900	640
Frankfurt a. M.	460	2620	1280	1380	560	410	990	1880	610	1320	1430	1080	—	590	910	500	1800	2320	820	420	2370	790	240	700	1840	730	1020	940	2410	400	1620	1410	2320	580	500	1310	540	1760	1440	220	790	860	1150	730	430
Genf/Genève	1040	2700	810	1460	1140	820	1300	2170	870	1570	1680	880	590	—	520	1090	2380	2400	1400	970	1950	1040	600	160	1420	400	1420	430	3000	590	1380	1990	1990	570	950	990	720	1840	2020	390	310	680	1730	1030	280
Genoa/Genova	1320	2500	890	1180	1170	1100	1150	1700	1220	1860	1870	270	910	520	—	1380	2700	2640	1670	1000	2170	1330	900	520	1520	160	1610	400	2980	690	740	2280	1580	1010	1090	530	740	1590	2330	700	170	360	1700	980	480
Hamburg	500	2950	1780	1790	290	660	1210	2060	870	1370	1490	1480	500	1090	1380	—	1290	2720	310	380	2770	840	640	1140	2440	1230	1160	1450	2150	780	2020	900	2720	970	640	1710	920	2180	930	730	1300	1260	880	1120	930
Helsinki	1860	3420	3070	2180	1430	1950	1780	2280	2150	2660	1810	2590	1800	2380	2700	1290	—	3010	980	1330	4060	2130	1930	2270	3520	2520	2460	2740	1140	2080	3080	910	4010	2260	1740	3010	2220	2560	360	2020	2600	2550	1110	1790	2220
Istanbul	2770	1210	3110	940	2260	2730	1340	730	2930	3630	3750	2550	2320	2400	2640	2720	3010	—	2720	2210	4380	3100	2500	2480	3730	2000	3920	2530	2650	1930	2590	3300	2140	2760	1910	1980	1790	560	3330	2310	2620	1730	2010	1600	2230
Copenhagen/København	810	3250	2090	2100	460	970	1390	2140	1170	1680	1230	1670	820	1400	1670	310	980	2720	—	590	3070	1150	950	1430	2540	1540	1440	1750	2220	1100	2280	600	3030	1280	810	2020	1230	2160	630	1040	1680	1570	960	1120	1240
Leipzig	780	2780	1740	1460	170	720	820	1630	940	1580	1970	1110	420	970	1000	380	1330	2210	590	—	3120	1050	730	1130	2370	950	1690	1420	2020	430	1600	1200	2430	960	240	1390	580	1870	1250	640	1080	960	740	790	690
Lisbon/Lisboa	2270	4680	1270	3440	2890	2090	3240	4150	2090	2790	2900	2430	2370	1950	2170	2770	4060	4380	3070	3120	—	2260	2120	1790	650	2370	2490	1840	4750	2530	2900	3670	3740	1790	2820	2730	2670	3820	3700	2200	2170	2650	3480	2980	2230
London	350	3400	1580	2160	1000	380	1770	2660	170	530	650	1600	790	1040	1330	840	2130	3100	1150	1050	2260	—	590	860	1730	1320	280	1240	2850	1170	2070	1740	2910	470	1290	1900	1310	2540	1770	810	1230	1590	1590	1510	1040
Luxembourg	410	2800	1270	1560	770	220	1230	2120	420	1130	1230	1060	240	600	900	640	1930	2500	950	730	2120	590	—	520	1590	740	930	940	2620	570	1560	1540	2330	330	740	1330	710	1940	1570	220	780	1020	1360	960	440
Lyon	990	2880	650	1570	1260	670	1490	2090	750	1390	1500	790	700	160	520	1140	2270	2480	1430	1130	1790	860	520	—	1270	470	1140	310	3060	750	1260	2040	2090	470	1100	1050	900	1980	2090	440	330	670	1940	1220	440
Madrid	1740	4030	620	2790	2360	1560	2710	3510	1560	2260	2370	1790	1840	1420	1520	2440	3520	3730	2540	2370	650	1730	1590	1270	—	1730	1930	1200	4220	2000	2250	3140	3090	1260	2290	2090	2140	3170	3170	1660	1520	2010	2950	2450	1700
Milan/Milano	1180	2300	1110	1060	1110	960	1090	1780	1140	1850	1960	330	730	400	160	1230	2520	2000	1540	950	2370	1320	740	470	1730	—	1450	530	2770	500	870	2130	1600	850	870	590	520	1450	2160	520	140	280	1500	830	300
Manchester	780	3940	1690	2460	1420	600	2160	2960	400	310	370	1880	1020	1420	1610	1160	2460	3920	1440	1690	2490	280	930	1140	1930	1450	—	1580	3240	1390	2350	2050	3180	670	1520	2970	3170	2870	2100	2560	1510	1770	1960	1890	1170
Marseille	1250	2830	580	1590	1490	1080	1620	2300	1070	1780	1890	640	940	430	400	1450	2740	2530	1750	1420	1840	1240	940	310	1200	530	1580	—	3350	1030	1130	2350	1890	780	1400	890	1050	1970	2380	720	410	800	2090	1360	710
Moscow/Moskva	2540	3220	3690	2150	1860	2650	1960	1920	2840	3390	3500	2890	2410	3000	2980	2150	1140	2650	2220	2020	4750	2850	2620	3060	4220	2770	3240	3350	—	2260	3400	2060	3790	2960	1900	3190	2260	2350	1500	2630	2960	2600	1270	2100	2570
Munich/München	850	2110	1390	990	590	800	710	1700	1000	1710	1820	680	400	590	690	780	2080	1930	1100	430	2530	1170	570	750	2000	500	1390	1030	2260	—	1190	1690	1930	830	370	930	140	1370	1720	380	670	470	1000	450	300
Naples/Napoli	2080	660	1630	1600	1760	1840	1570	2120	1950	2600	2710	510	1620	1380	740	2020	3080	2590	2280	1600	2900	2070	1560	1260	2250	870	2350	1130	3400	1190	—	2570	840	1710	1540	210	1210	2010	2320	1370	900	780	2120	1400	1190
Oslo	1400	3600	2680	2360	1040	1560	1960	2740	1770	2280	1270	2280	1410	1990	2280	900	910	3300	600	1200	3670	1740	1540	2040	3140	2130	2050	2350	2060	1690	2570	—	3620	1880	1390	2620	1830	2740	560	1630	2200	2160	1560	1700	1840
Palermo	2770	1580	2470	1640	2540	2550	2040	2350	2740	3440	3550	1350	2320	1990	1580	2720	4010	2140	3030	2430	3740	2910	2330	2090	3090	1600	3180	1890	3790	1930	840	3620	—	2440	2300	1010	1950	2030	3650	2120	1740	1540	2710	2260	1890
Paris	430	3060	1120	1820	1100	300	1560	2450	300	1000	1110	1250	580	570	1010	970	2260	2760	1280	960	1790	470	330	470	1260	850	670	780	2960	830	1710	1880	2440	—	1080	1440	970	2200	1910	460	800	1130	1690	1300	580
Prague/Praha	960	2210	1680	970	350	910	580	1460	1120	1820	1930	1040	500	950	1090	640	1740	1910	810	240	2820	1290	740	1100	2290	870	1520	1400	1900	370	1540	1390	2300	1080	—	1290	380	1350	1420	630	1020	780	630	310	670
Rome/Roma	1770	1420	1470	1320	1530	1550	1350	2040	1730	2440	2550	300	1310	990	530	1710	3010	1980	2020	1390	2730	1900	1330	1050	2090	590	2970	890	3190	930	210	2620	1010	1440	1290	—	950	1710	2650	1110	700	540	1920	1250	890
Salzburg	980	2090	1530	850	730	940	580	1570	1140	1840	1960	700	540	720	740	920	2220	1790	1230	580	2670	1310	710	900	2140	520	3170	1050	2260	140	1210	1830	1950	970	380	950	—	1230	1860	520	690	410	990	310	440
Sofia/Sofija	2220	870	2550	380	1700	2170	780	430	2370	3080	3190	1510	1760	1840	1590	2180	2560	560	2160	1870	3820	2540	1940	1980	3170	1450	2870	1970	2350	1370	2010	2740	2030	2200	1350	1710	1230	—	2770	1750	1580	1170	1450	1040	1670
Stockholm	1430	3630	2710	2390	1070	1590	1990	2770	1800	2310	1450	2340	1440	2020	2330	930	360	3330	630	1250	3700	1770	1570	2090	3170	2160	2100	2380	1500	1720	2320	560	3650	1910	1420	2650	1860	2770	—	1660	2320	2190	1590	1730	1870
Strasbourg	680	2610	1050	1370	780	440	1090	2080	640	1340	1460	860	220	390	700	730	2020	2310	1040	640	2200	810	220	440	1660	520	2560	720	2630	380	1370	1630	2120	460	630	1110	520	1750	1660	—	660	800	1370	820	230
Turin/Torino	1260	2550	890	1160	1280	1040	1140	1680	1120	1760	1870	460	790	310	170	1300	2600	2620	1680	1080	2170	1230	780	330	1520	140	1510	410	2960	670	900	2200	1740	800	1020	700	690	1580	2320	660	—	340	1680	970	450
Venice/Venezia	1310	2030	1390	790	1080	1230	820	1500	1420	2120	2240	270	860	680	360	1260	2550	1730	1570	960	2650	1590	1020	670	2010	280	1770	800	2600	470	780	2160	1540	1130	780	540	410	1170	2190	800	340	—	1340	650	580
Warsaw/Warszawa	1280	2310	2420	1070	590	1380	680	1180	1570	2120	2230	1610	1150	1730	1700	880	1110	2010	960	740	3480	1590	1360	1940	2950	1500	1960	2090	1270	1000	2120	1560	2710	1690	630	1920	990	1450	1590	1370	1680	1340	—	690	1300
Vienna/Wien	1180	1900	1840	660	660	1130	270	1150	1340	2040	2150	900	730	1030	980	1120	1790	1600	1120	790	2980	1510	960	1220	2450	830	1890	1360	2100	450	1400	1700	2260	1300	310	1250	310	1040	1730	820	970	650	690	—	750
Zurich/Zürich	880	2530	1090	1290	850	660	1020	2010	860	1570	1680	640	430	280	480	930	2220	2230	1240	690	2230	1040	440	440	1700	300	1170	710	2570	300	1190	1840	1890	580	670	890	440	1670	1870	230	450	580	1300	750	—

European North Sea

Barent Sea

Jan Mayen (Norw.)

Hammerfest

Kirkenes

Murmansk

Narvik

Lofoten

1:5 000 000

ICELAND

Reykjavik

128

NORWAY

129

RUSSIA

FINLAND

Trondheim

Färöer (Denm.)

1:3 000 000

SWEDEN

Tampere

Turku

Lake Ladoga

Åland

Rockall

Shetland Islands (GB)

Orkney Islands

Bergen

Helsinki

Saint Petersburg

Oslo

Stockholm

ESTONIA

Novgorod

North Sea

132

Vänern

Glasgow

Edinburgh

Gothenburg

Gotland

130

131

Riga

LATVIA

Belfast

Öland

Smolensk

IRLAND

GREAT BRITAIN

DENMARK

LITHUANIA

Dublin

Copenhagen

Born-holm

Vilnius

Cork

Liverpool

Kalinin-grad

RUSSIA

1:3 000 000

Minsk

133

Birmingham

London

NETHER-LANDS

Amsterdam

Hamburg

Rügen

Gdansk

Baltic Sea

BELARUS

Scilly

Exeter

Hannover

Berlin

Poznań

Warsaw

Channel Islands

134

Brussels

GERMANY

Leipzig

135

POLAND

144

Lublin

Chernobyl

Kiev

BELGIUM

Cologne

Frankfurt

Wrocław

Kraków

UKRAINE

LUXEMB.

Paris

Nürnberg

Prague

CZECH REPUBLIC

L'viv

Nantes

Strasbourg

Stuttgart

Munich

Danube

SLOVAKIA

Dniestr

FRANCE

136

Bern

Zürich

LIECH.

Vienna

AUSTRIA

Bratislava

Budapest

MOLDOVA

Chisinǎu

La Coruña

Bordeaux

Lyon

SWITZER-LAND

Graz

Ljubljana

HUNGARY

Cluj-Napoca

ROMANIA

Vigo

Gijón

Bilbao

Milan

Trieste

SLOV.

Zagreb

Timişoara

Brasov

Porto

Valladolid

Toulouse

137

Turin

Venice

Po

140

CROATIA

Bucharest

Danube

142

Varna

PORTUGAL

SPAIN

Zaragoza

ANDORRA

Marseille

Nice

MONACO

Genoa

Florence

SAN MARINO

BOSNIA HERZEG.

Sarajevo

Belgrade

SERBIA

MONT.

BULGARIA

Lisbon

138

Madrid

Barcelona

1:3 200 000

Corsica

Elba

ITALY

VATICAN

Rome

Adriatic Sea

Bari

Podgorica

KOS.

Kristina

Skopje

Sofia

Plovdiv

Istanbul

Tajo

Valencia

139

Menorca

Mallorca

Sardinia

Naples

Tarent

Tirana

MACED.

Sevilla

Córdoba

Alicante

Balearic Islands

Tyrrhenian Sea

ALBANIA

Saloniki

TURKEY

Cádiz

Málaga

Almería

Mediterranean

141

GREECE

143

Lesbos

Izmir

Tangier

Oran

Strait of Gibraltar

Palermo

Messina

Athens

Peloponnese

Rabat

Fes

Algiers

1:3 200 000

Sicily

1:3 000 000

1:3 000 000

Rhodes

Casablanca

Valletta

MALTA

Crete

MOROCCO

TUNISIA

Mediterranean Sea

Tripolis

ALGERIA

LIBYA

EGYPT

1:5 000 000

Atlantic Ocean

Bay of Biscaya

Loire

Rhône

Ebro

Rhine

Elbe

Oder

Vistula

Seine

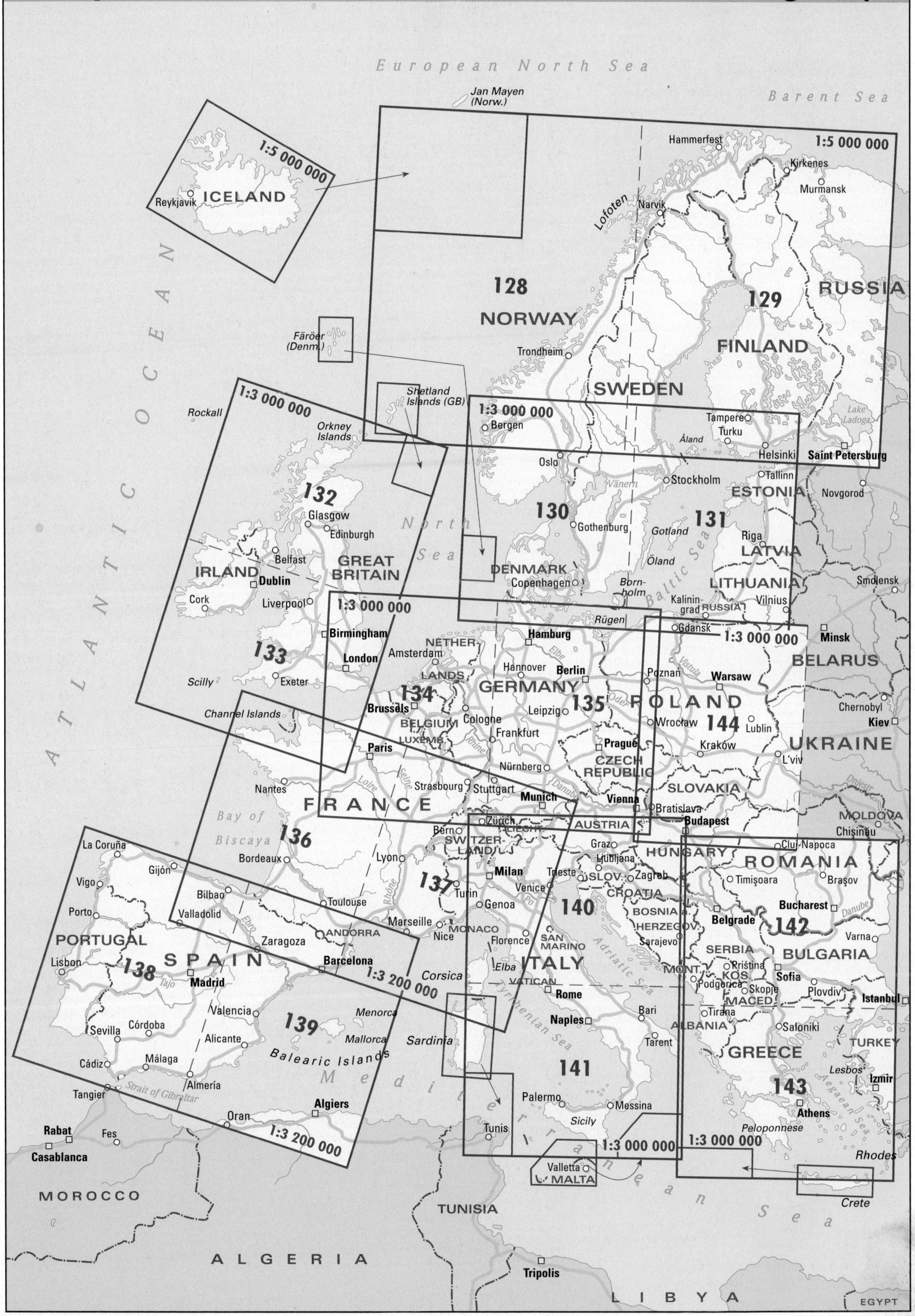

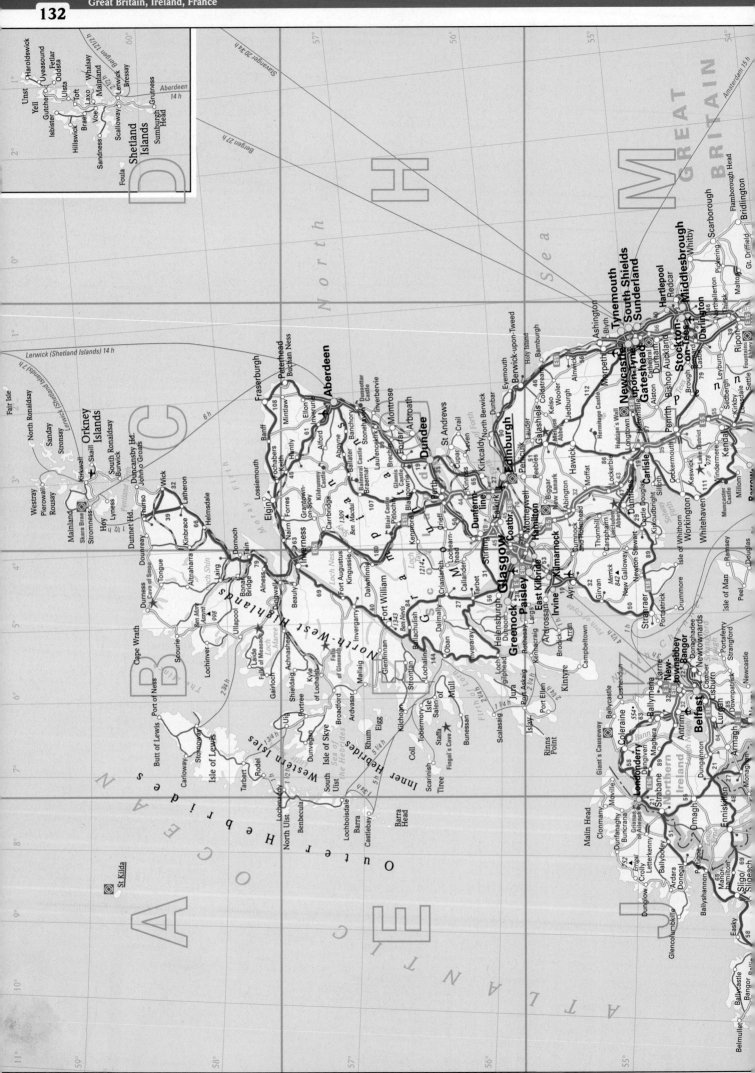

Shetland Islands

Orkney Islands

North Sea

ATLANTIC OCEAN

Outer Hebrides

Inner Hebrides

Western Isles

North-West Highlands

Scottish Highlands

Aberdeen
Dundee
Edinburgh
Glasgow
Paisley
Greenock
East Kilbride
Kilmarnock
Irvine
Inverness
Fort William
Oban
Perth
Stirling
Dunfermline
Falkirk
Motherwell
Hamilton
Ayr

Newcastle upon Tyne
Gateshead
Sunderland
South Shields
Tynemouth
Middlesbrough
Stockton-on-Tees
Hartlepool
Darlington
Carlisle

Belfast
Londonderry
Bangor
Newtownabbey
Northern Ireland

1:3 000 000   1cm ≙ 30 km

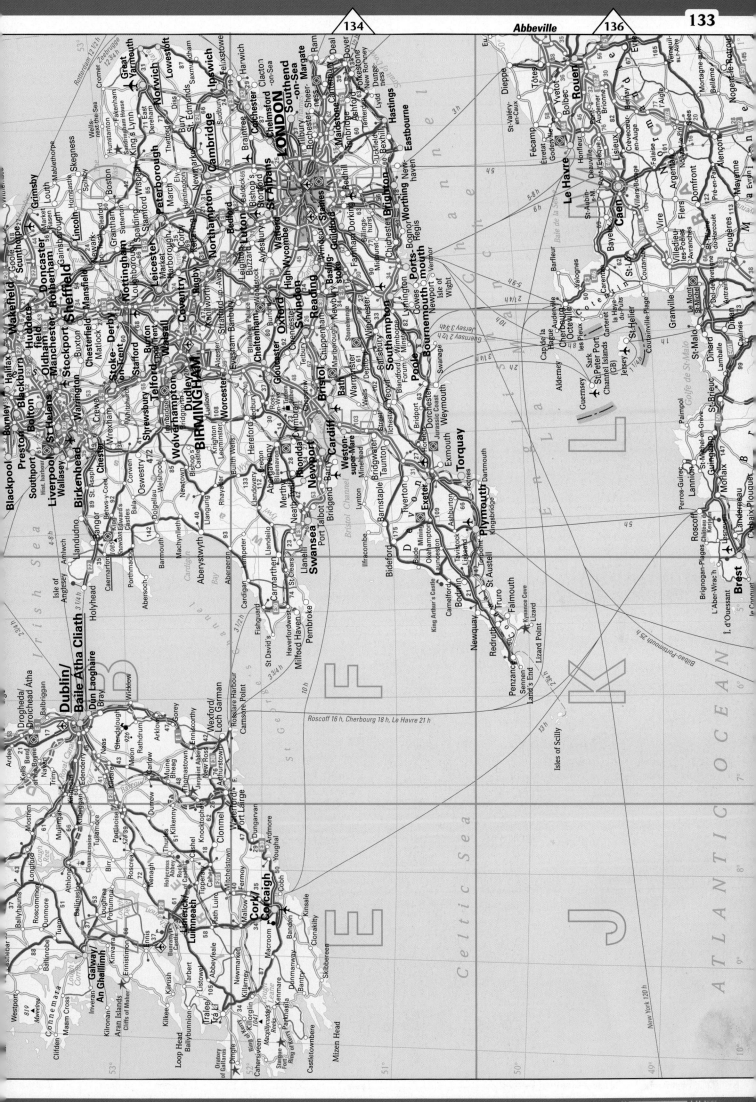

OCÉANO ATLÁNTICO

Ortigueira · Viveiro · Ribadeo · Luarca · Avilés · Gijón · Villaviciosa · Santander · Santoña · Laredo · S.Se
La Coruña / A Coruña · Ferrol · As Pontes de García Rodr. · Castropol · Pravia · Oviedo · Pola de Siero · Ribadesella · Llanes · Cuevas de Altamira · San Vicente de Barakaldo · Bilbao / Bilbo
Malpica de Berg. · Betanzos · Mondoñedo · Vegadeo · Tineo · Mieres · Langreo · Cangas de Onís · Unquera · Torrelavega · Solares · Viesgo · Durango · Eibar
Camariñas · Baio · Vilalba · Meira · A Fonsagrada · Belmonte · Cangas de Narcea · Pola de Lena · Pto. de Pajares · Riaño · Cabuérniga · Balmaseda · Bercedo · Vito Gast
Carballo · Ordes · Baamonde · Rábade · Grandas de Salime · La Pola de Gordón · Boñar · Cistierna · Reinosa · Corconte · Espinosa de los M. · Amurrio · Miranda de E. · Haro
Santiago de Compostela · Melide · Lugo · Guntín de Pallares · Sarria · Pedrafita do Cebreiro · León · Sta. María del Páramo · Guardo · Aguilar de Campoo · Osorno · Villadiego · Oña · Briviesca · Belorado
Muros · Noia · Padrón · A Golada · Monforte de Lemos · Astorga · Valencia de Don Juan · Saldaña · Herrera de Pisuerga · Villanueva · Burgos · Nájera · Mon.
Santa Uxía (Ribeira) · O Grove · Pontevedra · Lalín · Chantada · Ponferrada · Teleno · La Bañeza · Mayorga · Carrión de los Condes · Castrojeriz · S.Domingo de Silos · Lerma · Arandaⁿ
Vigo · Ourense · A Caniza · A Rúa · Las Médulas · Villada · Medina de Rioseco · Palencia · Quintana d.Puente · S.Leonardo de Yagüe · Salas de los Infantes
Pontevedra · Celanova · Xinzo de Limia · A Gudiña · Puebla de Sanabria · Benavente · Villalpando · Valladolid · Tórtoles de Esgueva · Roa · Peñafiel · S.Esteban de Gormaz · Ayllón
Tui · Verín · Vinhais · Bragança · Alcañices · Villardefrades · Toro · Tordesillas · Olmedo · Cuéllar · Sepúlveda · Riaza · Campisábalos
A Guarda · Santa Tekla · Caminha · Ponte da Barca · Gerês · Chaves · Mirandela · Miranda do Douro · Zamora · Medina del Campo · Arévalo · Castillo de Coca · Santa María la Real de Nieva · Sigüenza · Medinaceli
Viana do Castelo · Braga · Venda Nova · Macedo de Cavaleiros · Bermillo de Sayago · Fermoselle · Cañizal · Peñaranda de Bracamonte · Segovia · Guadalajara · Jadraque · Brihuega
Póvoa de Varzim · Vila do Conde · Barcelos · Guimarães · Amarante · Vila Real · Vila Flor · Ledesma · Salamanca · Alba de Tormes · Ávila · El Escorial · MADRID · Alcalá de Henares · Pastrana
Matosinhos · Vila Nova de Gaia · Porto · Penafiel · Paso da Régua · Lamego · Pinhão · Vila Nova de Foz Côa · Vitigudino · Lumbrales · Ciudad Rodrigo · Piedrahíta · S.Lorenzo de El Escorial · Móstoles · Getafe · Villarejo
Espinho · Ovar · Castelo de Paiva · Castro d'Aire · Moimenta da Beira · Barca d'Alva · La Alberca · Béjar · Jarandilla de la Vera · Naval carnero · Aranjuez · Ocaña · Tarancón
Aveiro · Albergaria-a-Velha · Vouzela · Viseu · Celorico da Beira · Almeida · Vila Formoso · El Barco de Ávila · Arenas de S.Pedro · Talavera de la Reina · Torrijos · Toledo · Quintanar de la Orden
Mira · Águeda · Tondela · Sta. Comba Dão · Guarda · Sabugal · Hoyos · Plasencia · Navalmoral de la Mata · Torrijos · Mora · Tembleque
Figueira da Foz · Mealhada · Oliveira do Hospital · Covilhã · Penamacor · Coria · Cañaveral · El Puente del A. · Orgaz · Madridejos · Alcázar de S.Juan
Coimbra · Condeixa · Conímbriga · Pampilhosa da Serra · Valverde del Fresno · Plasencia · Navalvillar de Pela · Guadalupe · La Nava de Ricomalillo · Corral de Cantos · El Molinillo · Puerto Lápice
Pedrógão · Pombal · Sertã · Castelo Branco · Segura · Piedras Albas · Navas del Madroño · Torrejón el Rubio · Trujillo · Miajadas · Puebla de Don Rodrigo · Daimiel · Tomelloso
Marinha Grande · Leiria · Mosteiro de Batalha · Tomar · Nisa · Zebreira · Herreruela · Cáceres · Guadalupe · Abenójar · Ciudad Real · Manzanares · Pedro Muñoz
Batalha · Fátima · Entroncamento · Alpalhão · Marvão · Valencia de Alcántara · Malpartida de Cáceres · Zorita · Monasterio de Guadalupe · Porzuna · Piedrabuena · Valdepeñas · La Solana
Nazaré · Alcobaça · Caldas da Rainha · Óbidos · Santarém · Portalegre · Arronches · Alburquerque · La Roca de la Sierra · Montánchez · Villanueva de la Serena · Puebla de Don Rodrigo · Almodóvar · Villaherm
Peniche · Lourinhã · Torres Vedras · Vila Franca de Xira · Montargil · Ponte de Sor · Fronteira · Campo Maior · Montijo · Miajadas · Puertollano · Villanueva de los Infantes · Villamanrique
Ericeira · Amadora · Sintra · Cascais · Lisboa · Almada · Infantado · Coruche · Mora · Estremoz · Elvas · Badajoz · La Albuera · Mérida · Don Benito · Castuera · Cabeza del Buey · Ciudad Real · Beas de Segura
Costa de Caparica · Barreiro · Vendas Novas · Arraiolos · Redondo · Olivenza · Almendralejo · Santa Marta · Hinojosa del Duque · Cardeña · La Carolina · Úbeda
Setúbal · Troia · Montemor-o-Novo · Évora · Reguengos de Monsaraz · Villanueva del Fresno · Zafra · Campillo de Llerena · Peñarroya-Pueblonuevo · Pozoblanco · Bailén · Linares · Villacarrillo · Cazorla
Sesimbra · Alcácer do Sal · Comporta · Mourão · Vidigueira · Moura · Jerez de los Caballeros · Los Santos de Maimona · Azuaga · Espiel · Santuario Virgen de la Cabeza · Andújar · Baeza · Jódar · Quesada
Grândola · Santo André · Torrão · Cuba · Portel · Jabugo · Fregenal de la Sierra · Fuente de Cantos · Llerena · Fuente Obejuna · Montoro · Porcuna · Jaén · Cabra · Úbeda
Sines · Ferreira do Alentejo · Beja · Vila Verde de Ficalho · Serpa · Aracena · Santa Olalla del Cala · Alanís · Constantina · Cardeña · Córdoba · Baena · Martos · Alcalá la Real · Moreda
Vila Nova de Milfontes · Santa Luzia · Ourique · Almodôvar · Mértola · Zalamea la Real · Nerva · Zafra · Santa Qlalla · Palma del Río · Écija · Aguilar · Lucena · Loja · Granada
Odemira · Alcoutim · Villanueva de los Castillejos · La Palma del Condado · Itálica · Sevilla · Carmona · Puente Genil · Estepa · Santa Fe · Guadix
Portimão · Silves · São Brás de Alportel · Ayamonte · Huelva · Almonte · Dos Hermanas · Morón de la Frontera · Campillos · Antequera · Vélez-Málaga · Nerja · Motril
Cabo de S.Vicente · Lagos · Albufeira · Faro · Olhão · Tavira · Punta Umbría · La Rábida · La Puebla del Río · Las Cabezas de San Juan · Algodonales · Ronda · Alora · Málaga · Torremolinos · Costa del Sol
Sagres · Golfo de Cádiz · Lebrija · Matalascañas · Sanlúcar de Barrameda · Chipiona · Arcos de la Frontera · Coín · Fuengirola · Berja · Adra
Jerez de la Frontera · Medina-Sidonia · Jimena de la Frontera · San Pedro de Alcántara · Marbella · Estepona
Cádiz · San Fernando · Puerto Real · San Roque · La Línea de la Concepción · Gibraltar (GB)
Cabo Trafalgar · Barbate de Franco · Tarifa · Punta de Europa · Algeciras · Ceuta (Sebta) (Esp.) · Isla del Alborán (Esp.)
Tanjah (Tanger) · Cap Spartel · Ksar-es-Seghir · MARUECOS

Beograd   **142**

Sassari   Cágliari   Sassari

0 ▬▬▬▬ 50 km

142

Hungary, Romania, Bulgaria, Serbia, Montenegro, Croatia, Bosnia and Herzegovina, Kosovo, Macedonia, Albania, Greece, Turkey, Ukraine, Moldova

İstanbul

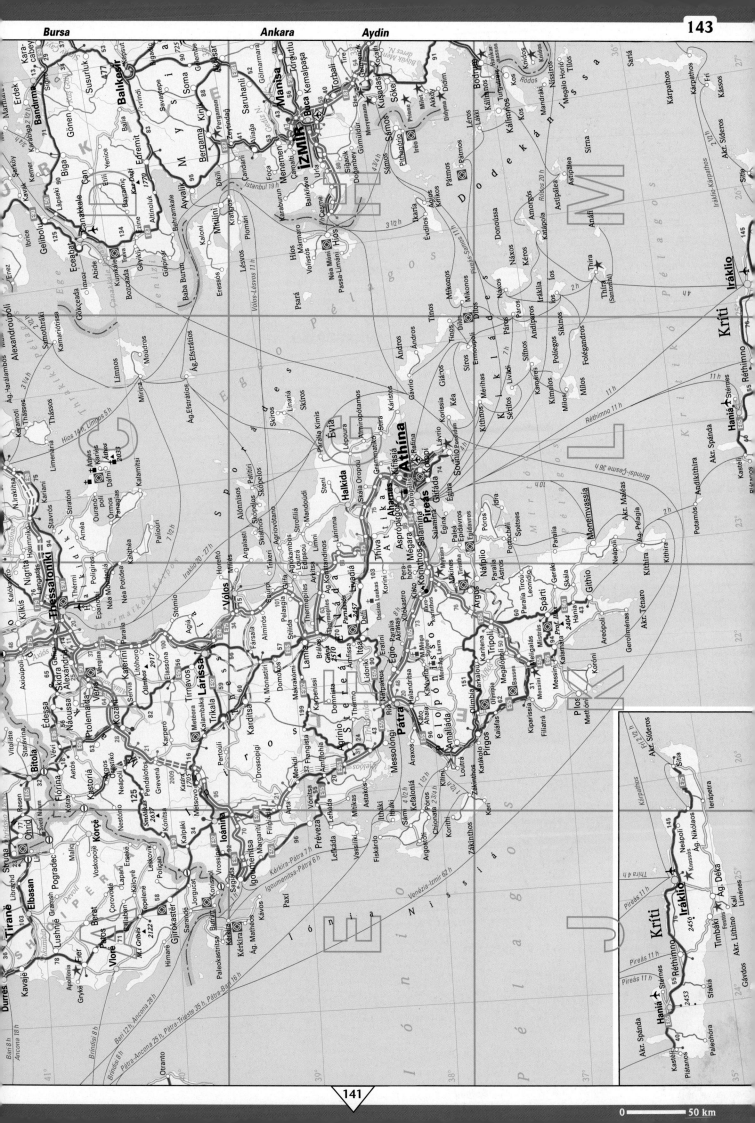

Index of places

The atlas contains three indexes of places.

1. Great Britain 1:301,000
2. Ireland 1:301,000
3. Europe 1:3,000,000 and 1:5,000,000 planning maps

For easier visibility, the index of places includes grey bars. The bar at the top indicates where the index for Great Britain begins, the centre bar indicates the index for Ireland and the bar at the bottom indicates the index for Europe.

The place names are given in their original language, for example, Roma for Rome or Lisboa for Lisbon.

All three indexes follow the same principle: to make places easy to locate, each entry is followed by a number and a letter. The number is the page of the appropriate map and the letter identifies the square in which the place is located.

A	B	C
D	E	F
G	H	J
K	L	M

For a better overview, the map pages are divided into fields of equal size, designated by a green grid. A letter is located in the centre of each square. This letter is given after the page number in each index entry.

The indexes of places contain the names of the cities shown in the maps section, independent and dependent municipalities, as well as city and municipal districts, in alphabetical order.

Spaces between letters are not taken into consideration. Thus, for example, "Villa del Río" is sorted as one word, "VilladelRío". Diacritical marks (letters with accents or other special signs) have no effect on alphabetization.

Abbreviations of the countries:

(A)	Austria	(KOS)	Kosovo
(AL)	Albania	(L)	Luxembourg
(AND)	Andorra	(LT)	Lithuania
(B)	Belgium	(LV)	Latvia
(BG)	Bulgaria	(M)	Malta
(BIH)	Bosnia and Herzegovina	(MA)	Morocco
(BLR)	Belarus	(MC)	Monaco
(CH)	Switzerland	(MD)	Moldova
(CZ)	Czech Republic	(MK)	Macedonia
(D)	Germany	(MNE)	Montenegro
(DK)	Denmark	(N)	Norway
(DZ)	Algeria	(NL)	Netherlands
(E)	Spain	(P)	Portugal
(EST)	Estonia	(PL)	Poland
(F)	France	(RO)	Romania
(FIN)	Finland	(RSM)	San Marino
(FL)	Liechtenstein	(RUS)	Russia
(GB)	Great Britain	(S)	Sweden
(GR)	Greece	(SK)	Slovakia
(H)	Hungary	(SLO)	Slovenia
(HR)	Croatia	(SRB)	Serbia
(I)	Italy	(TR)	Turkey
(IRL)	Ireland	(UA)	Ukraine
(IS)	Iceland		

Great Britain 1:301,000

A

A'Chill 69 K
Ab Kettleby 33 G
Abbas Combe 14 M
Abberley 23 B
Abberton 18 C
Abberton 23 F
Abberwick 54 L
Abbess Roding 18 A
Abbey 13 M
Abbey-cwrm-hir 30 K
Abbey Dore 22 J
Abbey Hulton 31 C
Abbeylands 37 B
Abbey Saint Bathans 54 D
Abbeystead 43 K
Abbey Town 47 J
Abbeyview 105 G
Abbey Village 38 B
Abbot's Salford 23 F
Abbotrule 53 L
Abbots Bickington 12 M
Abbots Bromley 32 G
Abbotsbury 6 F
Abbotsham 12 J
Abbotskerwell 5 E
Abbots Langley 17 B
Abbots Leigh 14 F
Abbotsley 25 J
Abbots Morton 23 F
Abbots Ripton 25 F
Abbotswood 8 A
Abdon 31 K
Aber 21 A
Aberaeron 29 K
Aberaman 21 M
Aberangell 29 F
Aberargie 58 E
Aberarth 29 K
Aberbanc 21 A
Aberbargoed 22 K
Aberbeeg 22 K
Abercanaid-Troedyrhiw 22 K
Abercarn-Newbridge 22 K
Abercastle Square and Compass 20 A
Abercegir 29 J
Aberchalder 64 C

Aberchirder 73 K
Abercraf 21 J
Abercrombie 59 G
Abercwmboi 21 M
Abercych 20 C
Abercynafon 22 G
Aber-Cywarch 30 D
Aberdalgie 58 E
Aberdare 21 M
Aberdaron 28 C
Aberdeen 67 E
Aberdour 58 L
Aberdulais 21 L
Aberdyfi 29 H
Aberedw 22 D
Abereiddy 20 A
Abererch 29 B
Aberfan 22 K
Aberfeldy 65 L
Aberffraw 36 H
Aberffrwd 29 L
Aberford 39 C
Aberfoyle 57 H
Abergavenny/Y Fenni 22 H
Abergele 37 H
Aber-Giâr 21 A
Abergorlech 21 E
Abergwesyn 21 C
Abergwili 21 D
Abergwydol 29 J
Abergwynant 29 F
Abergwynfi Croeserw 21 M
Abergwyngregyn 36 J
Abergynolwyn 29 F
Aberhafesp 30 G
Aberhosan 29 J
Aberkenfig 13 C
Aberlady 58 L
Aberlemno 59 A
Aberllefenni 29 F
Abermeurig 21 B
Abermule 30 H
Abernaint 30 E
Abernant 20 F
Abernant 21 M
Abernant 22 K
Abernethy 58 E
Abernyte 58 F
Aberporth 20 C
Abersky 71 L
Abersoch 29 A

Abersychan 22 L
Aberthin 13 C
Abertillery 22 L
Abertridwr 30 D
Abertridwr-Senghenydd 22 K
Abertysswg 22 K
Aberuthven 58 D
Aber-Village 22 G
Aberyscir 22 D
Aberystwyth 29 L
Abhainn Suidhe 74 J
Abingdon 16 B
Abinger Common 17 K
Abinger Hammer 17 K
Abington 52 H
Abington Pigotts 25 J
Abingworth 9 E
Ablington 23 M
Abney 39 L
Aboyne 66 J
Abram 38 E
Abriachan 71 K
Abridge 17 F
Abronhill 57 M
Abson 15 D
Abthorpe 24 J
Abune-the-Hill 79 D
Aby 34 A
Acaster Malbis 40 A
Acaster Selby 40 A
Accrington 38 C
Ach'yan Todhair 64 H
Acha Mòr 75 D
Achabraid 56 H
Achachork 69 H
Achahoish 56 G
Achanalt 70 F
Achandunie 71 E
Achany 71 B
Achaphubuil 64 E
Acharacle 63 J
Achargary 77 E
Acharn 57 C
Acharn 63 J
Acharn 66 H
Achath 67 D
Achavanich 78 H
Achavraie 70 H
Achduart 76 L
Achentoul 77 J
Achfary 76 J

Achgarve 70 B
Achiemore 77 A
Achiemore 77 F
Achiltibuie 76 L
Achina 77 E
Achindown 71 M
Achinduich 71 B
Achinduin 63 M
Achingills 78 E
Achintee 70 H
Achintraid 70 G
Achleck 63 G
Achleek 63 J
Achllader 64 M
Achluachrach 64 F
Achlyness 76 F
Achmelvich 76 H
Achmore 70 G
Achnaba 64 K
Achnabat 71 L
Achnacarnin 76 H
Achnacarry 64 E
Achnacloich 69 M
Achnacloich 56 B
Achnaconeran 65 A
Achnacreebeag 64 K
Achnacroish 63 M
Achnadrish 63 G
Achnafalnich 57 A
Achnagarron 71 E
Achnaha 63 E
Achnahanat 71 B
Achnahannet 65 C
Achnairn 77 K
Achnaluachrach 77 L
Achnamara 56 G
Achnasaul 64 E
Achnasheen 70 F
Achnashelloch 56 H
Achosnich 63 E
Achosnich 71 C
Achreamie 78 D
Achriabhach 64 H
Achriesgill 76 F
Achrimsdale 72 A
Achurch 25 D
Achuvoldrach 77 E
Achvaich 71 C
Achvarasdal 78 D
Ackergill 78 H
Acklam 45 K

Acklam 44 C
Ackleton 31 L
Acklington 49 C
Ackton 39 F
Ackworth Moor Top 39 F
Acle 27 C
Acock's Green 23 C
Acol 11 B
Acomb 49 D
Acomb 40 A
Aconbury 22 J
Acrefair 30 C
Acton 17 H
Acton 26 M
Acton 30 M
Acton 31 B
Acton 104 H
Acton Bridge 38 L
Acton Green 23 D
Acton Pigott 31 G
Acton Round 31 K
Acton Scott 30 M
Acton Trussell 31 J
Acton Turville 15 A
Adamhill 51 F
Adamthwaite 43 E
Adbaston 31 E
Adber 14 M
Adderbury 24 H
Adderley 31 B
Adderstone 54 H
Addiewell 52 C
Addingham 43 M
Addington 10 B
Addington 17 J
Addington 24 M
Addlestone 17 G
Addlethorpe 34 B
Adeney 31 H
Adfa 30 G
Adforton 22 C
Adisham 11 B
Adlestrop 24 G
Adlingfleet 40 E
Adlington 38 E
Admaston 31 G
Admaston 31 J
Admington 24 G
Adstone 24 J
Adversane 9 B
Advie 72 K

Adwell 16 C
Adwick le Street 40 G
Adwick upon Dearne 39 J
Adziel 73 L
Ae 47 B
Affleck 67 E
Affpuddle 7 D
Afon-wen 37 J
Agglethorpe 43 F
Aghadowey 108 H
Aghagallon 104 F
Aghalee 104 F
Aghamore 103 H
Aghavilly 104 G
Aghinlig 104 D
Aghmakane 104 L
Aghnagar 104 D
Aghyaran 107 K
Agivey 108 H
Aglionby 48 H
Ahoghill 108 M
Aidriehill 57 M
Aignis 75 E
Aike 40 C
Aikers 79 L
Aiketgate 48 H
Aikton 47 J
Ailsworth 25 B
Ainderby Quernhow 44 H
Ainderby Steeple 44 E
Aingers Green 19 A
Ainsdale 38 D
Ainstable 48 H
Ainsworth 38 F
Ainthorpe 45 D
Aintree 38 D
Aird 46 A
Aird 56 D
Aird 75 F
Aird a'Mhachair 68 K
Aird a'Mhulaidh 75 G
Aird Asaig 74 J
Àird Dhall 75 B
Aird Mhidhinis 68 K
Aird Mhighe 74 M
Aird Mhòr 68 K
Aird nan Sruban 68 B
Aird of Sleat 63 B
Aird Ruairidh 68 H
Aird Thunga 75 E
Aird Uig 74 F

Airdrie 52 B
Airdrie Mill 72 K
Airidh a Bhruaich 75 G
Airieland 47 D
Airlington 10 G
Airmyn 40 E
Airntully 58 B
Airor 63 C
Airth 58 K
Airton 43 J
Airyhassen 46 E
Aisby 33 H
Aisby 40 L
Aiskew 44 G
Aislaby 44 B
Aislaby 45 D
Aislaby 45 G
Aisthorpe 40 L
Aith 79 D
Aith 79 F
Aith 80 B
Aith 81 G
Aitham 38 C
Aithsetter 81 H
Aitnoch 72 K
Akeld 54 G
Akeley 24 J
Akenham 27 K
Albaston 4 F
Alberbury 30 F
Albourne 9 F
Albrighton 31 H
Albrighton 31 D
Alburgh 27 E
Albury 17 C
Albury End 17 C
Alby Hill 35 L
Alcaig 71 H
Alcaston 30 M
Alcester 23 F
Alcombe 13 J
Alconbury 25 F
Alconbury Weston 25 F
Aldborough 35 L
Aldborough 44 L
Aldborough Saint John 44 A
Aldbourne 15 F
Aldbrough 41 B
Aldbury 17 A
Aldclune 65 M

146 Great Britain 1:301,000

A B C D E F G H I J K L M N O P Q R S T U V W X Y Z

Aldeburgh 27 M
Aldeby 27 F
Aldenham 17 E
Alderbury 15 M
Alderford 35 K
Aldergrove 104 C
Alderholt 7 C
Alderley 15 A
Aldermaston 16 H
Aldermaston Soke 16 H
Aldermaston Wharf 16 H
Alderminster 24 D
Aldershot 16 M
Aldersley Green 38 K
Alderton 15 A
Alderton 23 J
Alderton 24 J
Alderton 27 L
Alderton 31 D
Alderwasley 32 B
Aldfield 44 G
Aldford 38 K
Aldham 18 C
Aldham 27 K
Aldie 71 F
Aldingbourne 9 D
Aldingham 42 H
Aldington 23 J
Aldington 11 D
Aldington Frith 11 D
Aldochlay 57 G
Aldreth 26 D
Aldridge 31 M
Aldringham 27 J
Aldsworth 23 M
Aldunie 66 A
Aldwak 44 L
Aldwark 32 B
Aldwick 9 D
Aldwincle 25 B
Aldworth 16 E
Alexandria 57 K
Alfardisworthy 12 L
Alfington 6 A
Alfold Crossways 9 B
Alford 9 B
Alford 14 M
Alford 34 B
Alford 66 F
Alfreton 32 B
Alfrick 23 D
Alfriston 10 G
Algarkirk 34 G
Alhampton 14 M
Alkborough 40 E
Alkerton 24 G
Alkham 11 E
Alkington 31 A
Alkmonton 32 D
Allaleigh 5 H
Allanaquoich 66 G
Allangrange Mains 71 H
Allanton 52 B
Allanton 54 D
Allardice 67 K
Allathasdal 68 K
All Cannings 15 H
Allen's Green 17 C
Allendale 57 M
Allendale Town 48 J
Allenheads 48 J
Allensford 49 G
Allensmore 22 F
Aller 14 L
Allerby 47 H
Allerford 5 A
Allerford 13 F
Allerston 45 G
Allerthorpe 40 B
Allerton 39 F
Allesley 24 A
Allestree 32 E
Allexton 33 K
Alley 22 E
Allgreave 39 K
Allhallows-on-Sea 18 H
Allhallows 18 H
Alligin Shuas 70 D
Allimore Green 31 H
Allington 15 H
Allington 15 M
Allington 33 D
Allithwaite 42 F
Allnabad 77 G
Alloa 58 G
Allonby 47 H
Allostock 38 M
Allow 32 B
Alloway 51 H
All Saints South Elmham 27 E
Allscott 31 L
All Stretton 30 J
Alltchaorunn 64 L
Alltforgan 30 D
Alltmawr 22 D
Alltnacaillich 77 D
Allt-nan-Sugh 70 K
Alltsigh 65 A
Alltwalis 21 D
Alltwen 21 L
Alltyblaca 21 A
Allwood Green 27 G
Almeley 22 E
Almer 7 E
Almington 31 E
Alminstone Cross 12 J
Almondbank 58 E
Almondbury 39 E
Almondsbury 14 C
Alne 44 L
Alness 71 E
Alnham 54 K
Alnmouth 54 M
Alnwick 54 L
Alphamstone 26 M
Alpheton 26 M
Alphington 5 C
Alport 32 B
Alpraham 38 L
Alresford 18 C
Alrewas 32 G
Alsager 31 B
Alsagers Bank 31 B
Alsop en le Dale 32 A
Alston 48 J
Alstone 14 H
Alstone 23 H
Alstonefield 32 A
Alswear 13 K
Altanduin 77 M
Altanghu 76 K
Altarnun 4 C
Altass 71 B
Alterwall 78 E
Altgaltraig 56 L
Althorne 18 F
Althorpe 40 H
Alticry 46 E
Altihaskey 108 K
Altnafeadh 64 L
Altnaharra 77 H
Altnamackan 104 K
Altnnabreac Sta 78 G
Altofts 39 F
Alton 7 A
Alton 16 L
Alton 32 B
Alton 32 D
Alton Barnes 15 J
Alton Priors 15 J
Altonside 72 H
Alton Towers 32 D
Altrincham Hale 38 J
Altrua 64 F
Alva 58 G
Alvanley 38 K
Alvaston 32 E
Alvechurch 23 C
Alvecote 32 K
Alvediston 15 L
Alveley 31 L
Alverdiscott 13 G
Alverstoke 8 E
Alverstone 8 H
Alverton 33 D
Alves 72 G
Alvescot 16 A
Alveston 14 C
Alveston 24 D
Alvie 65 F
Alvingham 41 K
Alvington 22 M
Alwalton 25 B
Alweston 7 A
Alwinton 54 K
Alyth 58 C
Am Baile 68 L
Amatnatua 71 B
Amber Hill 33 F
Ambergate 32 B
Amberley 9 D
Amberley 23 L
Amble 49 C
Amblecote 31 L
Ambleside 42 C
Ambleston 20 E
Ambrismore 56 L
Ambrosden 24 L
Amcotts 40 H
Amersham 17 A
Amesbury 15 M
Amisfield 47 B
Amlwch 36 E
Amlwch Port 36 E
Ammanford 21 H
Amotherby 45 K
Ampfield 8 A
Ampleforth 44 J
Ampney Crucis 15 C
Ampney Saint Mary 15 C
Ampney Saint Peter 15 C
Amport 15 M
Ampthill 25 L
Ampton 26 J
Amroth 20 H
Amulree 58 A
Anaheilt 63 J
Anancaun 70 E
An Ard 70 A
Ancaster 33 E
Anchor 30 L
An Cnoc 75 E
Ancroft 54 H
Ancrum 53 J
Ancton 9 D
Anderby 34 B
Anderby Creek 34 B
Anderson 7 E
Anderton 38 L
Andover 16 K
Andover Down 16 K
Andoversford 23 M
Andreas 37 B
Angarrack 3 H
Angersleigh 14 K
Angerton 47 F
Angle 20 G
Angmering 9 E
Angram 40 A
Angram 43 F
Anie 57 E
Ankerville 71 F
Anlaby 40 F
An Leth Meadhanach 68 H
Anmer 34 M
Ann- Abbotts 15 M
Anna Valley 15 M
Annaclone 104 J
Annacloy 105 G
Annahilt 104 J
Annalong 98 C
Annan 47 F
Annaside 42 E
Annat 70 D
Annat 56 C
Annbank 51 F
Annesley 32 C
Annesley Woodhouse 32 C
Annfield Plain 49 H
Annochie 67 B
Annsborough 104 M
Annscroft 30 J
Ansdell 38 A
Ansford 14 M
Ansley 32 K
Anslow 32 G
Anslow Gate 32 G
Anstey 25 M
Anstey 32 M
An t-Ob 74 M
Anston 39 M
Anstruther 59 G
Ansty 9 C
Ansty 15 L
Ansty 24 B
Ansty Cross 7 A
Anthill Common 8 C
Anthorn 47 F
Antingham 35 L
Anton's Gowt 34 D
Antony 4 J
Antrim 104 C
Antrobus 38 H
Anwick 33 F
Anwoth 46 F
Aoradh 55 H
Apethorpe 25 B
Apley 33 C
Apperknowle West 39 M
Apperley 23 H
Appersett 43 E
Appin 64 K
Appleby 40 J
Appleby-in-Westmorland 48 L
Appleby Magna 32 H
Appleby Parva 32 H
Applecross 69 J
Appledore 10 F
Appledore 12 J
Appledore 13 M
Appleford 16 B
Applegarthtown 47 C
Appleshaw 15 J
Applethwaite 47 M
Appleton 16 A
Appleton-le-Moors 45 G
Appleton-le-Street 44 M
Appleton Roebuck 40 A
Appleton Thorn 38 H
Appleton Wiske 44 E
Appletreehall 53 L
Appletreewick 43 M
Appley 13 M
Appley Bridge 38 E
Apse Heath 8 H
Apsley End 25 L
Apuldram 8 F
Aquhytnie 67 D
Arabella 71 F
Arbirlot 59 B
Arboll 71 F
Arborfield 16 J
Arborfield Cross 16 J
Arborfield Garrison 16 J
Arbroath 59 E
Arbuthnott 67 K
Archiestown 72 L
Arclid 38 M
Ardachu 71 C
Ardalanish 55 C
Ardallie 67 C
Ardanaiseig 56 C
Ardaneaskan 70 G
Ardarroch 70 G
Ardbeg 55 L
Ardbeg 56 J
Ardboe 104 B
Ardcharnich 70 C
Ardchiavaig 55 C
Ardchonnell 56 E
Ardchuilk 70 M
Ardchullarie More 57 E
Ardchyle 57 B
Ardclach 71 M
Ardclach 72 K
Ard-dhubh 69 J
Arddleen 30 F
Ardechive 64 E
Ardelve 70 K
Arden 57 G
Ardens Grafton 23 F
Ardentinny 56 J
Ardeonaig 57 C
Ardersier 71 J
Ardery 63 J
Ardessie 70 B
Ardeun 104 B
Ardfern 56 E
Ardfernal 55 J
Ardgartan 57 D
Ardgay 71 B
Ardgayhill 71 B
Ardglass 105 K
Ardgowan 56 M
Ardgye 72 H
Ardheslaig 70 D
Ardiecow 72 J
Ardindrean 70 C
Ardingly 9 C
Ardington 16 D
Ardishaig 56 H
Ardkeen 105 H
Ardlair 66 C
Ardleigh 18 C
Ardler 58 C
Ardley 24 L
Ardlui 57 D
Ardlussa 56 G
Ardmair 76 L
Ardmaleish 56 M
Ardmay 57 D
Ardmillan 105 H
Ardminish 55 M
Ardmolich 63 F
Ardmoney 103 E
Ardmore 55 L
Ardmore 57 K
Ardmore 71 F
Ardmore 107 J
Ardmore 108 G
Ardnacross 63 H
Ardnadam 56 J
Ardnagowan 56 F
Ardnagrask 71 G
Ardnarff 70 G
Ardnastang 63 J
Ardnave 55 H
Ardno 56 F
Ardo 67 B
Ardoch 52 L
Ardoch 58 B
Ardochrig 52 A
Ardoyne 67 A
Ardpeaton 56 J
Ardreagh 108 H
Ardress 104 E
Ardross 71 E
Ardrossan 51 B
Ardshankill 103 A
Ardshave 71 C
Ardshealach 63 J
Ardsley 39 J
Ardslignish 63 H
Ardstraw 107 L
Ardtalla 55 M
Ardtalnaig 57 C
Ardtaraig 56 J
Ardtoe 63 E
Ardtole 105 L
Ardtornish 63 M
Ardtrea 104 B
Ardtrostan 57 F
Arduaine 56 E
Ardullie 71 H
Ardvasar 63 C
Ardvorlich 57 F
Ardwell 46 D
Ardwell Mains 46 D
Areley Kings 23 B
Arford 16 M
Argoed 22 K
Argos Hill 10 E
Arichastlich 57 A
Arichonan 56 G
Aridhglas 55 B
Arieleod 62 J
Arieniskill 63 F
Arinacrinachd 70 D
Arinagour 62 J
Arion 79 G
Arisaig 63 F
Arkendale 44 L
Arkesden 26 K
Arkholme 43 G
Arkley 17 E
Arksey 40 G
Arkwright Town 39 M
Arlecdon 47 L
Arlesey 25 L
Arleston 31 G
Arley 38 H
Arlingham 23 K
Arlington 13 G
Arlington 23 M
Arlington Beccott 13 G
Armadale 52 C
Armadale 77 F
Armagh 104 G
Armaghbrague 104 G
Armathwaite 48 H
Arminghall 27 B
Armitage 32 G
Armoy 108 J
Armscote 24 G
Armston 25 B
Armthorpe 40 G
Arnabost 62 J
Arncliffe 43 J
Arncroach 59 G
Arne 7 E
Arnesby 24 C
Arney 103 D
Arngask 58 H
Arnicle 50 B
Arnisdale 64 A
Arnish 69 J
Arniston 53 B
Arnol 75 B
Arnold 32 F
Arnprior 57 H
Arnside 42 F
Aros Mains 63 L
Arpafeelie 71 H
Arrad Foot 42 F
Arram 40 C
Arrathorne 44 D
Arreton 8 H
Arrington 25 J
Arrivain 57 A
Arrochar 57 D
Arrow 23 F
Arscaig 77 K
Artafallie 71 H
Arthington 39 C
Arthingworth 25 A
Arthog 29 F
Arthrath 67 B
Arthurstone 58 C
Articlave 108 E
Artigarvan 107 J
Arundel 9 D
Aryhoulan 64 G
Asby 47 L
Ascog 56 M
Ascott 24 G
Ascott-under-Wychwood 24 K
Ascreavie 66 L
Asenby 44 H
Asfordby 33 G
Asfordby Hill 33 G
Asgarby 33 F
Asgarby 34 A
Ash 11 B
Ash 14 L
Ash 16 M
Ash 18 K
Ash 25 A
Ashampstead 16 E
Ash Barton 12 M
Ashbocking 27 K
Ashbourne 32 A
Ashbrittle 13 M
Ashburton 5 E
Ashbury 5 A
Ashbury 15 F
Ashby 40 H
Ashby by Partney 34 A
Ashby cum Fenby 41 K
Ashby de la Launde 33 F
Ashby-de-la-Zouch 32 H
Ashby Folville 33 K
Ashby Magna 24 C
Ashby Parva 24 B
Ashby Puerorum 34 A
Ashby Saint Ledgers 24 F
Ashby Saint Mary 27 B
Ashchurch 23 H
Ashcombe 5 F
Ashcott 14 H
Ashdon 26 K
Ashe 16 K
Asheldham 18 F
Ashen 26 L
Ashenden 24 M
Asheridge 17 A
Ashfield 21 E
Ashfield 57 J
Ashfield 104 J
Ashfield cum Thorpe 27 G
Ashfield Green 27 H
Ashford 5 H
Ashford 7 C
Ashford 11 D
Ashford 13 G
Ashford 17 G
Ashford Hill 16 H
Ashford-Bowdler 22 C
Ashford in the Water 39 L
Ashgill 52 B
Ashgreen 18 K
Ashill 13 M
Ashill 14 K
Ashill 26 C
Ashingdon 18 E
Ashington 9 E
Ashington 14 M
Ashington 49 F
Ashkirk 53 H
Ashleworth 23 H
Ashley 16 K
Ashley 15 B
Ashley 15 D
Ashley 25 A
Ashley 26 H
Ashley 31 E
Ashley Green 17 A
Ashley Heath 7 C
Ashley Heath 31 E
Ashley Rostherne 38 J
Ash Magna 31 A
Ashmanhaugh 35 L
Ashmansworth 16 G
Ashmansworthy 12 J
Ash Mill 13 L
Ashmore 7 B
Ashmore Green 16 G
Ashmore Park 31 M
Ash-Naphill 16 C
Ashorne 24 D
Ashover 32 B
Ashow 24 A
Ashperton 23 D
Ashprington 5 H
Ash Priors 14 K
Ashreigney 13 K
Ash Street 26 M
Ashtead 17 L
Ash Thomas 13 M
Ashton 3 H
Ashton 22 C
Ashton 24 J
Ashton 25 B
Ashton 33 L
Ashton 38 K
Ashton Common 15 G
Ashton in Makerfield 38 E
Ashton Keynes 15 B
Ashton under Hill 23 J
Ashton upon Mersey 38 J
Ashton-under-Lyne 39 G
Ashurst 9 E
Ashurst Wood 9 C
Ashurst Wood 10 D
Ashurst-Netley Marsh 8 A
Ashwater 4 C
Ashwell 25 M
Ashwell 33 K
Ashwellthorpe 27 A
Ashwick 14 J
Ashwicken 34 L
Ashybank 53 L
Askam in Furness 42 E
Askern 40 D
Askerswell 6 F
Askett 16 C
Askham 33 A
Askham 48 K
Askham Bryan 40 A
Askham Richard 40 A
Asknish 56 H
Askrigg 43 F
Askwith 44 K
Aslackby 33 J
Aslacton 27 D
Aslockton 33 D
Asloun 66 F
Aspall 27 G
Aspatria 47 J
Aspenden Westmill 25 M
Aspley Guise 25 K
Aspull 38 E
Assater 80 H
Asselby 40 E
Asserby 34 B
Assington 26 M
Astbury 31 C
Astcote 24 J
Asterby 34 A
Asterley 30 J
Asterton 30 M
Asthall 24 K
Astle 71 C
Astley 23 B
Astley 31 D
Astley 32 K
Astley Abbotts 31 L
Astley Cross 23 B
Astley Green 38 J
Aston 16 A
Aston 16 F
Aston 22 C
Aston 25 M
Aston 31 A
Aston 31 B
Aston 31 D
Aston 31 G
Aston 31 M
Aston 38 H
Aston 39 L
Aston 39 M
Aston Abbots 25 K
Aston Botterell 31 K
Aston-by-Stone 31 F
Aston Cantlow 23 F
Aston Clinton 17 A
Aston-Crews Lea 23 G
Aston End 25 M
Aston Eyre 31 K
Aston Fields 23 C
Aston Flamville 32 L
Aston-Ingham 23 G
Aston juxta Mondrum 31 B
Aston le Walls 24 H
Aston Magna 24 G
Aston Munslow 31 K
Aston on Clun 30 M
Aston-on-Trent 32 H
Aston Rogers 30 J
Aston Rowant 16 C
Aston Sandford 16 C
Aston Somerville 23 J
Aston-Sub-Edge 23 J
Aston Tirrod 16 E
Aston Upthorpe 16 E
Astwick 25 L
Astwood 25 G
Astwood Bank 23 F
Aswarby 33 H
Aswardby 34 A
Atcham 31 G
Atch-Lench 23 F
Athelington 27 H
Athelney 14 L
Athelstaneford 53 C
Atherington 13 G
Atherstone 32 L
Atherstone on Stour 24 D
Atherton 38 E
Athorn Hall 58 H
Attadale 70 G
Atterby 40 M
Attical 98 C
Attleborough 27 A
Attleborough 32 L
Attlebridge 35 K
Atwick 41 A
Atworth 15 D
Aubourn 33 B
Auchagallon 50 C
Auchallater 66 G
Aucharnie 67 A
Auchattie 67 G
Auchavan 66 K
Auchenblae 67 K
Auchenbrack 52 K
Auchenbreck 56 H
Auchencairn 47 B
Auchencairn 47 D
Auchencarroch 57 G
Auchencrow 54 D
Auchendinny 53 A
Auchengray 52 C
Auchengruith 52 H
Auchenhalrig 72 J
Auchenheath 52 E
Auchenhessnane 52 K
Auchenmalg 46 D
Auchensoul 51 L
Auchentiber 51 C
Auchenvennel 57 G
Auchenvey 47 A
Auchgourish 65 C
Auchindrain 56 F
Auchindrean 70 C
Auchininna 73 K
Auchinleck 46 C
Auchinleck 51 J
Auchinloch 57 L
Auchinroath 72 L
Auchintoul 66 F
Auchintoul 71 B
Auchiries 67 C
Auchlean 65 F
Auchlee 67 H
Auchleuchries 67 C
Auchleven 67 A
Auchlochan 52 E
Auchlossan 66 F
Auchlunies 67 H
Auchlunkart 72 L
Auchlyne 57 B
Auchmacoy 67 B
Auchmantle 46 A
Auchmillan 51 F
Auchmithie 59 B
Auchmore 57 C
Auchmuirbridge 58 H
Auchmull 66 M
Auchnabony 47 D
Auchnacree 66 L
Auchnagallin 72 K
Auchnagatt 67 B
Aucholzie 66 H
Auchronie 66 H
Auchterarder 58 D
Auchteraw 64 C
Auchterderran 58 H
Auchterhouse 58 C
Auchtermuchty 58 J
Auchterneed 71 G
Auchtertool 58 L
Auchtertyre 58 C
Auchtertyre 70 K
Auchtertyre 72 H
Auchtubh 57 E
Auckengill 78 F
Auckley 40 G
Audenshaw 39 G
Audlem 31 B
Audley 31 B
Auds 73 G
Aughamullan 104 E
Augher 103 F
Aughnacloy 103 F
Aughnamullan 104 F
Aughton 15 J
Aughton 38 D
Aughton 39 M
Aughton 40 B
Aughton 43 G
Aughton Park 38 D
Auldearn 71 J
Aulden 22 F
Auldgirth 47 B
Auldhame 59 K
Auldhouse 52 A
Auldyoch 67 A
Ault a'Chruinn 70 K
Aultanrynie 76 J
Aultbea 70 B
Aultdearg 70 F
Aultgrishan 70 A
Aultibea 78 K
Aultiphurst 77 F
Aultmore 72 M
Ault-na-goire 65 A
Aulton 66 C
Aultvoulin Inverie 63 C
Aundorach 65 C
Aunsby 33 H
Auquhorthies 67 B
Aust 14 C
Austerfield 40 K
Austrey 32 L
Austwick 43 H
Authorpe 34 A
Authorpe Row 34 B
Avebury 15 F
Avebury Trusloe 15 F
Aveley 18 G
Avening 15 B
Averham 33 D
Aveton Gifford 5 H
Avielochan 65 C
Aviemore 65 C
Avington 16 G
Avington 16 K
Avoch 71 H
Avon 7 F
Avonbridge 58 K
Avon Castle 7 F
Avon Dassett 24 E
Avonmouth 14 C
Avonwick 5 H
Awbridge 8 A
Awhirk 46 D
Awhirk 46 K
Awkley 14 C
Awliscombe 6 A
Awre 23 K
Awsworth 32 F

Axbridge 14 H
Axford 15 F
Axford 16 L
Axminster 6 B
Axmouth 6 E
Aycliffe Village 44 B
Aydon 49 D
Aylburton 22 M
Ayle 48 J
Aylesbeare 6 A
Aylesbury 16 C
Aylesby 41 G
Aylesford 10 C
Aylesham 11 E
Aylestone 32 M
Aylmerton 35 H
Aylsham 35 L
Aylton 23 G
Aymestrey 22 C
Aynho 24 H
Ayot Saint Lawrence 17 B
Ayot Saint Peter 17 B
Ayr 51 E
Aysgarth 43 F
Ayside 42 F
Ayston 33 K
Ayton 45 H
Ayton 54 D
Aywick 80 E
Azerley 44 G

B

Babbacombe 5 J
Babbinswood 30 F
Babcary 14 M
Babel 21 F
Babell 37 J
Babeny 5 E
Babraham 26 G
Babworth 40 K
Bac 75 E
Back of Keppoch 63 F
Backaland 79 E
Backaskaill 79 B
Backbarrow 42 F
Backburn 66 C
Backburn 67 G
Backfolds 73 M
Backford 38 K
Backhill 67 A
Backhill of Clackriach 67 B
Backhillof Trustach 66 J
Backies 71 C
Backlass 78 H
Backwell 14 F
Backworth 49 F
Bacon End 18 A
Baconsthorpe 35 H
Bacton 22 H
Bacton 27 G
Bacton 35 M
Bacton Green 27 G
Bacup 39 A
Badachro 70 A
Badavanich 70 E
Badbury 15 F
Badby 24 E
Badcall 76 F
Badcaul 70 B
Baddeley Green 31 C
Baddesley Clinton 24 A
Baddesley Ensor 32 K
Baddidarach 76 H
Baddoch 66 G
Badenscoth 67 A
Badenyon 66 A
Badger 31 L
Badgers Mount 10 A
Badgeworth 23 L
Badgworth 14 H
Badicaul 70 K
Badingham 27 H
Badlesmere 11 A
Badlipster 78 H
Badluarach 70 B
Badminton 15 A
Badnagie 78 K
Badninish 71 C
Badrallach 70 C
Badsey 23 J
Badshot Lea 16 M
Badsworth 39 F
Badwell Ash 26 J
Bag Enderby 34 A
Bagby 44 H
Bagedon 23 L
Baggrow 47 J
Bàgh Mòr 68 E
Bàgh Shiarabhagh 68 K
Baghasdal 68 H
Bagillt 37 J
Baginton 24 B
Baglan 21 L
Bagley 30 F
Bagnall 31 C
Bagnor 16 G
Bagpath 23 L
Bagshot 16 G
Bagshot 16 J
Bagstone 15 A
Bagthorpe 32 C
Bagthorpe 34 J
Bagworth 32 L
Bagwyllydiart 22 J
Bail Ard Bhuirgh 75 B
Bail Uachdraich 68 B
Bail'Ur Tholastaidh 75 C
Baildon 39 B
Baile a' Mhanaich 68 B
Baile Ailein 75 G
Baile an Truiseil 75 B
Bailebeag 65 A
Baile Boldheach 56 G
Baile Glas 68 B
Baile Mhàrtainn 68 B
Baile Mhic Phàil 68 C
Baile Mòr 62 M
Baile Mòr 68 B
Baile na Creige 68 K
Baile nan Cailleach 68 E
Baile Raghnill 68 B
Baileysmill 105 G
Bailiesward 66 C
Bailleston 52 A
Bainbrigde 43 F
Bainshole 67 A
Bainton 24 L
Bainton 33 L
Bainton 40 C
Bairnkine 53 M
Baker Street 18 G
Bakers End 17 C
Bakewell 39 L
Balachuirn 69 J
Balbeg 71 K
Balbeg Dalmorton 51 H
Balbeggie 58 E
Balbithan 67 D
Balblair 71 G
Balblair 71 H
Balcherry 71 F
Balchers 73 K
Balchladich 76 H
Balchraggan 71 K
Balchrick 76 C
Balcombe 9 C
Balcomie 59 G
Balcurvie 58 J
Baldersby 44 H
Balderston 38 B
Balderton 33 D
Baldhu 3 J
Baldinnie 59 G
Baldock 25 M
Baldovie 59 D
Baldrine 37 B
Baldslow 10 J
Baldwin 37 B
Baldwinholme 48 G
Baldwin's Gate 31 E
Bale 35 G
Balemartine 62 A
Balephuil 62 A
Balerno 53 A
Balevullin 62 A
Balfarg 58 J
Balfield 66 M
Balfour 79 H
Balfron 57 H
Balgaveny 67 A
Balgavies 59 A
Balgonar 58 G
Balgove 67 B
Balgowan 58 D
Balgowan 65 E
Balgown 69 B
Balgrochan 57 L
Balgy 70 D
Balhaldie 57 J
Balhalgardy 67 A
Balhary 58 C
Balhelvie 58 F
Baliasta 80 A
Baligill 77 F
Baligrundle 63 M
Balintore 66 K
Balintore 71 F
Balintraid 71 F
Balke 107 H
Balkeerie 58 C
Balkholme 40 E
Balkissock 51 K
Ball 30 F
Ballabeg 37 D
Ballacannell 37 B
Ballacarnane Beg 37 A
Ballachrink 37 D
Ballachulish 64 H
Ballafesson 37 D
Ballagyr 37 A
Ballajora 37 B
Ballakilpheric 37 D
Ballamodha 37 D
Ballantrae 51 K
Ballasalla 37 B
Ballasalla 37 D
Ballateare 37 B
Ballater 66 H
Ballaugh 37 B
Ballechin 65 M
Balleigh 71 F
Ballencreiff 53 B
Balleney 108 J
Ball Hill 16 G
Ballidon 32 A
Balliekine 50 C
Balliemeanoch 56 C
Balliemore 56 B
Balliemore 56 J
Balligan 105 H
Ballimore 56 H
Ballimore 57 E
Ballinaby 55 G
Ballinamallard 103 D
Ballindarragh 103 H
Ballindean 58 F
Ballinderry Bridge 104 B
Ballingdon 26 M
Ballinger Common 17 A
Ballingham 22 J
Ballingry 58 H
Ballinlea 108 F
Ballinlick 58 B
Ballinluig 65 M
Ballinran 98 C
Ballinteer 108 E
Ballintoy 108 F
Ballintuim 65 M
Ballytemple 108 H
Balloch 57 G
Balloch 57 M
Balloch 71 L
Ballochan 66 J
Ballochford 66 A
Ballochroy 56 K
Ballochule 56 J
Ballogie 66 J
Balloo Cross Roads 105 G
Ballooly 104 J
Balloolymore 104 J
Balls Cross 9 A
Ballsmill 104 K
Ballsmyre 57 K
Ballyallaght 108 F
Ballyalton 105 K
Ballyard 103 E
Ballyardel 98 C
Ballyarnet 107 J
Ballybogy 108 H
Ballyboy 103 C
Ballyboylands 108 J
Ballybrooky 104 G
Ballycarry 105 B
Ballycastle 109 D
Ballyclare 105 A
Ballyconnelly 108 M
Ballyeaston 105 A
Ballygalley 109 K
Ballygawley 103 F
Ballygelly 109 K
Ballyginniff 104 C
Bally-Gomartin 105 D
Ballygowan 98 C
Ballygowan 104 J
Ballygowan 105 D
Ballygown 63 K
Ballygrant 55 H
Ballyhalbert 105 H
Ballyhaugh 62 J
Ballyhoe Bridge 108 J
Ballyholme 105 E
Ballyhornan 105 L
Ballykeel 98 C
Ballykeel 104 J
Ballykeel 108 M
Ballykelly 108 G
Ballykilbeg 105 K
Ballykinler 105 K
Ballyknock 104 H
Ballyknock 108 J
Ballyknock 108 L
Ballyleny 104 H
Ballyleny 104 J
Ballylesson 105 D
Ballylintagh 108 H
Ballyloughbeg 108 F
Ballylucas 105 K
Ballylumford 105 B
Ballymacanallen 104 H
Ballymacilroy 108 M
Ballymacrevan 104 F
Ballymacron 108 D
Ballymacurn North 105 G
Ballymagorry 107 H
Ballymarama 104 G
Ballymartin 98 C
Ballymeanoch 56 E
Ballymena 108 M
Ballymoney 108 G
Ballymoney 108 J
Ballynabragget 104 J
Ballynagabog Bridge 108 J
Ballynaghy 104 H
Ballynahinch 105 G
Ballynamallaght 107 M
Ballynameen 108 H
Ballynasaggar 103 F
Ballynaskeagh 104 H
Ballynchatty 103 B
Ballyneaner 107 J
Ballynease 108 L
Ballyness 108 G
Ballynoe 105 K
Ballynure 105 A
Ballyrashane 108 E
Ballyreagh 103 E
Ballyreagh 108 M
Ballyrogan 108 H
Ballyrogully 104 B
Ballyronan 104 B
Ballyroney 104 J
Ballysallagh 104 J
Ballytrustan 105 H
Ballyvally 104 M
Ballyveagh 98 C
Ballyvester 105 E
Ballyvoy 109 D
Ballywaddan 105 H
Ballywalter 105 E
Ballyward 104 M
Ballywatticock 105 E
Ballyweely 104 M
Ballywilly 104 E
Balmacara 70 K
Balmacara Square 70 K
Balmaclellan 47 A
Balmacneil 58 B
Balmacqueen 69 B
Balmae 47 D
Balmaha 57 G
Balmalcolm 58 J
Balmeanach 69 H
Balmeanach 69 J
Balmedie 67 E
Balmerino 58 F
Balmerlawn 8 D
Balmichael 50 F
Balmore 57 L
Balmore 65 L
Balmore 71 K
Balmore 71 M
Balmullo 59 D
Balmungie 71 J
Balmurrie 46 A
Balnabruich 78 K
Balnacoil 77 L
Balnacra 70 H
Balnafoich 71 L
Balnagnall 71 F
Balnaguard 65 M
Balnaguisich 71 E
Balnahard 55 F
Balnahard 63 K
Balnain 71 K
Balnakail 77 A
Balnaknock 69 E
Balnamoan 65 M
Balnamoon 66 M
Balnamore Milltown 108 H
Balnapaling 71 F
Balnaut Inver 66 G
Balne 40 D
Balnespick 65 F
Balquhidder 57 E
Balsall Common 24 A
Balscote 24 G
Balsham 26 G
Baltasound 80 A
Balterley 31 B
Baltersan 46 B
Balthangie 73 L
Baltonsborough 14 M
Baluachraig 56 E
Balvaird 71 H
Balvarran 65 M
Balvicar 56 A
Balvraid 71 M
Bamber Bridge 38 B
Bamber's Green 18 A
Bamburgh 54 H
Bamff 58 C
Bamford 39 L
Bampton 13 M
Bampton 16 A
Bampton 48 K
Bampton Grange 48 L
Banbridge 104 J
Banbury 24 H
Banchor 71 M
Banchory 67 G
Banchory-Devenick 67 H
Bancyfelin 20 F
Bancyffordd 21 D
Banff 73 G
Bangor 36 J
Bangor 105 E
Bangor-is-y-coed 30 C
Banham 27 D
Bank 8 D
Bankend 47 E
Bankfoot 58 B
Bankglen 52 G
Bankhead 67 D
Bankhead 67 E
Bank Newton 43 L
Banknock 57 M
Banks 38 A
Banks 48 D
Bankshill 47 C
Bank Street 23 A
Bannfoot 104 E
Banningham 35 L
Bannister Green 18 B
Bannockburn 57 J
Banstead 17 L
Bantham 5 G
Banton 57 M
Banwell 14 E
Bapchild 11 A
Bapton 15 L
Barabhas 75 B
Baramore 63 F
Baranoilt 108 G
Barassie 51 E
Barbaraville 71 F
Barber Booth 39 K
Barbon 43 D
Barbrook 13 E
Barby 24 E
Barcaldine 64 K
Barcheston 24 G
Barcombe 9 F
Barcombe Cross 10 G
Barcombe Cross 9 F
Barden 44 D
Bardennoch 51 M
Bardfield End Green 26 K
Bardfield Saling 18 B
Bardister 80 J
Bardney 33 C
Bardon 32 H
Bardon Mill 48 F
Bardowie 57 L
Bardrainney 57 K
Bardsea 42 F
Bardsey 39 C
Bardsley 39 D
Bardwell 26 F
Barford 24 G
Barford 27 A
Barford Saint Martin 15 L
Barfrestone 11 E
Bargeddie 52 A
Bargoed 22 K
Bargrennan 46 B
Bar Hall 105 L
Barham 11 E
Barham 25 E
Bar Hill 25 J
Barholm 33 L
Barkby 32 M
Barkby Thorpe 32 M
Barkestone-le-Vale 33 G
Barkham 16 J
Barking 17 J
Barking 27 K
Barkingside 17 F
Barking Tye 27 K
Barkisland 39 D
Barkston 33 E
Barkston Ash 40 A
Barkway 25 M
Barlae 46 B
Barlaston 31 F
Barlavington 9 D
Barlborough 39 M
Barlby 40 D
Barlestone 32 L
Barley 25 M
Barley 38 C
Barleyhill 49 G
Barleythorpe 33 K
Barling 18 J
Barlow 39 L
Barlow 40 D
Barlow 49 H
Barmby Moor 40 B
Barmby on the Marsh 40 E
Barmer 34 J
Barming 10 C
Barmoor Lane End 54 H
Barmouth 29 E
Barmpton 44 B
Barmston 41 A
Barnaby Green 27 J
Barnacabber 56 J
Barnacarry 56 H
Barnack 33 L
Barnacle 24 B
Barnard Castle 43 C
Barnard Gale 24 K
Barnardiston 26 L
Barnburgh 39 J
Barnby 27 F
Barnby Dun 40 G
Barnby in the Willows 33 E
Barnby Moor 40 K
Barndennoch 47 B
Barndennoch 52 L
Barnes 17 H
Barnet 17 E
Barnetby le Wold 40 J
Barney 35 K
Barnham 26 F
Barnham 27 K
Barnham Broom 27 A
Barnhead 59 B
Barnhill 49 D
Barnhill 72 G
Barnhills 46 G
Barningham 26 F
Barningham 44 A
Barnmeen 104 M
Barnoldby le Beck 41 K
Barnoldswick 43 L
Barns Green 9 B
Barnsley 23 M
Barnsley 39 J
Barnstaple 13 G
Barnston 18 A
Barnston 37 J
Barnstone 33 D
Barnt Green 23 C
Barnton 38 L
Barnwell 25 B
Barnwood 23 L
Barr 51 L
Barr 104 L
Barrachan 46 E
Barrack 67 B
Barraer 46 B
Barraglom 75 D
Barrahormid 56 G
Barran 56 B
Barrapol 62 A
Barras 43 B
Barras 67 K
Barrasford 49 D
Barravullin 56 E
Barregarrow 37 B
Barrhead 51 C
Barrhead 52 A
Barrhill 51 L
Barrington 14 L
Barrington 25 J
Barripper 3 H
Barrmill 51 C
Barrock 78 E
Barrons Court 107 L
Barrow 31 G
Barrow 33 K
Barrow 38 C
Barroway Drove 26 B
Barrowburn 54 K
Barrowby 33 H
Barrowden 33 L
Barrowford 39 A
Barrow Great 26 H
Barrow Gurney 14 F
Barrow-in-Furness 42 H
Barrow Street 15 K
Barrow upon Humber 40 J
Barrow upon Soar 32 J
Barrow upon Trent 32 H
Barry 14 D
Barry 59 D
Barry Island 14 D
Barsby 32 M
Barsham 27 F
Barston 24 A
Bartford Saint John 24 H
Bartford Saint Michael 24 H
Barthol Chapel 67 B
Barthomley 31 B
Bartley 8 A
Bartlow 26 K
Barton 5 F
Barton 23 F
Barton 23 J
Barton 26 G
Barton 31 A
Barton 38 B
Barton 38 D
Barton 44 A
Barton Bendish 26 B
Barton Hartshorn 24 M
Barton in Fabis 32 F
Barton in the Beans 32 L
Barton-in-the-Clay 25 L
Barton-le-Street 44 M
Barton-le-Willows 44 M
Barton Mills 26 E
Barton Moss 38 J
Barton-on-the-Heath 24 G
Barton Saint David 14 M
Barton Seagrave 25 A
Barton Stacey 16 K
Barton Turf 35 M
Barton-under-Needwood 32 G
Barton-upon-Humber 40 F
Barway 26 D
Barwell 32 L
Barwick 6 C
Barwick 17 C
Barwick 44 B
Barwick in Elmet 39 C
Baschurch 30 F
Bascote 24 E
Bascote Heath 24 E
Basford Green 31 C
Bashall Eaves 43 K
Bashley 7 F
Basildon 18 D
Basingstoke 16 L
Baslow 39 L
Bason Bridge 14 H
Bassaleg 14 B
Bassenthwaite 47 M
Bassett 8 A
Bassingbourn 25 J
Bassingfield 32 F
Bassingham 33 B
Bassingthorpe 33 H
Basta 80 E
Baston 33 M
Bastwick 27 C
Batchcott 22 C
Batcombe 6 C
Batcombe 14 M
Bate Heath 38 L
Bath 15 D
Bathampton 15 D
Bathealton 13 M
Batheaston 15 D
Bathford 15 D
Bathgate 52 C
Bathley 33 A
Bathpool 4 F
Batley 39 E
Batsford 23 J
Batt's Corner 16 M
Battersby 44 F
Battersea 17 H
Battisborough Cross 5 G
Battisford 27 K
Battisford Tye 26 M
Battle 10 H
Battle 22 D
Battlefield 31 D
Battlesbridge Rawreth 18 E
Battlesden 25 K
Battleton 13 H
Battramsley 8 D
Bauds of Cullen 72 J
Baugh 62 A
Baughurst 16 H
Baugthon Ryall 23 E
Baulking 16 A
Baumber 34 A
Baunton 23 L
Baverstock 15 L
Bawburgh 27 B
Bawdeswell 35 K
Bawdrip 14 H
Bawdsey 27 L
Bawsey 34 L
Bawtry 40 K
Baxenden 38 C
Baxterley 32 K
Bayan 104 L
Baybridge 49 G
Baycliff 42 H
Bayford 14 M
Baydon 15 F
Bayford 17 C
Bayles 48 J
Baylham 27 K
Baynard's Green 24 L
Baysham 22 J
Bayston Hill 31 G
Baythorne End 26 L
Bayton 23 A
Bayworth 16 B
Beachampton 24 J
Beachamwell 26 C
Beachans 72 K
Beacharr 50 B
Beachley 14 C
Beacon 6 A
Beacon End 18 C
Beacon's Bottom 16 C
Beaconsfield 17 D
Beacrabhaic 74 M
Beadlam 44 J
Beadnell 54 M
Beaford 13 K
Beaghbeg 104 A
Beal 40 D
Beal 54 H
Beamhurst 32 D
Beaminster 6 C
Beamish 49 H
Beamsley 43 M
Bean 18 G
Beanacre 15 E
Beanley 54 L
Beaquoy 79 D
Beardiville 108 E
Beare Green 17 L
Bearley 24 D
Bearpark 49 L
Bearsbridge 48 J
Bearsden 57 L
Bearsted 10 C
Bearwood 7 E
Bearwood 22 C
Beattock 52 M
Beauchamp Acton 23 D
Beauchamp Roding 18 A
Beauchief 39 L
Beaufort 22 G
Beaulieu 8 D
Beauly 71 G
Beaumaris 36 J
Beaumont 9 M
Beaumont 48 D
Beaumont Leys 32 M
Beausale 24 A
Beauworth 8 B
Beaworthy 5 A
Beaworthy 12 M
Beazley End 18 B
Bebington 38 G
Bebside 49 F
Beccles 27 F
Becconsall 38 A
Beckbury 31 H
Beckenham 17 J
Beckermet 42 A
Beckermonds 43 H
Beckfoot 42 B
Beck Foot 43 D
Beckfoot 47 J
Beckford 23 H
Beckhampton 15 E
Beck Hole 45 D
Beckingham 33 E
Beckingham 40 L
Beckington 15 G
Beckley 10 J
Beckley 16 B
Beck Row 26 E
Beck Side 42 E
Beckton 17 J
Beckwithshaw 44 K
Becontree 17 J
Bedale 44 G
Bedburn 49 K
Bedchester 7 B
Beddau 14 A
Beddgelert 36 M
Beddingham 9 F
Beddingham 10 G
Beddington 17 H
Bedfield 27 H
Bedford 25 H
Bedhampton 8 F
Bedingfield 27 G
Bedlar's Green 18 A
Bedlington 49 F
Bedlinog 22 K
Bedmond 17 B
Bednall 31 J
Bedrule 53 L
Bedstone 30 M
Bedwas 14 A
Bedworth 24 B
Beeby 32 M
Beech 16 L
Beech 31 F
Beech Hill 16 H
Beech Hill 104 L
Beechingstoke 15 H
Beechworthy 12 L
Beedon 16 D
Beeford 41 A
Beeley 32 B
Beelsby 41 K
Beenham 16 H
Beer 6 D
Beer Crocombe 14 K
Beer Hackett 6 C
Beesands 5 L
Beesby 34 B
Beeson 5 L
Beeston 25 H
Beeston 34 M
Beeston 38 K
Beeston 39 C
Beeston Regis 35 H
Beeswing 47 B
Beetham 43 D
Beetley 35 K
Began 14 A
Begbroke 24 L
Begdale 34 K
Begelly 20 H

A B C D E F G H I J K L M N O P Q R S T U V W X Y Z

148 Great Britain 1:301,000

A B C D E F G H I J K L M N O P Q R S T U V W X Y Z

Beggar Hill 18 D
Beguildy 30 L
Beighton 27 C
Beighton 39 M
Beinn Casgro 75 H
Beith 51 C
Bekesbourne 11 B
Belaugh 27 B
Belbins 8 A
Belbroughton 23 B
Belchamo Saint Paul 26 L
Belchamp Otten 26 L
Belchamp Walter 26 L
Belchford 34 A
Belcoo 102 F
Belfast 105 D
Belfast City 105 D
Belford 54 H
Belhelvie 67 E
Belhinnie 60 C
Bellabeg 66 E
Bellaghy 108 L
Bellamore 51 L
Bellanaleck 103 D
Bellanoch 56 D
Bellaty 66 K
Bell Bar 17 B
Bell Busk 43 L
Belleau 34 A
Belleek 102 C
Belleek 104 L
Belleisle 103 B
Bell End 23 C
Bellerby 44 D
Bellever 5 E
Bellfield 52 E
Belliehill 66 M
Bellingdon 17 A
Bellingham 49 A
Belloch 50 B
Belloch 66 L
Bells Yew Green 10 E
Bellsbank 51 J
Bellshill 52 B
Bellshill 54 H
Bellspool 52 F
Bellsquerry 52 C
Belluton 14 F
Belmaduthy 71 H
Belmesthorpe 33 L
Belmont 38 F
Belmont 80 B
Belmont 105 D
Belnacraig 66 E
Belowda 4 D
Belper 32 E
Belper Cane End 32 E
Belsay 49 E
Belsford Lincombe 5 H
Belsize 17 A
Belstead 27 K
Belston 51 F
Belstone 5 B
Belsyde 58 K
Belthorn 38 C
Beltinge 11 B
Beltingham 48 F
Beltoft 40 H
Belton 27 C
Belton 32 H
Belton 33 E
Belton 40 H
Belton-in-Rutland 33 K
Beltoy 105 A
Belvedere 17 J
Belvoir 33 G
Bembridge 8 H
Bemersyde 53 J
Bempton 45 M
Benacre 27 F
Benbuie 52 K
Benburb 104 D
Benderloch 64 K
Bendish 25 L
Bendooragh 108 H
Benenden 10 F
Benfield 46 B
Benholm 67 K
Beningbrough 44 L
Benington 25 M
Benington 34 D
Benllech 36 F
Benmore 56 J
Benmore 57 B
Bennacott 4 C
Bennecarrigan 51 D
Benniworth 33 C
Benson 16 E
Benstonhall 79 E
Bent 66 M
Benthall 31 G
Bentham 23 L
Benthoul 67 G
Bentley 16 M
Bentley 27 K
Bentley 32 K
Bentley 40 F
Bentley 40 G
Bentley Hanbury 23 C
Benton 13 G
Bentpath 48 A
Bentworth 16 L
Benvie 58 F
Benwick 25 C
Beoley 23 C
Beoraidbeg 63 C
Bepton 9 A
Beragh 103 C
Berden 26 K
Berea 20 A
Bere Alston 5 D
Bere Ferrers 5 D
Berepper 3 L
Bere Regis 7 E
Bergh Apton 27 B
Berinsfiled 16 B
Berkeley 23 K
Berkhamsted 17 A
Berkley 15 G
Berkswell 24 A
Bermondsey 17 J
Bermuda 32 L
Bernera 70 K
Berners Roding 18 A
Bernice 56 J
Bernisdale 69 E
Berrick Salome 16 B
Berridale 78 K
Berrier 48 K
Berriew 30 H
Berrington 31 G
Berrington 54 H
Berrow 14 E
Berrow 23 H
Berrow Green 23 D
Berryfield 15 D
Berry Hill 22 M
Berryhillock 72 J
Berrynarbor 13 D
Berry Pomeroy 5 H
Bersham 30 C
Berstane 79 H
Bersted 9 D
Berwick 10 G
Berwick Bassett 15 F
Berwick Hill 49 E
Berwick Saint James 15 L
Berwick Saint John 15 K
Berwick Saint Leonard 15 K
Berwick-upon-Tweed 54 E
Berwyn 30 B
Besford 23 E
Besford 31 D
Bessacarr 40 G
Bessbrook 104 L
Bessels Leigh 16 B
Bessingham 35 L
Best Beech Hill 10 E
Besthorpe 27 A
Besthorpe 33 A
Bestwood Village 32 F
Beswick 40 C
Betchworth 17 L
Bethania 29 L
Bethel 36 H
Bethel 36 J
Bethersden 10 F
Bethesda 20 E
Bethesda 36 J
Bethlehem 21 E
Bethnal Green 17 F
Betley 31 B
Betsham 18 G
Betteshanger 11 E
Bettiscombe 6 B
Bettisfield 31 A
Bettws 14 B
Betton 30 J
Betton 31 E
Bettws 21 M
Bettws 22 H
Bettws Cedewain 30 H
Bettws Gwerfil Goch 30 B
Bettws Newydd 22 L
Bettyhill 77 E
Betws 21 H
Betws Bledrws 21 B
Betws Garmon 36 M
Betwsv 20 C
Betws-y-coed 37 K
Betws-yn-Rhos 37 G
Beulah 20 C
Beulah 21 C
Bevendean 9 F
Bevercotes 33 A
Beverley 40 C
Beverston 15 B
Bevington 15 A
Bewaldeth 47 J
Bewcastle 48 E
Bewdley 23 B
Bewerly 44 K
Bewholme 41 A
Bexhill 10 H
Bexley 17 J
Bexleyheath 17 J
Bexwell 26 B
Beyton 26 J
Bhaltos 74 F
Bhatarsaigh 68 K
Bibury 23 M
Bicester 24 L
Bickenhall 14 K
Bickenhill 24 A
Bicker 33 J
Bickershaw 38 E
Bickerstaffe 38 D
Bickerton 31 A
Bickerton 40 A
Bickham Bridge 5 H
Bickington 5 E
Bickington 13 G
Bickleigh 5 C
Bickleigh 5 D
Bickleigh 13 L
Bickleton 12 J
Bickley 17 J
Bickley Moss 31 A
Bickley Town 31 A
Bicknacre 18 E
Bicknoller 14 G
Bicknor 10 C
Bickton 7 C
Bicton 30 J
Bicton 30 L
Bidborough 10 B
Biddenden 10 F
Biddenham 25 H
Biddestone 15 D
Biddisham 14 H
Biddlesden 24 J
Biddlestone 54 K
Biddulph 31 C
Biddulph Moor 31 C
Bideford-Northam 12 J
Bidford-on-Avon 23 F
Bielby 40 B
Bieldside 67 H
Bierley 8 H
Bierton 16 C
Bierton 24 M
Big Balcraig 46 E
Big Bridge 107 K
Bigbury 5 G
Bigbury-on-Sea 5 G
Bigby 40 J
Biggar 42 H
Biggar 52 F
Biggin 32 A
Biggin 32 B
Biggin 40 A
Biggings 80 M
Biggin Hill 10 A
Biggins 43 G
Biggleswade 25 H
Bighouse 77 F
Bighton 16 L
Bignor 9 D
Bigods 18 A
Bigrigg 47 L
Big Sand 70 A
Bigton 81 H
Bilberry 4 D
Bilborough 32 F
Bilbrook 13 J
Bilbrook 31 H
Bilbrough 40 A
Bilbster 78 H
Bildershaw 44 A
Bildeston 26 M
Billericay 18 D
Billesdon 33 K
Billesley 23 F
Billesley 23 F
Billing 25 D
Billingborough 33 J
Billinge 38 E
Billingford 27 D
Billingford 35 K
Billingham 44 C
Billinghay 33 F
Billingley 39 J
Billingshurst 9 B
Billingsley 31 K
Billington 25 K
Billington 38 C
Billockby 27 C
Billsmoor Park 49 A
Billy 108 F
Billy Row 49 L
Bilsborrow 42 M
Bilsby 34 B
Bilsington 11 D
Bilsthorpe 33 A
Bilston 31 M
Bilston 53 A
Bilstone 32 L
Bilting 11 D
Bilton 24 B
Bilton 41 B
Bilton 54 L
Bilton in Ainsty 40 A
Bimbister 79 G
Binbrook 41 K
Bincombe 7 D
Bindal 72 D
Binegar 14 J
Binfield 16 J
Binfield Heath 16 F
Bingfield 49 D
Bingham 33 D
Bingham's Melcombe 7 A
Bingley 39 B
Bings Heath 31 D
Binham 35 G
Binley 16 G
Binley Willenhall 24 B
Binley Woods 24 B
Binniehill 57 M
Binstead 8 E
Binsted 16 M
Bintree 35 K
Binweston 30 J
Birch 18 C
Birch 38 F
Bircham Newton 34 J
Bircham Tofts 34 J
Birchanger 18 A
Bircher 22 C
Birchfield 71 B
Birch Green 17 C
Birch Green 18 C
Birchgrove 21 L
Birchington 11 B
Birchley Heath 32 K
Birchover 32 B
Birchtfield 65 C
Birch Vale 39 G
Birchwood 33 B
Bircotes 40 K
Birdbrook 26 L
Birdfield 56 E
Birdham 8 F
Birdholme 32 B
Birdingbury 24 E
Birdlip 23 L
Birdsall 45 K
Birdsgreen 31 L
Birdsmoorgate 6 B
Birdston 57 L
Birdwell 39 J
Birdwood 23 K
Birgham 54 G
Birkby 44 E
Birkdale 38 A
Birkenhead 37 J
Birkenhills 73 K
Birkenshaw 39 B
Birkenshaw 52 A
Birkhall 66 H
Birkhill 53 G
Birkhill-Muirhead 58 F
Birkholme 33 H
Birkin 40 D
Birley 22 F
Birling 10 B
Birling 49 C
Birling Gap 10 K
Birlingham 23 E
Birmingham 31 M
Birness 67 B
Birse 66 J
Birsemore 66 J
Birstall 32 M
Birstall 39 E
Birstwith 44 K
Birtley 22 C
Birtley 49 D
Birtley 49 H
Birts Street 23 G
Bisbrooke 33 K
Bisham 16 F
Bishampton 23 F
Bishop Auckland 49 L
Bishopbridge 40 M
Bishopbriggs 57 L
Bishop Burton 40 F
Bishop Middleham 49 M
Bishop Monkton 44 K
Bishop Norton 40 M
Bishopsbourne Kingston 11 E
Bishops Cannings 15 E
Bishop's Castle 30 M
Bishop's Caundle 7 A
Bishop's Cleeve 23 H
Bishops Court 105 L
Bishop's Frome 23 D
Bishop's Itchington 24 E
Bishops Lydeard 14 K
Bishop's Nympton 13 L
Bishop's Offley 31 E
Bishop's Stortford 18 A
Bishop's Sutton 16 L
Bishop's Sutton 8 C
Bishop's Tachbrook 24 D
Bishop's Tawton 13 G
Bishopsteignton 5 F
Bishopstoke 8 B
Bishopston 21 K
Bishopstone 9 J
Bishopstone 10 K
Bishopstone 15 F
Bishopstone 15 L
Bishopstone 16 C
Bishopstone 22 F
Bishopstrow 15 G
Bishop Sutton 14 F
Bishop's Waltham 8 B
Bishops-Wickham 18 B
Bishopswood 14 K
Bishop's Wood 31 H
Bishopsworth 14 F
Bishop Thornton 44 K
Bishopthorpe 40 A
Bishopton 44 B
Bishopton 57 K
Bishop Wilton 40 B
Bishton 14 B
Bisley 17 G
Bisley 23 L
Bispham 42 L
Bissoe 3 J
Bisterne 7 F
Bisterne Close 7 F
Bitchfield 33 H
Bittadon 13 D
Bittaford 5 H
Bittering 35 K
Bitterley 31 K
Bitterne 8 B
Bitteswell 24 C
Bitton 14 F
Bix 16 F
Bixter 81 G
Blaby 32 M
Blackacre 47 C
Blackadder 54 D
Blackawton 5 H
Blackborough 13 M
Blackborough End 34 L
Black Bourton 16 A
Blackboys 10 G
Blackbraes 58 K
Black Bridge 105 G
Blackbrook 32 B
Blackburn 38 C
Blackburn 52 C
Blackburn 67 D
Black Callerton 49 E
Blackcastle 71 J
Blackchambers 67 D
Blackcraig 47 A
Black Crofts 64 K
Blackden Heath 38 M
Black Dog 13 L
Blackdog 67 E
Blackdown 6 B
Blackford 14 H
Blackford 14 M
Blackford 48 D
Blackford 58 G
Blackfordby 32 H
Blackfort 103 B
Blackgang 8 G
Blackhall 67 G
Blackhall Colliery 49 M
Blackhall Mill 49 H
Blackhall Rocks 49 M
Blackhaugh 53 E
Blackheat 27 J
Blackheath 17 J
Blackheath 18 C
Blackheath 31 M
Black Heddon 49 E
Blackhill 69 E
Blackhill 73 M
Black Horse Drove 26 B
Blackjack 33 J
Blackland 15 E
Blackley 38 F
Blacklunans 66 K
Black Marsh 30 J
Blackmill 13 C
Blackmill 21 M
Blackmoor 8 C
Blackmoor 14 E
Blackmoor 14 K
Blackmoor Gate 13 D
Blackmore 18 D
Blackmore End 17 B
Blackmore End 26 L
Black Mount 64 L
Blackness 58 K
Blackness 67 G
Blackness 78 H
Blacknest 16 M
Black Notley 18 B
Blacko 39 A
Black Pill 21 K
Blackpool 38 A
Blackpool Gate 48 E
Blackridge 52 B
Blackrock 22 H
Blackrock 55 H
Blackrod 38 E
Blackshaw 47 E
Blackshaw Head 39 A
Blackshaw Moor 32 A
Black Skull 104 J
Blacksmith's Green 27 G
Blackstone 9 E
Blackthorn 24 L
Blackthorpe 26 J
Blacktoft 40 E
Blacktop 67 H
Black Torrington 12 M
Blacktown 107 L
Blackwater 3 J
Blackwater 8 H
Blackwater 16 J
Blackwaterfoot 50 F
Blackwatertown 104 D
Blackwell 23 C
Blackwell 24 G
Blackwell 32 C
Blackwell 39 K
Blackwood 22 K
Blackwood 52 E
Blackwood Hill 31 C
Blacon 38 K
Bladnoch 46 E
Bladon 24 L
Blaenannerch 20 C
Blaenau Ffestiniog 36 M
Blaenavon 22 L
Blaendyryn 21 F
Blaenffos 20 C
Blaengarw 21 M
Blaengwrach 21 M
Blaengwynfi 21 M
Blaenpennal 29 L
Blaenplwyf 29 L
Blaenporth 20 C
Blaenrhondda 21 M
Blaenwaun 20 F
Blaen-y-coed 20 F
Blagdon 5 H
Blagdon 14 F
Blagdon Hill 14 K
Blagh 108 E
Blaich 64 E
Blaina 22 L
Blair Atholl 65 L
Blair Drummond 57 J
Blairdaff 67 D
Blairglas 57 G
Blairgowrie 58 C
Blairhall 58 K
Blairhoyle 57 H
Blairingone 58 G
Blairlogie 57 J
Blairmore 56 J
Blairnamarrow 66 A
Blairpark 51 B
Blairquhomrie 57 G
Blairskaith 57 L
Blairvadach 57 G
Blairydryne 67 G
Blaisdon 23 K
Blakebrook 23 B
Blakedown 23 B
Blakelaw 49 H
Blakelaw 53 J
Blakemere 22 E
Blakeney 23 K
Blakeney 35 G
Blakenhall 31 B
Blakenhall 31 L
Blakenham 27 K
Blakeshall 31 L
Blakesley 24 J
Blanchland 49 G
Bland Hill 44 K
Blandford Camp 7 B
Blandford Forum 7 B
Blandford Saint Mary 7 B
Blanefield 57 L
Blaney 103 D
Blankney 33 F
Blàr a' Chaorainn 64 H
Blarghour 56 F
Blarmachfoldach 64 H
Blarnalearoch 70 C
Blashford 7 C
Blaston 25 A
Blatherwycke 25 B
Blawith 42 F
Blaxhall 27 L
Blaxton 40 G
Blaydon 49 H
Bleadon 14 E
Bleak Hey Nook 39 D
Blean 11 A
Bleary 104 H
Bleasby 33 D
Bleatharn 43 B
Blebocraigs 58 J
Bleddfa 22 B
Bledington 24 K
Bledlow 16 C
Bledlow Ridge 16 C
Blegbie 53 B
Blencarn 48 L
Blencogo 47 J
Blencow 48 K
Blendworth 8 C
Blennerhasset 47 J
Bletchingdon 24 L
Bletchingley 10 A
Bletchley 25 K
Bletchley 31 D
Bletherston 20 E
Bletsoe 25 H
Blewbury 16 E
Blickling 35 L
Blidworth 32 C
Blindburn 54 K
Blindcrake 47 J
Blindley Heath 10 A
Blinkbonny 72 G
Blisland 4 E
Bliss Gate 23 B
Blissford 7 C
Blisworth 24 J
Blithbury 32 G
Blo'Norton 27 D
Blockley 23 J
Blofield 27 B
Blofield Heath 27 B
Blore 32 A
Blount's Green 32 D
Bloxham 24 H
Bloxholm 33 F
Bloxwich 31 M
Bloxworth 7 E
Blubberhouses 44 K
Blue Anchor 13 J
Blundellsands 38 D
Blundeston 27 F
Blunham 25 H
Blunsdon Saint Andrew 15 C
Bluntisham-Colne 25 F
Blunts 4 F
Blyborough 40 L
Blyford 27 J
Blymhill 31 H
Blyte 53 F
Blyth 40 K
Blyth 49 F
Blyth Bridge 52 F
Blythburgh 27 J
Blythe Bridge 31 F
Blyton 40 L
Bo'ness 58 K
Boarhills 59 G
Boarhunt 8 E
Boars Hill 16 B
Boarshead 10 D
Boarstall 24 L
Boasley Cross 5 A
Boat of Garten 65 C
Boath 71 E
Bobbing 10 C
Bobbington 31 L
Bobbingworth 18 D
Bocaddon 4 E
Bochastle 57 E
Bocking 18 B
Bocking Churchstreet 18 B
Boconnoc 4 E
Boddam 67 C
Boddam 81 J
Boddington 23 H
Bodedern 36 E
Bodelwyddan 37 H
Bodenham 15 L
Bodenham 22 F
Bodenham Moor 22 F
Bodermid 28 C
Bodewryd 36 E
Bodfari 37 L
Bodffordd 36 H
Bodham 35 H
Bodiam 10 E
Bodicote 24 H
Bodieve 4 A
Bodior 36 G
Bodle Street Green 10 H
Bodmin 4 E
Bodney 26 C
Bodney Camp 26 C
Bodorgan 36 H
Bodsham 11 D
Boduan 29 A
Boduan 36 K
Bogach 68 K
Bogallan 71 H
Bogbrae 67 C
Bogend 51 F
Boghall 52 C
Boghead 52 E
Bogheat 66 J
Bogmoor 72 J
Bogniebrae 73 K
Bognor Regis 9 D
Bograxie 67 D
Bogrie 47 A
Bogside 52 B
Bogton 73 K
Bogue 47 A
Bohenie 64 F
Bohetherick 4 F
Boho 103 D
Bohortha 3 J
Bohuntine 64 F
Bolam 44 A
Bolberry 5 K
Bold Heath 38 H
Boldon 49 J
Boldon Colliery 49 J
Boldre 8 D
Boldron 43 C
Bole 40 L
Bolea 108 G
Bolehill 32 B
Boleside 53 H
Bolham 13 M
Bolham Water 14 K
Bolie 108 G
Bolingey 3 F
Bollington 39 K
Bolney 9 C
Bolnhurst 25 H
Bolshan 59 B
Bolsover 32 C
Bolsterstone 39 H
Bolstone 22 J
Boltby 44 H
Bolton 38 F
Bolton 40 B
Bolton 48 L
Bolton 53 B
Bolton 54 L
Bolton Abbey 43 M
Bolton Bridge 43 M
Bolton-by-Bowland 43 L
Boltonfellend 48 E
Boltongate 47 J
Bolton-le-Sands 42 J
Bolton Low Houses 47 J
Bolton-on-Swale 44 D
Bolton Percy 40 A
Bolton upon Dearne 39 J
Bolventor 4 B
Bombie 47 D
Bomere Heath 31 D
Bonar Bridge 71 B
Bonawe 56 C
Bonby 40 J
Boncath 20 C
Bonchester Bridge 53 L
Bonchurch 8 H
Bondleigh 13 K
Bonehill 32 K
Bonhill 57 K
Boningale 31 H
Bonjedward 53 J
Bonkle 52 B
Bonnington 11 D
Bonnington 53 A
Bonnybank 58 J
Bonnybridge 57 M
Bonnykelly 73 L
Bonnyrigg 53 A
Bonnyton 58 C
Bonnyton 59 A
Bonnyton 59 B
Bonnyton 67 A
Bonsall 32 B
Bont 22 H
Bontddu 29 F
Bont Dolgadfan 30 G
Bont-goch or Elerch 29 J
Bontnewydd 29 L
Bontne-wydd 36 L
Bontnewydd 37 H
Bontuchel 37 L
Bonvilston 13 C
Booker 16 F
Booley 31 D
Boor 70 A
Boosbeck 44 C
Boot 42 B
Boothby Graffoe 33 E
Boothby Pagnell 33 H
Booth of Toft 80 F
Boothstown 38 F
Booth Wood 39 D
Bootle 38 D
Bootle 42 E
Booton 35 K
Boquhan 57 H
Boraston 23 A
Borden 10 C
Bordley 43 J
Bordon 16 M
Boreham 15 G
Boreham 18 E
Boreham Street 10 H
Borehamwood 17 E
Boreland 46 B
Boreland 47 C

Boreland 57 B
Borgh 68 K
Borgh 74 L
Borghastan 75 D
Borgie 77 E
Borgue 78 K
Borley 26 M
Borley Green 26 J
Bornais 68 H
Bornesketaig 69 B
Borness 46 F
Boroughbridge 44 L
Borough Green 10 B
Borras Head 30 C
Borreraig 69 D
Borrowash 32 E
Borrowby 44 H
Borrowby 45 D
Borrowfield 67 G
Borstal 10 C
Borstal 18 K
Borth 29 H
Borthwick 53 B
Borthwickbrae 53 L
Borthwickshiels 53 L
Borth-y-Gest 29 B
Borve 69 E
Borwick 43 G
Bosavern 3 G
Bosbury 23 D
Boscastle 4 B
Boscombe 7 F
Boscombe 15 M
Bosham 8 F
Bosham Hoe 8 F
Bosherston Buckspool 20 G
Boskednan 3 G
Bosley 38 M
Bossal 44 M
Bossiney 4 B
Bossingham 11 E
Bossington 13 F
Bostadh 75 D
Bostock Green 38 L
Boston 34 D
Boston Spa 39 C
Boswednack 3 G
Boswinger 4 G
Botallack 3 G
Botany Bay 17 F
Botcheston 32 L
Botesdale 27 D
Bothal 49 E
Bothamsall 33 A
Bothel 47 J
Bothenhampton 6 F
Bothwell 52 A
Botley 16 B
Botley 17 A
Botloe's Green 23 G
Botolph Claydon 24 M
Botolphs 9 E
Bottacks 71 G
Bottesford 33 D
Bottesford 40 H
Bottisham 26 G
Bottomcraig 58 F
Botton 45 D
Botton Head 43 G
Botusfleming 4 F
Botwnnog 29 A
Boughspring 22 M
Boughton 24 F
Boughton 26 B
Boughton 33 A
Boughton Aluph 11 D
Boughton Lees 11 D
Boughton Malherbe 10 C
Boughton Monchelsea 10 C
Boughton Street 11 A
Boulby 45 A
Bouldon 31 K
Boulmer 54 M
Boulston 20 E
Boultenstone 66 E
Boultham 33 B
Bourgh le Marsh 34 E
Bourn 25 J
Bourne 33 J
Bourne End 25 G
Bournemouth 7 F
Bournes Green 23 L
Bournheath 23 C
Bournmoor 49 J
Bournville 23 C
Bourton 14 E
Bourton 15 C
Bourton 15 K
Bourton 31 K
Bourton-on-the-Hill 23 J
Bourton-on-the-Water 23 M
Bousd 63 D
Bouth 42 F
Bovedy 108 L
Boveney 17 D
Boverton 13 C
Bovevagh 108 G
Bovey Tracey 5 E
Bovingdon 17 A
Bovington Camp 7 D
Bow 5 B
Bow 17 J
Bow 79 G
Bowbank 43 C
Bow Brickhill 25 K
Bowburn 49 L
Bowcombe 8 H
Bowd 6 A
Bowdale 43 B
Bowden 5 H
Bowden 53 H
Bowden Hill 15 E
Bowdon 38 J
Bower 48 C
Bower 78 E
Bowerchalke 7 C
Bowerhill 15 E
Bower House Tye 26 M
Bowermadden 78 E
Bowers Gifford 18 H
Bowershall 58 L
Bowertower 78 E
Bowes 43 C
Bowgreave 42 M
Bowland 53 E
Bowland Bridge 42 F
Bowley 22 F
Bowlhead Green 16 M
Bowling 57 K
Bowling Bank 30 C
Bowmanstead 42 C
Bowmore 55 L
Bowness-on-Solway 47 F
Bowness-on-Windermere 42 C
Bow of Fife 58 J
Bowsden 54 H
Bow Street 29 H
Bowthorpe 27 B
Box 15 B
Box 15 D
Boxbush 23 K
Box End 25 H
Boxford 16 D
Boxford 26 M
Boxley 10 C
Boxted 18 C
Boxted 26 J
Boxted Cross 18 C
Boxworth 25 F
Boylestone 32 D
Boyndie 73 G
Boyndlie 73 L
Boynton 45 L
Boysack 59 B
Boyton 4 C
Boyton 15 L
Boyton 27 L
Boyton Cross 18 A
Bozeat 25 D
Braaid 37 D
Braal Castle 78 D
Brabling Green 27 H
BrabourneLees 11 D
Brabster 78 E
Bracadale 69 H
Bracara 63 C
Braceborough 33 L
Bracebridge Heath 33 B
Braceby 33 H
Bracewell 43 L
Brackenfield 32 B
Bracklamore 73 L
Brackletter 64 E
Brackley 24 H
Brackley 50 C
Brackley 71 J
Brackloch 76 H
Bracknell 16 J
Braco 58 D
Bracobrae 72 M
Bracon Ash 27 B
Bracorina 63 C
Bradbourne 32 A
Bradda 37 D
Bradden 24 J
Braddock 4 E
Bradenham 16 C
Bradenham 26 C
Bradenstoke 15 E
Bradfield 16 E
Bradfield 19 A
Bradfield 35 L
Bradfield Combust 26 J
Bradfield Green 31 B
Bradfield Heath 19 A
Bradfield Saint Clare 26 J
Bradfield Saint George 26 J
Bradford 12 M
Bradford 54 H
Bradford 39 B
Bradford Abbas 6 C
Bradford Leigh 15 D
Bradford-on-Avon 15 D
Bradford-on-Tone 14 K
Bradford Peverell 7 D
Brading 8 H
Bradley 16 L
Bradley 31 J
Bradley 37 M
Bradley 41 G
Bradley Green 23 F
Bradley in the Moors 32 D
Bradley Stoke 14 C
Bradmore 32 J
Bradninch 5 C
Bradnop 31 C
Bradnop 32 A
Bradpole 6 C
Bradshaw 38 F
Bradstone 4 C
Bradwall Green 38 M
Bradwell 18 B
Bradwell 25 G
Bradwell 27 C
Bradwell 39 L
Bradwell Grove 23 M
Bradwell Grove 24 K
Bradwell-on-Sea 18 F
Bradwell Waterside 18 F
Bradworthy 12 L
Brae 47 B
Brae 70 A
Brae 71 A
Brae 71 H
Brae 80 J
Braeantra 71 E
Braefield 71 K
Braegrum 58 E
Braehead 46 E
Braehead 52 C
Braehead 52 E
Braehead 59 B
Braehead 79 H
Braehoulland 80 H
Braemar 66 G
Braemore 70 C
Braemore 78 K
Brae Nook 109 K
Brae of Achnahaird 76 L
Braeside 56 M
Braes of Enzie 72 J
Braes of Ullapool 70 C
Braeswick 79 F
Braeval 57 H
Braewick 81 G
Brafferton 44 B
Brafferton 44 L
Brafield-on-the-Green 25 D
Bragar 75 A
Bragbury End 17 C
Bragenham 25 K
Bragleenmore 56 B
Braides 42 M
Braidley 43 J
Braidwood 52 E
Braigo 55 H
Brailsford 32 E
Braintree 18 B
Braiseworth 27 G
Braishfield 8 A
Braithwaite 40 G
Braithwaite 47 M
Braithwell 40 G
Bramber 9 E
Bramcote 24 B
Bramcote 32 F
Bramdean 8 B
Bramerton 27 B
Bramfield 17 C
Bramfield 27 H
Bramford 27 K
Bramhall 38 J
Bramham 39 C
Bramhope 39 C
Bramley 16 H
Bramley 39 J
Bramley and Wonersh 17 K
Bramley Green 16 H
Bramling 11 B
Brampford Speke 5 C
Brampton 25 A
Brampton 25 H
Brampton 27 F
Brampton 35 L
Brampton 39 J
Brampton 40 L
Brampton 48 E
Brampton 48 L
Brampton Abbotts 23 G
Brampton Bryan 22 C
Brampton en le Morthen 39 M
Brampton Street 27 F
Bramshall 32 D
Bramshaw 8 A
Bramshill 16 J
Bramshott 9 A
Bran End 18 A
Branault 63 E
Brancaster 34 J
Brancaster Staithe 34 J
Brancepeth 49 L
Branchill 72 K
Brand Green 23 G
Brandesburton 41 A
Brandeston 27 H
Brandis Corner 12 M
Brandiston 35 L
Brandon 24 B
Brandon 26 F
Brandon 33 E
Brandon 49 L
Brandon 54 L
Brandon Bank 26 B
Brandon Creek 26 B
Brandon Parva 27 A
Brandsby 44 M
Brandy Wharf 40 M
Brane 3 G
Branksome 7 E
Branksome Park 7 E
Bransby 40 L
Branscombe 6 D
Bransford 23 E
Bransgore 7 F
Bransholme 41 B
Branston 32 G
Branston 33 B
Branston 33 G
Branston Booths 33 C
Branstone 8 H
Brant Broughton 33 E
Brantham 19 A
Branthwaite 47 J
Branthwaite 47 L
Branthwaite 48 G
Brantingham 40 F
Branton 40 G
Branton 54 L
Branxholme 53 L
Branxton 54 G
Brassington 32 B
Brasted 10 A
Brathens 67 G
Bratoft 34 E
Brattleby 40 L
Bratton 15 H
Bratton Clovelly 5 A
Bratton Fleming 13 G
Bratton Seymour 14 M
Braughing 25 M
Braughing Friars 17 C
Braunston 24 E
Braunstone Town 32 M
Braunston-in-Rutland 33 K
Braunton 12 J
Brawby 45 G
Brawl 77 F
Brawlbin 78 D
Bray 17 D
Braybrooke 25 A
Braye 8 M
Brayford 13 G
Bray Shop 4 F
Braystones 42 A
Brayton 40 D
Brazacott 4 C
Breach 11 E
Breachwood Green 25 L
Breadsall 32 E
Breadstone 23 K
Bready 107 J
Breage 3 H
Breahaed 79 B
Breakachy 71 G
Breakish 69 M
Bream 22 M
Breamore 7 C
Brean 14 E
Breanais 74 F
Brearton 44 K
Breascleit 75 D
Breaston 32 F
Brechfa 21 D
Brechin 59 B
Brechin 66 M
Breckan 79 G
Breckles 26 C
Breck of Cruan 79 E
Breckrey 69 F
Brecon/Aberhonddu 22 D
Bredbury 39 G
Brede 10 J
Bredenbury 23 D
Bredfield 27 L
Bredgar 10 C
Bredhurst 10 C
Bredicot 23 E
Bredon 23 H
Bredon's Hardwick 23 H
Bredon's Norton 23 H
Bredwardine 22 E
Breedon on the Hill 32 H
Breibhig 75 E
Brèibhig 68 K
Breich 52 C
Breighton 40 E
Breiwick 81 D
Bremhill 15 E
Bremirehoull 81 H
Brenchley 10 E
Brenchoillie 56 F
Brendon 13 E
Brent Eleigh 26 M
Brentford 17 H
Brentingby 33 G
Brent Knoll 14 H
Brentwood 18 D
Brenzett 11 G
Brereton 31 J
Brereton Green 38 M
Brereton Heath 38 M
Bressingham 27 D
Bressingham Common 27 D
Bretby 32 H
Bretford 24 B
Bretforton 23 J
Bretherdale Head 43 A
Bretherton 38 B
Brettabister 81 D
Brettenham 26 F
Brettenham 26 J
Bretton 38 K
Brewlands Bridge 66 K
Brewood 31 J
Briantspuddle 7 D
Brickendon 17 C
Bricket Wood 17 B
Bricklehampton 23 J
Bride 37 B
Bride 46 L
Bridegtown 13 J
Bridekirk 47 J
Bridell 20 C
Bridestowe 5 A
Bridford 5 B
Bridge 11 B
Bridge End 33 J
Bridge End 49 G
Bridgefoot 47 L
Bridgefoot 58 F
Bridge Green 26 K
Bridgehampton 14 M
Bridgehaugh 66 A
Bridgemary 8 E
Bridgend 20 C
Bridgend 23 K
Bridgend 42 C
Bridgend 50 C
Bridgend 55 L
Bridgend 58 J
Bridgend 58 K
Bridgend 66 A
Bridgend 66 C
Bridgend 66 F
Bridgend 66 M
Bridgend 56 E
Bridgend of Lintrathen 58 C
Bridgend/Pen-y-bont ar Ogwr 13 C
Bridge of Allan 57 J
Bridge of Avon 72 L
Bridge of Balgie 65 K
Bridge of Brown 66 A
Bridge of Cally 58 B
Bridge of Canny 66 J
Bridge of Craigisla 58 C
Bridge of Dee 47 D
Bridge of Don 67 E
Bridge of Dun 59 B
Bridge of Dye 66 J
Bridge of Earn 58 E
Bridge of Ericht 65 K
Bridge of Feugh 67 G
Bridge of Forss 78 D
Bridge of Gairn 66 E
Bridge of Gaur 65 K
Bridge of Muchalls 67 H
Bridge of Muick 66 H
Bridge of Oich 64 C
Bridge of Orchy 57 A
Bridge of Tilt 65 L
Bridge of Walls 81 G
Bridge of Weir 57 K
Bridge Reeve 13 K
Bridgerule 12 L
Bridges 4 D
Bridges 30 J
Bridge Street 26 M
Bridgetown 4 C
Bridgetown 31 J
Bridge Trafford 38 K
Bridge Yate 15 D
Bridgham 26 F
Bridgnorth 31 L
Bridgwater 14 G
Bridlington 45 M
Bridport 6 F
Bridstow 22 J
Briedeswell 66 C
Brierfield 39 A
Brierley 22 C
Brierley 23 K
Brierley 39 J
Brierley Hill 31 M
Brierton 44 C
Brig o'Turk 57 E
Brigde Hewick 44 H
Brigdefoot 66 E
Brige of Alford 66 F
Brigg 40 J
Brigh 104 B
Brigham 41 A
Brigham 47 L
Brighouse 39 E
Brighouse 46 F
Brighstone 8 G
Brightgate 32 B
Brighthampton 16 A
Brightling 10 H
Brightlingsea 19 A
Brighton 4 D
Brighton 9 F
Brightons 58 K
Brightwalton 16 D
Brightwell 27 K
Brightwell Baldwin 16 B
Brightwell-cum-Sotwell 16 E
Brignall 44 A
Brigsley 41 K
Brigsteer 43 D
Brigstock 25 A
Brill 24 M
Brilley 22 E
Brimfield 22 C
Brimington 39 M
Brimley 5 E
Brimpsfield 23 L
Brimpton 16 H
Brims 79 K
Brimscombe 15 B
Brimscombe 23 L
Brimstage 37 J
Brind 40 E
Brindfey 31 A
Brindister 81 G
Brindister 81 H
Brindle 38 B
Brindley Ford 31 C
Brineton 31 H
Bringhurst 25 A
Brington 25 E
Brinian 79 E
Brinin̈gham 35 K
Brinkhill 34 A
Brinkley 26 H
Brinklow 24 B
Brinkworth 15 B
Brinmore 71 L
Brinscall 38 B
Brinsley 32 F
Brinsop 22 F
Brinsworth 39 M
Brinton 35 G
Brisco 48 G
Brisley 35 K
Brislington 14 F
Bristol 14 C
Briston 35 K
Britannia 39 D
Britford 15 M
Brithdir 29 F
Briton Ferry 21 L
Britwell Salome 16 E
Brixham 5 J
Brixton 5 G
Brixton 17 H
Brixton Deverill 15 K
Brixworth 24 F
Brize Norton 16 A
Broad Blunsdon 15 C
Broadbottom 39 G
Broadbridge 8 F
Broadbridge Heath 9 B
Broad Campden 23 J
Broad Chalke 15 L
Broadclyst 5 C
Broadfield 9 C
Broadford 69 M
Broadford Bridge 9 B
Broad Green 18 C
Broad Green 23 E
Broad Green 26 H
Broadhaugh 53 L
Broad Haven 20 D
Broadheath 38 J
Broad Heath Upper 23 A
Broadhembury 6 A
Broadhempston 5 E
Broad Hill 26 E
Broad Hinton 15 F
Broadholme 33 B
Broadlay 20 J
Broad Layings 16 G
Broadley 38 F
Broadley 72 J
Broadley Common 17 C
Broad-Marston 23 F
Broadmayne 7 D
Broadmeadows 53 H
Broadmere 16 L
Broadmoor 20 H
Broadoak 6 C
Broad Oak 7 A
Broad Oak 10 H
Broad Oak 10 J
Broad Oak 21 E
Broad Oak 22 J
Broad Oak 42 B
Broad's Green 18 B
Broadstairs 11 C
Broadstone 7 E
Broadstone 31 K
Broad Street 10 C
Broadstreet Common 14 B
Broad Street Green 18 E
Broad Town 15 F
Broadwas 23 E
Broadwater 9 E
Broadway 14 K
Broadway 20 J
Broadway 23 J
Broadway 27 H
Broadwell 16 A
Broadwell 23 J
Broadwell 24 E
Broadwey 7 D
Broadwindsor 6 C
Broadwoodkelly 13 K
Broadwoodwidger 4 C
Brobury 22 E
Brochel 69 J
Brochloch 51 M
Brochroy 56 C
Brock Hill 18 E
Brockagh Bridge 103 D
Brockbridge 8 B
Brockdish 27 E
Brockenhurst 8 D
Brocketsbrae 52 E
Brockford Street 27 G
Brockhall 24 F
Brockham 17 L
Brockhampton 23 M
Brockhampton 23 G
Brockholes 39 E
Brocklesby 41 G
Brockley 14 E
Brockley Corner 26 J
Brockley Green 26 J
Brockton 30 J
Brockton 30 M
Brockton 31 H
Brockton 31 K
Brockweir 22 M
Brockworth 23 L
Brocton 31 J
Brodick 51 A
Brodsworth 39 J
Brogborough 25 G
Brokenborough 15 B
Broken Cross 38 L
Broken Cross 38 M
Bromborough 38 G
Brome 27 D
Bromesberrow Heath 23 G
Brome Street 27 D
Bromeswell 27 L
Bromfield 30 M
Bromfield 47 J
Bromham 15 E
Bromham 25 H
Bromley Green 11 D
Brompton 18 L
Brompton 44 E
Brompton 45 H
Brompton-on-Swale 44 D
Brompton Ralph 13 J
Brompton Regis 13 J
Bromsash 23 G
Bromsgrove 23 B
Bromyard 23 D
Bromyard Downs 23 D
Bronaber 29 C
Bronant 29 L
Brongest 20 C
Bronington 31 A
Bronllys 22 D
Bronwydd Arms 21 D
Bronydd 22 E
Bronygarth 30 C
Brook 8 A
Brook 8 G
Brook 11 D
Brook 15 M
Brook 16 M
Brook 20 J
Brooke 27 B
Brooke 33 K
Brookeborough 103 E
Brookenby 41 K
Brookfield 57 K
Brookhorpe 23 L
Brookhouse 39 K
Brookhouse 43 G
Brookhouse Green 38 M
Brookland 11 G
Brooklands 47 A
Brookmans Park 17 B
Brooks 30 H
Brooks Green 9 B
Brook Street 9 C
Brook Street 18 D
Brookvale 104 H
Brookville 26 B
Brookwood 16 J
Broom 23 F
Broom 25 H
Broombrae 66 F
Broome 23 B
Broome 27 E
Broome 30 M
Broomedge 38 H
Broome Park 54 L
Broomer's Corner 9 B
Broomfield 11 B
Broomfield 14 G
Broomfield 18 B
Broomfield 67 B
Broomfleet 40 E
Broom Hill 7 E
Broomhill 49 C
Broomholm 35 M
Broom of Dalreoch 58 D
Broom's Green 23 G
Brora 72 A
Broseley 31 G
Brotherhill 20 H
Brothertoft 34 D
Brotherton 40 D
Brotton 45 A
Broubster 78 D
Brough 33 B
Brough 39 L
Brough 40 F
Brough 43 B
Brough 78 E
Brough 79 G
Brough 80 F
Brough 81 D
Brough 81 E
Broughall 31 A
Brough Lodge 80 B
Broughshane 108 M
Brough Sowerby 43 B
Broughton 13 C
Broughton 15 M
Broughton 24 H
Broughton 25 D
Broughton 25 F
Broughton 25 G
Broughton 37 M
Broughton 38 B
Broughton 38 J
Broughton 40 J
Broughton 45 K
Broughton 47 H
Broughton 52 F
Broughton 79 B
Broughton Astley 32 M
Broughton Beck 42 F
Broughton Gifford 15 D
Broughton Hackett 23 E
Broughton in Furness 42 E
Broughton Mills 42 E
Broughton Moor 47 H
Broughton Poggs 15 C
Broughtown 79 F
Broughty Ferry 59 D
Broughton 43 L
Brow Top 43 G
Browland 81 G
Brown Candover 16 L
Brown Edge 31 C
Brown Edge 38 A
Brownhill 38 C
Brownhill 67 B
Brownhills 31 J
Brownhills 59 G
Brownieside 54 L
Browninghill Green 16 H
Brownlow Heath 31 C
Brownmuir 67 K
Brownston 5 H
Browsburn 52 B
Broxa 45 H
Broxbourne 17 C
Broxburn 53 C
Broxburn 58 K
Broxholme 33 B
Broxted 18 A
Broxton 31 A
Broxwood 22 C
Broyle Side 9 F
Broyle Side 10 G
Brù 75 B
Bruachmary 71 M
Bruairnis 68 K
Bruan 78 H
Bruera 38 K
Bruern Abbey 24 K

Craiginorne 105 A
Craiglockhart 53 A
Craiglug 67 G
Craigmalloch 51 M
Craigmaud 73 L
Craigmillar 53 A
Craignant 30 C
Craigneuk 52 B
Craignure 63 M
Craigo 66 M
Craigow 58 H
Craigrothie 58 J
Craigruie 57 E
Craigs 108 M
Craigsimmie 58 F
Craigton 57 H
Craigton 58 C
Craigton 59 D
Craigton 67 G
Craigton 71 B
Craigtown 77 F
Craig-y-nos 21 J
Craik 53 K
Crail 59 G
Crailing 53 J
Crailinghall 53 J
Crakehall 44 D
Crakehill 44 H
Crambe 44 M
Cramlington 49 F
Cramond 58 L
Cramond Bridge 58 L
Cranage 38 M
Cranagh 107 M
Cranberry 31 E
Cranborne 7 C
Cranbourne 17 G
Cranbrook 10 F
Cranbrook Common 10 F
Cranfield 25 G
Cranford 12 J
Cranford Saint Andrew 25 D
Cranford Saint John 25 D
Cranham 18 D
Cranham 23 L
Crank 38 E
Cranleigh-Rowly 17 K
Cranmore 8 D
Cranna 73 K
Crannoch 72 M
Cranny 104 B
Cranoe 25 A
Cransford 27 H
Cranshaws 53 C
Cranslough 104 D
Cranstal 37 B
Cranstal 46 L
Cranstone Riddel 53 B
Crantock 3 F
Cranwell 33 E
Cranwich 26 C
Cranworth 27 A
Craobh Haven 56 E
Crapstone 5 D
Crarae 56 E
Crask of Aigas 71 K
Craskins 66 F
Craster 54 M
Craswall 22 E
Cratfield 27 H
Crathes 67 G
Crathie 65 D
Crathie 66 H
Crathorne 44 E
Craven Arms 30 M
Crawcrook 49 H
Crawford 38 E
Crawford 52 H
Crawfordjohn 52 H
Crawfordsburn 105 E
Crawick 52 G
Crawley 9 C
Crawley 16 K
Crawley 24 K
Crawley Down 9 C
Crawleyside 49 K
Crawshawbooth 38 C
Crawton 67 K
Cray 43 J
Cray 66 K
Cray's Pond 16 E
Crayford 17 J
Crayke 44 M
Crays Hill 18 E
Creacombe 13 L
Creag Ghoraidh 68 E
Creaganterve Mhòr 56 E
Creagen 64 K
Creagh 103 E
Creca 47 F
Credenhill 22 F
Crediton 5 C
Creech Heathfield 14 K
Creech Saint Michael 14 K
Creed 4 G
Creekmoor 7 E
Creekmouth 17 J
Creeting Saint Mary 27 G
Creeton 33 H
Creetown 46 F
Creggan 103 C
Creggan 104 K
Creggans 56 F
Cregneash 37 D
Cregrina 22 A
Creich 58 F
Creigiau 14 A
Cremyll 4 J
Creslow Whitchurch 24 M
Cressage 31 G
Cressbrook 39 L
Cresselly 20 H
Cressing 18 B
Cresswell 31 F
Cresswell 49 C
Cresswell Quay 20 H
Creswell 39 M
Cretingham 27 H
Cretshengan 56 K
Crewe 31 B
Crewe-by-Farndon 31 A
Crewgreen 30 F
Crewkerne 6 C
Crews Hill 17 F
Crianlarich 57 A
Cribyn 21 A
Criccieth 29 B
Crichie 67 B
Crichton 53 B
Crick 14 C
Crick 24 F
Crickadarn 22 D
Cricket Malherbie 6 B
Crickheath 30 F
Crickhowell 22 H
Cricklade 15 C
Cridling Stubbs 40 D
Crieff 58 D
Criggion 30 F
Crigglestone 39 F
Crilly 103 F
Crimond 73 M
Crimonmogate 73 M
Crimplesham 26 B
Crimscote 24 D
Crinan 56 D
Crindle 108 G
Cringleford 27 B
Crinow 20 H
Cripp's Corner 10 J
Cripplesease 3 H
Crix 18 B
Croasdale 47 L
Crock Street 14 K
Crockenhill 17 J
Crockernwell 5 B
Crockerton 15 G
Crocketford 47 A
Crockey Hill 40 A
Crockham Hill 10 A
Crockhurst Street 10 B
Crockleford Heath 18 C
Crockness 79 G
Croes y pant 22 L
Croes-an-wra 3 G
Croesau Bach 30 F
Croesgoch 20 A
Croeslan 21 A
Croesor 36 M
Croesyceiliog 21 G
Croesyceiliog 22 L
Croft 22 C
Croft 32 L
Croft 34 E
Croft 38 H
Croftamie 57 H
Croftgarbh 65 L
Croftgarbh 57 C
Croftinload 65 M
Crofton 15 J
Crofton 39 F
Croft-on-Tees 44 B
Crofts 47 A
Crofts of Benachielt 78 G
Crofts of Haddo 67 B
Crofty 21 K
Croggan 56 A
Croglin 48 H
Croick 71 A
Croick 77 F
Crois Dùghaill 68 H
Cromarty 71 J
Crombie 58 K
Cromblet 67 A
Cromdale 66 A
Cromer 25 M
Cromer 35 H
Cromer Hyde 17 B
Cromford 32 B
Cromhall 15 A
Cromhall Common 15 A
Cromor 75 H
Cromwell 33 A
Cronberry 52 G
Crondall 16 M
Cronkedooney 37 D
Cronk-y-Voddy 37 A
Cronton 38 G
Crook 42 F
Crook 49 L
Crookedholm 51 F
Crookgate Bank 49 H
Crookham 16 H
Crookham 54 G
Crookham Village 16 M
Crookhouse 53 J
Crooklands 43 D
Crook of Devon 58 G
Cropredy 24 H
Cropston 32 M
Cropthorne 23 F
Cropton 45 G
Cropwell Bishop 33 D
Cropwell Butler 33 D
Cros 75 B
Crosbost 75 H
Crosby 37 A
Crosby 38 D
Crosby 40 H
Crosby 47 H
Crosby Court 44 E
Crosby Garrett 43 B
Crosby-on-Eden 48 D
Crosby Ravensworth 43 A
Croscombe 14 J
Cross 14 E
Cross 103 E
Crossaig 50 C
Crossal 69 H
Crossapol 62 A
Cross Ash 22 J
Cross-at-Hand 10 F
Crossbush 9 D
Crosscanonby 47 H
Crossdale Street 35 H
Crossens 38 A
Crossflatts 39 B
Crossford 52 E
Crossford 58 L
Crossgar 105 G
Crossgare 108 H
Crossgate 33 J
Crossgatehall 53 B
Crossgates 22 A
Crossgates 58 L
Crossgill 43 G
Cross Green 4 C
Cross Green 26 M
Crosshands 20 F
Cross Hands 21 G
Crosshands 51 F
Crosshill 51 H
Crosshill 58 H
Cross Hills 43 M
Crosshouse 51 F
Cross Houses 31 G
Crossings 48 E
Cross in Hand 10 G
Cross Inn 14 A
Cross Inn 21 A
Cross Inn 29 L
Crosskeys 22 K
Crosskirk 78 D
Crosslands 30 F
Cross Lane Head 31 L
Cross Lanes 3 M
Cross Lanes 30 C
Cross Lanes 44 L
Crosslee 53 G
Crosslee 57 K
Crossmaglen 104 K
Crossmichael 47 A
Crossmoor 42 M
Cross o'th'hands 32 E
Cross of Jackston 67 A
Cross Roads 39 A
Crossroads 67 G
Crosston 59 A
Crossway 22 A
Crossway 22 H
Crossway 22 J
Crossway Green 23 B
Crossways 7 D
Crosswell 20 B
Crosswood 29 L
Croston 38 B
Crostwaith 42 F
Crostwick 27 B
Crostwight 35 M
Crothair 75 D
Crouch 10 B
Croughton 24 H
Crovie 73 H
Crow Hill 23 G
Crowan 3 H
Crowborough 10 D
Crowcombe 14 G
Crowdecote 32 A
Crowell 16 C
Crowell Hill 16 C
Crowfield 24 J
Crowfield 27 G
Crowhurst 10 A
Crowhurst 10 H
Crowland 33 M
Crowlas 3 H
Crowle 23 E
Crowle 40 H
Crowmarsh Gifford 16 E
Crown Corner 27 H
Crownhill 5 G
Crownland 27 G
Crownthorpe 27 A
Crowntown 3 H
Crowthorne 16 J
Crowton 38 L
Croxby 41 K
Croxdale 49 L
Croxden 32 D
Croxley Green 17 D
Croxton 25 J
Croxton 26 F
Croxton 31 E
Croxton 40 J
Croxton Kerrial 33 G
Croy 71 J
Croy 57 M
Croyde 12 J
Croydon 25 J
Croydon 17 J
Cruckton 30 J
Cruden Bay 67 C
Crudgington 31 G
Crudwell 15 B
Crug 30 L
Crugmeer 4 A
Crùlabhig 75 D
Crumlin 22 K
Crumlin 104 F
Crumplehorn 4 H
Crundale 11 D
Crundale 20 E
Cruntully Bridge 103 A
Cruwys Morchard 13 L
Crux Easton 16 G
Cruygbar 21 E
Crwbin 21 G
Crwt-y-gollen 22 H
Crya 79 G
Crymlyn 36 J
Crymych 20 F
Crynant 21 H
Cuaig 70 D
Cuan 56 A
Cubbington 24 D
Cubert 3 F
Cublington 25 K
Cuckfield 9 C
Cucklington 15 K
Cuckney 32 C
Cuckold's Green 27 F
Cuddesdon Denton 16 B
Cuddington 16 C
Cuddington 38 L
Cuddington Heath 31 A
Cuddy Hill 38 B
Cuddy Hill 42 M
Cudham 10 A
Cudlipptown 5 D
Cudworth 6 B
Cudworth 39 J
Cuffley 17 F
Cuidhir 68 K
Cuidhtinis 74 M
Cuidrach 69 E
Cuish 73 L
Cùl Doirlinn 63 F
Culbo 71 H
Culbokie 71 H
Culburnie 71 K
Culcabock 71 L
Culcairn 71 E
Culcharry 71 J
Culcheth 38 L
Culcronchie 46 F
Culdrain 66 C
Culduie 69 J
Culford 26 J
Culgaith 48 L
Culgower 77 M
Culham 16 B
Culkein 76 H
Culkerton 15 B
Cullachie 65 C
Cullaville 104 K
Cullen 72 J
Cullentra Cross Roads 103 E
Cullercoats 49 J
Cullicudden 71 H
Cullingworth 39 B
Cullion 107 J
Cullipool 56 A
Cullisse 71 F
Cullivoe 80 E
Culloch 57 F
Culloden 71 L
Cullybackey 108 M
Cullyhanna 104 K
Culmaily 71 C
Culmington Hayton's Bent 31 K
Culmstock 13 M
Culnacraig 76 L
Culnady 108 L
Culnaknock 69 F
Culrain 71 B
Culross 58 K
Culroy 51 H
Culsh 66 E
Culsh 66 F
Culshabbin 46 E
Culswick 81 G
Cultercullen 67 E
Cults 46 E
Cults 66 C
Cults 67 H
Culverstone Green 10 B
Culverthorpe 33 E
Culworth 24 H
Cumbernauld 57 M
Cumbernauld Village 57 M
Cumberworth 34 B
Cuminestown 73 L
Cumlewick 81 H
Cumloden 46 B
Cummersdale 48 G
Cummertrees 47 F
Cummingston 72 H
Cumnock 51 J
Cumnor 16 B
Cumrew 48 H
Cumwhinton 48 G
Cumwhitton 48 H
Cundall 44 H
Cunister 80 E
Cunningburn 105 E
Cunninghamhead 51 C
Cupar 58 J
Cupar Muir 58 J
Curbar 39 L
Curbridge 8 B
Curbridge 24 K
Curch Preen 31 G
Curchtown 42 M
Curdridge 8 B
Curglassan Cross Roads 104 B
Curland 14 K
Curland Common 14 K
Curraghamulkin 103 B
Curran 108 L
Currarie 51 K
Currie 53 A
Curry Mallet 14 K
Curry Rivel 14 L
Currysheskin 108 F
Curtisden Green 10 F
Curtisknowle 5 H
Cury 3 L
Cushendall 109 G
Cushendun 109 G
Cushnie 73 L
Cushuish 14 K
Cusop 22 E
Cutcloy 46 H
Cutcombe 13 J
Cutiau 29 E
Cutlers Green 26 K
Cutnall Green 23 B
Cutsdean 23 J
Cutthorpe 39 L
Cutts 81 H
Cuxham 16 B
Cuxton 18 K
Cuxwold 41 K
Cwm 22 K
Cwm 37 H
Cwmafan-Pontrhydyfen 21 L
Cwmaman 21 M
Cwmann 21 B
Cwmavon 22 L
Cwmbach 20 F
Cwmbach 22 E
Cwmbach 22 K
Cwmbelan 30 K
Cwmbrwyno 29 M
Cwmcarn 22 K
Cwmcarvan 22 M
Cwm-Cewydd 30 D
Cwm-Cou 20 C
Cwmcrawnon 22 G
Cwmdare 21 M
Cwmdu 21 E
Cwmdu 22 G
Cwmduad 21 D
Cwmerfyn 29 M
Cwmfelin Boeth 20 F
Cwmfelin Mynach 20 F
Cwmfelinfach 22 K
Cwmffrwd 21 G
Cwm Ffrwd-oer 22 L
Cwmgledd 21 H
Cwmgors 21 H
Cwmgwrach 21 M
Cwmifor 21 E
Cwm Irfon 21 C
Cwmisfael 21 G
Cwm-Llinau 29 F
Cwmllynfell 21 H
Cwmorgan 20 F
Cwmparc 21 M
Cwmpengraig 21 D
Cwm Penmachno 37 K
Cwmsych-bant 21 A
Cwmsymlog 29 M
Cwmtillery 22 L
Cwm-trwch Isaf 21 H
Cwm-twrch Uchaf 21 H
Cwm-y-glo 36 J
Cwmyoy 22 H
Cwmystwyth 29 M
Cwrt 29 J
Cwrtnewydd 21 A
Cwrt-y-cadno 21 B
Cyffylliog 37 L
Cyfronydd 30 H
Cymer 21 M
Cymmer 21 M
Cynghordy 21 F
Cynheidre 21 G
Cynwyd 30 B
Cynwyl Elfed 21 D

D

Daccombe 5 F
Dacre 44 K
Dacre 48 K
Dacre Banks 44 K
Daddry Shield 48 M
Dadford 24 J
Dadlington 32 L
Dafen 21 G
Daffy Green 27 A
Dagenham 17 J
Daglingworth 23 L
Dagnall 17 A
Dail Beag 75 A
Dail Mòr 75 A
Daill 55 L
Dailly 51 H
Dairsie or Osnaburgh 58 F
Dalabrog 68 H
Dalavich 56 E
Dalbeattie 47 D
Dalberg 65 B
Dalblair 52 G
Dalbog 66 M
Dalbury 32 E
Dalby 34 A
Dalby 37 A
Dalcairney 51 J
Dalchalloch 65 L
Dalchalm 72 A
Dalchenna 56 F
Dalchonzie 57 F
Dalchork 77 K
Dalchreichart 64 C
Dalchruin 57 F
Dalderby 34 A
Dale 20 G
Dale Abbey 32 E
Dale Head 48 K
Dalelia 63 J
Dale of Walls 81 K
Daless 71 M
Dalfaber 65 C
Dalgarven 51 B
Dalgig 51 J
Dalginross 57 F
Dalhalvaig 77 F
Dalham 26 H
Daligan 57 G
Dalivaddy 50 E
Dalkeith 53 B
Dallas 72 K
Dalleagles 51 J
Dallinghoo 27 L
Dallington 10 H
Dalmadilly 67 D
Dalmally 56 C
Dalmarnock 58 B
Dalmary 57 H
Dalmellington 51 J
Dalmeny 58 L
Dalmigavie 65 B
Dalmore 71 E
Dalnabreck 63 J
Dalnacroich 70 J
Dalnahaitnach 65 C
Dalnavie 71 E
Dalness 64 L
Dalnessie 77 L
Dalqueich 58 H
Dalquhairn 51 L
Dalquise 58 G
Dalreavoch 77 L
Dalroy 71 M
Dalry 51 B
Dalrymple 51 H
Dalserf 52 B
Dalston 48 G
Dalswinton 47 B
Dalton 38 E
Dalton 39 J
Dalton 44 A
Dalton 44 C
Dalton 44 H
Dalton 47 C
Dalton 49 E
Dalton 49 G
Dalton-in-Furness 42 E
Dalton-on-Tees 44 E
Dalvennan 51 J
Dalwhinnie 65 G
Dalwood 6 B
Damerham 7 C
Damgate 27 C
Damhead 108 H
Damnaglaur 46 G
Danaway 10 C
Danbury-Little Baddow 18 E
Danby 45 D
Danby Wiske 44 E
Dandalieth 72 L
Dandderwen 20 E
Danderhall 53 A
Dane End 17 C
Danebridge 39 K
Danesfield 16 F
Danskine 53 C
Darenth 18 G
Daresbury 38 H
Darfield 39 J
Dargate 11 A
Darite 4 F
Darkley 104 G
Darlaston 31 M
Darley 44 K
Darley Bridge 32 B
Darley Head 44 K
Darlingscott 24 G
Darlington 44 B
Darliston 31 D
Darlochan 50 E
Darlton 33 A
Darnford 67 G
Darnick 53 H
Darowen 29 J
Darra 73 K
Darras Hall 49 E
Darrington 39 F
Darsham 27 J
Dartford 17 J
Dartford Crossing 18 G
Dartington 5 H
Dartmeet 5 E
Dartmouth 5 H
Darton 39 F
Darvel 52 D
Darwen 38 C
Datchet 17 G
Datchworth 17 C
Daugh of Kinermony 72 L
Dauntsey 15 E
Dava 72 K
Davenham 38 L
Daventry 24 E
Davidston 71 J
Davidstow 4 B
Davington 53 K
Daviot 67 A
Daviot 71 L
Davoch of Grange 72 M
Dawlish 5 F
Dawlish Warren 5 F
Dawn 37 G
Daws Heath 18 H
Daw's House 4 C
Dawsmere 34 G
Daylesford 24 K
Ddôl Cownwy 30 D
Deadwater 48 C
Deaf Hill 49 M
Deal 11 F
Dean 5 E
Dean 7 B
Dean 8 B
Dean 47 L
Deanburnhaugh 53 K
Dean Doulting 14 J
Deane 16 L
Deanland 7 B
Dean Prior 5 H
Dean Row 38 M
Deans 52 C
Deanscales 47 L
Deanshanger 24 J
Deanston 57 J
Dearham 47 H
Dearne 39 J
Debach 27 L
Debden 26 K
Debden Green 26 K
Debenham 27 G
Dechmont 58 K
Deddington 24 H
Dedham 18 C
Dedham Heath 18 C
Dedridge 52 C
Deene 25 B
Deenethorpe 25 B
Deepcar 39 H
Deepcut 16 J
Deepdale 43 E
Deepin Saint Nickolas 33 M
Deeping Saint James 33 M
Deerhill 72 M
Deerhurst 23 H
Defynnog 21 F
Deganwy/Llandudno 37 G
Deighton 40 A
Deighton 44 E
Deiniolen 36 J
Delabole 4 B
Delamere 38 L
Delford 23 E
Delfrigs 67 E
Delliefure 66 A
Delly End 24 K
Delnabo 66 A
Delny 71 F
Delph 39 D
Delveich 57 F
Delves 49 H
Delvin End 26 L
Delvine 58 B
Dembleby 33 H
Den of Lindores 58 F
Denbigh 37 L
Denbury 5 E
Denby 32 E
Denby Dale 39 E
Denchworth 16 A
Dendron 42 H
Denehill 9 C
Denehill 10 D
Denend 67 A
Denford 25 E
Dengie 18 F
Denham 17 D
Denham 26 H
Denham 27 G
Denham Green 17 D
Denham Street 27 G
Denhead 59 G
Denhead 73 M
Denhead of Arbirlot 59 A
Denhead of Gray 58 F
Denholm 53 L
Denholme 39 B
Denholme Clough 39 B
Denmead 8 F
Denmill 67 E
Denmore 67 E
Dennington 27 H
Denny 57 M
Dennyloanhead 57 M
Denshaw 39 D
Denside 67 G
Densole 11 E
Denston 26 H
Denstone 32 D
Dent 43 E
Denton 11 E
Denton 25 C
Denton 25 D
Denton 27 E
Denton 33 G
Denton 39 G
Denton 43 M
Denton 44 A
Denver 26 B
Denwick 54 L
Deopham 27 A
Deopham Green 27 A
Depten 26 H
Deptford 15 L
Deptford 17 J
Derby 32 E
Derbyhaven 37 D
Dergoals 46 B
Deri 22 K
Derringstone 11 E
Derrington 31 F
Derry 105 H
Derryadd 104 E
Derryboy 104 L
Derryboye 105 G
Derrychrier 108 G
Derrycor 104 E
Derryfubble 104 D
Derrygonnelly 103 D
Derrygortrevy 104 D
Derryguaig 63 L
Derry Hill 15 E

154 Great Britain 1:301,000
A B C D E F G H I J K L M N O P Q R S T U V W X Y Z

Derrykeevan 104 E
Derrykeighan 108 J
Derrylin 103 G
Derrynacross 102 C
Derrynascobe 103 F
Derrynawilt 103 H
Derrynoose 104 G
Derryraine 104 G
Derrythorpe 40 H
Derrytrasna 104 E
Derryvore 103 G
Dersingham 34 H
Dervaig 63 G
Dervock 108 J
Derwen 37 L
Derwenlas 29 J
Desborough 25 A
Desertmartin 108 L
Desford 32 L
Detchant 54 H
Detling 10 C
Deuddwr 30 E
Deunant-isaf 37 L
Devauden 22 M
Devil's Bridge 29 M
Devitts Green 32 K
Devizes 15 H
Devonport 4 J
Devonside 58 G
Dewar 53 D
Dewartown 53 B
Dewlish 7 D
Dewsbury 39 E
Dhail bho Dheas 75 B
Dhoon 37 B
Dhoor 37 B
Dhowin 37 B
Dhowin 46 L
Dial Post 9 E
Dibden 8 D
Dibden Purlieu 8 D
Dickens Heath 23 C
Dickleburgh 27 D
Dickleburgh Moor 27 D
Didbrook 23 J
Didcot 16 B
Diddington 25 F
Diddlebury 31 K
Didley 22 J
Didling 8 C
Didmarton 15 A
Didsby 38 J
Didworthy 5 H
Digby 33 F
Diggle 39 D
Digswell 17 B
Dihewyd 21 A
Dilhorne 31 C
Dillham 35 M
Dilston 49 G
Dilton Marsh 15 G
Dilwyn 22 F
Dinas 20 F
Dinas 29 A
Dinas 36 L
Dinas Cross 20 B
Dinas Mawddwy 30 D
Dinas Powys 14 A
Dinder 14 J
Dinedor 22 F
Dines Green 23 E
Dingestow 22 M
Dingley 25 A
Dingwall 71 H
Dinlabyre 48 B
Dinnet 66 J
Dinnington 6 C
Dinnington 39 M
Dinnington 49 E
Dinorwig 36 M
Dinton 16 C
Dinton 15 L
Dinwoodie Mains 47 C
Dinworthy 12 L
Dippen 51 D
Dippenhall 16 M
Dipple 51 H
Dipple 72 H
Diptford 5 H
Dirdhu 66 A
Dirleton 59 K
Discoed 22 B
Disertowen 107 J
Diseworth 32 H
Dishes 79 F
Dishforth 44 H
Disley 39 G
Diss 27 D
Disserth 22 A
Distington 47 L
Ditcheat 14 M
Ditchingham 27 E
Ditchling 9 F
Ditteridge 15 D
Dittisham 5 H
Ditton 10 B
Ditton 17 G
Ditton 38 G
Ditton Green 26 H
Ditton Priors 31 K
Dixonfield 78 E
Dixton 22 M
Dixton 23 H
Doagh 105 A
Dobwalls 4 E
Doccombe 5 B
Dochgarroch 71 L
Docking 34 J
Docklow 23 A
Dockray 48 K
Dodburn 53 L
Doddinghurst 18 D
Doddington 11 A
Doddington 23 A
Doddington 33 B
Doddington 54 H
Doddington-Wimblington 26 A
Doddiscombsleigh 5 C
Dodford 23 B
Dodford 24 F
Dodington 15 A
Dodleston 38 K
Dodworth 39 H
Doe Lea 32 C
Dog Village 5 C
Dogdyke 33 F
Dogmersfield 16 M
Dolanog 30 E
Dolau 22 B
Dolbenmaen 36 L
Dolfach 30 K
Dol-fâch 30 G
Dolfor 30 L
Dol-fôr 29 F
Dolgarrog 37 G
Dolgellau 29 F
Dolgoch 29 E
Dolgran 21 D
Doll 72 A
Dollar 58 G
Dolley Green 22 B
Dollingstown 104 F
Dolphinholme 42 M
Dolphinton 52 F
Dolton 13 K
Dolwen 30 G
Dolwen 37 G
Dolwyddelan 36 M
Dol-y-bont 29 H
Dol-y-cannau 22 E
Dolyhir 22 B
Domgay 30 F
Donagh 103 H
Donaghadee 105 E
Donaghanic 103 C
Donaghcloney 104 J
Donaghey 104 A
Donaghmore 104 D
Doncaster 40 G
Donhead Saint Andrew 15 K
Donhead Saint Mary 15 K
Donibristle 58 L
Donington 33 J
Donington on Bain 34 A
Donington South Ing 33 J
Donisthorpe 32 H
Donkey Town 17 G
Donnington 8 F
Donnington 16 G
Donnington 23 J
Donnington 31 G
Donvaston 30 F
Donyatt 14 K
Doogary 103 C
Dooglen 104 J
Doonan 109 K
Doonfoot 51 E
Doonholm 51 H
Doons 104 A
Dopten Green 26 H
Dorchester 7 D
Dorchester 16 B
Dordon 32 K
Dore 39 L
Dores 71 L
Dorking 17 L
Dorking Tye 26 M
Dormans Park 9 C
Dormans Park 10 D
Dormansland 10 A
Dormanstown 44 C
Dormington 23 D
Dorney 17 D
Dornie 70 K
Dornoch 71 C
Dornock 47 F
Dorrery 78 D
Dorridge 24 A
Dorrington 30 J
Dorrington 31 B
Dorrington 33 F
Dorsell 66 F
Dorsington 23 F
Dorstone 22 E
Dorton 24 M
Dorusduain 70 L
Dosthill 32 K
Dothan 36 H
Dottery 6 C
Doublebois 4 E
Dougarie High 50 C
Doughton 15 B
Douglas 37 E
Douglas 52 E
Douglas and Angus 59 D
Douglas Bridge 107 L
Douglastown 59 A
Douglas Water 52 E
Dounby 79 D
Doune 57 J
Doune 65 C
Doune 71 A
Dounepark 73 K
Douneside 66 F
Dounie 71 B
Dounie 71 F
Dousland 5 D
Dove Holes 39 K
Dovenby 47 H
Dovendale 34 A
Dover 11 E
Dovercourt 19 A
Doverdale 23 B
Doveridge 32 D
Dowally 58 B
Dowdeswell 23 L
Dowland 13 K
Dowlands 6 E
Dowlish Wake 6 B
Down Ampney 15 C
Downderry 4 J
Downend 8 H
Downend 16 D
Downfield 58 F
Downgate 4 F
Downham 18 E
Downham 43 L
Downham 54 G
Downham Market 26 B
Down Hatherley 23 H
Downhead 14 J
Downhill 51 H
Downhill 108 E
Downholland Cross 38 D
Downholme 44 D
Downies 67 H
Downing 37 J
Downley 16 F
Downpatrick 105 G
Down Saint Mary 13 K
Down Thomas 5 G
Downton 7 C
Downton on the Rock 22 C
Downtown 8 D
Dowsby 33 J
Dowsdale 33 M
Dowthwaitehead 48 K
Doxford Park 49 J
Doynton 15 D
Draethen 14 A
Draffan 52 E
Dragon's Green 9 B
Drakeland Corner 5 G
Drakemyre 51 B
Drakes Broughton 23 E
Drakewalls 4 F
Draperstown 108 K
Draughton 25 A
Draughton 43 M
Drax 40 D
Draycot Cerne 15 E
Draycote 24 E
Draycott 14 H
Draycott 23 J
Draycott 32 E
Draycott in the Clay 32 D
Draycott in the Moors 31 F
Drayton 14 L
Drayton 16 B
Drayton 23 B
Drayton 23 F
Drayton 24 H
Drayton 25 A
Drayton 27 B
Drayton Bassett 32 K
Drayton Cosham 8 F
Drayton Parslow 25 K
Drayton Saint Leonard 16 B
Dreemskerry 37 B
Dreen 108 K
Dreenhill 20 D
Drefach 21 A
Drefach 21 G
Drefach 21 H
Drefelin 21 D
Dreggie 66 A
Dreghorn 51 F
Drem 59 K
Dreumasdal 68 E
Drewsteignton 5 B
Driby 34 A
Driffield 15 C
Driffield 40 C
Drift 3 G
Drigg 42 B
Drighlington 39 B
Drimnin 63 H
Drimsynie 56 F
Dringhoe 41 A
Drinisiadar 74 M
Drinkstone 26 J
Drinkstone Green 26 J
Drochaid Lusa 69 M
Drointon 31 F
Droitwich Spa 23 B
Droman 76 C
Dromara 104 J
Dromore 103 B
Dromore 104 J
Dromuie 69 E
Dron 58 E
Dronfield 39 M
Dronfield Woodhouse 39 L
Drongan 51 J
Dronley 58 F
Droop 7 A
Droxford 8 B
Droylsden 38 J
Druid 30 B
Druidston 20 D
Druimarbin 64 H
Druimavuic 64 K
Druimdrishaig 56 G
Druimindarroch 63 F
Druimkinnerras 71 K
Drum 56 H
Drum 58 H
Drum Manor 104 A
Druma Voulin 50 E
Drumahoe 107 J
Drumaness 105 G
Drumaroad 105 G
Drumbadmeen 102 C
Drumbee 104 G
Drumbeg 76 H
Drumbeg 105 D
Drumblade 67 A
Drumblair 73 K
Drumbo 105 D
Drumbuie 46 C
Drumbuie 70 K
Drumburgh 48 D
Drumcard 103 G
Drumcaw 105 K
Drumchapel 57 L
Drumchardine 71 H
Drumchork 70 B
Drumclog 52 D
Drumcullen 104 C
Drumderfit 71 H
Drumduff 103 A
Drumeldrie 58 J
Drumelzier 52 F
Drumfearn 69 M
Drumgavlin 105 G
Drumgley 59 A
Drumguish 65 E
Drumhirk 103 A
Drumin 66 A
Drumintee 104 L
Drumlassie 67 D
Drumlee 104 M
Drumlegagh 107 L
Drumlemble 50 E
Drumligair 67 E
Drumlithie 67 K
Drumlone 103 H
Drummannnon 104 E
Drummeny 104 B
Drummoney Bridge 103 A
Drummore 46 D
Drumnadrochit 71 K
Drumnagoon 104 E
Drumnagorrach 72 M
Drumnahive 66 F
Drumnakilly 103 C
Drumoak 67 G
Drumore 50 E
Drumphail 46 A
Drumquin 103 B
Drumrack 59 G
Drumraighland 108 G
Drumrash 47 A
Drumrunie 76 L
Drums 67 E
Drumsallie 64 D
Drumsaragh 108 H
Drumshang 51 H
Drumskinny 103 A
Drumsturdy 59 D
Drumsurn 108 G
Drumtroddan 46 E
Drumuillie 65 C
Drumvaich 57 J
Drumwhindle 67 B
Drunkendub 59 B
Drury 37 M
Drybeck 43 B
Drybridge 51 F
Drybridge 72 J
Drybrook-Ruardean 23 G
Dry Doddington 33 D
Dry Drayton 25 J
Dryhope 53 G
Drymen 57 H
Drymuir 67 B
Drynoch 69 H
Dryplaid 66 M
Dry Sandford 16 B
Dryslwyn 21 G
Dry Street 18 G
Dryton 31 G
Dubford 73 L
Dubhchladach 56 K
Dubton 59 B
Dubwath 47 M
Duchal Mains 57 K
Duck End 18 A
Duck's Cross 25 H
Duckington 31 A
Ducklington 16 A
Duddenhoe End 26 K
Duddingston 53 A
Duddington 33 L
Duddo 54 G
Duddon 38 K
Duddon Bridge 42 E
Dudleston Heath 30 C
Dudley 31 M
Dudley 49 F
Dudon 14 L
Duffield 32 E
Duffryn 14 B
Dufftown 72 L
Duffus 72 H
Dufton 48 L
Duggleby 45 K
Duirinish 70 K
Duisdalemore 69 M
Duisky 64 D
Dukestown 22 G
Dukinfield 39 G
Dulas 36 E
Dulcote 14 J
Dulford 6 A
Dull 65 L
Dullatur 57 M
Dullingham 26 H
Dulnain Bridge 65 C
Duloe 4 E
Duloe 25 H
Dulsie 71 M
Dulverton 13 H
Dulwich 17 J
Dumbarton 57 K
Dumbleton 23 J
Dumcrieff 52 M
Dumeath 66 C
Dumfin 57 G
Dumfries 47 B
Dumgoyne 57 H
Dummer 16 L
Dumpford 8 C
Dun 59 B
Dunadry 104 C
Dunaghy 108 J
Dunalastair 65 L
Dunan 69 M
Dunball 14 G
Dunbar 53 C
Dunbeath 78 K
Dunbeg 63 M
Dunblane 57 J
Dunbog 58 F
Duncanston 71 H
Duncanstone 66 C
Dun Chàrlabhagh 75 D
Dunchideock 5 C
Dunchurch 24 B
Duncote 24 J
Duncow 47 B
Duncrievie 58 H
Duncton 9 A
Dundee 59 D
Dundonald 51 F
Dundonald 105 D
Dundonnell 70 C
Dundraw 47 J
Dundreggan 64 C
Dundrennan 47 D
Dundrod 104 F
Dundrum 105 K
Dundry 14 F
Dunecht 67 D
Dunfallandy 65 M
Dunfermline 58 L
Dunfield 15 C
Dunford Bridge 39 H
Dungannon 104 D
Dungiven 108 G
Dungworth 39 H
Dunham-on-the-Hill 38 K
Dunham on Trent 33 B
Dunhampton 23 B
Dunham Town 38 J
Dunino 59 G
Dunipace 57 M
Dunira 57 F
Dunkeld-Birnam 58 B
Dunkerton 15 D
Dunkeswell 6 A
Dunk's Green 10 B
Dunlappie 66 M
Dunley 23 B
Dunlop 51 C
Dunloy 108 J
Dunmore 56 K
Dunmore 58 G
Dunmore 105 K
Dunmurry 104 F
Dunnamanagh 107 J
Dunnamore 104 A
Dunnet 78 E
Dunnichen 59 A
Dunning 58 E
Dunnington 23 F
Dunnington 40 B
Dunnington 41 A
Dunnockshaw 38 C
Dunnose 8 H
Dunollie 56 B
Dunoon 56 J
Dunragit 46 A
Duns 54 D
Duns Tew 24 L
Dunsby 33 J
Dunscore 47 B
Dunscroft 40 G
Dunsdale 44 C
Dunsfold 9 A
Dunsford 5 B
Dunshalt 58 J
Dunsinnan 58 E
Dunsley 45 D
Dunsop Bridge 43 K
Dunstable 25 K
Dunstall 32 G
Dunstall Green 26 H
Dunstan 54 M
Dunster 13 J
Dunston 27 B
Dunston 31 J
Dunston 33 C
Dunston 49 H
Dunstone 5 G
Dunstone 5 L
Dunsville 40 G
Dunswell 40 F
Dunsyre 52 F
Dunterton 4 C
Dunthrop 24 K
Duntisbourne-Abbots 23 L
Duntisbourne-Leer 23 L
Duntisbourne-Rouse 23 L
Duntish 7 A
Duntocher 52 A
Duntocher 57 L
Dunton 24 M
Dunton 25 J
Dunton 34 M
Dunton Bassett 24 C
Dunton Green 10 A
Dunton Wayletts 18 D
Duntulm 69 B
Dunturk 105 G
Dunure 51 H
Dunvant 21 K
Dunvegan 69 D
Dunwich 27 J
Durdar 48 G
Durdie 58 F
Durgates 10 E
Durham 49 L
Durisdeer 52 L
Durisdeermill 52 L
Durleigh 14 G
Durley 15 J
Durnamuck 70 B
Durness 77 A
Durno 67 A
Duror 64 G
Durran 56 E
Durran 78 E
Durrington 9 E
Durrington 15 M
Dursley 15 A
Durston 14 K
Durweston 7 B
Dury 81 D
Duston 24 F
Duthil 65 C
Dutlas 30 L
Duton Hill 18 A
Dutton 38 H
Duxford 26 G
Dwygyfylchi 37 G
Dwyran 36 H
Dyan 104 D
Dyce 67 E
Dyer's Green Kneesworth 25 J
Dyffryn 21 M
Dyffryn Ardudwy 29 B
Dyffryn Ceidrych 21 E
Dyffryn Cellwen 21 J
Dyke 33 J
Dyke 72 G
Dykehead 52 B
Dykehead 57 H
Dykehead 66 L
Dykelands 67 K
Dykend 66 K
Dykeside 73 K
Dylife 29 J
Dymchurch-Saint Mary's Bay 11 G
Dymock 23 G
Dyrham 15 D
Dysart 58 L
Dyserth 37 H

E

Eadar Dha Fhadhail 74 F
Eagland Hill 42 M
Eagle 33 B
Eagle Moor 33 B
Eaglescliffe 44 B
Eaglesfield 47 C
Eaglesfield 47 L
Eaglesfield 48 A
Eaglesham 52 A
Eairy 37 A
Eakring 33 A
Ealand 40 H
Ealing 17 E
Eamont Bridge 48 L
Earby 43 L
Earcroft 38 C
Eardington 31 L
Eardisland 22 C
Eardisley 22 E
Eardiston 23 A
Eardiston 30 F
Earith 26 D
Earle 54 G
Earlestown 38 H
Earlham 27 B
Earlish 69 E
Earls Barton 25 D
Earls Colne 18 B
Earl's Common 23 F
Earl's Croome 23 E
Earlsdon 24 A
Earlsferry 59 G
Earlsford 67 B
Earl's Green 27 G
Earl Shilton 32 L
Earl Soham 27 H
Earl Sterndale 39 K
Earlston 51 F
Earlston 53 J
Earl Stonham 27 G
Earlstoun 51 M
Earlswood 22 M
Earlswood 23 C
Earnley 8 F
Earsairidh 68 K
Earshaig 52 M
Earsham 27 E
Earswick 44 M
Eartham 9 D
Easby 44 F
Easebourne 9 A
Easenhall 24 B
Eashing 16 M
Easington 16 B
Easington 16 C
Easington 41 H
Easington 45 A
Easington 49 M
Easington 54 H
Easington Colliery 49 M
Easington Lane 49 M
Easingwold 44 L
Easole Street 11 E
Eassie 58 C
East Aberthaw 13 F
East Allington 5 H
East Anstey 13 H
East Ardsley 39 F
East Ashley 13 K
East Ashling 8 F
East Auchronie 67 D
East Barkwith 33 C
East Barnet 17 E
East Barsham 35 G
East Beckham 35 H
East Bedfont 17 G
East Bennan 51 D
East Bergholt 27 K
East Bilney 35 K
East Blatchington 10 K
East Boldon 49 J
East Boldre 8 D
Eastbourne 10 L
East Brent 14 H
Eastbridge 27 J
East Bridgford 33 D
East Buckland 13 G
East Budleigh 6 D
East Burrafirth 81 G
Eastburn 40 C
East Burton 7 D
Eastbury 16 D
Eastbury 17 D
East Butterwick 40 H
Eastby 43 M
East Cainbeg 67 K
East Calder 52 C
East Carlton 25 A
East Challow 16 D
East Charleton 5 L
East Chiltington 9 F
East Chinnock 6 C
East Chisenbury 15 J
East Cholderton 15 M
Eastchurch 18 M
East Clandon 17 K
East Claydon 24 M
East Coker 6 C
East Combe 14 G
Eastcombe 23 L
East Compton 14 J
East Cornworthy 5 H
Eastcote 17 E
Eastcote 24 A
Eastcote 24 F
Eastcott 12 L
Eastcott 15 H
East Cottingwith 40 B
Eastcourt 15 B
East Cowes 8 E
East Cowick 40 D
East Cowton 44 E
East Cramlington 49 F
East Cranmore 14 J
East Creech 7 E
East Croachy 71 L
East Croftmore 65 C
East Davoch 66 F
East Dean 8 A
East Dean 9 D
East Dean 10 K
East Dereham 27 A
East Down 13 D
East Drayton 33 A
East End 7 E
East End 8 D
East End 10 F
East End 14 F
East End 16 G
East End 19 A
East End 24 K
East End 26 K
Easter Quarff 81 H
Easter Ardross 71 E
Easter Balgedie 58 H
Easter Balmoral 66 H
Easter Boleskine 65 A
Easter Compton 14 C
Easter Culfosie 67 D
Easter Elchies 72 L
Easter Fearn 71 B
Easter Fodderletter 66 A
Easter Galcantray 71 M
Eastergate 9 D
Easter Howgate 53 A
Easter Kinkell 71 H
Easter Knox 59 D
Easter Lednathie 66 L
Easter Moniack 71 L
Eastern Green 24 A
Easter Ord 67 G
Easter Skeld 81 G
Easter Suddie 71 H
Easterton 15 H
Eastertown 14 E
Easter Whyntie 73 G
East Farleigh 10 C
East Farndon 24 C
East Ferry 40 H
Eastfield 45 H
Eastfield 52 B
Eastfield Hall 49 C
East Fortune 59 K
East Fulwood 57 K
East Garston 16 D
Eastgate 35 L
Eastgate 49 K
East Ginge 16 D
East Goscote 32 M
East Grafton 15 J
East Grimstead 15 M
East Grinstead 9 C
East Guldefort 10 J
East Haddon 24 F

East Hagbourne 16 E
East Halton 41 G
East Ham 17 J
Eastham 23 A
Eastham 38 G
Easthampstead 16 J
East Hanney 16 A
East Hanningfield 18 E
East Hardwick 39 F
East Harling 27 D
East Harlsey 44 E
East-Harptree 14 J
East Hartford 49 F
East Harting 8 C
East Hatley 25 J
East Hauxwell 44 D
East Haven 59 D
East Heckington 33 F
East Hedleyhope 49 L
East Helmsdale 78 K
East Hendred 16 D
East Heslerton 45 K
East Hoathly 10 G
Easthope 31 K
East Hope 43 C
Easthorpe 18 C
East-Horrington 14 J
East Horsley 17 K
East Huntspill 14 H
East Hyde 17 B
East Ilkerton 13 E
East Ilsley 16 E
Eastington 13 L
Eastington 23 K
Eastington 23 M
East Keal 34 D
East Kennett 15 F
East Keswick-Bardsey 39 C
East Kilbride 52 A
East Kirkby 34 D
East Knapton 45 K
East Knighton 7 D
East Knoyle 15 K
East Kyloe 54 H
East Lambrook 14 L
East Lamington 71 F
East Langdon 11 E
East Langton 24 C
East Langwell 71 C
East Lavington 9 D
East Layton 44 A
Eastleach 15 C
East Leake 32 J
East Learmouth 54 G
Eastleigh 8 B
Eastleigh 12 J
East Leigh 13 K
East Lexham 34 M
East Lilburn 54 L
Eastling 11 A
East Linton 53 C
East Liss 8 C
East Looe 4 J
East Lound 40 H
East Lulworth 7 D
East Lutton 45 K
East Lydford 14 M
East Lyng 14 K
East Mains 67 G
East Malling 10 B
East Marden 8 F
East Markham 33 A
East Marton 43 L
East Meon 8 C
East Mere 13 M
East Mersea 18 C
East Mey 78 E
East Molesey 17 H
East Morden 7 E
East Morton 39 B
East Ness 44 J
Eastney 8 F
Eastnor 23 G
East Norton 33 K
East Nynehead 14 K
East Oakley 16 L
Eastoft 40 H
East Ogwell 5 E
Easton 5 B
Easton 14 J
Easton 15 E
Easton 16 K
Easton 25 E
Easton 27 A
Easton 27 H
Easton 33 H
Easton 48 D
Easton Grey 15 B
Easton in Gordano 14 F
Easton Maudit 25 D
Easton on the Hill 33 L
Easton Royal 15 J
East Orchard 7 B
East Ord 54 E
East Panson 4 C
East Peckham 10 B
East Pennard 14 J
East Portlemouth 5 L
East Prawle 5 L
East Preston 9 E
East Putford 12 M
East Quantoxhead 14 G
East Rainton 49 M
East Ravendale 41 K
East Raynham 34 M
Eastriggs 47 F
Eastrington 40 E
East Rounton 44 E
East Rudham 34 M
East Runton 35 H
East Ruston 35 M
Eastry 11 B
East Saltoun 53 B
Eastside 79 L
East Sleekburn 49 F
East Somerton 27 C
East Stockwith 40 L
East Stoke 7 E
East Stoke 33 D
East Stour 15 K
East Stourmouth 11 B
East Stratton 16 K
East Studdal 11 E
East Taphouse 4 E
East-the-Water 12 J
East Thirston 49 B
East Tilbury 18 G
East Tisted 8 C
East Torrington 40 M
East Tuddenham 27 A
East Tullyfergus 58 C
East Tytherley 15 M
East Tytherton 15 E
East Village 5 C
Eastville 34 D
East Wall 31 K
East Walton 34 M
Eastwell 33 G
East Wellow 8 A
East Wemyss 58 J
East Whitburn 52 C
East Whitefield 58 B
Eastwick 17 C
Eastwick 80 J
East Williamston 20 H
East Wilton 44 G
East Winch 34 L
East Winterslow 15 M
East Wittering 8 F
Eastwood 18 H
Eastwood 32 F
Eastwood 39 A
East Woodburn 49 A
East Woodhay 16 G
East Worldham 16 L
East-Worlington 13 L
East Wretham 26 F
Eathorpe 24 E
Eaton 27 B
Eaton 30 M
Eaton 31 K
Eaton 33 G
Eaton 38 L
Eaton 38 M
Eaton 40 K
Eaton Bishop 22 F
Eaton Bray 25 K
Eaton Hall 38 K
Eaton Hastings 16 A
Eaton Socon 25 H
Eaton upon Tern 31 E
Eavestone 44 G
Ebberston 45 G
Ebbw Vale 22 K
Ebchester 49 H
Ebford 5 C
Ebrington 23 J
Ecchinswell 16 G
Ecclaw 54 A
Ecclefechan 47 C
Eccles 10 C
Eccles 38 J
Eccles 53 J
Ecclesfield 39 J
Ecclesgreig 67 K
Eccleshall 31 E
Ecclesmachan 58 K
Eccles on Sea 35 M
Eccles Road 27 D
Eccleston 38 B
Eccleston 38 G
Eccleston 38 K
Eccup 39 C
Echt 67 D
Eckford 53 J
Eckington 23 H
Eckington 39 M
Ecton 25 D
Edale 39 K
Eday 79 E
Edburton 9 E
Edderside 47 J
Edderton 71 F
Eddesbourne Wake 15 L
Eddington 11 B
Eddleston 53 D
Eden 105 A
Eden Park 17 J
Edenagarry 104 J
Edenbridge 10 A
Edenfield 38 F
Edenhall 48 L
Edenham 33 H
Edensor 39 L
Edentaggart 57 G
Edenthorpe 40 G
Edentrillick 104 J
Ederline 56 E
Edern 36 K
Ederney 103 A
Edgarley 14 J
Edgbaston 23 C
Edgcote 24 H
Edgcott 24 M
Edge 23 L
Edge 30 J
Edgebolton 31 D
Edge End 22 M
Edgefield 35 K
Edgefield Street 35 K
Edgehead 53 B
Edgehill 24 G
Edgerley 30 F
Edgeworth 23 L
Edgmond 31 E
Edgmond Marsh 31 E
Edgton 30 M
Edgware 17 E
Edgworth 38 F
Edinample 57 F
Edinbane 69 E
Edinbarnet 57 L
Edinburgh 61 F
Edingale 32 G
Edingley 33 A
Edingthorpe 35 M
Edington 14 H
Edington 15 H
Edistone 12 H
Edithmead 14 H
Edith Weston 33 L
Edlesborough 25 K
Edlingham 54 L
Edlington 34 A
Edmondsham 7 C
Edmondsley 49 L
Edmondthorpe 33 G
Edmonstone 79 H
Edmonton 4 A
Edmonton 17 F
Edmundbyers 49 G
Ednam 53 J
Ednaston 32 D
Edney Common 18 D
Edradynate 65 L
Edrom 54 D
Edstaston 31 D
Edstone 24 D
Edwalton 32 F
Edwardstone 26 M
Edwinsford 21 E
Edwinstowe 33 A
Edworth 25 M
Edwyn Loach 23 D
Edwyn Ralph 23 A
Edzell 66 M
Efail Isaf 14 A
Efailnewydd 29 A
Efail-rhyd 30 E
Efailwen 20 E
Efenechtyd 37 L
Effingham 17 K
Effirth 81 G
Efford 5 C
Egerton 10 F
Egerton 38 F
Egerton Forstal 10 F
Egerton Green 31 A
Eggborough 40 D
Egginton 25 K
Egginton 32 E
Egglescliffe 44 B
Eggleston 43 C
Egham 17 G
Egleton 33 K
Eglingham 54 L
Eglinton 107 J
Eglish 104 D
Egloshayle 4 D
Egloskerry 4 C
Eglwysbach 37 G
Eglwys-Brewis 13 C
Eglwys Cross 31 A
Eglwys Fach 29 J
Eglwyswen 20 C
Eglwyswrw 20 C
Egmanton 33 A
Egremont 47 L
Egton 45 D
Egton Brigde 45 D
Egypt 17 D
Eight Ash Green 18 C
Eilanreach 70 K
Eilean Darach 70 C
Einacleit 74 F
Eisgein 75 G
Eisingrug 29 C
Elan Village 22 A
Elberton 14 C
Elburton 5 G
Elcho 58 E
Elcombe 15 F
Eldernell 25 C
Eldersfield 23 H
Elderslie 57 K
Eldom Heath 24 A
Eldroth 43 H
Eldwick 39 B
Elevan Lane Ends 104 H
Elford 32 G
Elford 54 H
Elgin 72 H
Elgol 69 L
Elham 11 E
Elie 59 G
Elim 36 E
Elishaw 49 A
Elkesley 40 K
Elkstone 23 L
Ellan 65 C
Elland 39 E
Ellary 56 G
Ellastone 32 D
Ellemford 53 F
Ellen's Green 9 B
Ellenabeich 56 A
Ellenhall 31 E
Ellerbeck 44 E
Ellerby 45 D
Ellerdine Heath 31 D
Elleric 64 K
Ellerker 40 F
Ellerton 31 E
Ellerton 40 B
Ellesborough 16 C
Ellesmere 30 C
Ellesmere Port 38 G
Ellingham 7 C
Ellingham 27 E
Ellingham 54 L
Ellingstring 44 G
Ellington 25 E
Ellington 49 C
Ellioth 59 E
Ellisfield 16 L
Ellishadder 69 F
Ellister 55 K
Ellistown 32 H
Ellon 67 B
Ellonby 48 K
Ellough 27 F
Elloughton 40 F
Ellwood 22 M
Elm 34 K
Elmbridge 23 B
Elmdon 24 A
Elmdon 26 K
Elmesthorpe 32 L
Elmhurst 32 G
Elmley Castle 23 J
Elmley Lovett 23 B
Elmore 23 K
Elmore Back 23 K
Elm Park 18 G
Elmscott 12 H
Elmsett Burstallhill 27 K
Elmstead Market 18 C
Elmsted 11 D
Elmstone 11 B
Elmstone Hardwicke 23 H
Elmswell 26 J
Elmswell 40 C
Elmton 39 M
Elphhillock 66 F
Elphin 76 M
Elphinstone 53 B
Elrick 66 C
Elrick 67 D
Elrig 46 E
Elsdon 49 A
Elsecar 39 J
Elsenham 18 A
Elsfield 16 B
Elsham 40 J
Elsing 35 K
Elslack 43 L
Elsrickle 52 F
Elstead 16 M
Elsted 8 C
Elsthorpe 33 H
Elstob 44 B
Elston 33 D
Elston 38 B
Elstone 13 K
Elstow 25 H
Elstree 17 E
Elstronwick 41 B
Elswick 42 M
Elsworth 25 F
Elterwater Little 42 C
Eltisley 25 J
Elton 22 C
Elton 23 K
Elton 25 B
Elton 32 B
Elton 33 D
Elton 38 G
Elton 44 B
Elvanfoot 52 H
Elvaston 32 E
Elveden 26 F
Elvingston 53 B
Elvington 11 E
Elvington 40 B
Elwick 44 C
Elwick 49 M
Elwick 54 H
Elworth 38 L
Elworthy 13 J
Ely 14 A
Ely 26 D
Emberton 25 G
Embleton 47 M
Embleton 54 M
Embo 71 C
Emborough 14 J
Embsay 43 M
Emeraconart 55 H
Emery Down 8 A
Emley 39 E
Emley Moor 39 E
Emmer Green 16 F
Emneth 34 K
Emneth Hungate 34 K
Empingham 33 L
Empshott 8 C
Emsworth 8 F
Enchmarsh 31 G
End-Bourne 17 D
Enderby 32 M
Endmoor 43 D
Endon 31 C
Enfield 17 F
Enford 15 J
Engine Common 15 A
Englefield 16 H
Englefield Green 17 G
English Bicknor 22 M
Englishcombe 15 D
English Frankton 31 D
Engollan 4 D
Enham-Alamein 16 G
Enmore 14 G
Ennerdale Bridge 47 L
Enniskillen 103 D
Enochdhu 65 M
Ensay 63 G
Ensbury 7 F
Ensdon 30 F
Ensis 13 G
Enstone 24 K
Enterkinfoot 52 L
Enville 31 L
Eòlaigearraidh 68 K
Eorabus 55 C
Eòropaidh 75 C
Epperstone 33 D
Epping 17 F
Epping Green 17 C
Epping Upland 17 F
Eppleby 44 A
Eppping Green 17 C
Epsom and-Ewell 17 H
Epwell 24 G
Epworth 40 H
Erbistock 30 C
Erbusaig 70 K
Erchless Castle 71 K
Erdington 32 K
Eredine 56 E
Eriboll 77 D
Ericstane 52 M
Eridge Green 10 E
Eridge Sta 10 D
Erines 56 H
Eriswell 26 E
Erlestoke 15 H
Ermington 5 G
Erpingham 35 L
Errasallagh Cross Roads 103 H
Errogie 65 A
Errol 58 F
Erskine 57 K
Erveny 103 G
Ervey Cross Roads 107 J
Ervie 46 G
Erwarton 19 A
Erwood 22 D
Eryholme 44 E
Eryrys 37 M
Escomb 49 L
Escrick 40 A
Esgair 21 D
Esgairgeilog 29 F
Esh 49 L
Esher 17 H
Eshnadarragh 103 H
Eshnadeelada 103 H
Esholt 39 B
Eshott 49 B
Eshton 43 L
Esh Winning 49 L
Eshywulligan 103 H
Eskadale 71 K
Eskbank 53 A
Eskdale Green 42 B
Eskdalemuir 53 K
Eskham 41 L
Esknish 55 H
Eskragh 103 F
Esprick 42 M
Essendine 33 L
Essendon 17 C
Essich 71 L
Essington 31 J
Esslemont 67 B
Eston 44 C
Eswick 81 D
Etal 54 G
Etchilhampton 15 H
Etchingham 10 E
Etchinghill 11 E
Etchinghill 31 J
Etherly 49 L
Ethie Mains 59 B
Eton 17 D
Etteridge 65 E
Ettersgill 48 M
Ettington 24 D
Etton 33 M
Etton 40 C
Ettrick 53 K
Ettrickbridge 53 G
Ettrickdale 56 M
Ettrickhill 53 G
Etwall 32 E
Euston 26 F
Euxton 38 B
Evanton 71 E
Evedon 33 F
Evelix 71 C
Evenjobb 22 B
Evenley 24 H
Evenlode 24 G
Evenwood 44 A
Everbay 79 F
Evercreech 14 J
Everdon 24 F
Everingham 40 B
Everleigh 15 J
Everley 45 H
Eversholt 25 K
Evershot 6 C
Eversley 16 J
Eversley Centre 16 J
Eversley Cross 16 J
Everthorpe 40 F
Everton 8 D
Everton 25 H
Everton 40 K
Evertown 48 A
Evesbatch 23 D
Evesham 23 J
Evington 32 M
Ewart Newtown 54 G
Ewarts Cross Roads 104 L
Ewden Village 39 H
Ewell 11 E
Ewell Minnis 11 E
Ewelme 16 E
Ewen 15 B
Ewenny 13 C
Ewerby 33 F
Ewerby Thorpe 33 F
Ewes 48 A
Ewhurst 17 K
Ewhurst Green 10 J
Ewloe 37 M
Eworthy 5 A
Ewshot 16 M
Ewyas Harold 22 H
Exbourne 13 K
Exbury 8 D
Exebridge 13 M
Exelby 44 G
Exeter 5 C
Exford 13 H
Exhall 23 F
Exhall 24 B
Exminster 5 C
Exmouth 5 F
Exnaboe 81 J
Exning 26 H
Exton 5 F
Exton 8 B
Exton 13 J
Exton 33 L
Eyam 39 L
Eydon 24 H
Eye 22 C
Eye 27 G
Eye 33 M
Eye Green 33 M
Eyehorne Street 10 C
Eyemouth 54 D
Eyeworth 25 J
Eyke 27 L
Eynesbury 25 H
Eynort 69 H
Eynsford-Farningham 17 M
Eynsham 16 A
Eype 6 F
Eyre 69 E
Eythorne 11 E
Eyton 22 C
Eyton 30 C
Eyton 30 M

F

Faccombe 16 G
Faceby 44 F
Faddiley 31 A
Fadmoor 44 J
Faebait 71 G
Faerdre 21 L
Faifley 57 L
Failand 14 F
Failford 51 F
Failsworth 39 G
Fain 70 C
Fairbourne 29 E
Fairburn 39 F
Fairfield 23 B
Fairfield 23 C
Fairford 15 C
Fair Green 34 L
Fairlands 17 K
Fairlie 51 B
Fairlight 10 J
Fairlight Cove 10 J
Fairmile 6 A
Fairmilehead 53 A
Fairnington 53 J
Fair Oak 8 B
Fairoak 31 E
Fair Oak Green 16 H
Fairseat 10 B
Fairstead 18 B
Fairwarp 10 D
Fairy Cross 12 J
Fakenham 35 K
Fakenham Magna 26 F
Fala 53 B
Fala Dam 53 B
Falahill 53 E
Faldingworth 40 M
Falfield 15 A
Falfield 59 G
Falkenham 27 L
Falkirk 58 K
Falkland 58 J
Falla 53 M
Fallagh 107 M
Fallagloon 108 L
Fallgarrive 108 F
Fallgate 32 B
Fallin 57 J
Falls 105 D
Falmer 9 F
Falmouth-Penryn 3 J
Falstone 48 C
Fanagmore 76 F
Fancott 25 K
Fangdale Beck 44 F
Fangfoss 40 B
Fanmore 63 K
Fans 53 F
Farcet 25 C
Far Cotton 24 F
Farden 23 A
Fareham-Portchester 8 E
Farewell 32 G
Far Forest 23 B
Farforth 34 A
Far Gearstones 43 H
Faringdon 16 A
Farington 38 B
Farlam 48 E
Farlary 71 C
Farleigh 10 A
Farleigh 14 F
Farleigh Hungerford 15 G
Farleigh Wallop 16 L
Farlesthorpe 34 B
Farleton 43 D
Farleton 43 G
Farley 15 M
Farley 30 J
Farley 32 D
Farley Green 17 K
Farley Hill 16 J
Farleys End 23 K
Farlington 44 M
Farlough 104 C
Farlow 31 K
Farmborough 14 F
Farmcote 23 J
Farmington 23 M
Farmoor 16 B
Farmtown 72 M
Farnborough 16 D
Farnborough 16 M
Farnborough 17 J
Farnborough 24 H
Farncombe 17 K
Farndish 25 D
Farndon 33 D
Farndorn 31 A
Farnell 59 B
Farnham 7 B
Farnham 16 M
Farnham 17 D
Farnham 18 A
Farnham 27 H
Farnham 44 L
Farnham Common 17 D
Farnham Green 18 A
Farnley 39 B
Farnley Tyas 39 E
Farnsfield 33 A
Farnworth 38 F
Farnworth 38 G
Farr 65 F
Farr 71 L
Farr 77 E
Farrancassidy 102 C
Farringdon 5 C
Farrington Gurney 14 J
Farsley 39 B
Farthinghoe 24 H
Farthingloe 11 E
Farthingstone 24 F
Farway 6 A
Fasach 69 D
Fascadale 63 E
Fasnacloich 64 K
Fasque 66 M
Fassfern 64 D
Fatfield 49 J
Fattahead 73 K
Faugh 48 H
Fauldhouse 52 C
Faulkbourne 18 B
Faulkland 15 G
Fauls 31 D
Faversham 11 A
Favillar 66 A
Fawdington 44 H
Fawdon 49 E
Fawfieldhead 32 A
Fawkham Green 18 K
Fawler 24 K
Fawley 8 D
Fawley 16 D
Fawley 16 F
Fawley Chapel 23 G
Fawney 107 J
Fawsyde 67 K
Faxfleet 40 E
Faygate 9 B
Fazeley 32 K
Fearby 44 G
Fearn 71 F
Fearnan 57 C
Fearnbeg 70 D
Fearnhead 38 B
Fearnmore 70 D
Fearn Station 71 F
Featherstone 31 J
Featherstone 39 F
Feckenham 23 F
Feeny 108 K
Feetham 43 F
Feizor 43 H
Felbridge 9 C
Felbrigg 35 H
Felcourt 9 C
Felden 17 A
Felindre 21 A
Felindre 21 E
Felindre 21 G
Felindre 21 L
Felindre 30 L
Felindre Farchog 20 B
Felinfach 21 B
Felinfach 22 D
Felinfoel 21 G
Felingwmuchaf 21 D
Felixkirk 44 H
Felixstowe 19 B
Fell End 43 E
Fell Side 47 J
Felldownhead 4 C
Fellgate 49 J
Felling 49 H
Fellington 54 G
Felmersham 25 H

Felmingham 35 L
Felpham 9 D
Felsham 26 J
Felstead 18 B
Feltham 17 G
Felthorpe 35 L
Felton 14 F
Felton 23 D
Felton 49 B
Felton Butler 30 F
Feltwell 26 B
Fenay Bridge 39 E
Fence 38 C
Fence Houses 49 M
Fencott 24 L
Fen Ditton 26 G
Fen Drayton 25 F
Fen End 24 A
Fenhouses 33 J
Feniscowles 38 B
Feniton 6 A
Fenny Bentley 32 A
Fenny Bridges 6 A
Fenny Compton 24 E
Fenny Drayton 32 L
Fenny Stratford 25 K
Fenrother 49 B
Fenstanton 25 F
Fenstead End 26 L
Fenton 25 F
Fenton 31 C
Fenton 33 B
Fenton 33 E
Fenton 54 G
Fenton Barns 59 K
Fenwick 40 D
Fenwick 49 E
Fenwick 51 C
Fenwick 54 H
Feochaig 50 F
Feock 3 J
Feolin 55 J
Ferindonald 63 C
Feriniquarrie 69 D
Fern 66 L
Ferndale 21 M
Ferndown 7 F
Ferness 72 K
Fernham 16 A
Fernhill Heath 23 E
Fernhurst 9 A
Fernie 58 J
Ferniegair 52 B
Fernilea 69 H
Fernilee 39 K
Ferrensby 44 L
Ferriby Sluice 40 F
Ferring 9 E
Ferry Keils 55 J
Ferrybridge 39 F
Ferryden 59 B
Ferryhill 49 L
Ferryside 20 J
Fersfield 27 D
Fersit 64 J
Feshiebridge 65 F
Fetcham 17 K
Fetterangus 73 M
Fettercairn 66 M
Feumore 104 F
Fewston 44 K
Feystown 109 K
Ffairfach 21 H
Ffair-Rhos 29 M
Ffaldybrenin 21 B
Ffarmers 21 B
Ffawyddog 22 H
Ffordd-las 37 L
Fforest 21 G
Fforestfach 21 L
Ffostrasol 21 A
Ffridd Uchaf 36 M
Ffrith 37 M
Ffynnonddrain 21 D
Ffynnongroyw 37 J
Fidden 55 B
Fiddes 67 K
Fiddington 14 G
Fiddington 23 H
Fiddleford 7 A
Fiddler's Green 73 M
Fiddlers Hamlet 17 F
Field 31 F
Field Broughton 42 F
Field Dalling 35 G
Field Head 32 M
Fifehead Magdalen 15 K
Fifehead Neville 7 A
Fifield 16 J
Fifield 24 K
Fifield Bavant 15 L
Filby 27 C
Filching 10 K
Filey 45 L
Filgrave 25 G
Filkins 15 C
Filleigh 13 G
Filleigh 13 L
Fillingham 40 L
Fillongley 24 A
Filton 14 C
Fimber 45 K
Finaghy 105 D
Finavon 59 A
Fincarn 108 K
Finchairn 56 E
Fincham 26 B
Finchampstead 16 J
Finchdean 8 F
Finchingfield 26 L
Finchley 17 E
Findern 32 E
Findhorn 72 G
Findhorn Bridge 65 C
Findochty 72 J
Findo Gask 58 D
Findon 9 E
Findon 67 H
Findon Mains 71 H
Findrassie 72 H
Finedon 25 D
Fingal Street 27 H
Fingask 67 A
Fingest 16 F
Finghall 44 D
Fingland 47 F
Fingland 52 G
Finglesham 11 E
Fingringhoe 18 C
Finlarig 57 C
Finlaystone 57 K
Finmere 24 M
Finnart 65 K
Finningham 27 G
Finningley 40 G
Finnis 104 J
Finnygaud 73 K
Finsbury 17 F
Finsthwaite 42 F
Finstown 79 G
Fintona 103 B
Fintry 57 H
Fintry 73 K
Finvoy 108 H
Finzean 66 J
Fionnsabhagh 74 M
Fioscabhaig 69 G
Fir Tree 49 L
Firbank 43 D
Firbeck 40 K
Firgrove 39 D
Firle 9 F
Firle 10 G
Firsby 34 E
Firsdown 15 M
First Coast 70 B
Firth 80 F
Fishbourne 8 E
Fishbourne 8 F
Fishburn 49 M
Fishcross 58 G
Fisherford 67 A
Fisherstreet 9 A
Fisherton 51 H
Fisherton 71 J
Fisherton de la Mere 15 L
Fishguard/Abergwaun 20 B
Fishlake 40 G
Fishleigh Barton 13 G
Fishpond Botton 6 B
Fishpool 38 F
Fishtoft 34 G
Fishtoft Drove 34 D
Fishwick 54 D
Fiskerton 33 C
Fiskerton 33 D
Fitling 41 B
Fittleton 15 J
Fittleworth 9 A
Fitton End 34 K
Fitz 30 F
Fitzhead 13 M
Fitzwilliam 39 F
Fiunary 63 L
Five Ashes 10 D
Fivehead 14 L
Fivelanes 4 C
Fivemiletown 103 E
Five Oaks 9 B
Five Oaks 9 M
Five Roads 21 G
Fladbury 23 F
Fladda 80 H
Fladdabister 81 H
Flagg 39 K
Flamborough 45 M
Flamstead 17 B
Flansham 9 D
Flasby 43 M
Flash 39 K
Flashader 69 E
Flaunden 17 A
Flawborough 33 D
Flawith 44 L
Flax Bourton 14 F
Flaxby 44 L
Flaxley 23 K
Flaxpool 14 G
Flaxton 44 M
Fleckney 32 M
Flecknoe 24 E
Fleet 6 F
Fleet 16 M
Fleet 34 K
Fleet Hargate 34 G
Fleetwood 42 L
Fleggburgh/Burgh Saint Margaret 27 C
Flemingston 13 C
Flemington 52 A
Flempton 26 J
Fleoideabhagh 74 M
Fletchertown 47 J
Fletching 9 F
Fletching 10 D
Flexbury 12 L
Flexford 16 M
Flimby 47 H
Flimwell 10 E
Flint 37 J
Flint Cross 25 M
Flintham 33 D
Flint Mountain 37 M
Flinton 41 B
Flitcham 34 M
Flitton 25 L
Flitwick 25 L
Flixborough 40 H
Flixborough Stather 40 H
Flixton 27 E
Flixton 38 J
Flixton 45 L
Flockton 39 E
Flodaigh 68 E
Flodden 54 G
Flodigarry 69 B
Flookburgh 42 F
Flordon 27 B
Flore 24 F
Floshelyg 29 L
Flotterton 49 A
Flowton 27 K
Flugarth 80 F
Flurrybridge 104 L
Flush 104 M
Flush House 39 E
Flushing 3 J
Flushing 3 M
Flushing 67 C
Flyford Flavell 23 F
Flyingthorpe 45 E
Fobbing 18 G
Fochabers 72 H
Fochriw 22 K
Fockerby 40 E
Fodderty 71 G
Foel 30 D
Fofannybane 104 M
Foffarty 59 A
Foggathorpe 40 B
Fogo 54 D
Fogorig 54 D
Fogwatt 72 H
Foindle 76 F
Folda 66 K
Fold Hill 34 E
Fole 31 F
Foleshill 24 B
Folke 7 A
Folkestone 11 E
Folkingham 33 H
Folkington 10 G
Folksworth 25 B
Folkton 45 L
Folla Rule 67 A
Follifoot 44 K
Folly Gate 5 A
Fonthill Bishop 15 K
Fonthill Gifford 15 K
Fontmell Magne 7 B
Fontwell 9 D
Foodieash 58 J
Foolow 39 L
Foots Cray 17 J
Forbestown 66 E
Force Forge 42 F
Forcett 44 A
Ford 5 L
Ford 9 D
Ford 15 D
Ford 15 M
Ford 16 C
Ford 23 J
Ford 30 J
Ford 32 A
Ford 38 D
Ford 54 G
Ford 56 E
Fordcombe 10 D
Fordell 58 L
Forden 30 H
Ford End 26 K
Forder Green 6 E
Fordham 18 C
Fordham 26 B
Fordham 26 E
Fordingbridge 7 C
Fordington 34 A
Fordon 45 L
Fordoun 67 K
Ford Street 14 K
Fordton 5 C
Fordwells 24 K
Ford Woodtown 12 J
Fordyce 73 G
Foremark 32 H
Forest 9 K
Forestburn Gate 49 B
Forest Coal Pit 22 H
Forest Gate 17 F
Forest Green 17 K
Forest Head 48 H
Forest Hill 16 B
Forest-in-Teesdale 48 M
Forest Mill 58 G
Forest Row 9 C
Forest Row 10 D
Forestside 8 F
Forest Town 32 C
Forfar 59 A
Forgandenny 58 E
Forge 29 J
Forge Side 22 L
Forgie 72 M
Forgue 73 K
Forkill 104 L
Formal 58 C
Formby 38 D
Formil Bridge 103 C
Forncett End 27 D
Forncett Saint Mary 27 D
Forncett Saint Peter 27 D
Forneth 58 B
Fornham All Saints 26 J
Fornham Saint Genevieve 26 J
Fornham Saint Martin 26 J
Fornighty 71 J
Forres 72 G
Forrestfield 52 B
Forry's Green 26 L
Forsbrook 31 F
Forse 78 L
Forsinard 77 J
Forston 7 D
Fort Augustus 64 C
Forter 66 K
Forteviot 58 E
Fort George 71 J
Forth 52 C
Forthampton 23 H
Fortingall 65 L
Forton 6 B
Forton 30 F
Forton 31 E
Forton 42 M
Fortrie 67 B
Fortrie 73 K
Fortrose 71 H
Fortuneswell 7 G
Fort William 64 H
Fortwilliam 104 J
Forward Green 27 G
Fosbury 16 G
Foscot 24 K
Fosdyke 34 G
Fossebridge 23 M
Foss-y-ffin 29 K
Foster Street 18 A
Foston 32 D
Foston 33 D
Foston 44 M
Foston on the Wolds 41 A
Fotherby 41 K
Fotheringhay 25 B
Foubister 79 H
Foul Mile 10 H
Foulden 26 C
Foulden 54 D
Foulridge 39 A
Foulsham 35 K
Foundry 108 M
Fountainhall 53 E
Four Ashes 27 G
Four Ashes 31 J
Four Crosses 23 K
Four Crosses 30 G
Four Crosses 31 J
Four Elms 10 A
Four Forks 14 G
Four Gotes 34 K
Four Lanes 3 J
Fourlanes End 31 B
Four Marks-Medstead 16 L
Four Mile Bridge 36 G
Four Oaks 10 J
Four Oaks 24 A
Four Oaks 31 M
Fourpenny 71 C
Fourstones 49 D
Fovant 15 L
Foveran 67 E
Fowey 4 H
Fowlis 58 F
Fowlis Wester 58 D
Fowlmere 26 G
Fownhope 22 J
Fox Corner 17 K
Fox Street 18 C
Foxash Estate 19 A
Foxcombe Hill 16 B
Foxcote 23 L
Foxdale 37 A
Foxearth 26 L
Foxfield 15 F
Foxfield 42 E
Foxham 15 E
Foxholes 45 L
Foxhunt Green 10 G
Foxley 15 B
Foxley 35 K
Foxt 32 A
Foxton 24 C
Foxton 25 J
Foxton 44 B
Foxup 43 H
Foxwist Green 38 L
Foy 23 G
Foyers 65 A
Fraddon 4 D
Fradley 32 G
Fradswell 31 F
Fraisthorpe 41 A
Framfield 10 G
Framingham Earl 27 B
Framingham Pigot 27 B
Framlingham 27 H
Frampton 6 F
Frampton 34 G
Frampton Mansell 23 L
Frampton-on-Severn 23 K
Frampton West-End 34 G
Framsden 27 G
Frankby 37 J
Frankley 23 C
Frankton 24 B
Frankville 105 G
Frant 10 E
Fraserburgh 73 M
Frating Green 19 A
Fratton 8 F
Freathy 4 J
Freckenham 26 E
Freckleton-Warton 38 A
Freeby 33 G
Freeland 24 K
Freester 81 D
Freethorpe 27 C
Freiston 34 G
Freiston Shore 34 G
Fremington 12 J
Fremington 43 F
Frenchbeer 5 B
Frensham 16 M
Fresgoe 78 D
Freshfield 38 D
Freshford 15 D
Freshwater East 20 H
Fressingfield 27 H
Freston 27 K
Freswick 78 F
Fretherne 23 K
Frettenham 27 B
Freuchie 58 J
Freystrop 20 G
Friar's Gate 10 D
Friday Bridge 26 A
Fridaythorpe 45 K
Friern Barnet 17 E
Friesland 62 J
Friesthorpe 40 M
Frieth 16 F
Frilsham 16 E
Frindsbury 18 G
Fring 34 J
Fringford 24 L
Frinsted 10 C
Frinton-on-Sea 19 A
Friockheim 59 B
Frisby on the Wreake 33 G
Friskney 34 D
Friskney Eaudyke 34 E
Friskney Tofts 34 E
Friston 10 K
Friston 27 H
Fritchley 32 B
Frith Bank 34 D
Frith Common 23 A
Fritham 8 A
Frithelstock 12 M
Frithelstock Stone 12 M
Frithville 34 D
Frittenden 10 F
Fritton 27 E
Fritton 27 F
Fritwell 24 L
Frizington 47 L
Frocester 23 K
Frodesley 31 G
Frodsham 38 H
Froggatt 39 L
Froghall 32 A
Frogham 7 C
Frogmore 5 L
Frogmore 16 J
Frogmore 17 B
Frogpool 3 J
Frog Pool 23 B
Frolesworth 24 B
Frome 15 G
Frome Saint Quitin 6 C
Fromes Hill 23 D
Fron 22 A
Fron 30 H
Fron 36 K
Froncysyllte 30 C
Frongoch 30 A
Frostenden 27 F
Frosterley 49 K
Frotoft 79 E
Froxfield Green 8 C
Fryerning 18 D
Fryton 44 M
Fulbeck 33 E
Fulbourn 26 G
Fulbrook 24 K
Fulford 14 K
Fulford 31 F
Fulford 40 A
Fulham 17 H
Fulking 9 E
Full Sutton 40 B
Fuller Street 18 B
Fuller's Moor 31 A
Fullerton 16 K
Fulletby 34 A
Fullwood 51 C
Fulmer 17 D
Fulmodeston 35 K
Fulnetby 33 C
Fulready 24 G
Fulstow 41 K
Fulwell 24 K
Fulwell 49 J
Fulwood 38 B
Fulwood 39 L
Fundenhall 27 A
Funtington 8 F
Funtley 8 E
Funzie 80 B
Furley 6 B
Furnace 29 J
Furnace 56 F
Furness Vale 39 K
Furneux Pelham 25 M
Furzebrook 7 E
Furzehill 13 E
Furzey Lodge 8 D
Fyfett 14 K
Fyfield 15 C
Fyfield 15 F
Fyfield 15 M
Fyfield 18 A
Fynydd 30 K
Fyvie 67 A

G

Gabhsann bho Dheas 75 B
Gabhsann bho Thuath 75 B
Gablon 71 C
Gabroc Hill 51 C
Gaddesby 32 M
Gadfa 36 E
Gaer 22 G
Gaer-fawr 22 M
Gaerwen 36 H
Gagingwell 24 K
Gailey 31 J
Gainford 44 A
Gainsborough 40 L
Gainsford End 26 L
Gair 53 K
Gairloch 70 A
Gairlochy 64 E
Gairney Bank 58 H
Gaisgill 43 A
Gaitsgill 48 G
Galashiels 53 H
Galbally 104 A
Galdanagh 109 K
Galgate 42 M
Galgorm 108 M
Galhampton 14 M
Gallachoile 56 G
Gallagh Wood 103 F
Gallanach 56 B
Gallatown 58 L
Galleywood 18 E
Gallowfauld 59 A
Gallowstree Common 16 E
Galltair 70 K
Galmisdale 63 E
Galmpton 5 J
Galmpton 5 K
Galphay 44 G
Galscwm 22 B
Galsson 42 J
Galston 51 F
Galtrigill 69 D
Gamble's Green 18 B
Gamblesby 48 H
Gameslay 39 G
Gamlingay 25 J
Gammaton 12 J
Gammersgill 43 J
Gamston 32 F
Gamston 40 K
Ganarew 22 M
Ganavan 56 B
Ganllwyd 29 C
Gannochy 66 M
Gansclet 78 H
Ganstead 41 B
Ganthorpe 44 M
Ganton 45 L
Garbat 71 C
Garbhallt 56 F
Garboldisham 27 D
Gardenstown 73 L
Gardenvale 108 J
Garderhouse 81 G
Gardiner's Cross Roads 103 E
Gare Hill 15 G
Garelochhead 57 G
Garford 16 A
Garforth 39 C
Gargrave 43 L
Gargunnock 57 J
Gariochsford 67 A
Garlieston 46 F
Garlogie 67 D
Garmond 73 L
Garmony 63 L
Garmouth 72 H
Garn 29 A
Garnant 21 H
Garndolbenmaen 36 L
Garnett Bridge 43 A
Garnkirk 57 L
Garn-yr-erw 22 L
Garpel 52 D
Garrabost 75 E
Garraburn 72 M
Garrachra 56 J
Garra Eallabus 55 H
Garraron 56 E
Garras 3 M
Garreg 29 C
Garreg Bank 30 J
Garrick 58 D
Garrigill 48 J
Garrison 102 C
Garroch 46 C
Garros 69 F
Garrow 58 A
Garryduff 108 J
Garrygualach 64 B
Garryhorn 51 M
Garsdale 43 E
Garsdale Head 43 E
Garsdon 15 B
Garshall Green 31 F
Garsington 16 B
Garstang 42 M
Garston 38 G
Garswood 38 E
Gartachoil 57 H
Gartbeck 55 L
Gartcosh 57 M
Garth 21 M
Garth 22 A
Garth 30 C
Garth 37 A
Garth 80 M
Garthbrengy 22 D
Gartheli 21 B
Garthmyl 30 H
Garthorpe 33 G
Garthorpe 40 E
Gartly 66 C
Gartmore 57 H
Gartnagrenach 56 K
Gartnatra 55 L
Gartness 52 B
Gartness 57 H
Gartocharn 57 G
Garton 41 B
Garton-on-the-Wolds 40 C
Gartymore 77 M
Gartymore 78 K
Garvagh 108 H
Garvaghy 103 F
Garvald 53 C
Garvard 55 E
Garvary 103 D
Garvary Bridge 102 C
Garve 71 G
Garvestone 27 A
Garvock 57 K
Garwaldwaterfoot 53 K
Garway 22 J
Garway Hill 22 J
Gask 67 C
Gass 51 J
Gastard 15 D
Gasthorpe 26 F
Gatcombe 8 G
Gate 39 F
Gatebeck 43 D
Gate Burton 40 L
Gateford 40 K
Gateforth 40 D
Gatehead 51 F
Gate Helmsley 40 B
Gatehouse 48 C
Gatehouse of Fleet 46 F
Gatelawbridge 52 L
Gateley 35 K
Gatenby 44 H
Gateshead 49 H
Gatesheath 38 K
Gateside 51 C
Gateside 58 H
Gateside 59 A
Gateside 66 F
Gathurst 38 E
Gatley 38 J
Gattonside 53 H
Gaufron 22 A
Gaulby 32 M
Gauldry 58 F
Gauls 58 B
Gaunt's Common 7 B
Gaunton's Bank 31 A
Gautby 33 C
Gavinton 54 D
Gawber 39 J
Gawcott 24 M
Gawsworth 38 M
Gawthrop 43 E
Gawthwaite 42 E
Gay Street 9 B
Gaydon 24 D
Gayfield 79 B
Gayhurst 25 G
Gayle 43 E
Gayles 44 A
Gayton 24 F
Gayton 31 F
Gayton 34 M
Gayton 37 J
Gayton le Marsh 34 B
Gayton Thorpe 34 M
Gaywood 34 L
Gazeley 26 H
Gearraidh Bhaird 75 H
Geàrraidh ma Mònadh 68 H
Gearraidh na h-Aibhne 75 D
Geary 69 D
Gedding 26 J
Geddington 25 A
Gedintailor 69 H
Gedney 34 K
Gedney Broadgate 34 K
Gedney Drove End 34 G
Gedney Dyke 34 G
Gedney Hill 34 K
Gee Cross 39 G
Geilston 57 K
Geirinis 68 E
Geisiader 74 F
Geldeston 27 F
Gell 29 B
Gell 37 G
Gellanach 62 J
Gelli 20 E
Gellifor 37 L
Gelligaer 22 K
Gellilydan 29 C
Gellioedd 30 A
Gellyburn 58 B
Gellywen 20 F
Gelston 47 D
Gembling 41 A
Genesis Green 26 H
Genoch Mains 46 A
Gentlesham 31 J
Geocrab 74 M
Georgeham 12 F
Georgia 3 H
Germansweek 5 A
Germoe 3 H
Gerrans 3 J
Gerrards Cross 17 D
Gestingthorpe 26 L
Geuffordd 30 E
Geufron 29 M

Great Britain 1:301,000 157

Gibbieston 60 D
Gibraltar 16 C
Gibraltar 34 E
Gibraltar Swilland 27 K
Gidea Park 18 D
Gidleigh 5 B
Giffirdland 51 B
Gifford 53 C
Giffordtown 58 J
Giggleswick 43 H
Gilberdyke 40 E
Gilchriston 53 B
Gilcrux 47 J
Gildersome 39 B
Gildingwells 40 K
Gileston 13 F
Gilfach Goch 21 M
Gilfachreda 21 A
Gilford 104 H
Gilgarran 47 L
Gill 51 B
Gillamoor 44 J
Gillan 3 M
Gillen 69 D
Gilling East 44 J
Gilling West 44 D
Gillingham 10 C
Gillingham 15 K
Gillingham 27 F
Gill of Garth 79 H
Gillow Heath 31 C
Gills 78 E
Gill's Green 10 F
Gillygooly 103 B
Gillyholme 103 D
Gilmanscleuch 53 G
Gilmerton 53 A
Gilmerton 58 D
Gilmilnscroft 51 F
Gilmonby 43 C
Gilmorton 24 C
Gilsland 48 E
Gilston 17 C
Gilston 53 E
Gilwern 22 H
Gimingham 35 L
Giosla 74 F
Gipping 27 G
Gipsey Bridge 34 D
Girlsta 81 G
Girsby 44 E
Girthon 46 F
Girton 26 G
Girton 33 B
Girvan 51 G
Gisburn 43 L
Gisleham 27 F
Gislingham 27 G
Gissing 27 D
Gittisham 6 A
Gladestry 22 B
Gladsmuir 53 B
Glais 21 L
Glaisdale 45 D
Glame 69 J
Glamis 59 A
Glanaman 21 H
Glan Conwy 37 K
Glancraig 58 H
Glan Denys 21 B
Glandford 35 G
Glandwr 20 F
Glandy Cross 20 E
Glanmule 30 L
Glanrhyd 20 C
Glanton 54 L
Glanton Pyke 54 L
Glanvilles Wootton 7 A
Glan-y-don 37 J
Glan-yr-afon 30 A
Glapthorn 25 B
Glapwell 32 C
Glarryford 108 M
Glas-allt-Shiel 66 H
Glasbury 22 E
Glaschoil 72 K
Glascoed 22 L
Glascoed 30 H
Glascoed 37 H
Glascorrie 66 H
Glascote 32 K
Glasdrum 64 K
Glasdrumman 98 C
Glasdrumman 104 M
Glasdrummond 104 G
Glasdrummond 104 H
Glasfryn 37 K
Glasgow 60 E
Glasinfryn 36 J
Glasnakille 69 L
Glaspwll 29 J
Glassburn 71 K
Glassdrumman 104 K
Glasserton 46 H
Glassford 52 A
Glasshouse Hill 23 G
Glasshouses 44 K
Glasslaw 73 L
Glasslie 58 J
Glasson 47 F
Glassonby 48 H
Glasterlaw 59 B
Glaston 33 K
Glastonbury 14 H
Glastry 105 H
Glatton 25 C
Glazebury 38 H
Glazeley 31 K
Gleadless 39 M
Gleadsmoss 38 M
Gleann Dail bho Dheas 68 H
Gleann dail bho Tuath 68 H
Gleann Tholastaidh 75 F
Gleaston 42 H
Glebe 108 D
Glecknabae 56 L
Gledheather 108 M
Glemsford 26 L
Glen 46 F
Glen 47 A
Glen 103 E
Glenancross 63 C
Glenariff Glen 109 G
Glenariff or Waterfoot 109 G
Glenarm 66 L
Glenarm 109 K
Glenastle 55 L
Glen Auldyn 37 B
Glenavy 104 F
Glenbank House 109 G
Glenbarr 50 B
Glenbeg 63 H
Glenbeg 66 A
Glen Bernisdale 69 E
Glenbervie 67 K
Glenboig 57 M
Glenborrodale 63 H
Glenbranter 56 F
Glenbreck 52 J
Glenbuck 52 D
Glenburn 51 C
Glencaple 47 E
Glencarse 58 E
Glencat 66 J
Glenceitlein 64 L
Glencoe 64 H
Glencrosh 52 K
Glendevon 58 G
Glendoebeg 65 A
Glendoick 58 F
Glenduckie 58 F
Glenee 46 C
Glenegedale 55 L
Glenelg 70 K
Glenfarg 58 H
Glenfern 103 B
Glenfield 32 M
Glenfinnan 64 D
Glenfoot 58 E
Glengarnock 51 C
Glengennet 51 L
Glengolly Geise 78 D
Glengrasco 69 H
Glenhead 108 G
Glenhoul 51 M
Glenhull 107 M
Glenkerry 53 K
Glenkindie 66 F
Glenlair 47 A
Glenlatterach 72 L
Glenlean 56 J
Glenlee 66 H
Glenlichorn 57 F
Glenlivet 66 A
Glenlochar 47 D
Glenluce 46 A
Glenmallan 57 G
Glenmavis 57 M
Glenmaye 37 A
Glenmidge 47 B
Glenmoor 37 A
Glen Mona 37 B
Glenmore 56 B
Glenmore 56 L
Glenmore 69 H
Glen Moriston 64 C
Glenmoy 66 L
Glennasheevar 102 C
Glenochar 52 H
Glenoe 105 A
Glen of Newmill 72 M
Glenogil 66 L
Glen Parva 32 M
Glenprosen Village 66 L
Glenquiech 66 L
Glenrazie 46 B
Glenreasdell Mains 56 K
Glenridding 48 K
Glen Rossal 77 K
Glenrothes 58 J
Glensaugh 66 M
Glen Sluain 56 F
Glenstriven 56 J
Glentham 40 M
Glenton 67 D
Glentress 53 D
Glentrool Village 46 B
Glentruan 37 B
Glentruan 46 L
Glentworth 40 L
Glenuig 63 F
Glenurquhart 71 J
Glenvale 108 M
Glen Village 58 K
Glenville 104 L
Glen Vine 37 B
Glen-yr-afon 30 B
Glespin 52 E
Gletness 81 D
Glewstone 22 J
Glinton 33 M
Glooston 33 K
Glororum 54 H
Glossop 39 G
Gloster Hill 49 C
Gloucester 23 L
Gloup 80 D
Glusburn 39 A
Glutt 78 G
Glympton 24 L
Glyn Ceiriog 30 B
Glynarthen 20 C
Glyncoch 22 K
Glyncorrwg 21 M
Glynde 9 F
Glynde 10 G
Glyndesbourne 10 G
Glyndesbourne 9 F
Glyndyfrdwy 30 B
Glynllan 21 M
Glynn 105 A
Glynneath 21 J
Glynogwr 21 M
Glyntaff 14 A
Glyntaff 22 K
Glyntawe 21 J
Glyntwymyn 29 J
Gnosall 31 E
Gnosall Heath 31 H
Goadby 33 K
Goadby Marwood 33 G
Goadhail 63 L
Goatacre 15 E
Goathill 7 A
Goathland 45 D
Goathurst 14 G
Gobhaig 74 J
Gobowen 30 C
Godalming 17 K
Godington 24 M
Godmanchester 25 F
Godmanstone 7 D
Godmersham 11 D
Godnestone 11 B
Godney 14 H
Godolphin Cross 3 H
Godshill 7 C
Godshill 8 H
Godstone 10 A
Goerge Nympton 13 G
Goff's Oak 17 C
Gogar 58 L
Gogarth 37 G
Goginan 29 L
Golan 36 L
Golant 4 E
Golberdon 4 F
Golcar 39 E
Goldborne 38 H
Goldcliff 14 B
Golden Cross 10 G
Golden Green 10 B
Golden Grove 21 H
Goldenhill 31 C
Golden Pot 16 L
Golden Valley 23 H
Golders Green 17 E
Goldfinch Bottom 16 G
Goldhanger 18 F
Golding 31 G
Goldsborough 44 L
Goldsborough 45 D
Goldsithney 3 H
Goldthorpe 39 J
Goldworthy 12 J
Gollanfield 71 J
Golspie 71 C
Golval 77 F
Gomeldon 15 M
Gomersal 39 E
Gomshall 17 K
Gonalstone 33 D
Gonfirth 80 J
Good Easter 18 A
Gooderstone 26 C
Goodleigh 13 G
Goodmanham 40 C
Goodnestone 11 A
Goodrich 22 J
Goodrington 5 J
Goodwick 20 B
Goodworth Clatford 16 K
Goodyers End 24 B
Goole 40 E
Goonbell 3 F
Goonhavern 3 F
Goose Green 27 D
Gooseham 12 H
Goosey 16 A
Goosnargh 38 B
Goostrey 38 M
Gordieston 47 B
Gordon 53 F
Gordonbush 71 C
Gordonstown 67 A
Gordonstown 73 K
Gorebridge 53 B
Gorefield 34 K
Gorey 9 M
Goring 16 E
Goring-by-Sea 9 E
Gorleston-on-Sea 27 C
Gorrachie 73 K
Gorran Churchtown 4 G
Gorran Haven 4 G
Gorsedd 37 J
Gorseinon 21 K
Gorseness 79 E
Gorsgoch 21 A
Gorslas 21 G
Gorsley 23 G
Gorsley Common 23 G
Gorstan 71 C
Gortaclare 103 C
Gortagilly 104 B
Gortantaoid 55 H
Gortin 107 M
Gortmullan 103 G
Gortnacross 108 G
Gortnageeragh 108 M
Gorton 38 J
Gortreagh 104 A
Gosbeck 27 K
Gosberton 33 J
Gosberton Clough 33 J
Gosfield 18 D
Gosforth 42 B
Gosforth 49 H
Gosheden 107 J
Gosmore 25 L
Gosport 8 E
Gossabrough 80 E
Goswick 54 H
Gotham 32 J
Gotherington 23 H
Gott 81 G
Goudhurst 10 E
Goulceby 34 A
Gourdas 67 A
Gourdon 67 K
Gourock 56 M
Govan 57 L
Goveton 5 H
Govilon 22 H
Gowanhill 73 M
Gowdall 40 D
Gowerton 21 K
Gowkhall 58 K
Goxhill 40 J
Goxhill 41 A
Goxhill Haven 41 B
Grabhair 75 H
Graby 33 J
Gracehill 108 M
Graemeshall 79 H
Graffham 9 A
Grafham 25 E
Grafton 16 A
Grafton 22 F
Grafton 23 A
Grafton 44 L
Grafton Flyford 23 F
Grafton Regis 24 J
Grafton Underwood 25 A
Grafty Green 10 C
Graianrhyd 37 M
Graig 37 G
Graig 37 H
Graig-fechan 37 L
Graig Penllyn 13 C
Grain 18 H
Grainsby 41 K
Grainthorpe 41 L
Graizelound 40 H
Gramasdail 68 E
Grampound 4 G
Granborough 24 M
Granby 33 D
Grandborough 24 E
Grandes Rocques 9 K
Grandtully 65 M
Grange 18 L
Grange 37 J
Grange 47 M
Grange 58 F
Grange Blundel 104 D
Grange Crossroads 72 M
Grange Hill 17 F
Grangemill 32 B
Grange Moor 39 E
Grangemouth 58 K
Grange of Lindores 58 F
Grange-Over-Sands 42 F
Grangepans 58 K
Grangetown 44 C
Grange Villa 49 H
Grangewalls 105 K
Granish 65 C
Gransha 105 B
Gransha 105 D
Gransmoor 41 A
Granstop 20 A
Grantchester 26 G
Grantham 33 H
Grantlodge 67 D
Granton 58 L
Grantown-on-Spey 66 A
Grantshouse 54 A
Granville 104 D
Grappenhall 38 H
Grasby 40 J
Grasmere 42 C
Grasscroft 39 D
Grassendale 38 G
Grassholme 43 C
Grassington 43 M
Grassmoor 32 B
Grassthorpe 33 A
Grateley 15 M
Gratwich 31 F
Graveley 25 F
Graveley 25 L
Gravelly Hill 31 M
Gravels 30 J
Graven 80 F
Graveney 11 A
Gravesend 18 G
Grayingham 40 L
Grayrigg 43 D
Grays 18 G
Grayshott 9 A
Grayson Green 47 L
Graystone 66 H
Grayswood 9 A
Graythorp 44 C
Grazeley 16 H
Greasbrough 39 J
Great Abington 26 G
Great Addington 25 D
Great-Alne 23 F
Great Altcar 38 D
Great Asby 43 B
Great Ashfield 26 J
Great Ayton 44 F
Great Baddow 18 E
Great Bardfield 26 L
Great Barford 25 H
Great Barr 31 M
Great-Barrington 23 M
Great Barrow 38 K
Great Barton 26 J
Great Barugh 45 G
Great Bavington 49 D
Great Bealings 27 K
Great Bedwyn 15 J
Great Bentley 19 A
Great Bircham 34 J
Great Blakenham 27 K
Great Bolas 31 D
Great Bookham 17 K
Great Bosullow 3 G
Great Bourton 24 H
Great Bowden 25 A
Great Bradley 26 H
Great Braxted 18 B
Great Bricett 26 M
Great Brickhill 25 K
Great Bridgeford 31 F
Great Brington 24 F
Great Bromley 19 A
Great Broughton 44 F
Great Broughton 47 H
Great Budworth 38 L
Great Burdon 44 B
Great Burstead 18 D
Great Busby 44 F
Great Canfield 18 A
Great Carlton 34 A
Great Casterton 33 L
Great Chart 11 D
Great Chatwell 31 H
Great Chesterford 26 K
Great Cheverell 15 H
Great Chishill 25 M
Great Clacton 19 D
Great Clifton 47 L
Great-Comberton 23 H
Great Corby 48 H
Great Cornard 26 M
Great Cotes 41 G
Great Cowden 41 B
Great Coxwell 16 A
Great Cransley 25 A
Great Cressingham 26 C
Great Crosby 38 D
Great Cubley 32 D
Great Dalby 33 K
Great Doddington 25 D
Great Dunham 34 M
Great Dunmow 18 A
Great Durnford 15 L
Great Easton 18 A
Great Easton 25 A
Great Eccleston 42 M
Great Edstone 44 J
Great Ellingham 27 A
Great Elm 15 G
Great Eversden 25 J
Great Fencote 44 D
Great Finborough 26 J
Greatford 33 L
Great Fransham 34 M
Great Gaddesden 17 A
Great Gate 32 D
Great Gidding 25 B
Great Givendale 40 B
Great Glemham 27 H
Great Glen 32 M
Great Gonerby 33 E
Great Gransden 25 J
Great Green 26 J
Great Habton 45 K
Great Hale 33 F
Great Hallingbury 18 A
Greatham 8 C
Greatham 9 D
Greatham 44 C
Great Hampden 16 C
Great Harrowden 25 D
Great Harwood 38 C
Great Hatfield 41 B
Great Hautbois 35 L
Great Haywood 31 J
Great Heck 40 D
Great Henny 26 M
Great Hinton 15 H
Great Hockham 26 F
Great Holland 19 A
Great Horkesley 18 C
Great Hormead 25 M
Great Horwood 24 M
Great Houghton 25 D
Great Houghton 39 J
Great Hucklow 39 L
Great Kelk 41 A
Great Kimble 16 C
Great Kingshill 17 A
Great Langton 44 E
Great Leigh 18 B
Great Limber 41 G
Great Linford 25 G
Great Livermere 26 J
Great Longstone 39 L
Great Lumley 49 L
Great Lynn 30 J
Great Malvern 23 E
Great Maplestead 26 L
Great Marton 38 A
Great Massingham 34 M
Great Milton 16 B
Great Missenden-Prestwood 17 A
Great Mitton 38 C
Great Mongeham 11 E
Great Moulton 27 D
Great Munden 17 C
Great Musgrave 43 B
Great Ness 30 F
Great Notley 18 B
Great Oakley 19 A
Great Oakley 25 A
Great Offley 25 L
Great Ormside 43 B
Great Orton 48 G
Great Ouseburn 44 L
Great Oxendon 24 C
Great Palgrave 34 M
Great Parndon 17 C
Great Paxton 25 F
Great Plumstead 27 B
Great Ponton 33 H
Great Preston-Kippax 39 F
Great Raveley 25 F
Great-Rissington 23 M
Great Ryburgh 35 K
Great Ryle 54 K
Great Ryton 31 G
Great Saling 18 B
Great Salkeld 48 L
Great Sampford 26 L
Great Sankey 38 H
Great Shefford 16 D
Great Shelford 26 G
Great Snoring 35 G
Great Somerford 15 B
Great Stainton 44 B
Great Stambridge 18 E
Great Staughton 25 E
Great Steeping 34 D
Great Stonar 11 B
Greatstone-on-Sea 11 G
Great Strickland 48 L
Great Stukeley 25 F
Great Sturton 33 C
Great Sutton 31 K
Great Swinburne 49 D
Great Tew 24 K
Great Tey 18 C
Great Thirkleby 44 H
Great Thurlow 26 H
Great Torrington 12 M
Great Tosson 49 B
Great Totham 18 B
Great Urswick 42 E
Great Wakering 18 J
Great Waldingfield 26 M
Great Walsingham 35 G
Great Waltham 18 B
Great Warley 18 D
Great Washbourne 23 H
Great Welnetham 26 J
Great Wenham 27 K
Great Whittington 49 D
Great Wigborough 18 C
Great Wilbraham 26 G
Great Wishford 15 L
Great-Witcombe 23 L
Great Witley 23 B
Great-Wolford 24 G
Greatworth 24 H
Great Wratting 26 L
Great Wymondley 25 L
Great Wyrley 31 J
Great Wytheford 31 D
Great Yarmouth 27 C
Great Yeldham 26 L
Greeba 37 A
Greenan 51 H
Greenbank 80 D
Greenburn 52 C
Greencastle 98 C
Greencastle 103 C
Greendykes 54 H
Green End 17 C
Greenfield 16 F
Greenfield 25 L
Greenfield 37 J
Greenfield 39 G
Greenfield 64 B
Greenford 17 E
Greengairs 57 M
Greenham 16 G
Green Hammerton 44 L
Greenhaugh 48 C
Green Haughton 31 G
Greenhead 48 F
Greenhill 10 E
Greenhill 11 B
Green Hill 15 B
Greenhill 17 E
Greenhill 39 M
Greenhill 57 M
Greenhite 18 G
Greenholm 52 D
Greenholme 43 A
Greenhouse 53 H
Greenhow 43 M
Greenigoe 79 H
Greenisland 105 A
Greenland 78 E
Greenlands 16 F
Green Lane 23 D
Green Lane 30 H
Greenlaw 53 F
Greenlaw 73 K
Greenloaning 58 G
Greenmeadow 22 L
Greenmount 38 F
Greenmow 81 H
Greenock 57 K
Greenodd 42 F
Green Ore 14 J
Greens Norton 24 J
Greenside 49 H
Greensidehill 54 K
Greenskares 73 L
Greenspot 67 A
Greenstead Green 18 B
Greensted 18 D
Green Street 17 E
Green Street Green 17 M
Green Tye 17 C
Greenway 14 K
Greenwich 17 J
Greeny 79 D
Greet 23 J
Greete 23 B
Greetham 33 L
Greetham 34 A
Greetland 39 D
Greevy 107 L
Gregoy's Lane 104 C
Gregson Lane 38 B
Grèin 68 K
Greinetobht 68 B
Gremista 81 D
Grenaby 37 D
Grendon 25 D
Grendon 32 K
Grendon Common 32 K
Grendon Green 23 D
Grendon Underwood 24 M
Grenofen 5 D
Grenoside 39 J
Greosabhagh 74 M
Gresham 35 H
Greshornish 69 E
Gressenhall 35 K
Gressingham 43 G
Greta Bridge 44 A
Gretna 48 D
Gretna Green 48 D
Gretton 23 J
Gretton 25 A
Gretton 31 K
Grewelthorpe 44 G
Greyabbey 105 E
Greyfriars 17 K
Greygarth 44 G
Greynor 21 H
Greys Green 16 F
Greysouthen 47 L
Greysteel 108 G
Greystoke 48 K
Greystone 43 L
Greystone 59 A
Greystone 104 D
Greywell 16 L
Griais 75 E
Grianan 75 E
Gribthorpe 40 E
Griff 24 B
Griffithstown Sebastapol 22 L
Grimbister 79 H
Grimeford Village 38 E
Grimethorpe 39 J
Griminis 68 E
Griminis 74 K
Grimister 80 E
Grimley 23 E
Grimmet 51 H
Grimness 79 H
Grimoldby 41 L
Grimpo 30 F
Grimsargh 38 B
Grimsby 41 G
Grimscote 24 F
Grimscott 12 L
Grimsthorpe 33 H
Grimston 33 G
Grimston 34 M
Grimston 41 B
Grimstone 6 F
Grindale 45 L
Grindigar 79 H
Grindiscol 81 E
Grindle 31 H
Grindleford 39 L
Grindleton 43 L
Grindley 31 F
Grindley Brook 31 A
Grindlow 39 L
Grindon 32 A
Grindon 54 G
Gringley on the Hill 40 K
Grinsdale 48 D
Grinshill 31 D
Grinton 43 F
Griomsidar 75 E
Grisedale 43 E
Grishipoll 62 J
Gristhorpe 45 H
Griston 26 C
Gritley 79 H
Grittenham 15 E
Grittleton 15 D
Grizebeck 42 E
Grizedale 42 F
Grobister 79 F
Groby 32 M
Groes 21 L
Groes 37 L
Groesfaen 14 A
Groesffordd 36 K
Groeslon 36 L
Grogport 50 C
Gromford 27 L
Gronant 37 H
Groombridge 10 D
Groomsport 105 E
Grosmont 22 J
Grosmont 45 D
Groton 26 M
Grouville 9 M
Grove 7 G
Grove 11 B
Grove 40 K
Grove End 32 K
Grove Hill 104 J
Grovesend 21 K
Grudie 71 C

A B C D E F G H I J K L M N O P Q R S T U V W X Y Z

Gruids 71 B
Gruinart Flats 55 H
Grula 69 H
Gruline 63 L
Grumbla 3 G
Grunasound 81 H
Grundisburgh 27 K
Gruting 81 G
Grutness 81 J
Gualachulain 64 L
Guardbridge 59 D
Guarlford 23 E
Guay 58 B
Gubbergill 42 B
Guestling Green 10 J
Guestwick 35 K
Guestwick Green 35 K
Guide Post 49 F
Guilden Morden 25 J
Guilden Sutton 38 K
Guildford 17 K
Guildtown 58 E
Guilsborough Coton 24 F
Guilsfield 30 H
Guineaford 13 G
Guisborough 44 C
Guiseley-Yeadon 39 B
Guist 35 K
Guiting Power 23 J
Gulladuff 108 L
Gullane 59 K
Gulval 3 H
Gumfreston 20 H
Gumley 24 C
Gunby 33 H
Gunby 40 E
Gundleton 16 L
Gunn 13 G
Gunnerside 43 F
Gunnerton 49 D
Gunness 40 H
Gunnislake 4 F
Gunnista 81 D
Gunthorpe 33 D
Gunthorpe 35 K
Gunwalloe Chyanvounder 3 L
Gunwalloe Fishing Cove 3 L
Gurdworth 32 K
Gurnard 8 E
Gurney Slade 14 J
Gurnos 21 H
Gussage-All Saints 7 B
Gussage-Saint Michael 7 B
Guston 11 E
Gutcher 80 E
Guthram Gowt 33 J
Guthrie 59 A
Guyhirn 26 A
Guyhirn Gull 26 A
Guy's Head 34 K
Guy's Marsh 15 K
Guyzance 49 C
Gwaelod-y-Garth 14 A
Gwaenysgor 37 H
Gwalchmai 36 H
Gwarallt 21 D
Gwardafolog 21 A
Gwaun-Cae-Gurwen 21 H
Gwbert 20 C
Gweek 3 M
Gwehelog 22 L
Gwenddwr 22 D
Gwennap 3 J
Gwenter 3 M
Gwernaffield 37 M
Gwernafon 30 G
Gwernesey 22 L
Gwernogle 21 D
Gwernymynydd 37 M
Gwersyllt 30 C
Gwespyr 37 J
Gwinear 3 H
Gwithian 3 H
Gwndwn 21 D
Gwyddelwern 30 B
Gwyddgrug 21 D
Gwynfryn 29 B
Gwystre 22 A
Gwytherin 37 K
Gyfelia 30 C
Gyffin 37 G

H

Habberley 23 B
Habberley 30 J
Habrough 41 G
Haccombe 5 F
Haceby 33 H
Hacheston 27 H
Hackford 27 A
Hackforth 44 D
Hackland 79 E
Hackleton 25 G
Hackness 45 H
Hackness 79 G
Hackney 17 F
Hackthorn 40 M
Haconby 33 J
Hadden 54 G
Haddenham 16 C
Haddenham 26 D
Haddington 33 B
Haddington 53 B
Haddiscoe 27 F
Haddon 25 B
Hademore 32 G
Hadfield 39 G
Hadham Cross 17 C
Hadham Ford 17 C
Hadleigh 18 H
Hadleigh 26 M
Hadleigh Heath 26 M
Hadley 31 G
Hadley End 32 G
Hadlow 10 B
Hadlow Down 10 D
Hadnall 31 D
Hadstock 26 K
Hadzor 23 E
Haffenden Quartier 10 F
Hafod-Dinbych 37 K
Hafod-y-Green 37 H
Haggbeck 48 E
Haggerston 54 H
Haggrister 80 J
Hagley 22 F
Hagley 23 B
Hagworthingham 34 A
Haighton Green 38 B
Hailes 23 J
Hailsham 10 H
Haimer 78 E
Hainault 17 F
Hainford 35 L
Hainton 41 K
Haisthorpe 45 L
Halam 33 A
Halberton 13 M
Halcro 78 E
Hale 7 C
Hale 16 M
Hale 38 G
Hale Bank 38 G
Halebarns 38 J
Hales 31 E
Halesowen 31 M
Hales Place 11 B
Hales Raveningham 27 F
Halesworth 27 H
Halewood 38 G
Halford 24 G
Halford 30 M
Halfpenny Green 31 L
Halfway 16 G
Halfway 21 E
Halfway 21 F
Halfway House 30 J
Halfway Houses 18 H
Halifax 39 E
Halistra 69 D
Halket 51 C
Halkirk 78 D
Halkyn 37 M
Hall 51 C
Halland 10 G
Hallaton 33 K
Hallatrow 14 J
Hallbankgate 48 E
Hall Cross 38 A
Hall Dunnerdale 42 B
Hallen 14 C
Halliburton 53 F
Hallin 69 D
Halling 10 B
Hallington 41 K
Hallington 49 D
Hall of Clestrain 79 G
Hall of Tankerness 79 H
Hall of the Forest 30 L
Halloughton 33 D
Hallow 23 E
Hallrule 53 L
Halls 53 C
Hallsands 5 L
Hall's Green 25 M
Hallthwaites 42 E
Hall Weston 25 E
Hallworthy 4 B
Hallyne 53 D
Halmer End 31 B
Halmore 23 K
Halmyre Mains 53 D
Halnaker 9 D
Halsall 38 D
Halse 14 K
Halse 24 H
Halsetown 3 H
Halsham 41 B
Halsinger 13 G
Halstead 18 B
Halstead 33 K
Halstock 6 C
Haltham 34 D
Haltoft End 34 D
Halton 17 A
Halton 30 C
Halton 38 H
Halton 42 J
Halton 49 D
Halton Camp 17 A
Halton East 43 M
Halton Gill 43 H
Halton Holegate 34 D
Halton Lea Gate 48 H
Halton West 43 L
Haltwhistle 48 F
Halvergate 27 C
Halvosso 3 J
Halwell 5 H
Halwill 12 M
Halwill Junction 12 M
Ham 11 E
Ham 16 G
Ham 17 H
Ham 23 K
Ham 78 E
Ham 81 C
Hambleden 16 F
Hambledon 17 K
Hambledon 8 C
Hamble-le-Rice 8 E
Hambleton 42 M
Hambridge 14 L
Hambrook 8 F
Hambrook 14 C
Hameringham 34 A
Hamerton 25 E
Hametoun 81 C
Ham Green 14 F
Ham Green 23 C
Hamilton 52 A
Hamiltonsbawn 104 H
Hammersmith 17 H
Hammerwich 31 J
Hammond Street 17 C
Hammoon 7 B
Hamnavoe 80 F
Hamnavoe 80 H
Hamnavoe 81 H
Hampen 23 M
Hamperden End 26 K
Hampnett 23 M
Hampole 40 G
Hampreston 7 E
Hampstead 17 E
Hampstead Norreys 16 E
Hampsthwaite 44 K
Hampton 17 H
Hampton 23 J
Hampton 25 C
Hampton 31 L
Hampton Bishop 22 F
Hampton Heath 31 A
Hampton in Arden 24 A
Hampton Lovett 23 B
Hampton Lucy 24 D
Hampton on the Hill 24 D
Hampton Poyle 24 L
Hamptworth 8 A
Hamsey 9 F
Hamstall Ridware 32 G
Hamstead 8 D
Hamstead 31 M
Hamstead Marshall 16 G
Hamsterley 49 H
Hamsterley 49 K
Hamstreet 11 D
Ham Street 14 M
Hamworthy 7 E
Hanbury 32 D
Hanbury Woodend 32 G
Hanchett Village 26 L
Hanchurch 31 F
Handbridge 38 K
Handcross 9 C
Handforth 38 J
Handley 38 K
Handley 39 M
Handsacre 32 G
Handsworth 31 M
Handsworth 39 M
Hanford 31 F
Hangersley 7 C
Hanging Houghton 24 F
Hanging Langford 15 L
Hanham 14 F
Hankelow 31 B
Hankerton 15 B
Hankham 10 H
Hanley 31 C
Hanley Child 23 A
Hanley-Castle 23 E
Hanley-Swan 23 E
Hanley William 23 A
Hanlith 43 L
Hanmer 31 A
Hannah 34 B
Hannahstown 105 D
Hannington 15 C
Hannington 16 H
Hannington 25 D
Hannington Wick 15 C
Hanslope 25 G
Hanwell 24 H
Hanwood 30 J
Hanworth 17 H
Hanworth 35 L
Happendon 52 E
Happisburgh 35 M
Happisburgh Common 35 M
Hapsford 38 K
Hapton 27 E
Hapton 38 C
Harberton 5 H
Harbertonford 5 H
Harbledown 11 A
Harborne 31 M
Harborough Magna 24 B
Harbottle 49 A
Harbourneford 5 H
Harbridge 7 C
Harbury 24 E
Harby 33 B
Harby 33 G
Harcombe 6 A
Harcourt 3 J
Harcourts Hill 104 H
Harden 39 B
Hardendale 43 A
Hardgate 47 A
Hardgate 67 G
Hardham 9 D
Hardhorn 42 M
Hardingham 27 A
Hardings Wood 31 B
Hardingstone 25 D
Hardington 15 G
Hardington Mandeville 6 C
Hardington Marsh 6 C
Hardley 8 D
Hardley Street 27 C
Hardmead 25 G
Hardraw 43 E
Hardstoft 32 C
Hardway 8 E
Hardway 14 M
Hardwick 24 L
Hardwick 24 M
Hardwick 25 D
Hardwick 25 J
Hardwick 27 E
Hardwick 39 F
Hardwick Village 40 K
Hardwicke 22 E
Hardwicke 23 H
Hardwicke 23 K
Hardy's Green 18 C
Hareby 34 A
Hareden 43 K
Harefield 17 D
Hare Hatch 16 F
Harehope 54 L
Harelaw 52 E
Harescombe 23 L
Haresfield 23 K
Hareshaw 52 D
Hare Street 25 M
Hare Street Ardeley 25 M
Harewood 4 F
Harewood 39 C
Harewood End 22 J
Harford 5 G
Hargate 27 D
Hargrave 25 E
Hargrave 26 H
Hargrave 38 K
Harker 48 D
Harkstead 19 A
Harlaston 32 G
Harlaw 67 A
Harlaxton 33 H
Harle Syke 39 A
Harlech 29 B
Harlesden 17 E
Harleston 5 H
Harleston 26 J
Harleston 27 E
Harlestone 24 F
Harley 31 G
Harlington 25 L
Harlington 39 J
Harlosh 69 G
Harlow Hill 49 E
Harlow-Sawbridgeworth 18 A
Harlthorpe 40 B
Harlton 25 J
Harlyn 4 A
Harman's Cross 7 H
Harmby 44 D
Harmer Green 17 B
Harmer Hill 31 D
Harmondsworth 17 G
Harmston 33 B
Harnham 15 L
Harnhill 15 C
Harold Hill 18 D
Haroldston West 20 D
Haroldswick 80 A
Harold Wood 18 D
Harome 44 J
Harpenden 17 B
Harpford 6 A
Harpham 41 A
Harpham 45 L
Harpley 23 A
Harpley 34 M
Harpole 24 F
Harpsdale 78 D
Harpsden 16 F
Harpswell 40 L
Harpur Hill 39 K
Harpurthey 38 J
Harrapool 69 M
Harrier 81 C
Harrietfield 58 D
Harrietsham 10 C
Harrington 25 A
Harrington 34 A
Harrington 47 D
Harringworth 25 A
Harris 63 A
Harriseahead 31 C
Harriston 47 J
Harrold 25 G
Harrowbarrow 4 F
Harrowden 25 H
Harrow on the Hill 17 E
Harston 33 G
Hart 49 M
Hartburn 49 E
Hartest 26 J
Hartfield 10 D
Hartford 25 F
Hartford 38 L
Hartfordbridge 16 J
Hartforth 44 D
Harthill 31 A
Harthill 39 M
Harthill 52 B
Hartington 32 A
Hartland 12 H
Hartlebury 23 B
Hartlepool 44 C
Hartlepool 49 M
Hartley 10 F
Hartley 18 G
Hartley 43 B
Hartley 49 F
Hartley Wespall 16 H
Hartley Wintney 16 J
Hartlip 10 C
Harton 30 M
Harton 44 M
Harton 49 J
Hartpury 23 G
Hartshill 32 L
Hartshorne 32 H
Hartside 54 K
Hartsop 42 C
Hartwell 24 J
Hartwood 52 B
Harvel 10 B
Harvington 23 B
Harvington 23 F
Harwell 16 E
Harwich 19 A
Harwood 38 F
Harwood 48 M
Harwood 49 A
Harwood Dale 45 H
Harworth-Tickhill 40 K
Hascombe 17 K
Haselbech 24 C
Haselbury Plucknett 6 C
Haseley 24 D
Haselot 23 F
Hasfield 23 H
Hasguard 20 G
Haskayne 38 D
Hasketon 27 L
Hasland 32 B
Haslemere 9 A
Haslingden 38 C
Haslingden Grane 38 C
Haslingfield 25 J
Haslington 31 B
Hass 53 M
Hassall 31 B
Hassall Green 31 B
Hassell Street 11 D
Hassendean 53 H
Hassingham 27 C
Hassocks 9 F
Hassop 39 L
Haster 78 H
Hastigrow 78 E
Hastingleigh 11 D
Hastings 10 J
Hastingswood 18 A
Hastoe 17 A
Haswell 49 M
Haswell Plough 49 M
Hatch 15 K
Hatch 16 L
Hatch 25 H
Hatch Beauchamp 14 K
Hatch End 17 E
Hatching Green 17 B
Hatchmere 38 L
Hatcliffe 41 K
Hatfield 17 B
Hatfield 18 B
Hatfield 23 A
Hatfield 40 G
Hatfield Broad Oak 18 A
Hatfield Woodhouse 40 G
Hatford 16 A
Hatherden 16 G
Hatherleigh 12 M
Hathern 32 J
Hatherop 15 C
Hathersage 39 L
Hatherton 31 B
Hatherton 31 J
Hatley Saint George 25 J
Hatston 79 H
Hatt 4 F
Hattencrook 67 E
Hattingley 16 L
Hatton 17 G
Hatton 24 D
Hatton 30 M
Hatton 33 C
Hatton 38 H
Hatton 67 C
Hatton Heath 38 K
Hatton of Fintray 67 E
Haugham 34 A
Haugh Head 54 K
Haughhead 57 L
Haughley 27 G
Haughley Green 27 G
Haugh of Glass 72 M
Haugh of Urr 47 D
Haughton 30 F
Haughton 31 J
Haughton 31 K
Haughton 33 A
Haughton Green 39 G
Haughton Moss 31 A
Haultwick 17 C
Haunn 63 G
Haunton 32 G
Hauxton 26 G
Havant 8 F
Haven 22 C
Havenstreet 8 H
Haverfordwest/Hwlffordd 20 D
Haverhill 26 L
Haverigg 42 E
Havering-atte-Bower 18 D
Haveringland 35 L
Haversham 25 G
Haverthwaite 42 F
Hawarden 38 K
Hawes 43 E
Hawford 23 E
Hawick 53 L
Hawkchurch 6 B
Hawkedon 26 H
Hawkenbury 10 F
Hawkeridge 15 G
Hawkerland 6 A
Hawkesbury 15 A
Hawkesbury 24 B
Hawkesbury Upton 15 A
Hawkes End 24 A
Hawkhill 54 L
Hawkhurst 10 F
Hawkinge 11 E
Hawkley 8 C
Hawkridge 13 H
Hawkshead 42 C
Hawksland 52 E
Hawkswick 43 J
Hawkswick Cote 43 J
Hawksworth 33 D
Hawksworth 39 B
Hawkwell 18 E
Hawley 18 G
Hawley Fox Lane 16 J
Hawling 23 M
Hawn 79 E
Hawnby 44 J
Haworth 39 A
Hawsker 45 E
Hawstead Whepstead 26 J
Hawthorn 49 M
Hawthorn Hill 16 J
Hawthorn Hill 33 F
Hawthorpe 33 H
Hawton 33 D
Haxby 44 M
Haxey 40 H
Haydock 38 H
Haydon 7 A
Haydon Bridge 48 F
Haydon Wick 15 C
Haye 4 F
Hayes 17 D
Hayes 17 J
Hayfield 39 G
Hay Green 34 L
Hayhillock 59 A
Hayle 3 H
Haynes 25 H
Haynes Church End 25 H
Hay-on-Wye 22 E
Hayscastle 20 D
Hayscastle Cross 20 D
Hay Street 25 M
Hayton 40 B
Hayton 40 K
Hayton 47 J
Hayton 48 H
Haytor Vale 5 E
Haytown 12 M
Haywards Heath 9 C
Haywood Oaks 32 C
Hazelbury Bryan 7 A
Hazeleigh 18 E
Hazel End 18 A
Hazeley 16 J
Hazel Grove 39 G
Hazelrigg 54 H
Hazelside 52 E
Hazelslade 31 J
Hazelton Walls 58 F
Hazelwood 32 E
Hazlemere-Tylers Green 17 D
Hazlerigg 49 E
Hazleton 23 M
Hazlewood 43 M
Heacham 34 H
Head of Muir 57 M
Headcorn 10 F
Headingley 39 C
Headington 16 B
Headlam 44 A
Headless Cross 23 C
Headley 16 G
Headley 16 M
Headley 17 L
Headley Down 16 M
Headley on the Hill 49 H
Headon 40 K
Heads Nook 48 H
Heage 32 B
Healaugh 40 A
Healaugh 43 F
Heald Green 38 J
Heale 13 D
Healey 39 D
Healey 44 G
Healey 49 G
Healeyfield 49 G
Healing 41 G
Heamoor 3 G
Heanor 32 E
Heanton Punchardon 13 G
Heapham 40 L
Hearthstane 52 J
Heasley Mill 13 H
Heaste 69 M
Heath 10 C
Heath 14 A
Heath 32 C
Heath and Reach 25 K
Heathcot 67 H
Heathcote 32 A
Heath Durley 8 B
Heath End 16 H
Heath End 16 M
Heather 32 H
Heatherfield 69 H
Heathfield 5 E
Heathfield 10 H
Heathfield 57 K
Heathfield Allerford 14 K
Heath-Flackwell 16 F
Heathhall 47 B
Heath Hayes 31 J
Heath Hill 31 H
Heath House 14 H
Heath-Iver 17 D
Heathon 31 L
Heatley 38 H
Heaton 31 C
Heaton 42 J
Heaton 49 J
Heaton Moor 38 J
Heaverham 10 B
Heaviley Offerton Green 38 J
Hebburn 49 J
Hebden 43 M
Hebden Brigde 39 A
Hebden Green 38 L
Hebing End 17 C
Hebron 20 F
Hebron 49 B
Heck 47 C
Heckfield 16 H
Heckfordbridge 18 C
Heckington 33 F
Heckmondwike 39 E
Heddington 15 E
Heddish 38 J
Heddle 79 G
Heddon-on-the-Wall 49 H
Hedenham 27 E
Hedge End-Botley 8 B
Hedgehog Bridge 33 F
Hedgerley 17 D
Hedging 14 K
Hednesford 31 J
Hedon 41 B
Hegdon Hill 23 D
Heggerscales 43 B
Heglibister 81 G
Heigh 38 E
Heighington 44 A
Heighington-Washingborough 33 C
Heights of Kinlochewe 70 E
Heilam 77 D
Heiton 53 J
Hele 5 C
Hele 13 D
Hele Barton 13 L
Helen's Bay 105 E
Helensburgh 57 G
Helford 3 M
Helford Passage 3 M
Helhoughton 34 M
Helions Bumpstead 26 L
Hellaby 39 J
Helland 4 E
Hellesdon 27 B
Hellidon 24 E
Hellifield 43 L
Hellingly 10 H
Hellington 27 B
Hellister 81 G
Helmdon 24 H
Helmingham 27 G
Helmsdale 78 K
Helmshore 38 F
Helmsley 44 J
Helperby 44 L
Helperthorpe 45 L
Helpringham 33 J
Helpston 33 L
Helsby 38 K
Helston 3 H
Helstone 4 B
Helton 48 K
Helwith Brigde 43 H
Hemblington 27 B
Hemel Hempstead 17 A
Hemingbrough 40 D
Hemingby 34 A
Hemingford Abbots 25 F
Hemingford Grey 25 F
Hemingstone 27 K
Hemington 15 G
Hemington 25 B
Hemington 33 K
Hemley 27 L
Hemlington 44 C
Hempholme 41 A
Hempnall 27 E
Hempnall Green 27 E
Hempriggs 72 G
Hempstead 26 K
Hempstead 35 G
Hempstead 35 M
Hempsted 23 L
Hempton 24 H
Hempton 34 M
Hemsby 27 C
Hemswell 40 L
Hemswell Cliff 40 L
Hemsworth 39 F
Hemyock 13 M
Henbury 38 M
Henderland 47 B
Hendersyde Park 53 J
Hendon 17 E
Hendon 49 J
Hendra 3 J
Hendre 37 M
Hendre-forgan 21 M
Hendy 21 G
Heneglwys 36 H
Henfield 9 E
Henford 4 C
Hengoed 22 B
Hengoed 22 K
Hengoed 30 C
Hengrave 26 J
Henham 26 K

A B C D E F G H I J K L M N O P Q R S T U V W X Y Z

Huntly 66 C
Huntly 72 M
Huntly 104 H
Huntlywood 53 F
Hunton 10 B
Hunton 44 D
Hunton 79 F
Hunton Bridge 17 B
Hunt's Cross 38 G
Huntsham 13 M
Huntshaw 12 J
Huntspill 14 H
Huntworth 14 G
Hunwick 49 L
Hunworth 35 K
Hurdsfield 38 M
Hurley 16 F
Hurley 32 K
Hurlford 51 F
Hurliness 79 K
Hurn 7 F
Hursley 8 B
Hurst 16 J
Hurst 39 G
Hurst 43 F
Hurstbourne Priors 16 K
Hurstbourne Tarrant 16 G
Hurst Green 10 A
Hurst Green 10 E
Hurst Green 38 C
Hurstpierpoint-Keymer 9 F
Hurworth-on-Tees 44 B
Hury 43 C
Husbands Bosworth 24 C
Husborne Crawley 25 K
Husthwaite 44 H
Hustwood 39 A
Hutcherleigh 5 H
Huthwaite 32 C
Hutoft 34 B
Hutton 18 D
Hutton 38 B
Hutton 48 K
Hutton 54 D
Hutton Bonville 44 E
Hutton Buscel 45 H
Hutton Conyers 44 G
Hutton Cranswick 40 C
Hutton End 48 G
Hutton Henry 49 M
Hutton-le-Hole 44 J
Hutton Magna 44 A
Hutton Roof 43 D
Hutton Roof 48 K
Hutton Rudby 44 E
Huttons Ambo 45 K
Hutton Sessay 44 H
Hutton Wandesley 40 A
Huxley 38 K
Huxter 81 D
Huxter 81 G
Huyton-With-Roby 38 G
Hycemoor 42 E
Hyde 7 C
Hyde 23 L
Hyde 39 G
Hyde Heath 17 A
Hydestile 17 K
Hyndlee 53 L
Hynford Bridge 52 E
Hynish 62 A
Hyssington 30 J
Hythe 8 D
Hythe 11 E
Hythe End 17 G
Hythie 73 M

I

Ibberton 7 A
Ible 32 B
Ibsley 7 C
Ibstock 32 H
Ibstone 16 F
Ibthorpe 16 G
Ibworth 16 H
Ickburgh 26 C
Ickenham 17 D
Ickford 16 B
Ickham 11 B
Ickleford 25 L
Icklesham 10 J
Ickleton 26 K
Icklingham 26 E
Ickwell 25 H
Icomb 23 M
Idbury 24 K
Iddesleigh 13 K
Ide Hill 10 A
Ideford 5 F
Iden 10 J
Iden Green 10 E
Iden Green 10 F
Idlicote 24 G
Idmiston 15 M
Idridgehay 32 B
Idrigill 69 E
Idstone 15 F
Idvies 59 A
Ifield 9 C
Ifold 9 A
Iford 9 F
Ifton Heath 30 C
Ightfield 31 A
Ightham 10 B
Iken 27 L
Ilam 32 A
Ilchester 14 L
Ilderton 54 K
Ilford 17 F
Ilfracombe 13 D
Ilkeston 32 F
Ilketshall Saint Andrew 27 E
Ilketshall Saint Lawrence 27 E
Ilketshall Saint Margaret 27 E
Ilkley 43 M
Illey 23 C
Illington 26 F
Illingworth 39 B
Illogan 3 J
Illston on the Hill 32 M
Ilmer 16 C
Ilmington 24 G
Ilminster 14 L
Ilsington 5 E
Ilston 21 K
Ilton 14 L
Ilton 44 G
Imachar 50 C
Imeroo Cross Roads 103 E
Immingham 41 G
Impington 26 G
Ince 38 G
Ince Blundell 38 D
Ince in Makerfield 38 E
Inchbare 66 M
Inchberry 72 L
Inchcailloch 57 G
Incheril 70 E
Inchfad 57 G
Inchgrundle 66 H
Inchina 70 B
Inchindown 71 E
Inchinnan 57 L
Inchlaggan 64 B
Inchlonaig 57 G
Inchlumpie 71 E
Inchmore 71 K
Inchmurrin 57 G
Inchnadamph 76 J
Inch of Arnhall 66 M
Inchree 64 G
Inchture 58 F
Inchyra 58 E
Indian Queens 4 D
Inerrval 50 A
Ingatestone 18 D
Ingbirchworth 39 H
Ingham 26 J
Ingham 35 M
Ingham 40 L
Ingleborough 34 K
Ingleby 32 H
Ingleby 44 B
Ingleby Arncliffe 44 E
Ingleby Greenhow 44 F
Inglesbatch 15 D
Inglesham 15 C
Ingleton 43 G
Ingleton 44 A
Inglewhile 42 M
Ingliston 58 L
Ingoe 49 D
Ingoldisthorpe 34 H
Ingoldmells 34 B
Ingoldsby 33 H
Ingon 24 D
Ingram 54 K
Ings 42 C
Ingst 14 C
Ingworth 35 L
Inishrush 108 L
Injebreck 37 B
Inkberrow 23 F
Inkhorn 67 B
Inkpen 16 G
Inkstack 78 E
Innellan 56 M
Inner Hope 5 K
Innerhadden 65 K
Innerleithen 53 D
Innerleven 58 J
Innermessan 46 A
Innerwick 54 A
Innerwick 65 K
Innsworth-Churchdown 23 L
Insch 67 A
Insh 65 E
Inshegra 76 F
Inshore 77 A
Inskip 42 M
Instow 12 J
Inver 58 B
Inver 71 F
Inver 78 K
Inverailort 63 F
Inveraldie 59 D
Inverallgin 70 D
Inverallochy 73 M
Inveramsay 67 A
Inveran 71 B
Inveraray 56 F
Inverardran 57 B
Inverarish 69 J
Inverarity 59 A
Inverarnan 57 D
Inverasdale 70 A
Inverbervie 67 K
Inverbrough 71 M
Invercassley 71 B
Inverchoran 70 J
Invercrhnan 64 L
Invercreran 64 K
Inverdruie 65 C
Inverebrie 67 B
Inveresk 53 B
Inverey 66 G
Inverfarigaig 71 K
Invergarry 64 C
Invergelder 66 G
Invergeldie 57 C
Invergordon 71 E
Invergowie 58 F
Inverguseran 63 C
Inverharroch 66 A
Inverhervie 57 A
Inverinan 56 C
Inverinate 70 K
Inverkeilor 59 B
Inverkeithing-Dalgety Bay 58 L
Inverkeithny 73 K
Inverkip 56 M
Inverkirkaig 76 H
Inverlael 70 C
Inverlaidnan 65 C
Inverlauren 57 G
Inverlochlarig 57 E
Inverlochy 57 A
Invermoidart 63 F
Invermoriston 65 A
Invernaver 77 E
Inverneill 56 H
Inverness 71 L
Invernoaden 56 F
Inverquharity 66 L
Inverquhomery 67 C
Inverroy 64 F
Invershiel 70 K
Invershin 71 B
Inversnaid 57 D
Inverugie 67 C
Inveruglas 57 D
Inverurie 67 D
Invervar 65 K
Inverythan 67 A
Inwardleigh 5 A
Inworth 18 C
Iochdar 68 E
Iping 9 A
Ipplepen 5 E
Ipsden 16 E
Ipstones 32 A
Ipswich 27 K
Irby 37 J
Irby in the Marsh 34 E
Irby Upon Humber 41 G
Irchester 25 D
Ireby 43 G
Ireby 47 J
Ireland 79 G
Ireland 81 H
Ireleth 42 E
Ireshopeburn 48 M
Irlam 38 J
Irnham 33 H
Iron Acton 15 A
Ironbridge 31 G
Iron Cross 23 F
Ironmacannie 47 A
Ironside 73 L
Ironville 32 C
Irstead 35 M
Irthington 48 E
Irthlingborough 25 D
Irton 45 H
Irvine 51 E
Irvinestown 103 A
Isauld 78 D
Isbister 79 D
Isbister 79 H
Isbister 80 E
Isbister 80 F
Isfield 9 F
Isfield 10 G
Isham 25 D
Isle Abbotts 14 L
Isle Brewers 14 L
Isle of Dogs 17 J
Isle of Man/Ronaldsway 37 D
Isle of Whithorn 46 H
Isleham 26 E
Isleham Marina 26 E
Isleornsay or Eilean Iarmain 69 M
Islesburgh 80 J
Islesteps 47 B
Isleworth 17 H
Isley Walton 32 H
Islibhig 74 F
Islington 17 E
Islip 24 L
Islip 25 B
Istead Rise 18 G
Isycoed 31 A
Itchen Abbas 16 K
Itchen Stoke 16 K
Itchingfield 9 B
Itchington 15 A
Itteringham 35 L
Itton 5 B
Itton Common 22 M
Ivegill 48 G
Ivelet 43 F
Iver-Heath 17 D
Iveston 49 H
Ivinghoe Aston 25 K
Ivinghoe-Pitstone 17 A
Ivington 22 C
Ivington Green 22 C
Ivy Todd 26 C
Ivybridge 5 G
Ivychurch 11 G
Iwade 10 C
Iwerne Courtney or Shroton 7 B
Iwerne Minster 7 B
Ixworth 26 J
Ixworth Thorpe 26 F

J

Jack Hill 44 K
Jackstown 67 A
Jackton 52 A
Jacobs Well 17 K
Jacobstow 12 L
Jacobstowe 13 K
Jameston 20 H
Jamestown 53 K
Jamestown 57 K
Jamestown 71 G
Janefield 71 H
Jarrow 49 J
Jarvis Brook 10 D
Jawcraig 57 M
Jayes Park 17 K
Jaywick 19 D
Jedburgh 53 J
Jeffreyston 20 H
Jemimaville 71 H
Jerbourg 9 K
Jerrettspass 104 L
Jersay 52 B
Jesmond 49 H
Jevington 10 K
Jewell's Marhamchurch Cross 12 L
Jockey End 17 A
Jodrell Bank 38 M
Johnby 48 K
John o'Gaunt 33 K
John o'Groats 78 F
Johnshaven 67 K
Johnston 20 G
Johnstone 57 K
Johnstonebridge 52 M
Jonesborough 104 L
Jordans 17 D
Jordanston 20 A
Jump 39 J
Juniper 49 G
Juniper Green 53 A
Juniper Hill 24 H
Jurby East 37 B
Jurby West 37 B

K

Kaber 43 B
Kaimes 53 A
Kames 52 D
Kames 56 L
Katesbridge 104 J
Kea 3 J
Keadby 40 H
Keady 104 G
Keal Cotes 34 D
Kearsley 38 F
Kearstwick 43 D
Kearton 43 F
Kearvaig 76 C
Keasden 43 H
Keddington 41 K
Kedington 26 L
Kedleston 32 E
Keelby 41 G
Keele 31 B
Keeley Green 25 H
Keeres Green 18 A
Keeston 20 D
Keevil 15 H
Kegworth 32 J
Kehelland 3 H
Keig 66 F
Keighley 39 B
Keilarsbrae 58 G
Keilhill 73 K
Keillmore 56 G
Keillor 58 C
Keillour 58 D
Keills 55 H
Keinton Mandeville 14 L
Keir Mill 52 L
Keisby 33 H
Keiss 78 E
Keith 72 M
Keithkock 66 M
Kelbrook 43 L
Kelby 33 E
Keld 43 A
Keld 43 F
Keldholme 44 J
Kelfield 40 A
Kelham 33 D
Kellan 63 L
Kellas 59 D
Kellas 72 L
Kellaton 5 L
Kelleth 43 B
Kelleythorpe 40 C
Kelling 35 G
Kellingley 40 D
Kellington 40 D
Kelloe 49 M
Kelly 4 C
Kelly Bray 4 F
Kelmarsh 24 C
Kelmscott 15 C
Kelsale 27 H
Kelsall 38 K
Kelshall 25 M
Kelsick 47 J
Kelso 53 J
Kelstedge 32 B
Kelstern 41 K
Kelston 15 D
Keltneyburn 65 L
Kelton 43 C
Kelton 47 B
Kelty 58 H
Kelvedon 18 B
Kelvedon Hatch 18 D
Kemacott 13 D
Kemback 58 J
Kemberton 31 H
Kemble 15 B
Kemerton 23 H
Kemeys Commander 22 L
Kemnay 67 D
Kempley 23 G
Kempley Green 23 G
Kempsey 23 E
Kempsford 15 C
Kempston 25 H
Kempston Hardwick 25 H
Kempton 30 M
Kemp Town 9 F
Kemsley 11 A
Kenardington 11 D
Kencott 16 A
Kendal 43 D
Kendram 69 B
Kenfig 13 B
Kenfig Hill 13 B
Kenilworth 24 A
Kenknock 57 B
Kenley 17 L
Kenley 31 G
Kenmore 58 A
Kenmore 70 D
Kenn 5 F
Kenn 14 E
Kennacraig 56 K
Kennerleigh 13 L
Kennet 58 G
Kennethmont 66 C
Kennett 26 H
Kennford 5 C
Kenninghall 27 D
Kennington 11 D
Kennington 16 B
Kennoway 58 J
Kenny Hill 26 E
Kennythorpe 45 K
Kenovay 62 A
Kensaleyre 69 E
Kensington 17 H
Kensworth 17 A
Kentallen 64 G
Kentchurch 22 J
Kentford 26 H
Kentisbeare 6 A
Kentisbury 13 D
Kentisbury Ford 13 D
Kentmere 43 A
Kenton 5 F
Kenton 17 E
Kenton 27 G
Kentra 63 F
Kents Bank 42 F
Kentsboro 15 M
Kent's Green 23 G
Kent's Oak 8 A
Kenwick 30 F
Kenwyn 3 J
Kenyon 38 H
Keoldale 77 A
Keppanach Onlch 64 G
Keppoch 70 K
Keprigan 50 E
Kepwick 44 H
Keresley 24 A
Kerne Bridge 22 J
Kerridge 39 K
Kerris 3 G
Kerry 30 L
Kerrycroy 56 M
Kerrymenoch 56 M
Kerrysdale 70 A
Kerry's Gate 22 J
Kersall 33 A
Kersey 26 M
Kershopefoot 48 B
Kersoe 23 J
Kerswell 6 A
Kerswell Green 23 E
Kesgrave 27 K
Kesh 103 A
Kessingland 27 F
Kestle Mill 4 D
Keston 17 J
Keswick 27 B
Keswick 35 M
Keswick 47 M
Kettering 25 A
Ketterinham East 27 B
Kettins 58 C
Kettlebaston 26 M
Kettlebridge 58 J
Kettleburgh 27 H
Kettlehill 58 J
Kettleholm 47 C
Kettleness 45 D
Kettleshulme 39 K
Kettlesing Bottom 44 K
Kettlestone 35 K
Kettlethorpe 33 B
Kettletoft 79 F
Kettlewell 43 J
Ketton 33 L
Kew 17 H
Kewstoke 14 E
Kexbrough 39 E
Kexby 40 B
Kexby 40 L
Key Green Timbersbrook 38 M
Keycol 10 C
Keyham 32 M
Keyhaven 8 D
Keyingham 41 B
Keynsham 14 F
Keysoe 25 E
Keysoe Row 25 E
Keyston 25 E
Keyworth 32 J
Kibblesworth 49 H
Kibworth Beauchamp 24 C
Kibworth Harcourt 32 M
Kidbrooke 17 J
Kiddal Lane End 39 C
Kiddemore Green 31 H
Kidderminster 23 B
Kiddington 24 K
Kidlington 24 L
Kidmore End 16 F
Kidsgrove 31 C
Kidstones 43 J
Kidwelly 21 G
Kiel Crofts 64 K
Kielder 48 C
Kikburn 40 C
Kilbarchan 57 K
Kilbeg 63 C
Kilberry 56 K
Kilbirnie 51 B
Kilbride 69 M
Kilbride 56 B
Kilbride 56 L
Kilburn 32 E
Kilburn 44 H
Kilby 32 M
Kilchamaig 56 K
Kilchattan 55 E
Kilchattan Bay 51 B
Kilchenzie 50 E
Kilcheran 63 M
Kilchiaran 55 K
Kilchoan 63 H
Kilchoman 55 G
Kilchrenan 56 C
Kilclief 105 L
Kilconquhar 59 G
Kilcoo 104 M
Kilcot 23 G
Kilcoy 71 H
Kilcreggan 56 J
Kilcross 104 C
Kildale 44 F
Kildalloig 50 F
Kildary 71 F
Kildavanan 56 L
Kildonan 51 D
Kildonnan 63 E
Kildowney 108 M
Kildress 104 A
Kildrummy 66 F
Kildwick 43 M
Kilfinan 56 H
Kilfinnan 64 F
Kilgetty 20 H
Kilgwrrwg Common 22 M
Kilham 45 L
Kilham 54 G
Kilkeel 98 C
Kilkenneth 62 A
Kilkerran 51 H
Kilkhampton 12 L
Kilkinamurry 104 J
Killadeas 103 D
Killagan Bridge 108 J
Killaloo 107 J
Killamarsh 39 M
Killarbran 103 E
Killard 105 L
Killay 21 K
Killbeg 63 L
Killead Corners 104 C
Killean 50 B
Killearn 57 H
Killeen 104 E
Killeen 104 G
Killeen 107 L
Killellan Park 50 E
Killen 71 H
Killen 107 L
Killens 103 F
Killerby 44 A
Killeter 107 K
Killichonan 65 K
Killiechonate 64 F
Killiechronan 63 L
Killiecrankie 65 M
Killiemor 63 L
Killilan 70 K
Killimster 78 H
Killin 57 B
Killinallan 55 H
Killinchy 105 H
Killinghall 44 K
Killington 43 D
Killochyett 53 E
Killocraw 50 B
Killough 105 K
Killowen 98 B
Killycanavan 104 B
Killycarn 109 K
Killycolpy 104 B
Killyfaddy 103 F
Killyflugh 108 M
Killygony 105 G
Killykergan 108 H
Killylane Upper 108 G
Killylea 104 G
Killyleagh 105 H
Killymore Bridge 107 M
Killymuck 104 B
Kilmacolm 57 K
Kilmacrew 104 J
Kilmahog 57 E
Kilmahumaig 56 D
Kilmalieu 64 G
Kilmaluag 69 B
Kilmany 58 F
Kilmarie 69 L
Kilmarnock 51 F
Kilmartin 56 E
Kilmaurs 51 C
Kilmelford 56 B
Kilmeny 55 H
Kilmersdon 14 J
Kilmeston 8 B
Kilmichael 50 E
Kilmichael Glassary 56 E
Kilmichael of Inverlussa 56 G
Kilmington 6 B
Kilmington 15 K
Kilmington Common 15 K
Kilmoluaig 62 A
Kilmonivaig 64 E
Kilmorack 71 G
Kilmore 56 B
Kilmore 63 C
Kilmore 104 E
Kilmore 105 G
Kilmore 109 G
Kilmory 51 D
Kilmory 56 G
Kilmory 63 A
Kilmory 63 E
Kilmuir 69 B
Kilmuir 69 D
Kilmuir 71 F
Kilmuir 71 H
Kilmun 56 J
Kiln Pit Hill 49 G
Kilnaslee 104 D
Kilnave 55 H
Kilncadzow 52 B
Kilndown 10 E
Kilnhurst 39 J
Kilninian 63 G
Kilninver 56 B
Kilnsea 41 H
Kilnsey 43 J
Kilnwick 40 C
Kiloran 55 E
Kilpatrick 50 F
Kilpatrick 63 M
Kilpeck 22 J
Kilphedir 77 M
Kilpin 40 E
Kilraghts 108 J
Kilrea 108 L
Kilrenny 59 G
Kilsally 104 B
Kilsby 24 F
Kilskeery 103 E
Kilspindie 58 F
Kilsyth 57 M
Kiltarlilty 71 K
Kilton 14 G
Kiltyrie 57 C
Kilundine 63 H
Kilvaxter 69 B
Kilve 14 G
Kilvington 33 D
Kilwaughter 105 A
Kilwinning 51 B
Kimberley 27 A
Kimberley 32 F
Kimblesworth 49 L
Kimble Wick 16 C
Kimbolton 22 C
Kimbolton 25 E
Kimcote 24 C
Kimmeridge 7 H
Kimmerston 54 G
Kimpton 15 M
Kimpton 17 B
Kinawley 103 G
Kinbrace 77 J
Kinbuck 57 J
Kincaple 59 D
Kincardine 58 K
Kincardine 71 B
Kincardine O'Neil 66 J
Kinclaven 58 B
Kincorth 67 H
Kincraig 65 F
Kincraigie 58 B
Kindallachan 58 B
Kinerras 71 K
Kineton 23 J
Kineton 24 D
Kinfauns 58 E
King Edward 73 K
Kingarth 56 M
Kingcoed 22 M
Kingerby 40 M
Kingham 24 K
Kingholm Quay 47 B
Kinghorn 58 L
Kinglassie 58 H
Kingoodie 58 F
Kings 17 F
King's Acre 22 F
Kingsand 4 J
Kingsbarns 59 G
Kingsbridge 5 H
Kingsbridge 13 J
King's Bromley 32 G
Kingsburgh 69 E

Great Britain 1:301,000 161

Kingsbury 17 E
Kingsbury 32 K
Kingsbury Episcopi 14 L
King's Caple 22 J
Kingscavil 58 K
Kingsclere 16 H
King's Cliffe 25 B
Kings Clipstone 32 C
Kingscote 15 A
Kingscott 13 K
King's Coughton 23 F
Kingscross 51 D
Kingsdon 14 L
Kingsdown 11 F
Kingseat 58 L
Kingsey 16 C
Kingsfold 9 B
Kingsford 31 L
Kingsford 51 C
Kingsford 66 F
King's Green 23 G
Kingshall Street 26 J
King's Heath 23 C
Kings Hill 10 B
Kingshouse 57 E
Kingside Hill 47 J
Kingskerswell 5 F
Kingskettle 58 J
Kingsland 22 C
Kings Langley 17 A
Kingsley 16 M
Kingsley 31 C
Kingsley 38 L
Kingsley Green 9 A
King's Lynn 34 L
King's Meaburn 48 L
Kingsmill 104 B
King's Mills 9 K
Kings Muir 53 D
Kingsmuir 59 A
Kingsnorth 11 D
Kingsnorth 18 H
King's Norton 32 M
King's Norton 23 C
King's Nympton 13 K
Kings Ripton 25 F
King's Somborne 16 K
King's Stag 7 A
King's Sutton 24 H
King Sterndale 39 K
Kingstanding 31 M
Kingsteignton 5 F
Kingsteps 71 J
King's Thorn 22 J
Kingsthorpe 24 F
Kingston 5 G
Kingston 7 A
Kingston 7 F
Kingston 7 H
Kingston 8 G
Kingston 25 J
Kingston 59 K
Kingston 72 J
Kingston Blount 16 C
Kingston by Sea 9 E
Kingston Deverill 15 K
Kingstone 14 L
Kingstone 22 F
Kingstone 32 D
Kingston Gorse 9 E
Kingston Lisle 16 D
Kingston near Lewes 9 F
Kingston on Soar 32 J
Kingston Saint Mary 14 K
Kingston Seymour 14 E
Kingston upon Hull 41 D
Kingston upon Thames 17 H
Kingstown 48 D
King's Walden 25 L
Kingswear 5 J
Kingswell 51 C
Kingswells 67 E
Kingswinford 31 L
Kingswood 10 C
Kingswood 14 F
Kingswood 15 A
Kingswood 17 L
Kingswood 22 B
Kingswood 24 A
Kingswood 24 M
Kingswood 30 H
Kings Worthy 16 K
Kingthorpe 33 C
Kington 22 B
Kington 23 F
Kington Langley 15 E
Kington Magna 15 K
Kington Saint Michael 15 E
Kingussie 65 E
Kingweston 14 L
Kinharrachie 67 B
Kinkell Bridge 58 D
Kinknockie 67 C
Kinlet 31 L
Kinloch 58 B
Kinloch 58 C
Kinloch 58 J
Kinloch 63 B
Kinloch 69 M
Kinloch 76 J
Kinlochard 57 E
Kinlochbervie 76 F
Kinlocheil 64 D
Kinlochewe 70 E
Kinloch Hourn 64 A
Kinloch Laggan 65 D
Kinlochleven 64 H
Kinlochmoidart 63 F
Kinlochmore 64 H
Kinloch Rannoch 65 K
Kinlochspelve 56 A
Kinloss 72 G
Kinmel Bay 37 H
Kinmuck 67 D
Kinmundy 67 E
Kinnadie 67 B
Kinnaird 58 F
Kinneff 67 K
Kinnelhead 52 M
Kinnell 59 B
Kinnerley 30 F
Kinnersley 22 E
Kinnersley 23 E
Kinnerton 22 B
Kinnesswood 58 H
Kinninvie 44 A
Kinnordy 59 A
Kinoulton 33 G
Kinross 58 H
Kinrossie 58 E
Kinsbourne Green 17 B
Kinsey Heath 31 B
Kinsham 22 C
Kinsley 39 F
Kinson 7 F
Kintbury 16 G
Kintessack 72 G
Kintillo 58 E
Kintocher 66 F
Kinton 22 C
Kinton 30 F
Kinton 30 M
Kintore 67 D
Kintour 55 L
Kintra 55 L
Kintra 63 K
Kintraw 56 E
Kinuachdracht 56 D
Kinveachy 65 C
Kinver 31 L
Kippen 57 J
Kippford 47 D
Kirbuster 79 F
Kirby Bedon 27 B
Kirby Bellars 33 G
Kirby Cane 27 E
Kirby Cross 19 A
Kirby Grindalythe 45 K
Kirby Hill 44 D
Kirby Hill 44 L
Kirby Knowle 44 H
Kirby-le-Soken 19 A
Kirby Misperton 45 G
Kirby Muxloe 32 M
Kirby Row 27 E
Kirby Sigston 44 E
Kirby Underdale 45 K
Kirby Wharfe 40 A
Kirby Wiske 44 H
Kircubbin 105 H
Kirdford 9 A
Kirk 78 E
Kirkabister 81 E
Kirkandrews 46 F
Kirkandrews-on-Eden 48 D
Kirkbampton 48 D
Kirkbean 47 E
Kirkbister 79 G
Kirk Bramwith 40 G
Kirkbride 47 F
Kirkbuddo 59 A
Kirkburn 53 D
Kirkburton 39 E
Kirkbuster 79 D
Kirkby 38 D
Kirkby 40 M
Kirkby 44 F
Kirkby Fleetham 44 D
Kirkby Green 33 F
Kirkby in Ashfield 32 C
Kirkby-in-Furness 42 E
Kirkby la Thorpe 33 F
Kirkby Lonsdale 43 G
Kirkby Malham 43 L
Kirkby Mallory 32 L
Kirkby Malzeard 44 G
Kirkby Mills 44 J
Kirkbymoorside 44 J
Kirkby on Bain 33 F
Kirkby Stephen 43 B
Kirkby Thore 48 L
Kirkby Underwood 33 H
Kirkcaldy 58 L
Kirkcambeck 48 E
Kirkcarswell 47 D
Kirkcolm 46 A
Kirkconnell 47 E
Kirkconnel 52 G
Kirkcowan 46 B
Kirkcudbright 47 D
Kirk Deighton 39 C
Kirk Ella 40 F
Kirkfieldbank 52 E
Kirkgunzeon 47 E
Kirkham 38 A
Kirkham 44 M
Kirkhamgate 39 F
Kirk Hammerton 44 L
Kirkharle 49 D
Kirkheaton 39 E
Kirkheaton 49 D
Kirkhill 59 B
Kirkhill 66 A
Kirkhill 71 H
Kirkhill Pendicle 67 B
Kirkhills 108 J
Kirkhope 53 G
Kirkhouse 53 G
Kirkibost 69 L
Kirkinch 58 C
Kirkinner 46 E
Kirkintilloch-Lenzie 57 L
Kirk Ireton 32 B
Kirkistown 105 H
Kirkky Overblow 39 C
Kirkland 47 L
Kirkland 48 L
Kirkland 52 G
Kirkland 52 K
Kirklands 59 G
Kirk Langley 32 E
Kirkleatham 44 C
Kirklevington 44 E
Kirkley 27 F
Kirklington 33 A
Kirklington 44 H
Kirklinton 48 D
Kirkliston 58 L
Kirkmaiden 46 D
Kirk Merrington 49 L
Kirk Michael 37 B
Kirkmichael 51 H
Kirkmichael 65 M
Kirkmichael Main 47 B
Kirkmuirhill 52 E
Kirknewton 52 C
Kirknewton 54 G
Kirkney 66 C
Kirk of Shotts 52 B
Kirkon of Largo or Upper Largo 58 J
Kirkoswald 48 H
Kirkoswald 51 H
Kirkpatrick Durham 47 A
Kirkpatrick-Fleming 48 D
Kirk Sandall 40 G
Kirksanton 42 E
Kirk Smeaton 40 D
Kirkstile 66 D
Kirkstyle 78 F
Kirkton 47 B
Kirkton 52 H
Kirkton 53 L
Kirkton 57 H
Kirkton 58 D
Kirkton 58 F
Kirkton 59 A
Kirkton 59 B
Kirkton 67 A
Kirkton 70 G
Kirkton 70 K
Kirkton 71 C
Kirkton 71 J
Kirkton 73 K
Kirkton 73 M
Kirkton Manor 53 D
Kirkton of Rayne 67 A
Kirkton of Airlie 58 C
Kirkton of Auchterhouse 58 C
Kirkton of Auchterless 67 A
Kirkton of Barevan 71 M
Kirkton of Bourtie 67 A
Kirkton of Collace 58 F
Kirkton of Culsalmond 67 A
Kirkton of Durris 67 G
Kirkton of Glenbuchat 66 E
Kirkton of Glenisla 66 K
Kirkton of Kingoldrum 58 C
Kirkton of Lethendy 58 B
Kirkton of Logie Buchan 67 B
Kirkton of Maryculter 67 G
Kirkton of Menmuir 66 M
Kirkton of Monikie 59 D
Kirkton of Skene 67 D
Kirkton of Tough 66 F
Kirktown 73 M
Kirktown of Alvah 73 K
Kirktown of Deskford 72 J
Kirktown of Fetteresso 67 G
Kirkwall 79 H
Kirkwhelpington 49 D
Kirk Yetholm 54 G
Kirmington 40 J
Kirminnoch 46 G
Kirmond le Mire 41 K
Kirn 56 J
Kirriemuir 59 A
Kirstead Green 27 E
Kirtlebridge 47 F
Kirtling Green 26 H
Kirtlington 24 L
Kirtomy 77 F
Kirton 27 L
Kirton 33 A
Kirton 34 G
Kirton End 34 G
Kirton Holme 33 J
Kirton in Lindsey 40 M
Kislingbury 24 F
Kites Hardwick 24 E
Kittle 21 K
Kittybrewster 67 E
Kitwood 16 L
Kiveton Park 39 M
Knaith 40 L
Knaphill 17 G
Knapp 14 K
Knapp 58 F
Knapton 35 L
Knapton 40 A
Knapton Green 22 F
Knapwell 25 J
Knaresborough-Harrogate 44 K
Knarsdale 48 J
Knaven 67 B
Knayton 44 H
Knebworth 17 B
Knedlington 40 E
Kneesall 33 A
Kneeton 33 D
Knelston 21 K
Knettishall 26 F
Knightacott 13 G
Knightcote 24 E
Knighton 5 G
Knighton 22 B
Knighton 31 B
Knighton 31 E
Knighton 32 M
Knightwick 23 D
Knill 22 B
Knipton 33 G
Knitsley 49 H
Kniveton 32 A
Knochenkelly 51 D
Knock 48 L
Knock 72 M
Knock 63 L
Knockaholet 108 J
Knockally 78 K
Knockan 76 M
Knockandhu 66 A
Knockando 72 L
Knockanully 108 M
Knockbain 71 H
Knockbreck 71 F
Knockbrex 46 F
Knockcloghrim 108 L
Knockdolian 51 K
Knockdow 56 M
Knockdown 15 A
Knockenstob 52 G
Knockentiber 51 F
Knockholt 10 A
Knockholt Pound 10 A
Knockin 30 F
Knocklearn 47 A
Knockmelder 105 H
Knockmoyle 103 C
Knocknaha 50 E
Knocknain 46 G
Knocknalling 51 M
Knockrome 55 J
Knocks 103 H
Knocksharry 37 A
Knockshinnoch 51 J
Knodishall 27 H
Knolls Green 38 M
Knolton 30 C
Knook 15 H
Knossington 33 K
Knott End-on-Sea 42 M
Knotting 25 E
Knotting Green 25 E
Knottingley 40 D
Knotty Green 17 D
Knowbury 23 A
Knowe 46 B
Knowehead 51 M
Knowesgate 49 D
Knoweside 51 H
Knowes of Elrick 73 K
Knowetownhead 53 L
Knowhead 51 F
Knowhead 73 L
Knowle 5 B
Knowle 6 D
Knowle 13 G
Knowle 23 A
Knowle 14 F
Knowle-Bentley Heath 24 A
Knowle Green 38 C
Knowle Village 8 E
Knowl Hill 16 F
Knowlton 11 E
Knowl Wall 31 F
Knowsley 38 D
Knowstone 13 L
Knucklas 30 L
Knutsford 38 M
Knypersley 31 C
Küggar 3 M
Kyleakin 69 M
Kyle of Lochalsh 70 K
Kylerhea 70 K
Kylesku 76 J
Kylestrome 76 J
Kynnersley 31 H
Kyre 23 A

L

Labby 108 K
Labost 75 A
Lacasaidh 75 G
Lacasdail 75 E
Laceby 41 G
Lacey Green 16 C
Lach Dennis 38 L
Lache 38 K
Lack 103 B
Lackford 26 H
Lackhampstead 16 D
Lacock 15 E
Ladbroke 24 E
Laddingford 10 B
Lade Bank 34 D
Ladock 4 D
Lady 79 F
Ladybank 51 H
Ladybank 58 J
Ladybrook 105 D
Ladycross 4 C
Ladykirk 54 D
Ladysford 73 L
Lady's Green 26 H
Laga 63 H
Lagavara 108 F
Lagavulin 55 L
Lagg 51 D
Lagg 51 H
Lagg 55 J
Laggan 55 L
Laggan 64 F
Laggan 65 D
Lagganulva 63 K
Laghey Corner 104 D
Laghtyowen Bridge 104 A
Lagrae 52 G
Laide 70 B
Laindon 18 D
Lair 66 K
Lair 70 H
Lairg 77 K
Lairgmore 71 L
Laithhes 48 K
Lake 13 G
Lake 15 L
Lakenham 27 B
Lakenheath 26 E
Lakes End 26 A
Lakeside 42 F
Laleham 17 G
Laleston 13 C
Lalnwinio 20 F
Lamancha 53 D
Lamarsh 26 M
Lamas 35 L
Lamb Corner 18 C
Lambden 53 F
Lambeg 104 F
Lamberhurst 10 E
Lamberton 54 E
Lambeth 17 J
Lambfell Moar 37 A
Lambley 32 F
Lambley 48 J
Lambourn 16 D
Lambourn Woodlands 16 D
Lambourne End 17 F
Lambs Green 9 B
Lambston 20 D
Lamerton 5 D
Lamesley 49 H
Lamington 52 F
Lamington 71 F
Lamlash 51 D
Lamloch 51 M
Lamonby 48 K
Lamorna 3 G
Lamorran 4 G
Lampeter 21 B
Lampeter Velfrey 20 H
Lamphey 20 H
Lamplugh 47 L
Lamport 25 D
Lamyatt 14 M
Lana 4 C
Lana 12 L
Lanark 52 E
Lancaster 42 J
Lanchester 49 L
Lancing 9 E
L'Ancresse 9 K
Landbeach 26 G
Landcross 12 J
Landerberry 67 D
Landford 8 A
Landhallow 78 K
Landimore 21 K
Landkey 13 G
Landore 21 L
Landrake 4 F
Landscove 5 E
Landshipping 20 H
Landulph 4 F
Landwade 26 H
Landywood 31 J
Laneast 4 C
Lane End 5 A
Lane End 10 A
Lane End 16 F
Lane End 18 G
Lane End 42 B
Lane Green 31 J
Laneham 33 A
Lane Head 39 E
Lanehead 48 C
Lane Head West 44 A
Lanercost 48 E
Laneshaw Brigde 39 A
Langar 33 G
Langbank 57 K
Langbar 43 M
Langcliffe 43 H
Langdale 42 C
Langdale End 45 H
Langdon Beck 48 M
Langdon Cross 4 C
Langdon Hills 18 G
Langdyke 58 J
Langenhoe 18 C
Langford 6 A
Langford 15 C
Langford 18 E
Langford 25 L
Langford 33 A
Langford Budville 13 M
Langham 18 C
Langham 26 J
Langham 33 K
Langham 35 G
Langho 38 C
Langholm 48 A
Langhouse 56 M
Langlee 53 H
Langleeford 54 K
Langley 8 C
Langley 8 D
Langley 10 C
Langley 17 D
Langley 24 D
Langley 25 L
Langley 26 K
Langley 38 M
Langley Burrell 15 E
Langley Marsh 13 J
Langley Mill 32 F
Langley Park 49 L
Langley Street 27 C
Langloft 33 M
Langney 10 L
Langold 40 K
Langore 4 C
Langport 14 L
Langrick 34 D
Langridge 15 D
Langridgeford 13 G
Langrigg 47 J
Langrish 8 C
Langsett 39 H
Langshaw 53 E
Langside 57 F
Langskaill 79 E
Langstone 8 F
Langstone 14 B
Langthorne 44 D
Langthorpe 44 L
Langthwaite 43 F
Langtoft 45 L
Langton 34 A
Langton 44 A
Langton 45 K
Langton by Wragby 33 C
Langton Green 10 E
Langton Herring 6 F
Langton Matravers 7 H
Langtree 12 M
Langwathby 48 L
Langwith 32 C
Langwith Junction 32 C
Langworth 33 C
Lanivet 4 E
Lanjeth 4 D
Lanlivery 4 E
Lanner 3 J
Lanreath 4 E
Lanrick 57 J
Lansallos 4 H
Lansdown 15 D
Lanteglos 4 B
Lanton 53 J
Lanton 54 G
Lapford 13 K
Lapford Cross 13 K
Laphroaig 55 L
Lapley 31 J
Lapworth 24 A
Larachbeg 63 M
Larbert 57 M
Larches 38 B
Larden Green 31 A
Largie 67 A
Largiemore 56 H
Largoward 59 G
Largs 56 M
Largybeg 51 D
Largymore 51 D
Larkfield 56 M
Larkhall 52 B
Larkhill 15 L
Larling 27 D
Larne 105 A
Larrick 4 C
Larriston 48 B
Lartington 43 C
Lary 66 E
Lasham 16 L
Lassington 23 G
Lasswade 53 A
Lastingham 45 G
Latchford 17 C
Latchingdonn 18 E
Latchley 4 F
Lately Common 38 H
Lathallan Mill 59 G
Lathbury 25 G
Latheron 78 L
Latheronwheel 78 K
Lathones 59 G
Latimer 17 A
Latteridge 15 A
Lattiford 14 M
Latton 15 C
Lauchintilly 67 D
Lauder 53 E
Laugharne 20 J
Laughterton 33 B
Laughton 24 C
Laughton 10 G
Laughton 40 L
Laughton Common 39 M
Laughton-en-le-Morthen 39 M
Launcells 12 L
Launceston 4 C
Launde Abbey 33 K
Launton 24 L
Laurelvale 104 H
Laurencekirk 67 K
Laurieston 47 A
Lavant 9 D
Lavendon 25 G
Lavenham 26 M
Laverhay 52 M
Lavernock 14 D
Laversdale 48 E
Laverstock 15 M
Laverstoke 16 K
Laverton 15 G
Laverton 23 J
Laverton 44 G
Law 52 B
Lawers 58 D
Lawers 57 C
Lawford 19 A
Lawhead 59 G
Lawhitton 4 C
Lawkland 43 H
Lawley 31 G
Lawnhead 31 E
Lawrencetown 104 H
Lawrenny 20 H
Lawshall 26 J
Lawton 22 C
Laxey 37 B
Laxfield 27 H
Laxfirth 81 D
Laxford Bridge 76 F
Laxo 80 F
Laxton 25 B
Laxton 33 A
Laxton 40 E
Laycock 39 A
Layer Breton 18 C
Layer de la Haye 18 C
Layer Marney 18 C
Layham 26 M
Laytham 40 B
Layton 44 A
Lazenby 44 C
Lazonby 48 H
le Croc 9 M
Lea 15 B
Lea 30 J
Lea 30 M
Lea 32 B
Lea 40 L
Leac a' Li 74 M
Leachel Cushmie 66 F
Leachkin 71 L
Leadburn 53 A
Leaden Roding 18 A
Leadenham 33 E
Leadgate 48 J
Leadgate 49 H
Leadhills 52 H
Leafield 24 K
Leagrave 25 L
Leake Commonside 34 D
Leake Hurn's End 34 D
Lealands 10 H
Lealholm 45 D
Lea Line 23 G
Lealt 69 F
Lealt 56 D
Lea Marston 32 K
Leamington Hastings 24 E
Leanach 56 F
Leanaig 71 H
Leargybreck 55 J
Leasgill 43 D
Leasingham 33 E
Leaston 53 B
Leatherhead 17 L
Leathley 39 B
Leaton 31 D
Lea Town 38 B
Lea Valley 17 B
Leaveland 11 A
Leavenheath 26 M
Leavening 45 K
Leaves Green 10 A
Leaves Green 17 M
Lebberston 45 H
Lechlade on Thames 15 C
Leck 43 G
Leckford 16 K
Leckfurin 77 E
Leckhampstead 24 J
Leckhampton 23 L
Leckie 70 E
Leckmelm 70 C
Leckwith 14 A
Leconfield 40 C
Ledaig 64 K
Ledburn 25 K
Ledbury 23 G
Ledcharrie 57 B
Ledgemoor 22 F
Ledicot 22 C
Ledmore 76 M
Lednagullin 77 F
Ledsham 38 G
Ledsham 39 F
Ledston 39 F
Ledwell 24 L
Lee 8 A
Lee 12 F
Lee 30 F
Lee 43 K
Lee 55 C
Leeans 81 G
Leebotten 81 H
Leebotwood 30 J
Lee Brockhurst 31 D
Leece 42 H
Lee Clump 17 A
Leeds 10 C
Leeds 39 C
Leedstown 3 H
Leek 31 C
Leek Wootton 24 A
Lee Mill 5 G
Leeming 39 A
Leeming 44 G
Leeming Bar 44 D
Lee Moor 5 D
Lee-on-the-Solent 8 E
Lees 32 E
Lees 39 D
Leesthorpe 33 K
Leeswood 37 M
Leetown Cottown 58 F
Leftwich 38 L

A B C D E F G H I J K L M N O P Q R S T U V W X Y Z

A B C D E F G H I J K L M N O P Q R S T U V W X Y Z

Legamaghery 103 E
Legars 53 J
Legbourne 34 A
Legburthwaite 48 K
Legerwood 53 F
Leggs 102 C
Legland 103 B
Legsby 40 M
Leicester 32 M
Leicester Forest East 32 M
Leigh 7 A
Leigh 10 B
Leigh 15 C
Leigh 17 L
Leigh 23 E
Leigh 24 K
Leigh 30 J
Leigh 38 E
Leigh Beck 18 H
Leigh Commen 14 M
Leigh Green 10 F
Leigh-on-Sea 18 H
Leigh Sinton 23 E
Leighterton 15 A
Leighton 14 J
Leighton 30 H
Leighton 31 G
Leighton Bromswold 25 E
Leighton Buzzard 25 K
Leigh upon Mendip 14 J
Leigh Wood 14 F
Leim 50 B
Leinthall Earls 22 C
Leinthall Starkes 22 C
Leintwardine 22 C
Leire 24 B
Leirinmore 77 A
Leiston 27 J
Leitfie 58 C
Leith 58 L
Leitholm 54 D
Leitrim 104 M
Lelant 3 H
Lelley 41 B
Lem Hill 23 A
Lempitlaw 54 G
Lenaderg 104 H
Lenchwick 23 F
Lendalfoot 51 K
Lenham 10 C
Lenie 71 K
Lennel 54 G
Lennoxtown 57 L
Lenton 33 H
Lenton 32 F
Lenwade 35 K
Leoch 58 C
Leominster 22 C
Leonard Stanley 23 K
Leorin 55 L
Leoville 9 L
Lepe 8 D
Lephin 69 D
Lephinmore 56 H
Leppington 45 K
Lepton 39 E
L'Erée 9 K
Lerryn 4 E
Lerwick 81 D
Lesbury 54 M
Leschangie 67 D
Lescrow 4 H
Leslie 58 J
Leslie 66 C
Leslie Hill 104 G
Lesmahagow 52 E
Lesnewth 4 B
Lessendrum 72 M
Lessingham 35 M
Lessonhall 47 J
Leswalt 46 G
L'Etacq 9 L
Letchmore Heath 17 E
Letchworth 25 L
Letcombe Bassett 16 D
Letcombe Regis 16 D
Letham 58 J
Letham 59 A
Letham Grange 59 B
Lethem 53 M
Lethenty 67 B
Letheringham 27 L
Letheringsett 35 G
Lettaford 5 B
Lettan 79 F
Letterbreen 103 D
Letterewe 70 E
Letterfearn 70 K
Letterfinlay 64 F
Letterloan 108 H
Lettermore 63 H
Letters 70 C
Letterston 20 D
Lettoch 66 A
Letton 22 C
Letton 22 E
Letton Green 27 A
Letty Green 17 C
Letwell 40 K
Leuchars 59 D
Leumrabhagh 75 H
Levallymore 104 L
Levaneap 80 F
Leven 41 A
Leven 58 J
Levens 43 D
Levenshulme 38 J
Levenwick 81 H
Leverburgh/ An t-Ob 74 M
Leverington 34 K
Leverton 34 D
Leverton Highgate 34 D
Leverton Lucasgate 34 D
Leverton Outgate 34 D
Levington 27 K
Levisham 45 G
Levishie 65 A
Lew 16 A
Lewaigue 37 B
Lewannick 4 C
Lewdown 5 A
Lewes 9 F
Leweston 20 D
Lewisham 17 J
Lewiston 71 K
Lewistown 21 M
Lewknor 16 C
Leworthy 13 G
Lewtrenchard 5 A
Ley 4 E
Ley 66 F
Leybourne 10 B
Leyburn 44 D
Leycett 31 B
Ley Green 25 L
Leyland 38 B
Leylodge 67 D
Leys 58 C
Leys 66 F
Leys 73 M
Leysdown-on-Sea 11 A
Leysmill 59 B
Leys of Cossans 59 A
Leysters 23 A
Leyton 17 F
Lezant 4 C
Lhanbryde 72 H
Liatrie 70 M
Libanus 22 G
Libberton 52 F
Liberton 53 A
Liceasto 74 M
Lichfield 32 G
Lickey 23 C
Lickey End 23 C
Lickford 9 A
Liddel 79 L
Liddesdale 63 J
Liddington 15 F
Lidgate 26 H
Lidgate 39 L
Lidlington 25 G
Lieurary 78 D
Liff 58 F
Lifton 4 C
Liftondown 4 C
Lighthorpe 24 D
Lightwater 17 G
Lightwood Green 30 C
Lightwood Green 31 B
Lilbourne 24 C
Lilburn Tower 54 L
Lilleshall 31 H
Lilley 25 L
Lilliesleaf 53 H
Lillingstone Dayrell 24 J
Lillingstone Lovell 24 J
Lillington 7 A
Lilstock 14 G
Lilyhurst 31 H
Limavady 108 G
Limbrick 38 E
Limefield 38 F
Limekilnburn 52 A
Limekilns 58 L
Limerigg 57 M
Liminary 108 M
Limington 14 L
Limmerhaugh Muir 52 D
Limpenhoe 27 C
Limpley Stoke 15 D
Limpsfield 10 A
Linchmere 9 A
Lincluden 47 B
Lincoln 33 B
Lincomb 23 B
Lincombe 13 D
Lindal in Furness 42 E
Lindale 42 F
Lindean 53 H
Lindfield 9 C
Lindifferon 58 F
Lindores 58 F
Lindridge 23 A
Lindsell 18 A
Lindsey 26 M
Lindsey Tye 26 M
Linfairn 51 H
Linford 7 C
Linford 18 G
Lingague 37 D
Lingdale 45 A
Lingen 22 C
Lingfield 10 A
Lingreabhagh 74 M
Lingwood 27 C
Linhope 54 K
Linicro 69 B
Linkenholt 16 G
Linkhill 10 F
Linkinhorne 4 F
Linklater 79 L
Linksness 79 G
Linksness 79 H
Linktown 58 L
Linley 30 M
Linley Green 23 D
Linlithgow 58 K
Linlithgow Bridge 58 K
Linshiels 54 K
Linsiadar 75 D
Linsidemore 71 B
Linslade 25 K
Linstead 27 H
Linstock 48 D
Linthwaite 39 E
Lintlaw 54 D
Lintmill 72 J
Linton 10 C
Linton 23 G
Linton 26 K
Linton 39 C
Linton 43 M
Linton 49 C
Linton 53 J
Linton-on-Ouse 44 L
Linton Overseal 32 G
Linwood 7 C
Linwood 40 M
Linwood 57 K
Lionacleit 68 E
Lional 75 C
Liphook 9 A
Lisbane 105 G
Lisbellaw 103 D
Lisboy Bridge 103 C
Lisburn 104 F
Liscloon 107 J
Liscolman 108 F
Liscombe 13 H
Lisconrea 103 E
Lisdoart 103 F
Liskeard 4 F
Lislea 108 L
Lismoyle 108 L
Lisnacree 98 C
Lisnafin 107 L
Lisnahunshin 108 M
Lisnamalligan 104 M
Lisnamuck 108 L
Lisnarrick 103 A
Lisnaskea 103 H
Liss 8 C
Lissan 104 A
Liss Forest 8 C
Lissington 40 M
Liston 26 M
Listooder 105 G
Lisvane 14 A
Litcham 34 M
Litchborough 24 F
Litchfield 16 G
Litherland 38 D
Litlington 10 K
Litlington 25 M
Little Abington 26 G
Little Addington 25 D
Little-Alne 23 F
Little Asby 43 B
Little Atherfield 8 G
Little Ayre 79 G
Little-Ayre 80 J
Little Ayton 44 F
Little Badminton 15 A
Little Ballinluig 65 M
Little Bampton 47 F
Little Bampton 48 D
Little Bardfield 26 L
Little Barford 25 H
Little Barningham 35 L
Little-Barrington 23 M
Little Barugh 45 G
Little Bealings 27 K
Littlebeck 45 D
Little Bedwyn 15 J
Little Bentley 19 A
Little Berkhamsted 17 C
Little-Birch 22 J
Little Blakenham 27 K
Little Bollington 38 J
Littleborough 39 D
Littlebourne 11 B
Little Bowden 25 A
Little Bradley 26 H
Little Brampton 30 M
Little Braxted 18 B
Little Brechin 66 M
Littlebredy 6 F
Little Brickhill 25 K
Little Brington 24 F
Little Bromley 19 A
Little Budworth 38 L
Little Burstead 18 D
Littlebury 26 K
Littlebury Green 26 K
Little Bytham 33 L
Little Carlton 34 A
Little Casterton 33 L
Little Cawthorpe 34 A
Little Chalfont 17 D
Little Chart 11 D
Little Chesterford 26 K
Little Cheverell 15 H
Little Chishill 25 M
Little Clacton 19 A
Little-Comberton 23 E
Little-Compton 24 G
Little Cornard 26 M
Little Cowarne 23 D
Little Coxwell 16 A
Little Creich 71 B
Little Cressingham 26 C
Little Crosby 38 D
Little Cubley 32 D
Little Dalby 33 K
Littledean 23 K
Little Dens 67 C
Little Dewchurch 22 J
Little Downham 26 D
Little Driffield 40 C
Little Duchrae 47 A
Little Dunham 34 M
Little Dunkeld 58 B
Little Dunmow 18 A
Little Easton 18 A
Little Eaton 32 E
Little Eccleston 42 M
Little Ellingham 27 A
Little End 18 D
Little Eversden 25 J
Little Faringdon 15 C
Little Fencote 44 D
Little Fenton 40 A
Littleferry 71 C
Little Finborough 26 J
Little Fransham 26 C
Little Gaddesden 17 A
Little Gidding 25 B
Little Glenshee 58 B
Little Gransden 25 J
Little Gruinard 70 B
Little Habton 45 K
Little Hadham 17 C
Little Hale 33 F
Little Hallingbury 18 A
Littleham 5 F
Littleham 12 J
Little Hampden 16 C
Littlehampton 9 D
Little Harrowden 25 D
Little Haseley 16 B
Little Hatfield 41 A
Little Hautbois 35 L
Little Haven 20 D
Little Hay 32 K
Little Hayfield 39 G
Little Haywood-Colwich 31 J
Littlehempston 5 H
Little Henny 26 M
Little Hereford 23 A
Little Horkesley 18 C
Little Hormead 25 M
Little Horsted 10 G
Little Horwood 24 M
Little Houghton 25 D
Littlehoughton 54 M
Little Hucklow 39 L
Little Hulton 38 F
Little Kimble 16 C
Little Kineton 24 D
Little Kingshill 17 A
Little Langford 15 L
Little Laver 18 A
Little Leigh 38 L
Little Leighs 18 B
Little Lever 38 F
Little London 10 H
Little London 16 G
Little London 16 H
Little London 33 M
Little Longstone 39 L
Little Lynturk 66 F
Little Malvern 23 D
Little Maplestead 26 L
Little-Marcle 23 G
Littlemark 51 J
Little Marlow 16 F
Little Massingham 34 M
Little Melton 27 B
Little Mill 22 L
Littlemill 51 J
Littlemill 66 H
Littlemill 71 M
Little Missenden 17 A
Littlemore 16 B
Little Musgrave 43 B
Little Ness 30 K
Little Newcastle 20 E
Little Newsham 44 A
Little Oakley 19 A
Little Oakley 25 A
Little Orton 48 G
Little Ouse 26 B
Little Ouseburn 44 L
Littleover 32 E
Little Paxton 25 E
Little Petherick 4 A
Little Pill 13 G
Little Pitlurg 72 M
Little Plumstead 27 B
Little Ponton 33 H
Littleport 26 D
Little Rahane 57 G
Little Raveley 25 F
Little Ribston 44 L
Little-Rissington 23 M
Little Ryburgh 35 K
Little Ryle 54 K
Little Salkeld 48 L
Little Sampford 26 L
Little Saxham 26 H
Little Scatwell 71 G
Little Shelford 26 G
Little Smeaton 40 D
Little Snoring 35 K
Little Sodbury 15 A
Little Somerford 15 B
Little Stainton 44 B
Little Stanney 38 K
Little Staughton 25 E
Little Steeping 34 D
Littlester 80 F
Littlestone-on-Sea 11 G
Little Stonham 27 G
Little Street 27 L
Little Stretton 30 M
Little Stretton 32 M
Little Strickland 48 L
Little Stukeley 25 F
Little Swinburne 49 D
Little Tew 24 K
Little Tey 18 C
Little Thetford 26 D
Little Thirkleby 44 H
Littlethorpe 32 M
Littlethorpe 44 K
Little Thurlow 26 H
Little Thurrock 18 G
Littleton 14 L
Littleton 16 K
Littleton 17 G
Littleton 38 K
Littleton 58 F
Littleton Drew 15 D
Littleton Panell 15 H
Littleton-upon-Severn 14 C
Little Torboll 71 C
Little Torrington 12 M
Little Totham 18 C
Little Town 47 M
Littletown 49 M
Little Wakering 18 J
Little Walden 26 K
Little Waldingfield 26 M
Little Walsingham 35 G
Little Waltham 18 B
Little Warley 18 D
Little Weighton 40 F
Little Welnetham 26 J
Little Wenlock 31 G
Little Whittingham Green 27 H
Littlewick Green 16 F
Little Wilbraham 26 G
Little-Witcombe 23 L
Little-Witley 23 B
Little Wittenham 16 B
Little-Wolford 24 G
Littleworth 9 E
Littleworth 16 A
Littleworth 23 E
Little Wratting 26 L
Little Wymondley 25 L
Little Wyrley 31 J
Little Yeldham 26 L
Littley Green 18 B
Litton 14 J
Litton 39 L
Litton 43 H
Litton Cheney 6 F
Liurbost 75 E
Liverpool 38 G
Liverton 5 E
Liverton 45 D
Liverton Street 10 C
Livingston 52 C
Livingston Village 52 C
Lixwm 37 M
Lizard 3 L
Llaingarreglwyd 21 A
Llaithddu 30 K
Llan 30 G
Llanaber 29 E
Llanaelhaearn 36 L
Llanafan 29 L
Llanafanfawr 22 A
Llanallgo 36 F
Llananno 30 K
Llanarmon 29 B
Llanarmon Dyffryn Ceiriog 30 B
Llanarmon-yn-Ial 37 M
Llanarth 21 A
Llanarth 22 L
Llanarthne 21 G
Llanasa 37 J
Llanbabo 36 E
Llanbadarn 30 K
Llanbadarn Fawr 29 L
Llanbadarn-y-garreg 22 D
Llanbadrig 36 E
Llanbedr 22 D
Llanbedr 22 H
Llanbedr 29 B
Llanbedr-Dyffryn-Clwyd 37 L
Llanbedrgoch 36 J
Llanbedrog 29 A
Llanbedr-y-cennin 37 G
Llanberis 36 M
Llanbister 30 K
Llanblethian 13 C
Llanboidy 20 F
Llanbradach 22 K
Llanbrynmair 30 G
Llanbydderi 13 C
Llancarfan 13 C
Llancayo 22 L
Llancynfelyn 29 H
Llandaff 14 A
Llandanwg 29 B
Llandarcy 21 L
Llandawke 20 J
Llanddaniel Fab 36 H
Llanddarog 21 G
Llanddeiniol 29 L
Llanddeiniolen 36 J
Llandderfel 30 A
Llanddeusant 21 H
Llanddeusant 36 E
Llanddew 22 D
Llanddewi 21 K
Llanddewi Brefi 21 B
Llanddewi'r Cwm 22 D
Llanddewi Rhydderch 22 L
Llanddewi Velfrey 20 E
Llanddewi Ystradenni 22 A
Llanddoged 37 K
Llanddona 36 J
Llanddowror 20 J
Llanddulas 37 G
Llanddwywe 29 E
Llanddyfnan 36 J
Llandefaelog 22 D
Llandefaelog tre'r-graig 22 G
Llandefalle 22 D
Llandegai 36 J
Llandegfan 36 J
Llandegla 37 M
Llandegley 22 B
Llandegveth 22 L
Llandegwning 29 A
Llandeilo 21 H
Llandeilo Graban 22 D
Llandeilo'r-Fan 21 F
Llandeloy 20 D
Llandevaud 14 B
Llandevenny 14 B
Llandinabo 22 J
Llandinam 30 K
Llandissilio 20 E
Llandogo 22 M
Llandough 13 C
Llandough 14 A
Llandovery/Llanymddyfri 21 F
Llandow 13 C
Llandre 21 E
Llandre 29 H
Llandrillo 30 B
Llandrillo-yn-Rhos 37 G
Llandrindod Wells 22 A
Llandrinio 30 F
Llandudno-Junction 37 G
Llandudwen 29 A
Llandwrog 36 L
Llandybie 21 H
Llandyfaelog 21 G
Llandyfriog 20 C
Llandyfrydog 36 E
Llandygwydd 20 C
Llandyrnog 37 L
Llandyssil 30 H
Llandysul 21 A
Llanedwen 36 H
Llanegan 29 A
Llaneglwys 22 D
Llanegryn 29 E
Llanegwad 21 D
Llanelian-yn-Rhos 37 G
Llanelidan 37 L
Llanelieu 22 E
Llanellen 22 L
Llanelli 21 K
Llanelltyd 29 F
Llanelly 22 H
Llanelly Hill 22 H
Llanelwedd 22 A
Llanenddwyn 29 B
Llanerchymedd 36 E
Llanerfyl 30 D
Llanfabon 22 K
Llanfachreath 36 E
Llanfachreth 29 F
Llanfaelog 36 H
Llanfaelrhys 29 A
Llanfaes 36 J
Llanfaethlu 36 E
Llanfaglan 36 L
Llanfair 29 B
Llanfair Caereinion 30 H
Llanfair Clydogau 21 B
Llanfair Dyffryn Clwyd 37 L
Llanfairfechan 36 J
Llanfair Kilgeddin 22 L
Llanfair-Nant-Gwyn 20 C
Llanfair Pwllgwyngyll 36 J
Llanfair Talhaiarn 37 H
Llanfair Waterdine 30 L
Llanfairyneubwll 36 H
Llanfairynghornwy 36 E
Llanfallteg 20 E
Llanfaredd 22 A
Llanfarian 29 L
Llanfechain 30 E
Llanfechan 22 A
Llanfechell 36 E
Llanfendigaid 29 E
Llanferres 37 M
Llan Ffestiniog 29 C
Llanfflewyn 36 E
Llanfigael 36 E
Llanfihangel-ar-arth 21 D
Llanfihangel Glyn Myfyr 37 L
Llanfihangel Nant Bran 21 F
Llanfihangel-Nant-Melan 22 B
Llanfihangel Rhydithon 22 B
Llanfihangel Rogiet 14 C
Llanfihangel Talyllyn 22 G
Llanfihangel uwch-Gwili 21 D
Llanfihangel-y-Creuddyn 29 L
Llanfihangel-yng-Ngwynfa 30 E
Llanfihangel yn Nhowyn 36 H
Llanfihangel-y-pennant 29 F
Llanfihangel-y-pennant 36 L
Llanfihangel-y-Traethau 29 B
Llanfilo 22 D
Llanfoist 22 H
Llanfor 30 A
Llanfrechfa 22 L
Llanfrothen 29 C
Llanfrynach 22 G
Llanfwrog 36 E
Llanfwrog 37 L
Llanfyllin 30 E
Llanfynydd 21 D
Llanfynydd 37 M
Llanfyrnach 20 F
Llangadfan 30 D
Llangadog 21 E
Llangadwaladr 30 E
Llangadwaladr 36 H
Llangaffo 36 H
Llangain 21 G
Llangammarch Wells 21 F
Llangan 13 C
Llangarron 22 J
Llangasty Talyllyn 22 G
Llangathen 21 E
Llangattock 22 H
Llangattock Lingoed 22 H
Llangattock-Vibon-Avel 22 J
Llangedwyn 30 E
Llangefni 36 H
Llangeinor 21 M
Llangeitho 21 B
Llangeler 21 A
Llangelynnin 29 E
Llangennech 21 K
Llangennith 21 K
Llangenny 22 H
Llangernyw 37 G
Llangian 29 A
Llangiwg 21 H
Llangloffan 20 A
Llanglydwen 20 F
Llangoed 36 J
Llangoedmor 20 C
Llangollen 30 C
Llangolman 20 E
Llangorse 22 G
Llangorwen 29 H
Llangovan 22 M
Llangower 30 A
Llangranog 20 C
Llangristiolus 36 H
Llangrove 22 J
Llangua 22 J
Llangunnor 21 D
Llangwm 20 H
Llangwm 22 L
Llangwm 22 M
Llangwm 30 A
Llangwyfan 37 L
Llangwyllog 36 H
Llangwyryfon 29 L
Llangybi 21 B
Llangybi 22 L
Llangybi 36 L
Llangyfelach 21 L
Llangyndeyrn 21 G
Llangynhafal 37 L
Llangynidr 22 G
Llangynin 20 F
Llangynog 20 J
Llangynog 30 E
Llangynwyd 21 M
Llanhamlach 22 G
Llanharan 13 C
Llanharry 13 C
Llanhennock 14 B
Llanhilleth 22 L
Llanidloes 30 K
Llaniestyn 29 A
Llanigon 22 E
Llanilar 29 L
Llanilid 13 C
Llanishen 22 M
Llanllawddog 21 D
Llanllechid 36 J
Llanllowell 22 L
Llanllugan 30 G
Llanllwch 21 G
Llanllwchaiarn 30 H
Llanllwni 21 D
Llanllyfni 36 L
Llanmadoc 21 K
Llanmaes 13 C
Llanmartin 14 B
Llanmerewig 30 H
Llanmihangel 13 C
Llanmiloe 20 J
Llanmorlais 21 K
Llannefydd 37 H
Llannerch-y-môr 37 J
Llannon 21 G
Llannor 29 A
Llanon 29 L
Llanover 22 L
Llanpumsaint 21 D
Llanrhaeadr 37 L
Llanrhaedr-ym-Mochnant 30 E
Llanrhian 20 A
Llanrhidian 21 K
Llanrhos 37 G
Llanrhyddlad 36 E
Llanrhystud 29 L
Llanrothal 22 J
Llanrug 36 J
Llanrwst 37 K
Llansadurnen 20 J
Llansadwrm 21 E
Llansadwrn 36 J
Llansaint 20 J
Llansamlet 21 L
Llansanffraid Glan Conwy 37 G
Llansannan 37 L
Llansannor 13 C
Llansantffraed 22 G
Llansantffraed 29 L
Llansantffraed-Cwmdeuddwr 22 A
Llansantffraed-Cwmdeuddwr 30 K
Llansantffraed-in-Elwel 22 A
Llansantffraid-ym-Mechain 30 E
Llansawel 21 E
Llansilin 30 E
Llansoy 22 M
Llanspyddid 22 D
Llanstadwell 20 G

Mappleborough Green 23 C
Mappleton 41 A
Mappowder 7 A
Màraig 75 G
Marazion 3 H
Marbhig 75 H
Marbury 31 A
March 26 A
Marcham 16 A
Marchamley 31 D
Marchington 32 D
Marchington Woodlands 32 D
Marchlands 52 E
Marchwiel 30 C
Marchwood 8 A
Marcross 13 C
Marden 10 F
Marden 15 H
Marden 22 F
Marden Thron 10 F
Mardu 30 L
Mardy 22 H
Marefield 33 K
Mareham le Fen 34 D
Mareham on the Hill 34 A
Marehill 9 B
Marfleet 41 B
Margam 21 L
Margaret Marsh 7 B
Margaret Roding 18 A
Margaretting 18 D
Margate 11 C
Margnaheglish 51 D
Margreig 47 B
Marham 26 B
Marham 34 L
Marholm 33 M
Marianglas 36 F
Mariansleigh 13 L
Marishader 69 F
Mark 14 H
Mark Causeway 14 H
Mark Cross 10 E
Markbeech 10 A
Markby 34 B
Market Bosworth 32 L
Market Deeping 33 M
Market Drayton 31 E
Market Harborough 24 C
Markethill 58 C
Markethill 104 H
Market Lavington 15 H
Market Overton 33 K
Market Rasen 40 M
Market Stainton 34 A
Market Warsop 32 C
Market Weighton 40 C
Market Weston 26 F
Markfield 32 L
Markham 22 K
Markham Moor 33 A
Markinch 58 J
Markington 44 K
Marks Tey 18 C
Marksbury 14 F
Markwell 4 F
Markyate 17 B
Marlborough 15 F
Marlcliff 23 F
Marldon 5 J
Marlesford 27 L
Marley Green 31 A
Marley Hill 49 H
Marlingford 27 A
Marloes 20 G
Marlow 16 F
Marlow Botton 16 F
Marlpit Hill 10 A
Marnhull 7 A
Marnoch 73 K
Marnock 57 M
Marple 39 G
Marr 39 J
Marrick 43 F
Marrister 80 F
Marros 20 J
Marrywell 67 H
Marsden 39 D
Marsett 43 F
Marsfield 10 D
Marshalsea 6 B
Marsham 35 L
Marshaw 43 K
Marsh Baldon 16 B
Marshbrook 30 M
Marshchapel 41 L
Marshfield 14 B
Marshfield 15 D
Marshgate 4 B
Marsh Gibbon 24 M
Marsh Green 6 A
Marsh Green 10 A
Marsh Green 31 G
Marshland Saint James 34 K
Marsh Lane 22 M
Marsh Lane 39 M
Marshside 11 B
Marshside 38 A
Marshwood 6 B
Marske 44 D
Marske-by-the-Sea 44 C
Marston 15 H
Marston 16 B
Marston 22 C
Marston 31 F
Marston 31 H
Marston 32 K
Marston 33 E
Marston 38 L
Marston Doles 24 E
Marston Green 24 A
Marston Magna 14 M
Marston Meysey 15 C
Marston Montgomery 32 D
Marston Moretaine 25 G
Marston on Dove 32 D
Marston Saint Lawrence 24 H
Marston Stannett 23 D
Marston Trussell 24 C
Marstow 22 J
Marsworth 17 A
Marten 15 J
Marthall 38 M
Martham 27 C
Martin 7 C
Martin 11 E
Martindale 48 K
Martin Dales 33 F
Martin Drove End 7 C
Martinhoe 13 D
Martin Hussingtree 23 E
Martin Mill 11 E
Martinscroft 38 H
Martinstown 108 M
Martinstown or Winterborne Saint Martin 7 D
Martlesham 27 L
Martlesham Heath 27 K
Martletwy 20 H
Martley 23 B
Martock 14 L
Marton 12 E
Marton 30 J
Marton 38 M
Marton 40 L
Marton 42 E
Marton 44 C
Marton 44 L
Marton 45 G
Marton Abbey 44 M
Marton-le-Moor 44 H
Marwick 79 D
Marwood 13 G
Mary Tavy 5 D
Marybank 71 G
Maryburgh 71 H
Maryfield 81 D
Marygold 54 D
Marykirk 66 M
Marylebone 38 E
Marypark 72 L
Maryport 46 G
Maryport 47 H
Marystow 5 A
Maryton 59 A
Maryton 59 B
Marywell 59 B
Marywell 66 J
Masham 44 G
Mashborough 11 B
Mashbury 18 A
Masongill 43 G
Mastin Moor 39 M
Mastrick 67 E
Matching 18 A
Matching Green 18 A
Matching Tye 18 A
Matfen 49 D
Matfield 10 E
Mathern 14 C
Mathon 23 D
Mathry 20 A
Matlaske 35 L
Matlock 32 B
Matlock Bath 32 B
Matson 23 L
Matterdale End 48 K
Mattersey 40 K
Mattingley 16 J
Mattishall 27 A
Mattishall Burgh 27 A
Mauchline 51 F
Maud 73 L
Maugersbury 23 M
Maughold 37 B
Mauld 71 K
Maulden 25 L
Maulds Meaburn 43 A
Maunby 44 H
Maund Bryan 23 D
Maundown 13 J
Mautby 27 C
Mavesyn Ridware 32 G
Mavis Enderby 34 A
Mawbray 47 J
Mawcarse 58 H
Mawdesley 38 D
Mawdlam 13 B
Mawgan 3 M
Mawgan Porth 4 D
Mawla 3 J
Mawley 23 A
Mawnan 3 M
Mawnan Smith 3 M
Mawthorpe 34 B
Maxey 33 M
Maxstoke 24 A
Maxton 53 J
Maxwellheugh 53 J
Maxworthy 4 C
Maybole 51 H
Mayfield 10 E
Mayfield 32 D
Mayfield 53 B
Mayford 17 K
Mayland 18 F
Maylandsea 18 F
Mayobridge 104 L
Maypole 3 A
Maypole 11 B
Maypole 22 J
Maypole Green 27 F
May's Corner 104 J
Maywick 81 H
Mazetown 104 F
McCreadys Corner 104 D
McGregor's Corner 108 M
McLaughlins Corner 108 H
Mead End 15 L
Meadle 16 C
Meadowtown 30 J
Mealabost 75 E
Mealabost Bhuigh 75 B
Mealasta 74 F
Meal Bank 43 D
Mealsgate 47 J
Mearbeck 43 L
Meare 14 H
Meare Green 14 L
Mears Ashby 25 D
Measham 32 H
Meathop 42 F
Meaux 41 B
Meavy 5 D
Medbourne 25 A
Medburn 49 E
Meddon 12 H
Meden Vale 32 C
Medlam 34 D
Medmenham 16 F
Medomsley 49 H
Meenagorp Bridge 107 M
Meerbrook 31 C
Meer End 24 A
Meesden Brent 25 M
Meeth 13 K
Meggethead 52 J
Meidrim 20 F
Meifod 30 E
Meigh 104 L
Meigle 58 C
Meikle Earnock 52 B
Meikle Grenach 56 M
Meikle Obney 58 B
Meikleour 58 B
Meikle Strath 66 M
Meikle Tarty 67 B
Meikle Wartle 67 A
Meikle Whitefield 58 B
Meinciau 21 G
Meir 31 F
Meir Heath 31 F
Melbourn 25 J
Melbourne 32 H
Melbourne 40 B
Melbury Abbas 7 B
Melbury Bubb 6 C
Melbury Osmond 6 C
Melbury Sampford 6 C
Melby 80 M
Melchbourne 25 E
Meldon 5 A
Meldon 49 E
Meldreth 25 J
Melfort 56 B
Melgarve 65 D
Meliden 37 H
Melinbrynrhedyn 29 J
Melincourt 21 M
Melin-y-coed 37 K
Melin-y-ddol 30 H
Melin-y-Wig 30 B
Melkinthorpe 48 L
Melkridge 48 F
Melksham 15 E
Melldalloch 56 H
Melling 38 D
Melling 43 G
Mellis 27 G
Mellon Charles 70 A
Mellon Udrigle 76 K
Mellor 38 C
Mellor 39 G
Mellor Brook 38 B
Mells 15 G
Mells Wenhaston 27 H
Melmerby 43 J
Melmerby 44 H
Melmerby 48 L
Melplash 6 C
Melrose 53 H
Melsetter 79 K
Melsonby 44 A
Meltham 39 E
Melton 27 L
Meltonby 40 B
Melton Constable 35 K
Melton Mowbray 33 G
Melton Roos 40 J
Melvaig 70 A
Melverley 30 F
Melverley Green 30 F
Melvich 77 F
Membury 6 B
Memsie 73 M
Memus 66 L
Menabilly 4 H
Menai Bridge 36 J
Mendham 27 E
Mendlesham 27 G
Mendlesham Green 27 G
Menheniot 4 F
Menithwood 23 A
Menna 4 D
Mennock 52 H
Menston 39 B
Menstrie 58 G
Mentmore 25 K
Meoble 63 F
Meole Brace 31 G
Meonstoke 8 B
Meopham 18 K
Mepal 26 D
Meppershall 25 L
Merbach 22 E
Mercaston 32 E
Mere 15 K
Mere 38 H
Mere Brow 38 A
Mereclough 39 A
Mere Green 32 K
Mereworth 10 B
Mergie 67 G
Meriden 24 A
Merkadale 69 H
Merkland 47 A
Merkland 51 L
Merley 7 E
Merlins Bridge 20 D
Merrington 31 D
Merrion 20 G
Merriott 6 C
Merrivale 5 D
Merry Hill 17 E
Merrymeet 4 F
Mersham 11 D
Merstham 17 L
Merston 9 D
Merstone 8 H
Merther 3 J
Merthyr 20 F
Merthyr Cynog 22 D
Merthyr Dyfan 14 A
Merthyr Mawr 13 C
Merthyr Tydfil/Merthyr Tudful 22 M
Merthyr Vale 22 K
Merton 12 M
Merton 17 H
Merton 24 L
Merton 26 C
Mervinslaw 53 M
Meshaw 13 L
Messing 18 C
Messingham 40 H
Metcombe 6 A
Metfield 27 E
Metfield Common 27 E
Metheringham 33 C
Methil 58 J
Methlem 28 C
Methley 39 F
Methlick 67 B
Methven 58 E
Methwold 26 B
Methwold Hythe 26 B
Mettingham 27 E
Metton 35 L
Mevagissey 4 G
Mexborough 39 J
Mey 78 E
Meysey Hampton 15 C
Miabhaig 74 F
Miabhaig 74 J
Miabhaig 74 M
Michaelchurch 22 J
Michaelchurch Escley 22 E
Michaelchurch-on-Arrow 22 E
Michaelston-le-Pit 14 A
Michaelston-y-Fedw 14 A
Michaelstow 4 B
Micheldever 16 K
Michelmersh 8 A
Mickfield 27 G
Mickle Trafford 38 K
Micklebring 39 J
Mickleby 45 D
Micklefield 39 C
Mickleham 17 L
Mickleover 32 E
Mickleton 23 J
Mickleton 43 C
Mickletown 39 F
Mickley 44 G
Mickley Square 49 H
Mid Ardlaw 73 L
Midbea 79 E
Mid Beltie 66 J
Mid Calder 52 C
Mid Clyth 78 H
Mid Culbeuchly 73 K
Middle Assendon 16 F
Middle Aston 24 L
Middle Barton 24 L
Middlebie 47 C
Middle Claydon 24 M
Middle-Crackington 12 L
Middle Cragabus 55 L
Middle Drums 59 B
Middleham 44 D
Middle Handley 39 M
Middle Harling 27 D
Middlehill 4 F
Middlehope 31 K
Middle Kames 56 H
Middle-Littleton 23 F
Middle Maes-coed 22 E
Middlemarsh 7 A
Middle Mill 20 D
Middlemuir 67 E
Middle Rasen 40 M
Middlesbrough 44 C
Middleshaw 43 D
Middlesmoor 43 J
Middlestone Moor 49 L
Middlestown 39 E
Middleton 16 K
Middleton 21 K
Middleton 25 A
Middleton 27 J
Middleton 30 F
Middleton 30 J
Middleton 31 K
Middleton 32 A
Middleton 32 B
Middleton 32 K
Middleton 34 L
Middleton 38 F
Middleton 39 F
Middleton 42 J
Middleton 43 D
Middleton 43 M
Middleton 45 G
Middleton 49 E
Middleton 53 B
Middleton 54 H
Middleton 56 M
Middleton 58 B
Middleton 58 H
Middleton 62 A
Middleton 67 E
Middleton Bank Top 49 E
Middleton Carbonell 23 A
Middleton Cheney 24 H
Middleton Green 31 F
Middleton Hall 54 K
Middleton-in-Teesdale 49 K
Middleton-on-Leven 44 E
Middleton-on-Sea 9 D
Middleton on the Hill 23 A
Middleton-on-the-Wolds 40 C
Middleton Priors 31 K
Middleton Saint George 44 B
Middleton Scriven 31 K
Middleton Stoney 24 L
Middleton Tyas 44 D
Middletown 30 J
Middletown 42 A
Middletown 104 G
Middle Tysoe 24 G
Middle Wallop 15 M
Middlewich 38 L
Middle Winterslow 15 M
Middle Woodford 15 L
Middlewood Green 27 G
Middlezoy 14 L
Middridge 44 B
Midfield 77 E
Mid Garrary 46 C
Mid Garth 79 F
Midge Hall 38 B
Midgeholme 48 H
Midgham 16 H
Midgley 39 A
Midgley 39 E
Midhopestones 39 H
Midhurst 9 A
Midlem 53 H
Mid Main 71 K
Midpark 56 L
Midsomer Norton 14 J
Midtown 70 A
Midtown of Buchromb 72 L
Mid Urchany 71 M
Midville 34 D
Mid Walls 81 K
Mid Yell 80 E
Migdale 71 B
Migvie 66 F
Milarrochy 57 G
Milborne Port 14 M
Milborne Saint Andrew 7 D
Milborne Wick 14 M
Milbourne 15 B
Milbourne 49 E
Milburn 48 L
Milbury Heath 15 A
Milcombe 24 H
Milden 26 M
Mildenhall 15 F
Mildenhall 26 E
Milebush 10 F
Milebush 105 A
Mile Elm 15 E
Mile End 18 C
Mile End 22 M
Mile-end Borgue 46 F
Mileham 34 M
Mile Oak 9 E
Milesmark 58 L
Milfield 54 G
Milford 12 H
Milford 31 J
Milford 32 E
Milford 104 G
Milford Haven/Aberdaugleddau 20 G
Milford on Sea 8 D
Milford-Witley 16 M
Milking Nook 33 M
Milkwall 22 M
Milland 9 A
Mill Bank 39 D
Millbank 105 A
Millbay 105 B
Millbeck 47 M
Millbounds 79 E
Millbreck 67 C
Millbrex 67 B
Millbridge 16 M
Millbrook 4 J
Millbrook 8 A
Millbrook 9 M
Millbrook 25 K
Millbrook 39 G
Millbrook 105 A
Millburn 51 F
Millcombe 5 H
Mill Common 27 F
Milldale 32 A
Milldens 59 A
Mill End 16 F
Mill End 25 M
Millerhill 53 B
Miller's Dale 39 K
Mill Green 18 D
Mill Green 27 G
Mill Green 31 E
Millheugh 52 B
Mill Hill 17 E
Mill Hill 103 E
Mill Hill 105 G
Millholme 43 D
Millhouse 48 G
Millhouse 56 L
Millhousebridge 47 C
Mill Houses 43 G
Millikenpark 57 K
Millington 40 B
Millisle 105 E
Mill Lane 16 M
Millmeece 31 E
Millness 71 K
Mill of Balrownie 66 M
Mill of Kingoodie 67 B
Mill of Uras 67 K
Millom 42 E
Mill Park 50 H
Millpool 4 E
Millport 51 B
Mills 108 J
Mill Side 42 F
Mill Street 35 K
Millthorpe 33 J
Millthorpe 39 L
Millthrop 43 D
Milltown 13 G
Milltown 32 B
Milltown 41 A
Milltown 71 M
Milltown 78 F
Milltown 103 A
Milltown 103 C
Mill Town 104 C
Milltown 104 E
Milltown 104 G
Milltown 104 H
Milltown 104 J
Milltown 104 L
Milltown 107 J
Milltown 108 J
Milltown 108 L
Milltown 109 G
Milltown 109 K
Milltown of Aberdalgie 58 E
Milltown of Craigston 73 L
Milltown of Edinvillie 72 L
Milltown of Rothiemay 72 M
Milltown of Towie 66 F
Milnathort 58 H
Milngavie 57 L
Milnquarter 57 M
Milnrow 39 D
Milnthorpe 43 D
Milo 21 H
Milrig 51 F
Milson 23 A
Milstead 10 C
Milston 15 J
Milton 16 B
Milton 20 H
Milton 24 H
Milton 26 G
Milton 31 C
Milton 32 H
Milton 33 A
Milton 46 D
Milton 47 B
Milton 48 E
Milton 57 H
Milton 57 K
Milton 58 A
Milton 59 A
Milton 66 A
Milton 70 J
Milton 71 F
Milton 71 H
Milton 71 K
Milton 72 G
Milton 72 J
Milton 78 H
Milton Abbas 7 A
Milton Abbot 4 C
Milton Bridge 53 A
Milton Bryan 25 K
Milton Clevedon 14 M
Milton Coldwells 67 B
Milton Combe 5 D
Milton Common 16 B
Milton Damerel 12 M
Miltonduff 72 H
Milton Ernest 25 H
Milton Green 38 K
Milton Hill 16 B
Miltonise 46 A
Milton Keynes 25 G
Milton Keynes Village 25 G
Milton Lilbourne 15 J
Milton Malsor 24 F
Milton Morenish 57 C
Milton of Auchinhove 66 F
Milton of Balgonie 58 J
Milton of Buchanan 57 H
Milton of Campfield 66 J
Milton of Campsie 57 L
Milton of Corsindae 67 D
Milton of Cushnie 66 F
Milton of Dalcapon 65 M
Milton of Edradour 65 M
Milton of Gollanfield 71 J
Milton of Lesmore 66 C
Milton of Machany 58 D
Milton of Murtle 67 H
Milton of Noth 66 C
Milton of Tullich 66 E
Milton on Stour 15 K
Milton Regis 10 C
Milton-under-Wychwood 24 K
Milverton 13 M
Milwich 31 F
Milwr 37 J
Minard 56 E
Minchington 7 B
Minchinhampton 15 B
Mindrum 54 G
Minehead 13 J
Minera 30 C
Minerstown 105 K
Minety 15 B
Minffordd 29 B
Mingarrypark 63 J
Mingary 63 H
Mingearraidh 68 H
Miningsby 34 D
Minions 4 F
Minishant 51 H
Minley Manor 16 J
Minllyn 30 D
Minnes 67 E
Minnigaff 46 B
Minnonie 73 L
Minshull Vernon 38 L
Minstead 8 A
Minster 18 J
Minsteracres 49 G
Minsterley 30 J
Minster Lovell 24 K
Minster-Manston 11 B
Minsterworth 23 K
Minterburn 104 D
Minterne Magna 7 A
Mintfordd 29 F
Minting 33 C
Mintlaw 73 M
Mintlaw Station 73 M
Minto 53 H
Minton 30 M
Minwear 20 H
Minworth 32 K
Mirbister 79 D
Mireland 78 E
Mirfield 39 E
Miserden 23 L
Miskin 14 A
Misson 40 K
Misterton 6 C
Misterton 24 C
Misterton 40 L
Mistley 19 A
Mitcham 17 H
Mitchel Troy 22 M
Mitcheldean 23 G
Mitchell 4 D
Mitchelland 42 F
Mitford 49 E
Mithian 3 F
Mitton 31 J
Mixbury 24 H
Mixon 32 A
Moat 48 D
Mobberley 38 M
Moccas 22 E
Mochdre 30 K
Mochdre 37 G
Mochrum 46 E
Mockbeggar 7 C
Mockerkin 47 L
Modbury 5 G
Moddershall 31 F
Moelfre 30 E
Moelfre 36 F
Moffat 52 M
Moggerhanger 25 H
Moghan Bridge 104 D
Moira 32 H
Moira 104 F
Molash 11 A
Mold /Yr Wyddgrug 37 M
Molehill Green 18 A
Molescroft 40 C
Molesworth 25 E
Molland 13 H
Mollington 24 H
Mollington 38 K
Mollinsburn 57 M
Mona 36 H
Monachiyle 57 E
Monachty 29 K
Monaughty 22 B
Monboddo 67 K
Mondynes 67 K
Monea 103 D
Monevechadan 56 F
Monewden 27 H
Moneydie 58 E
Moneydig 108 H
Moneyglass 104 C
Moneyhaw 104 B
Moneymore 104 B
Moneyneany 108 K
Moneyreagh 105 D
Moneysharvan 108 L
Moneyslane 104 J
Moniaive 52 K
Monifieth 59 D
Monikie 59 D
Monimail 58 J
Monington 20 C
Monken Hadley 17 E
Monk Fryston 40 D
Monkhopton 31 K
Monkland 22 C
Monkleigh 12 J
Monknash 13 C
Monkokehampton 13 K

A B C D E F G H I J K L **M** N O P Q R S T U V W X Y Z

Newtonmill 66 M
Newtonmore 65 E
Newton Morell 44 A
Newton of Ardtoe 63 F
Newton of Balcanquhal 58 H
Newton of Falkland 58 J
Newton-on-Ouse 44 L
Newton-on-Rawcliff 45 G
Newton on the Moor 49 B
Newton on Trent 33 B
Newton Poppleford 6 A
Newton Purcell 24 M
Newton Redhill 67 A
Newton Regis 32 K
Newton Reigny 48 K
Newton Saint Boswells 53 H
Newton Saint Cyres 5 C
Newton Saint Faith 27 B
Newton Saint Loe 15 D
Newton Saint Petrock 12 M
Newton Solney 32 H
Newton Stacey 16 K
Newton Stewart 46 B
Newton Toney 15 M
Newton Tracey 13 G
Newton under Roseberry 44 F
Newton upon Derwent 40 B
Newton Valence 8 C
Newton-with-Scales 38 A
Newtown 16 G
Newtown 8 A
Newtown 8 B
Newtown 8 D
New Town 10 G
Newtown 15 K
Newtown 23 D
New Town 23 J
Newtown 31 C
Newtown 31 D
Newtown 37 D
Newtown 39 G
Newtown 48 E
Newtown 49 B
New Town 53 B
Newtown 54 L
Newtown 64 C
Newtown 56 F
Newtown 7 E
Newtown Unthank 32 L
Newtown/Y Drenewydd 30 H
Newtownabbey 105 A
Newtownards 105 E
Newtownbutler 103 H
Newtown-Crommelin 108 M
Newtownhamilton 104 K
Newtown-in-Saint Martin 3 M
Newtownsaville 103 F
Newtownstewart 107 L
New Tredegar 22 K
New Trows 52 E
Newtyle 58 C
New Ulva 56 G
New Waltham 41 K
New Winton 53 B
New Yatt 24 K
New York 33 F
New York 34 D
New York 49 J
Neyland 20 G
Nibley 15 A
Nibon 80 J
Nicholashayne 13 M
Nicholaston 21 K
Nidd 44 K
Nigg 67 H
Nigg 71 F
Nigg Ferry 71 F
Niggards 81 C
Nilig 37 L
Nine Ashes 18 D
Ninebanks 48 J
Nine Mile Bridge 103 C
Nine Mile Burn 53 A
Ninfield 10 H
Ningwood 8 D
Nisbet 53 J
Nisthouse 79 G
Niton 8 H
Nitshill 52 A
Niwbwrch 36 H
Noak Bridge 18 D
Noak Hill 18 D
Noblehill 47 B
Nobottle 24 F
Nocton 33 C
Noke 24 L
Nolton 20 D
Nolton Haven 20 D
No Man's Heath 31 A
No Man's Heath 32 G
Nomansland 8 A
Nomansland 13 L
Noneley 31 D
Nonington 11 E
Nook 43 D
Nook 48 B
Noonsbrough 81 G
Noranside 66 L
Norbury 30 M
Norbury 31 E
Norbury 32 D
Norbury Common 31 A
Norchard 23 B
Nordelph 26 B
Norden 7 E
Norden 38 F
Nordley 31 L
Norham 54 D
Norley 38 L
Norleywood 8 D
Normanby 40 H
Normanby 45 G
Normanby-by-Spital 40 M
Normanby le Wold 40 M
Norman Cross 25 C
Normandy 16 M
Norman's Green 6 A
Normanton 32 E
Normanton 33 A
Normanton 33 D
Normanton 33 E
Normanton 33 L
Normanton 39 F
Normanton le Heath 32 H
Normanton on Soar 32 J
Normanton on Trent 33 A
Normanton-on-the-Wolds 32 J
Normoss 42 L
Norris Hill 32 H
Northacre 27 A
Northallerton 44 E
Northampton 24 F
North Ascot 16 J
North Aston 24 L
Northaw 17 E
North Baddesley 8 A
North Ballachulish 64 G
North Balloch 51 L
North Barrow 14 M
North Barsham 35 G
North Benfleet 18 E
North Berwick 59 K
North Blyth 49 F
North Boarhunt 8 E
Northborough 33 M
Northbourne 11 E
North Bovey 5 B
North Bradley 15 G
North Brentor 5 A
North Brewham 14 M
Northbrook 24 L
North Brora Muir 72 A
North Buckland 12 F
North Burlingham 27 C
North Cadbury 14 M
North Cairn 46 G
North Carlton 33 B
North Cave 40 F
North Cerney 23 L
Northchapel 9 A
North Charford 7 C
North Charlton 54 L
North-Cheriton 14 M
North Chideock 6 E
Northchurch 17 A
North Cliffe 40 E
North Clifton 33 B
North Cockerington 41 L
North Coker 6 C
North Connel 64 K
North Cornelly 13 B
Northcote Manor 13 K
North Cotes 41 L
Northcott 4 C
North Cove 27 F
North Cowton 44 E
North Cranna 73 K
North Crawley 25 G
North Cray 17 J
North Creake 34 J
North Curry 14 K
North Dalton 40 C
North Dawn 79 H
North Deighton 44 L
North Duffield 40 B
Northdyke 79 D
North Dykes 48 L
North Elkington 41 K
North Elmham 35 K
North Emsall 39 F
North End 8 F
North End 9 E
North End 14 E
Northend 15 D
Northend 16 F
North End 16 G
North End 18 A
Northend 24 E
North Erradale 70 A
North Fambridge 18 E
North Fearns 69 J
North Ferriby 40 F
Northfield 23 C
Northfield 54 A
Northfield 67 E
Northfleet 18 G
North Flobbets 67 A
North Frodingham 41 A
Northgate 33 J
North Gluss 80 J
North Gorley 7 C
North Green 27 E
North Greetwell 33 B
North Grimston 45 K
North Halley 79 H
North Hayling 8 F
North Hazelrigg 54 H
North Heasley 13 H
North Heath 9 B
North Hill 4 F
North Hill 26 D
North Hinksey Village 16 B
North Holmwood 17 L
North Huish 5 H
North Hykeham 33 B
Northiam 10 J
Northill 25 H
Northington 16 L
North Kelsey 40 J
North Kessock 71 H
North Killimster 78 H
North Killingholme 41 G
North Kilvington 44 H
North Kilworth 24 C
North Kyme 33 F
North Lancing 9 E
Northlands 34 D
Northleach 23 M
North Lee 16 C
Northleigh 6 A
North Leigh 24 K
North Leverton with Habblesthorpe 40 L
Northlew 5 A
North-Littleton 23 F
North Lopham 27 D
North Luffenham 33 L
North Marden 8 C
North Marston 24 M
North Middleton 53 B
North Middleton 54 K
Northmoor 16 A
Northmoor Green or Moorland 14 L
North Molton 13 H
North Moreton 16 E
Northmuir 59 A
North Mundham 9 D
North-Muskham 33 A
North Newbald 40 F
North Newington 24 H
North Newnton 15 J
North Newton 14 K
North Nibley 15 A
North Oakley 16 H
North Ockendon 18 G
Northolt 17 E
Northop 37 M
Northop Hall 37 M
North Ormsby 41 K
Northorpe 33 J
Northorpe 33 L
Northorpe 40 L
North Owersby 40 M
Northowram 39 B
North Perrott 6 C
North Petherton 14 G
North Petherwin 4 C
North Pickenham 26 C
North Piddle 23 F
Northpound 81 H
North Queensferry 58 L
North Radworthy 13 H
North Rauceby 33 E
Northrepps 35 H
North Reston 34 A
North Rigton 44 K
North Rode 38 M
North Roe 80 E
North Runcton 34 L
North Sandwick 80 E
North Scale 42 H
North Scarle 33 B
North Seaton 49 F
North Shian 64 K
North Shields 49 J
North Shoebury 18 J
North Shore 42 L
North Side 25 C
North Skelton 45 A
North Somercotes 41 L
North Stainley 44 G
North Stainmore 43 B
North Stifford 18 G
North Stoke 16 E
North Stoke 9 D
North Stoke 15 D
North Street 11 A
North Street 16 L
North Sunderland 54 J
North Tamerton 4 C
North Tawton 5 B
North Thoresby 41 K
North Tidworth 15 J
Northtown 79 H
North Tuddenham 27 A
Northwall 79 F
North Walsham 35 L
North Waltham 16 L
North Warnborough 16 L
North Water Bridge 66 M
North Watten 78 E
Northway 12 J
Northway 23 H
North Weald Bassett 18 D
North Wheatley 40 L
North Whilborogh 5 F
Northwich 38 L
Northwick 14 C
North Wick 14 F
North Widcombe 14 F
North Willingham 41 K
North Wingfield 32 B
North Witham 33 H
Northwold 26 B
Northwood 17 E
Northwood 31 D
Northwood 32 B
Northwood Green 23 K
North Wootton 7 A
North Wootton 14 J
North Wootton 34 L
North Wraxall 15 D
Norton 8 D
Norton 9 D
Norton 15 B
Norton 22 B
Norton 23 E
Norton 23 F
Norton 23 H
Norton 24 F
Norton 25 L
Norton 26 J
Norton 30 M
Norton 31 G
Norton 31 H
Norton 32 C
Norton 38 H
Norton 39 M
Norton 40 D
Norton 44 B
Norton Bavant 15 G
Norton Bridge 31 F
Norton Canes 31 J
Norton Canon 22 F
Norton Disney 33 B
Norton Ferris 15 K
Norton Fitzwarren 14 K
Norton Green 8 D
Norton Hawkfield 14 F
Norton Heath 18 D
Norton in Hales 31 E
Norton-in-the-Moors 31 C
Norton-Juxta-Twycross 32 L
Norton-le-Clay 44 H
Norton Lindsey 24 D
Norton Malreward 14 F
Norton Mandeville 18 D
Norton-on-Derwent 45 K
Norton Saint Philip 15 G
Norton sub Hamdon 14 L
Norton Subcourse 27 F
Norwell 33 A
Norwell Woodhouse 33 A
Norwich 27 B
Norwick 80 A
Norwood 39 M
Norwood Green 17 H
Norwood Hill 17 L
Noseley 33 K
Noss 81 J
Noss Mayo 5 G
Nosterfield 44 G
Nostie 70 K
Notgrove 23 M
Noth Otterington 44 H
Nottage 13 B
Nottingham 32 F
Nottington 7 D
Notton 15 E
Notton 39 F
Nounsley 18 E
Nowton 26 J
Nox 30 J
Nuffield 16 E
Nunburnholme 40 B
Nuneaton 32 L
Nuneham Courtenay 16 B
Nun Monkton 44 L
Nunney 15 G
Nunnington 44 J
Nunnykirk 49 B
Nuns Quarter 105 H
Nunthorpe 44 C
Nunton 15 L
Nunwick 49 D
Nursling 8 A
Nursted 8 C
Nutbourne 8 F
Nutbourne 9 B
Nuthall 32 F
Nuthampstead 25 M
Nuthurst 9 B
Nuthurst 24 A
Nutley 9 C
Nutley 10 D
Nutwell 40 G
Nyadd 57 J
Nybster 78 F
Nyetimber 9 D
Nyewood 8 C
Nymet Rowland 13 K
Nymet Tracey 5 B
Nympsfield 23 K
Nynehead 14 K
Nyton 9 D

O

Oadby 32 M
Oad Street 10 C
Oak Cross 5 A
Oakamoor 32 A
Oakbank 52 C
Oakdale-Pont-llanfraith 22 K
Oake Hillfarrance 14 K
Oaken 31 H
Oakenclough 42 M
Oakengates-Donnington 31 H
Oakenshaw 49 L
Oakenshaw Wyke 39 E
Oakerthorpe 32 B
Oakford 13 L
Oakford 21 A
Oakfordbridge 13 L
Oakgrove 38 M
Oakham 33 K
Oakhanger 16 M
Oakhill 14 J
Oakington-Longstanton 26 D
Oaklands 17 B
Oaklands 37 K
Oakle Street 23 K
Oakley 7 E
Oakley 16 B
Oakley 16 L
Oakley 25 H
Oakley 27 D
Oakley 58 K
Oakley Green 17 G
Oakridge Lynch 23 L
Oaks 30 J
Oaksey 15 B
Oakthorpe 32 H
Oakwood 49 D
Oakwoodhill 9 B
Oakworth 39 A
Oare 11 A
Oare 13 E
Oare 15 J
Oasby 33 H
Oatfield 50 E
Oathlaw 59 A
Oborne 14 M
Occlestone Green 38 L
Occold 27 G
Occumster 78 L
Ochiltree 51 J
Ochtermuthill 58 D
Ochtertyre 58 D
Ockbrook 32 E
Ockham 17 K
Ockle 63 E
Ockley 9 B
Ocle Pychard 23 D
Ocraquoy 81 H
Odcombe 6 C
Oddendale 43 A
Oddingley 23 E
Oddington 24 K
Oddington 24 L
Odd Town 15 D
Odell 25 G
Odie 79 F
Odiham 16 M
Odstock 15 L
Odstone 32 L
Offchurch 24 E
Offenham 23 F
Offham 9 F
Offord Cluny 25 F
Offord D'Arcy 25 F
Offton 27 K
Offwell 6 A
Ogbourne Maizey 15 F
Ogbourne Saint Andrew 15 F
Ogbourne Saint George 15 F
Ogil 66 L
Ogle 49 E
Ogmore 13 C
Ogmore-by-Sea 13 C
Ogmore Vale 21 M
Okeford Fitzpaine 7 A
Okehampton 5 A
Okehampton Camp 5 A
Olantigh 11 D
Old 25 D
Old Aberdeen 67 E
Old Alresford 16 L
Old Arley 32 K
Old Basing 16 L
Old Beetley 35 K
Old Belses 53 H
Oldberrow 23 C
Old Bewick 54 L
Old Bolingbroks 34 D
Oldborough 13 L
Old Brampton 39 L
Old Bridge of Urr 47 A
Old Buckenham 27 D
Old Burghclere 16 G
Oldbury 31 L
Oldbury 32 K
Oldbury-on-Severn 14 C
Oldbury on the Hill 15 A
Oldbury-Smethwick 31 M
Old Byland 44 J
Oldcastle 22 H
Oldcastle Heath 31 A
Old Castleton 48 B
Old Cleeve 13 J
Old Colwyn 37 G
Oldcotes 40 K
Old Court 22 E
Old Craighall 53 A
Oldcroft 23 K
Old Crombie 73 K
Old Dailly 51 H
Old Dalby 32 J
Old Deer 73 L
Old Denaby 39 J
Old Dowg 14 C
Old Duffus 72 H
Old Ellerby 41 B
Old Felixstowe 19 B
Oldfield 23 B
Oldfield 39 A
Oldford 15 G
Old Gore 23 G
Oldham 39 D
Oldhamstocks 54 A
Old Hunstanton 34 J
Oldhurst 25 F
Old Huttont 43 D
Old Kea 3 J
Old Kilpatrick 57 K
Old Kinnerrie 67 D
Old Knebworth 17 B
Oldland 14 F
Old Leake 34 D
Old Malton 45 K
Oldmeldrum 67 A
Old Micklefield 39 C
Old Milverton 24 D
Old Monkland 52 B
Old Newton 27 G
Old Park 31 G
Old Park 105 D
Old Philpstoun 58 K
Old Radnor 22 B
Old Rattray 73 M
Old Rayne 67 A
Old Romney 11 G
Old Scone 58 E
Oldshore Beg 76 F
Oldshoresmore 76 F
Old Sodbury 15 A
Old Somerby 33 H
Oldstead 44 J
Old Stratford 24 J
Old Swarland 49 B
Old Town 3 A
Old Town 43 D
Oldtown 66 C
Oldtown of Ord 73 K
Oldwalls 21 K
Old Warden 25 H
Oldways End 13 L
Old Weston 25 E
Oldwhat 73 L
Old Windsor-Horton 17 G
Old Wives Lees 11 A
Oldwood 23 A
Olgrinmore 78 D
Oliver 52 J
Oliver's Battery 8 B
Ollaberry 80 H
Ollerton 31 D
Ollerton 33 A
Ollerton 38 M
Olney 25 G
Olton 23 C
Olveston 14 C
Omagh 103 C
Ombersley 23 B
Ompton 33 A
Onchan 37 B
Onecote 32 A
Onehouse 27 G
Ongar Hill 34 L
Ongar Street 22 C
Onibury 30 M
Onllwyn 21 J
Onneley 31 B
On Thames 16 E
Onslow Village 17 K
Onziebust 79 E
Opinan 70 A
Opinan 76 K
Orange Lane 54 D
Orasaigh 75 G
Orbliston 72 H
Orbost 69 D
Orby 34 E
Orcas 14 M
Orchard Leigh 17 A
Orchard Portman 14 K
Orchard's Town 107 J
Orcheston 15 H
Orcop 22 J
Orcop Hill 22 J
Ord 69 M
Ordhead 67 D
Ordie 66 F
Ordiquish 72 L
Ordley 73 K
Ord Muir 71 H
Ore 10 J
Oreton 31 K
Orford 27 L
Orford 38 H
Orgreave 32 G
Orlestone 11 D
Orleton 22 C
Orleton 23 A
Orlingbury 25 D
Ormesby 27 C
Ormesby 44 C
Ormesby Saint Michael 27 C
Ormidale 56 H
Ormiscaig 70 B
Ormiston 53 B
Ormsaigmore 63 H
Ormsary 56 G
Ormskirk 38 D
Orphir 79 G
Orpington 17 J
Orrell 38 E
Orritor 104 A
Orroland 47 D
Orsett 18 G
Orslow 31 H
Orston 33 D
Orton 25 A
Orton 25 C
Orton 43 A
Orton 72 L
Orton-on-the-Hill 32 L
Orwell 25 J
Osbaldeston 38 B
Osbaston 32 L
Osbournby 33 H
Oscroft 38 K
Ose 69 G
Osgathorpe 32 H
Osgodby 40 D
Osgodby 40 M
Osgodby 45 H
Osisdale 71 C
Oskaig 69 J
Oskamull 63 K
Osmaston 32 D
Osmington 7 D
Osmington Mills 7 D
Osmotherley 44 E
Ospringe 11 A
Ossett 39 E
Ossington 33 A
Ostend 18 F
Ostend 35 M
Oswaldkirk 44 J
Oswaldtwistle 38 C
Oswestry 30 F
Otford 10 B
Othery Pathe 14 L
Otley 27 K
Otley 39 B
Otterburn 43 L
Otterburn 49 A
Otterburn Camp 49 A
Otter Ferry 56 H
Otterham 4 B
Otterhampton 14 G
Ottershaw 17 G
Otterswick 80 E
Otterton 6 D
Ottery Saint Mary 6 A
Ottringham 41 G
Oughterby 48 D
Oughtershaw 43 H
Oughtibridge 39 H
Oulston 44 J
Oulton 27 F
Oulton 31 F
Oulton 35 L
Oulton 39 F
Oulton 47 J
Oulton Broad 27 F
Oulton Street 35 L
Oundle 25 B
Ousby 48 L
Ousdale 78 K
Ousden 26 H
Ousefleet 40 E
Ouston 49 H
Outer Hope 5 K
Outertown 79 G
Outgate 42 C
Outhgill 43 E
Outlands 31 E
Outlane 39 E
Out Newton 41 H
Out Rawcliffe 42 M
Outwell 26 A
Outwood 17 L
Outwood 39 F
Outwoods 31 H
Ovenden 39 B
Over 14 C
Over 25 F
Overbister 79 F
Overbury 23 H
Over Compton 14 M
Over Green 32 K
Over Haddon 32 A
Over Kellet 43 G
Over Kiddington 24 K
Over Norton 24 G
Over Peover 38 M
Over Silton 44 E
Oversland 11 A
Oversley Green 23 F
Overstone 25 D
Overstrand 35 H
Over Stratton 14 L
Overthorpe 24 H
Overton 16 K
Overton 22 C
Overton 30 C
Overton 42 J
Overton 47 E
Overton 67 D
Overton 67 E
Overtown 15 E
Overtown 52 B
Over Wallop 15 M
Over Whitacre 32 K
Over Worten 24 H
Overy 32 M
Oving 9 D
Oving 24 M
Ovingdean 9 F
Ovingham 49 H
Ovington 16 K
Ovington 26 C
Ovington 26 L
Ovington 44 A
Ovington 49 G
Ower 8 A
Owermoigne 7 D
Owler Bar 39 L
Owlswick 16 C
Owmby-by-Spital 40 M
Owslebury 8 B
Owston 33 K
Owston Ferry 40 H
Owstwick 41 B
Owthorpe 33 G
Owton Manor 44 C
Oxborough 26 B
Oxcombe 34 A
Oxen End 26 L
Oxenholme 43 D
Oxenhope 39 A
Oxen Park 42 F
Oxenton 23 H
Oxenwood 15 J
Oxford 16 B
Oxhill 24 G
Oxley 31 M
Oxnam 53 M
Oxspring 39 H
Oxted 10 A
Oxton 32 F
Oxton 53 E
Oxwich 21 K

Oxwich Green 21 K
Oxwick 34 M
Oykel Bridge 71 A
Oyne 67 A

P

Pabail Iarach 75 E
Packington 32 H
Padanaram 59 A
Padbury 24 M
Paddington 17 E
Paddlesworth 11 E
Paddock Wood 10 E
Paddockhaugh 72 H
Paddolgreen 31 D
Padeswood 37 M
Padiham 38 C
Padside 44 K
Padstow 4 A
Padworth 16 H
Pagham 9 D
Paglesham Churchend 18 F
Paglesham Eastend 18 J
Pagnell 25 G
Paibeil 68 B
Paignton 5 J
Pailton 24 B
Paincastle 22 E
Painshawfield 49 G
Painswick 23 L
Painter's Forstal 11 A
Paisley 57 L
Pakefield 27 F
Pakenham 26 J
Pale 30 A
Palestine 15 M
Paley Street 16 J
Palgrave 27 D
Palmerstown 14 D
Palnackie 47 D
Palnure 46 C
Palterton 32 C
Pamber End 16 H
Pamber Green 16 H
Pamber Heath 16 H
Pamington 23 H
Pampisford 26 G
Pan 79 G
Panbride 59 D
Pancras 7 A
Pancrasweek 12 L
Pandy 22 H
Pandy 30 B
Pandy 30 G
Pandy Tudur 37 K
Panfield 18 B
Pangbourne 16 E
Pannal 44 K
Pant 30 F
Pant Glâs 36 L
Pant Mawr 29 M
Panteg 20 A
Pant-glas 29 J
Pantgwyn 20 C
Pantherthog 29 F
Pant-lasau 21 L
Pant-Meredith 21 E
Panton 33 C
Pant-y-dwr 30 K
Pantyffridd 30 H
Pantyffynnon 21 H
Panxworth 27 C
Papcastle 47 M
Papil 81 H
Papple 53 C
Papworth Everard 25 J
Papworth Saint Agnes 25 F
Parbold 38 E
Parbrook 14 J
Parc 30 A
Parc-Henri 21 D
Parcllyn 20 C
Parc Seymour 14 B
Pardshaw 47 L
Parham 27 H
Parish Holm 52 D
Park 52 L
Park 108 K
Park Bernisdale 69 E
Park Corner 16 F
Parkadeil 103 H
Parkend 22 M
Park End 49 D
Parkeston 19 A
Park Farm 11 D
Park Gate 8 E
Parkgate 17 L
Parkgate 37 J
Parkgate 47 C
Parkgate 104 C
Parkham 12 J
Parkham Ash 12 J
Parkhouse 22 M
Parkhurst 8 E
Parkmill 21 K
Parkstone 7 E
Parley Cross 7 F
Parracombe 13 D
Parrog 20 B
Parsonby 47 J
Parson Cross 39 J
Parson Drove 34 K
Partick 57 L
Partington 38 J
Partney 34 A
Parton 47 A
Parton 47 L
Partridge Green 9 E
Partrishow 22 H
Parva 27 H
Parwich 32 A
Passenham 24 J
Passingford Bridge 18 D
Paston 35 M
Patcharn 9 F
Patching 9 E
Patchole 13 D
Patchway 14 C
Pateley Brigde 44 K
Path of Condie 58 H
Pathfinder Village 5 C
Pathhead 52 G
Pathhead 53 B
Pathhead 58 L
Pathlow 24 D
Patmore Heath 25 M
Patna 51 J
Patney 15 H
Patrick 37 A
Patrick Brompton 44 D
Patrington 41 G
Patrixbourne 11 B
Patterdale 48 K
Pattingham 31 L
Pattishall 24 F
Pattiswick 18 B
Patton Bridge 43 D
Paul 3 G
Paulerspury 24 J
Paull 41 B
Paulton 14 J
Pauperhaugh 49 B
Pavenham 25 H
Pawlett 14 G
Pawston 54 G
Paxford 23 J
Paxton 54 D
Payhembury 6 A
Paythorne 43 L
Peacehaven 9 J
Peak Dale 39 K
Peak Forest 39 K
Peakirk 33 M
Pean Hill 11 A
Pearsie 66 L
Pease Pottage 9 C
Peasedown Saint John 15 G
Peasemore 16 D
Peasenhall 27 H
Peaslake 17 K
Peasmarsh 10 J
Peaston 53 B
Peastonbank 53 B
Peat Inn 59 G
Peathill 73 L
Peatling Magna 24 C
Peatling Parva 24 C
Peaton 31 K
Peats Corner 27 G
Pebmarsh 26 M
Pebworth 23 F
Pecket Well 39 A
Peckforton 31 A
Peckleton 32 L
Pedwell 14 H
Peebles 53 D
Peel 37 A
Peggs Green 32 H
Pegsdon 25 L
Pegswood 49 E
Peinchorran 69 H
Peinlich 69 E
Pelaw 49 J
Pelcomb Cross 20 D
Peldon 18 C
Pelham 25 M
Pelsall 31 M
Pelton 49 H
Pelutho 47 J
Pelynt 4 H
Pembrey 21 G
Pembridge 22 C
Pembroke 20 G
Pembroke Dock/Doc Penfro 20 G
Pembury 10 E
Penallt 22 M
Penally 20 H
Penare 4 G
Penarth 14 A
Pen-bont Rhydybeddau 29 L
Penbryn 20 C
Pencader 21 D
Pencaitland 53 B
Pencarreg 21 A
Pencelli 22 G
Penclawdd 21 K
Pencoed 13 C
Pencombe 23 D
Pencoyd 22 J
Pencraig 22 J
Pencraig 30 E
Pencroesoped 22 L
Pendas Fields 39 C
Penderyn 21 J
Pendine 20 J
Pendlebury 38 F
Pendleton 38 C
Pendock 23 G
Pendoggett 4 B
Pendomer 6 C
Pendoylan 14 A
Penegoes 29 J
Penelewey 3 J
Penffordd 20 E
Penffridd 36 L
Penge 17 J
Pengorffwysfa 36 E
Pengover Green 4 F
Pengwern 37 H
Penhale 4 D
Penhallick 3 M
Penhallow 3 F
Penhalurick 3 J
Penhow 14 B
Penhurst 10 H
Penicuik 53 A
Peniel 37 L
Penifiler 69 H
Peninver 50 F
Penisa'r Waun 36 J
Penistone 39 H
Penjerrick 3 J
Penketh 38 H
Penkevil 3 J
Penkill 51 H
Penkridge 31 J
Penley 30 C
Penllech 29 A
Penllergaer 21 K
Penllyn 13 C
Pen-llyn 36 E
Penmachno 37 K
Penmaen 21 K
Penmaen 22 K
Penmaenpool 29 F
Penmark 13 C
Penmon 36 J
Penmorfa 29 B
Penmynydd 36 J
Penn 17 D
Penn Street 17 D
Pennal 29 J
Pennan 73 L
Pennant 29 L
Pennant 30 G
Pennant 37 K
Pennant Melangell 30 D
Pennard 21 K
Pennerley 30 J
Pennington 42 E
Penny Bridge 42 F
Pennycross 55 C
Pennygate 35 M
Pennygown 63 L
Pennymoor 13 L
Pennyvenie 51 J
Penparc 20 C
Penparcau Rhydyfelin 29 L
Penperlleni 22 L
Penpillick 4 E
Penpol 3 J
Penpoll 4 H
Penponds 3 H
Penpont 52 L
Penre-bach 21 B
Penrherber 20 C
Penrhiwceiber 22 K
Penrhiw-llan 21 A
Penrhiwpal 21 A
Penrhos 22 M
Penrhos 29 A
Penrhos 36 D
Penrhyn Bay 37 G
Penrhyncoch 29 H
Penrhyndeudraeth 29 C
Penrhynside 37 G
Penrhys 21 M
Penrice 21 K
Penrith 48 L
Penrose 4 D
Penruddock 48 K
Pensarn 37 H
Pensarn 36 L
Pensarn Pentre 29 B
Pensax 23 A
Pensby 37 J
Penselwood 15 K
Pensford 14 F
Pensham 23 E
Penshaw 49 J
Penshurst 10 A
Pensilva 4 F
Penston 53 B
Pentewan 4 G
Pentir 36 J
Pentire 3 F
Pentland Hills 53 A
Pentlepoir 20 H
Pentlow 26 L
Pentney 34 L
Penton Mewsey 16 G
Pentraeth 36 J
Pentre 30 B
Pentre 30 C
Pentre 30 F
Pentre 30 K
Pentrebach 21 F
Pentrebach 21 H
Pentrebach 22 K
Pentre Berw 36 H
Pentre-bont 36 M
Pentrecagal 20 C
Pentrecelyn 30 G
Pentre-celyn 37 L
Pentreclwydau 21 M
Pentre-cwrt 21 D
Pentre Dolau Honddu 22 D
Pentredwr 21 L
Pentredwr 30 B
Pentrefelin 29 B
Pentrefelin 30 E
Pentrefelin 37 G
Pentre-felin 21 E
Pentrefoelas 37 K
Pentre Galar 20 F
Pentregat 21 A
Pentre-Gwenlais 21 H
Pentre Halkyn 37 J
Pentreheyling 30 H
Pentre Isaf 37 G
Pentre-Llanrhaeadr 37 L
Pentre Llifior 30 H
Pentre-llwyn-llwyd 22 A
Pentre-llyn 29 L
Pentre-llyn-cymmer 37 L
Pentre-mawr 37 H
Pentre-Morgan 21 D
Pentre'rbeirdd 30 E
Pentre'rfelin 21 F
Pentre-tafarn-y-fedw 37 K
Pentre-ty-gwyn 21 F
Pentrich 32 B
Pentridge 7 C
Pentwyn 14 A
Pentyrch 14 A
Penuwch 29 L
Penwithick 4 D
Penwyllt 21 J
Pen-y-banc 21 E
Penybont 22 A
Pen-y-bont 20 F
Pen-y-bont Llanerch Emrys 30 E
Penybontfawr 30 E
Pen-y-bryn 20 C
Penybryn 22 K
Pen-y-bryn 29 F
Penycae 30 C
Pen-y-cae 21 J
Pen-y-cae-mawr 22 L
Pen-y-cefn 37 H
Pen-y-clawdd 22 M
Pen-y-coedcae 14 A
Penycwm 20 D
Pen-y-fai 13 C
Penyffordd 37 M
Pen-y-ffordd 37 J
Pen-y-gârn 21 E
Penygarnedd 30 E
Pen-y-garnedd 36 J
Penygraig 21 M
Pen-y-graig Llangwnnadl 29 A
Penygroes 36 L
Pen-y-groes 21 G
Pen-y-lan 13 C
Pen-y-Mynydd 21 G
Pen-y-Park 22 E
Pen-yr-heol 22 M
Penysarn 36 E
Pen-y-stryt 30 C
Penywaun 21 M
Penzance 3 G
Peopleton 23 E
Peover Heath 38 M
Peper Harow 16 M
Peplow 31 D
Perceton 51 C
Percie 66 J
Percyhorner 73 M
Perham Down 15 J
Perivale 17 E
Perkhill 66 F
Perlethorpe 33 A
Perran Downs 3 H
Perranarworthal 3 J
Perranporth 3 F
Perranuthnoe 3 H
Perranwell 3 J
Perranzabuloe 3 F
Perry 25 E
Perry Barr 31 M
Perry Green 17 C
Perrystone Hill 23 G
Pershall 31 E
Pershore 23 E
Pert 66 M
Pertenhall 25 E
Perth 58 E
Perthy 30 F
Perton 31 L
Peterborough 25 C
Peterburn 70 A
Peterchurch 22 E
Peterculter Milltimber 67 G
Peterhead 67 C
Peterlee 49 M
Petersfield 8 C
Peter's Green 17 B
Peters Marland 12 M
Peterstone Wentlooge 14 B
Peterston-super-Ely 14 A
Peterstow 22 J
Peter Tavy 5 D
Petertown 79 G
Petham 11 D
Petrockstowe 12 M
Pett 10 J
Pettaugh 27 G
Pettinain 52 F
Pettistree 27 L
Petton 13 M
Petton 30 F
Petts Wood 17 J
Petty 67 A
Pettycur 58 L
Pettymuick 67 E
Petworth 9 A
Pevensey Bay 10 L
Peverel 18 B
Pewsey 15 J
Pharis 108 J
Philham 12 H
Philiphaugh 53 H
Phillack 3 H
Philleigh 3 J
Philpstoun 58 K
Phocle Green 23 G
Phoenix Green 16 J
Piblae 73 M
Pica 47 L
Piccadilly Corner 27 E
Piccotts End 17 A
Pickerells 18 A
Pickering 45 G
Picket Piece 16 K
Picket Post 7 C
Pickhill 44 H
Picklescott 30 J
Pickletillem 59 D
Pickmere 38 L
Pickney 14 K
Pickstock 31 E
Pickwell 12 F
Pickwell 33 K
Pickworth 33 H
Pickworth 33 L
Picton 38 K
Picton 44 E
Piddinghoe 9 J
Piddington 16 F
Piddington 24 M
Piddington 25 G
Piddlehinthide 7 A
Piddlehinton 7 D
Pidley 25 F
Piercebridge 44 A
Piercy 44 C
Pierowall 79 B
Pigdon 49 E
Pikehall 32 A
Pikes 42 B
Pikes 42 C
Pilgrims Hatch 18 D
Pilham 40 L
Pill 14 C
Pillaton 4 F
Pillerton-Hersey 24 D
Pillerton-Priors 24 D
Pilleth 22 B
Pilley 8 D
Pilley 39 J
Pilling 42 M
Pilling Lane 42 M
Pilning 14 C
Pilsbury 32 A
Pilsdon 6 B
Pilsgate 33 L
Pilsley 32 C
Pilsley 39 L
Pilton 14 J
Pilton 25 B
Pilton 33 K
Pilton Green 21 K
Pimperne 7 B
Pinchbeck 33 J
Pinchbeck West 33 J
Pinfold 38 D
Pinhay 6 E
Pinhoe 5 C
Pinley Green 24 D
Pinminnoch 51 K
Pinmore 51 L
Pinn 6 D
Pinner Harrow 17 E
Pinvin 23 E
Pinwherry 51 K
Pinxton 32 B
Pipe and Lyde 22 F
Pipe Gate 31 B
Piperhall 56 M
Piperhill 71 J
Pipe Ridware 32 G
Pipers Pool 4 C
Pipewell 25 A
Pippacott 13 G
Pipton 22 E
Pirnmill 50 C
Pirton 23 E
Pirton 25 L
Pisgah 29 L
Pishill 16 F
Pistyll 36 K
Pitagowan 65 L
Pitcairngreen 58 E
Pitcalnie 71 F
Pitcaple 67 A
Pitchcombe 23 L
Pitchcott 24 M
Pitchford 31 G
Pitch Place 17 K
Pitcombe 14 M
Pitcox 53 C
Pitcur 58 C
Pitfichie 67 D
Pitforthie 67 K
Pitgrudy 71 C
Pitkennedy 59 A
Pitkevy 58 J
Pitlessie 58 J
Pitlochry 65 M
Pitmachie 67 A
Pitmedden 67 B
Pitminster 14 K
Pitmuies 59 A
Pitmunie 67 D
Pitney 14 L
Pitscottie 58 J
Pitsea 18 H
Pitsford 24 F
Pitsford Hill 13 J
Pittendreich 72 H
Pittentrail 71 C
Pittenweem 59 G
Pittington 49 M
Pitton 15 M
Pitton 21 K
Pittulie 73 J
Pityme 4 A
Pity Me 49 L
Pixey Green 27 H
Place Newton 45 K
Plaidy 73 K
Plains 52 B
Plains 57 M
Plaish 31 G
Plaistow 9 A
Plaitford 8 A
Plâs Brondanw 36 M
Plas Fawr 21 D
Plas Gogerddan 29 H
Plas Gwynant Bethania 36 M
Plâs Llwyngwern 29 F
Plas Llysyn 30 G
Plas Nantyr 30 B
Plas-rhiw-Saeson 30 G
Plastow Green 16 H
Plawsworth 49 L
Plaxtol 10 B
Playden 10 J
Playford 27 K
Play Hatch 16 F
Playing Place 3 J
Plealey 30 J
Plean 57 M
Pleasington 38 B
Pleasley 32 C
Plenderleith 53 M
Plenmeller 48 F
Pleshey 18 A
Plockton 70 G
Plocrapol 74 M
Plowden 30 M
Ploxgreen 30 J
Pluckley 10 F
Pluckley Thorne 10 F
Plumbland 47 J
Plumbridge 107 M
Plumley 38 L
Plumpton 9 F
Plumpton 38 A
Plumpton 48 L
Plumpton Green 9 F
Plumpton Head 48 L
Plumstead 17 J
Plumstead 35 L
Plumton Rocks 44 L
Plumtree 32 J
Plungar 33 G
Plush 7 A
Plwmp 21 A
Plymouth 5 G
Plympton 5 G
Plymstock 5 G
Plymtree 6 A
Pockley 44 J
Pocklington 40 B
Pockthorpe 34 M
Pode Hole 33 M
Podimore 14 M
Podington 25 D
Podmore 27 A
Podmore 31 E
Point Clear 19 A
Pointon 33 J
Pokesdown 7 F
Pol a' Charra 68 L
Polapit Tamar 4 C
Polbae 46 B
Polbain 76 L
Polbathic 4 J
Polbeth 52 C
Polchar 65 F
Poldean 52 M
Polebrook 25 B
Polegate 10 G
Poles 71 C
Polesworth 32 K
Polglass 76 L
Polgooth 4 G
Poling 9 D
Polkerris 4 H
Polla 77 D
Poll Beg 103 D
Pollington 40 D
Pollo 71 F
Polloch 63 J
Pollokshaws 52 A
Pollokshields 57 L
Polmassick 4 G
Polmont 58 K
Polnessan 51 J
Polperro 4 H
Polruan 4 H
Polsham 14 H
Polskeoch 52 K
Polstead 26 M
Polstead Heath 26 M
Poltalloch 56 E
Poltimore 5 C
Polton 53 A
Polwarth 53 F
Polyphant 4 C
Polzeath 4 A
Pomeroy 104 A
Ponde 22 D
Pondersbridge 25 C
Ponders End 17 F
Pond Street 26 K
Ponsanooth 3 J
Ponsongath 3 M
Ponsworthy 5 E
Pont Aberglaslyn 36 M
Pontamman 21 H
Pontantwn 21 G
Pontardawe-Clydach 21 H
Pontarddulais 21 G
Pontarsais 21 D
Pont Creuddyn 21 B
Pont Crugnant 30 G
Pont Cyfyng 36 M
Pontefract 39 F
Ponteland 49 E
Ponterwyd 29 M
Pontesbury 30 J
Pontesford 30 J
Pontfadog 30 C
Pontfaen 20 B
Pont-faen 22 D
Pontgarreg 21 A
Pont Henri 21 G
Ponthir 22 L
Ponthirwaun Bryngwyn 20 C
Pont Llanio 21 B
Pontlliw 21 L
Pont Llogel 30 D
Pontllyfni 36 L
Pontlottyn 22 K
Pontneddfechan 21 J
Pont Pen-y-benglog 36 M
Pontrhydfendigaid 29 M
Pont Rhyd-y-cyff 21 M
Pont-rhyd-y-groes 29 M
Pontrilas 22 J
Pontrobert 30 E
Pontrug 36 H
Ponts Green 10 H
Pontshill 23 G
Pont-Sian 21 A
Pontsticill 22 G
Pontyates 21 G
Pontyberem 21 G
Pontybodkin 37 M
Pontyclun-Llantrisant 13 C
Pontycymer 21 M
Pontymister 14 B
Pont-y-pant 37 K
Pontypool-Cwmbran 22 L
Pontypridd 22 K
Pont-yr-hafod 20 D
Pontywaun 22 K
Pooksgreen 8 A
Pool 3 J
Pool 39 C
Poole 7 E
Poole Keynes 15 B
Poolewe 70 A
Pooley Bridge 48 K
Poolhill 23 G
Pool of Muckhart 58 G
Pool Quay 30 H
Poorton 6 C
Pope Hill 20 D
Popeswood 16 J
Popham 16 L
Poplar 17 J
Porchfield 8 D
Poringland 27 B
Porkellis 3 J
Porlock 13 E
Porlock Weir 13 E
Portachoillan 56 K
Portadown 104 E
Portaferry 105 H
Port-an-eorna 70 G
Port Ann 56 H
Port Appin 64 K
Port Askaig 55 H
Portavadie 56 L
Portavogie 105 H
Portballintrae 108 F
Port Bannatyne 56 M
Port Carlisle 47 F
Port Charlotte 55 L
Portclair 65 A
Port Driseach 56 H
Port Ellen 55 L
Port Elphinstone 67 D
Portencalzie 46 A
Portencross 51 B
Port Erin 37 D
Portesham 6 F
Port e Vullen 37 B
Port-Eynon 21 K
Portfield Gate 20 D
Portgate 5 A
Port Gaverne 4 A
Port Glasgow 57 K
Portglenone 108 L
Portgordon 72 J
Portgower 77 M
Porth 21 M
Porthallow 3 M
Porthcawl 13 B
Porthcothan 4 A
Porthcurno 3 K
Port Henderson 70 A
Porthgain 20 A
Porthkerry 14 D
Porthleven 3 L
Porthllechog 36 E
Porthmadog 29 B
Porthmeor 3 G
Porth Navas 3 M
Portholland 4 G
Porthoustock 3 M
Porthpean 4 G
Porthtowan 3 F
Porthyrhyd 21 E
Porthyrhyd 21 G
Porth-y-waen 30 F
Portincaple 57 G
Portington 40 E
Portinnisherrich 56 E
Portinscale 47 M
Port Isaac 4 A
Portishead 14 B
Portknockie 72 J
Portlethen 67 H
Portlethen Village 67 H
Portloe 4 G
Port Logan 46 D
Portmahomack 72 D

Rock Ferry 38 G
Rockfield 22 M
Rockfield 72 D
Rockhampton 15 A
Rockhill 30 L
Rock House 104 F
Rockingham 25 A
Rockland All Saints 27 A
Rockland Saint Mary 27 B
Rockland Saint Peter 27 A
Rockley 15 F
Rockwell End 16 F
Rockwell Green 13 M
Rodbourne 15 B
Rodbourne 15 C
Rodd 22 B
Roddam 54 L
Rodden 6 F
Roddymoor 49 L
Rode 15 G
Rode Heath 31 B
Rodeheath 38 M
Roden 31 G
Rodhuish 13 J
Rodington 31 G
Rodley 23 K
Rodmarton 15 B
Rodmell 9 F
Rodmersham 11 A
Rodney Stoke 14 H
Rodsley 32 D
Roecliffe Minskip 44 L
Roehampton 17 H
Roesound 80 J
Roffey 9 B
Rogart 71 C
Rogate 8 C
Rogerstone 14 B
Rogerton 52 A
Roghadal 74 M
Rogiet 14 C
Roke 16 B
Roker 49 J
Rollesby 27 C
Rolleston 32 D
Rolleston 33 D
Rolleston 33 K
Rolston 41 A
Rolstone 14 E
Rolvenden 10 F
Romaldkirk 43 C
Romanby 44 E
Romannobridge 53 D
Romansleigh 13 L
Romford 17 F
Romiley 39 G
Romsey 8 A
Romsley 23 C
Romsley 31 L
Ronague 37 D
Rookby 43 B
Rookery Hill 10 G
Rookery Hill 9 J
Rookhope 49 K
Rookley 8 H
Rooks Bridge 14 H
Roos 41 B
Roosebeck 42 H
Roosecote 42 H
Rootpark 52 C
Ropley 8 C
Ropley Dean 8 C
Ropsley 33 H
Rora 73 M
Rorandle 67 D
Rorrington 30 J
Rosarie 72 M
Rose 3 F
Roseacre 42 M
Rose Ash 13 L
Rosebank 52 B
Rosebrough 54 L
Rosebush 20 E
Rosedale Abbey 45 G
Roseden 54 L
Rosefield 71 J
Rosehall 71 B
Rosehearty 73 H
Rosehill 31 E
Rosehill 66 J
Roseisle 72 H
Rosemarket 20 G
Rosemarkie 71 H
Rosemary Lane 14 K
Rosemount 51 F
Rosemount 58 C
Rosenannon 4 D
Rosepool 20 D
Rosetta 105 D
Rosewell 53 A
Roseworthy 3 H
Rosgill 43 A
Roshven 63 F
Roskhill 69 D
Rosley 48 G
Roslin 53 A
Roslin Hill 108 M
Rosliston 32 G
Rosneaht 57 G
Ross 46 F
Ross 54 H
Ross 57 F
Rossett 38 K
Rossglass 105 K
Rossie Ochill 58 E
Rossington 40 G
Rossland 57 K
Rosslea 103 H
Ross-on-Wye 23 G
Roster 78 H
Rosthwaite 47 M
Roston 32 D
Rostrevor 104 L
Rosudgeon 3 H
Rosyth 58 L
Rothbury 49 B
Rotherby 32 J
Rotherfield 10 D
Rotherfield Greys 16 F
Rotherfield Peppard 16 F
Rotherham 39 J
Rothersthorpe 24 F
Rotherwas 22 F
Rotherwick 16 H
Rothes 72 L
Rothesay 56 M
Rothiebrisbane 67 A
Rothienorman 67 A
Rothiesholm 79 E
Rothley 32 J
Rothley 49 B
Rothmaise 67 A
Rothwell 25 A
Rothwell 39 F
Rothwell 41 K
Rotsea 41 A
Rottal 66 L
Rottingdean 9 J
Rottington 47 L
Roud 8 H
Rougham 26 J
Rougham 34 M
Rougham Green 26 J
Roughburn 64 F
Rough Close 31 F
Rough Common 11 A
Rough Haugh 77 E
Roughlee 39 A
Roughley 32 K
Roughsike 48 E
Roughton 31 L
Roughton 34 A
Roughton 35 L
Roundbush Green 18 A
Roundhay 39 C
Roundstreet Common 9 B
Roundway 15 H
Rousdon 6 E
Rousham 24 L
Rousky 107 M
Rous Lench 23 F
Routdaneburn 51 B
Routenburn 56 M
Routh 41 A
Row 42 F
Rowanburn 48 A
Rowde 15 E
Rowen 37 D
Rowfoot 48 F
Rowhedge 18 C
Rowhook 9 B
Rowington 24 A
Rowland 39 L
Rowlands Castle 8 F
Rowlands Gill 49 H
Rowledge 16 M
Rowlestone 22 H
Rowley 30 J
Rowley 49 G
Rowley Regis 31 M
Rowney Green 23 C
Rowsham 25 K
Rowsley 32 B
Rowston 33 F
Rowthorne 32 C
Rowton 30 J
Rowton 31 D
Rowton 38 K
Roxborough 104 K
Roxburgh 53 J
Roxby 40 J
Roxby 45 D
Roxhill 104 C
Roxton 25 H
Roxwell 18 A
Royal 17 D
Royal Leamington Spa 24 D
Royal's Green 31 B
Royal Tunbridge Wells 10 E
Roybridge 64 F
Roydon 17 C
Roydon 27 D
Roydon 34 L
Royston 25 M
Royston 39 F
Royton 39 D
Ruabon 30 C
Ruaig 62 J
Ruan Lanihorne 4 G
Ruan Major 3 L
Ruan Minor 3 M
Ruardean Woodside 23 K
Rubane 105 H
Rubery 23 C
Rubha Ghaisinis 68 E
Ruckcroft 48 H
Ruckland 34 A
Rucklers Lane 17 A
Ruckley 31 G
Ruddington 32 F
Rudford 23 G
Rudge 15 G
Rudgeway 14 C
Rudgwick 9 B
Rudhall 23 G
Rudheath Woods 38 L
Rudley Green 18 E
Rudloe 15 D
Rudry 14 A
Rudston 45 L
Rudyard 31 C
Rufford 38 D
Rufforth 40 A
Rugby 24 B
Rugeley 31 J
Ruilick 71 G
Ruishton Ham 14 K
Ruisigearraidh 74 L
Ruislip 17 E
Ruislip Common 17 D
Rumbling Bridge 58 G
Rumburgh 27 E
Rumford 4 D
Rumney 14 A
Rumwell 14 K
Runcorn 38 G
Runcton 9 D
Runcton Holme 34 L
Runfold 16 M
Runhall 27 A
Runham 27 C
Runnington 13 M
Runswick Bay 45 D
Runtaleave 66 K
Runwell 18 E
Ruscombe 16 F
Rushall 15 J
Rushall 23 G
Rushall 27 E
Rushall 31 M
Rushbrooke 26 J
Rushbury 31 K
Rushden 25 D
Rushden 25 M
Rushford 26 F
Rush Green 17 F
Rush Hall 108 G
Rushlake Green 10 H
Rushmere 27 F
Rushmere Saint Andrew 27 K
Rushmoor 16 M
Rushock 23 B
Rusholme 38 J
Rushton 25 A
Rushton 31 G
Rushton 38 L
Rushton Spencer 31 C
Rushwick 23 E
Rushyford 44 B
Ruskie 57 J
Ruskington 33 F
Rusland 42 F
Rusper 9 B
Ruspidge 23 K
Russel's Water 16 F
Rustington 9 D
Ruston Parva 45 L
Ruswarpe 45 E
Rutherend 52 A
Rutherford 53 J
Rutherglen 52 A
Ruthernbridge 4 D
Ruthers of Howe 78 E
Ruthin/Rhuthun 37 L
Ruthrieston 67 H
Ruthven 58 C
Ruthven 65 E
Ruthven 71 M
Ruthven 72 M
Ruthvenfield 58 E
Ruthvoes 4 D
Ruthwell 47 F
Ruyton-XI-Towns 30 F
Ryal 49 D
Ryal Fold 38 C
Ryall 6 B
Ryarsh 10 B
Rydal 42 C
Ryde 8 E
Rye 10 J
Ryefield 71 H
Rye Foreign 10 J
Rye Harbour 10 J
Ryehill 41 B
Ryhall 33 L
Ryhill 39 F
Ryhope 49 J
Ryhope Colliery 49 J
Rylstone 43 M
Ryme Intrinseca 6 C
Ryther 40 A
Ryton 23 G
Ryton 31 H
Ryton 45 K
Ryton 49 H
Ryton-on-Dunsmore 24 B

S

Saasaig 63 C
Sabden 38 C
Sackers Green 26 M
Sacombe 17 C
Sacriston 49 L
Sadberge 44 B
Saddell 50 C
Saddington 24 C
Saddle Bow 34 L
Sadgill 43 A
Saffron Walden 26 K
Sageston 20 H
Saham Toney 26 C
Saighdinis 68 C
Saighton 38 K
Saint Abbs 54 A
Saint Agnes 3 A
Saint Agnes 3 F
Saint Albans 17 B
Saint Allen 3 F
Saint Andrew 9 K
Saint Andrews 59 G
Saint Andrews Major 14 A
Saint Angelo 103 D
Saint Ann's 52 M
Saint Ann's Chapel 4 F
Saint Anne 8 M
Saint Annes 38 A
Saint Anthony 3 M
Saint Arvans 22 M
Saint Asaph/Llanelwy 37 H
Saint Athan 13 C
Saint Aubin 9 M
Saint Austell 4 D
Saint Bees 47 L
Saint Blazey Gate 4 E
Saint Blazey-Par 4 E
Saint Boswells 53 J
Saint Brelade 9 L
Saint Breock 4 D
Saint Breward 4 B
Saint Briavels 22 M
Saint Bride's Major 13 C
Saint Bride's-super-Ely 14 A
Saint Brides 20 D
Saint Brides Wentlooge 14 B
Saint Budeaux 4 J
Saintbury 23 J
Saint Buryan 3 G
Saint Catherine 15 D
Saint Catherines 56 F
Saint Clears/Sanclêr 20 J
Saint Cleer 4 F
Saint Clement 3 J
Saint Clément 9 M
Saint Clether 4 B
Saint Colmac 56 L
Saint Columb Major 4 D
Saint Columb Minor 4 D
Saint Columb Road 4 D
Saint Combs 73 M
Saint Cross South Elmham 27 E
Saint Cyrus 67 K
Saint David's 20 L
Saint David's 58 D
Saint Day 3 J
Saint Dennis 4 D
Saint Dogmaels 20 C
Saint Dominick 4 F
Saint Donat's 13 C
Saint Endellion 4 A
Saint Enoder 4 D
Saint Erme 3 J
Saint Erth 3 H
Saint Erth Praze 3 H
Saint Ervan 4 D
Saint Eval 4 D
Saint Ewe 4 G
Saint Fagans 14 A
Saint Fergus 73 M
Saintfield 105 G
Saint Fillans 57 F
Saint Florence 20 H
Saint Gennys 12 L
Saint George 37 H
Saint George's 14 A
Saint Germans 4 J
Saint Giles in the Wood 13 K
Saint Giles on the Heath 4 C
Saint Harmon 30 K
Saint Helen Auckland 44 A
Saint Helens 8 H
Saint Helens 38 G
Saint Helier 9 M
Saint Hilary 3 H
Saint Hilary 13 C
Saint Hill 9 C
Saint Ippollyts 25 L
Saint Ishmael 20 J
Saint Ishmael's 20 G
Saint Issey 4 A
Saint Ive 4 F
Saint Ives 3 H
Saint Ives 7 C
Saint Ives 25 F
Saint James South Elmham 27 E
Saint John 4 J
Saint John 9 M
Saint John's 37 A
Saint John's Chapel 48 M
Saint John's Town of Dalry 47 A
Saint John's Chapel 13 G
Saint John's Fen End 34 L
Saint John's Highway 34 L
Saint Johns 23 E
Saint Judes 37 B
Saint Just 3 G
Saint Just in Roseland 3 J
Saint Keverne 3 M
Saint Kew 4 A
Saint Kew Highway 4 B
Saint Keyne 4 E
Saint Lawrence 4 E
Saint Lawrence 8 H
Saint Lawrence 9 M
Saint Lawrence 18 F
Saint Leonards 10 J
Saint Leonards 7 F
Saint Leonards 17 A
Saint Levan 3 K
Saint Lythans 14 A
Saint Mabyn 4 E
Saint Madoes 58 E
Saint Margaret 27 C
Saint Margaret South Elmham 27 E
Saint Margaret's Hope 79 H
Saint Margaret's at Cliffe 11 F
Saint Margarets 22 E
Saint Mark's 37 D
Saint Martin 3 M
Saint Martin 4 J
Saint Martin 9 K
Saint Martin 9 M
Saint Martin 27 L
Saint Martin's 30 C
Saint Martins 58 E
Saint Mary Bourne 16 G
Saint Mary Church 13 C
Saint Mary Cray 17 J
Saint Mary Hill 13 C
Saint Mary in the Marsh 11 G
Saint Mary's 79 H
Saint Mary's Croft 46 A
Saint Mary's Hoo 18 H
Saint Mawes 3 J
Saint Mawgan 4 D
Saint Mellion 4 F
Saint Mellons 14 A
Saint Merryn 4 A
Saint Mewan 4 G
Saint Michael Caerhays 4 G
Saint Michael South Elmham 27 E
Saint Michael's on Wyre 42 M
Saint Michaels 10 F
Saint Michaels 23 A
Saint Michaels 59 D
Saint Minver 4 A
Saint Monans 59 G
Saint Neot 4 E
Saint Neots 25 H
Saint Newlyn East 3 F
Saint Nicholas 20 A
Saint-Nicholas at Wade 11 B
Saint Nicholas Downs 14 A
Saint Ninians 57 J
Saint Olaves 27 F
Saint-Osyth 19 A
Saint Ouen 9 L
Saint Owen's Cross 22 J
Saint Paul's Cray 17 J
Saint Paul's Walden 25 L
Saint Peter 9 M
Saint Peter's 9 K
Saint Peter's 11 C
Saint Petrox 20 G
Saint Pinnock 4 E
Saint Quivox 51 F
Saint Sampson 9 K
Saint Saviour 9 M
Saint Stephen 4 D
Saint Stephens 4 C
Saint Stephens 4 J
Saint Teath 4 B
Saint Tudy 4 B
Saint Twynnells 20 G
Saint Veep 4 E
Saint Vigeans 59 B
Saint Wenn 4 D
Saint Weonards 22 J
Saint Winnow 4 E
Salcombe 5 L
Salcombe Regis 6 D
Salcott-cum-Virley 18 C
Sale 38 J
Saleby 34 B
Sale Green 23 E
Salehurst 10 H
Salem 21 E
Salem 29 H
Salen 63 J
Salen 63 L
Salesbury 38 C
Salford 24 G
Salford 25 G
Salford 38 J
Salford Priors 23 F
Salfords 17 M
Salhouse 27 B
Saline 58 G
Salisbury 15 L
Salkeld Dykes 48 L
Sallachy 70 K
Sallachy 77 K
Salle 35 K
Salmonby 34 A
Salmond's Muir 59 D
Salperton 23 M
Salph End 25 H
Salsburgh 52 B
Salt 31 F
Saltash 4 F
Saltburn 71 F
Saltburn-by-the-Sea 44 C
Saltby 33 G
Saltcoats 51 B
Saltdean 9 J
Salter 43 G
Salterforth 43 L
Salterhill 72 H
Salterswall 38 L
Saltfeet 41 L
Saltfeetby All Saints 41 L
Saltfeetby Saint Clement 41 L
Saltfeetby Saint Peter 41 L
Saltford 14 F
Salthouse 35 G
Saltmarshe 40 E
Salton 44 J
Saltwick 49 E
Saltwood 11 D
Salum 62 J
Salwarpe 23 B
Salwayash 6 C
Sambourne 23 F
Sambrook 31 E
Samhla 68 B
Samlesbury 38 B
Samlesbury Bottoms 38 B
Sampford Arundel 13 M
Sampford Brett 13 J
Sampford Courtenay 5 B
Sampford Peverell 13 M
Sampford Spiney 5 D
Samuelston 53 B
Sanachan 70 G
Sanaigmore 55 H
Sancreed 3 G
Sancton 40 C
Sand 70 B
Sand 81 G
Sandaig 63 C
Sandbach 38 L
Sandbank 56 J
Sandbanks 7 E
Sandend 73 G
Sanderstead 17 M
Sandford 5 C
Sandford 7 E
Sandford 8 H
Sandford 14 E
Sandford 14 M
Sandford 43 B
Sandford 52 D
Sandford Saint Martin 24 K
Sandfordhill 67 C
Sandford-on-Thamas 16 B
Sandgate 11 E
Sandgreen 46 F
Sandhaven 73 M
Sandhead 46 D
Sandhoe 49 D
Sand Hole 40 E
Sandhole 56 E
Sandholes 104 A
Sandholme 34 G
Sandholme 40 E
Sandhurst 10 F
Sandhurst 16 J
Sandhurst 23 H
Sandhutton 44 H
Sand Hutton 44 M
Sandiacre 32 F
Sandilands 34 B
Sandiway 38 L
Sandleheath 7 C
Sandling 10 C
Sandness 80 M
Sandon 18 E
Sandon 25 M
Sandon 31 F
Sandown-Shanklin 8 H
Sandplace 4 E
Sandridge 17 B
Sandringham 34 L
Sandsend 45 D
Sandsound 81 G
Sandtoft 40 H
Sandvoe 80 H
Sandway 10 C
Sandwich 11 B
Sandwick 48 K
Sandwick 79 L
Sandwick 81 H
Sandwith 47 L
Sandy 25 H
Sandycrott 37 M
Sandygate 5 F
Sandygate 37 B
Sandy Haven 20 G
Sandyhills Colvend 47 E
Sandy Lane 15 E
Sangobeg 77 A
Sanna 63 E
Sanndabhaig 68 E
Sanndabhaig 75 E
Sannox 51 A
Sanquhar 52 G
Santon 40 J
Santon Bridge 42 B
Santon Downham 26 F
Sapcote 32 L
Sapey 23 A
Sapey Common 23 A
Sapiston 26 F
Sapperton 23 L
Sapperton 33 H
Sarclet 78 H
Sarisbury 8 E
Sarn 13 C
Sarn 30 L
Sarnau 20 C
Sarnau 20 F
Sarnau 22 D
Sarnau 30 A
Sarnau 30 E
Sarn Bach 29 A
Sarnesfield 22 F
Sarn Meyllteyrn 29 A
Saron 21 D
Saron 21 G
Saron 37 L
Sarrat 17 A
Sarre 11 B
Sarsden 24 K
Sarsgrum 77 A
Satley 49 L
Satran 69 H
Satterleigh 13 K
Satterthwaite 42 F
Sauchen 67 D
Saucher 58 F
Sauchie 58 G
Sauchieburn 66 M
Sauchrie 51 H
Saughall 38 K
Saughtree 48 B
Saul 23 K
Saul 105 G
Saundby 40 L
Saundersfoot 20 H
Saunderton 16 C
Saunton 12 J
Sausthorpe 34 A
Saval 77 K
Savary 63 L
Saverley Green 31 F
Sawbridge 24 E
Sawdon 45 H
Sawley 32 F
Sawley 43 L
Sawley 44 K
Sawrey 42 C
Sawston 26 G
Sawtry 25 C
Saxby 33 G
Saxby 40 M
Saxby All Saints 40 J
Saxelbye 33 G
Saxham 26 H
Saxham Street 27 G
Saxilby 33 B
Saxlingham 27 E
Saxlingham 35 G
Saxlingham Green 27 E
Saxlingham Nethergate 27 E
Saxmundham 27 H
Saxon Street 26 H
Saxtead 27 H
Saxtead Green 27 H
Saxthorpe 35 K
Saxton 40 A
Sayers Common 9 F
Scackleton 44 M
Scadabhagh 74 M
Scaddy 105 G
Scaftworth 40 K
Scagglethorpe 45 K
Scalasaig 55 E
Scalby 45 H
Scalby Mills 45 H
Scaldwell 25 D
Scaleby 48 D
Scaleby Hill 48 D
Scale Houses 48 H
Scales 42 H
Scales 48 K
Scalford 33 G
Scaling 45 D
Scallastle 63 M
Scalloway 81 G
Scamblesby 34 A
Scamodale 63 F
Scampston 45 K
Scampton 40 L
Scapa 79 H
Scar 79 F
Scarborough 45 H
Scarcewater 4 D
Scarcliffe 32 C
Scarcroft 39 C
Scardroy 70 J
Scarff 80 H
Scarfskerry 78 E
Scargill 43 C
Scarisbrick 38 D
Scarning 27 A
Scarnish Heanish 62 A
Scarrington 33 D
Scarth Hill 38 D
Scartho 41 G
Scarva 104 H
Scatness 81 J
Scatraig 71 L
Scawby 40 J
Scawton 44 J
Scayne's Hill 9 C
Scethrog 22 G
Scholar Green 31 C
Scholes 39 C
Scholes 39 E
Schoolhill 67 G
Schoolhill 67 H
Scleddau 20 B
Sco Ruston 35 L
Scofton 40 K
Scole 27 D
Scolpaig 74 K
Scolton 20 E
Scone 58 E
Scoor 55 C
Scopwick 33 F
Scoraig 76 K
Scorborough 40 C
Scorrier 3 J
Scorriton 5 E
Scorton 42 M
Scorton 44 D
Scotbheinn 68 E
Scotby 48 G
Scotch Corner 44 D
Scotch Street 104 E
Scotch Town 107 M
Scotforth 42 J
Scothern 33 C
Scotlandwell 58 H
Scots Gap 49 E
Scotsburn 71 F
Scotscraig 59 D
Scotston 58 A
Scotston 67 K
Scotstown 63 J
Scottas 63 C
Scotter 40 H
Scotterthorpe 40 H
Scotton 40 H

A B C D E F G H I J K L M N O P Q R S T U V W X Y Z

Great Britain 1:301,000 171

South Ferriby 40 F
Southfields 18 G
Southfleet 18 G
South Garvan 64 D
Southgate 17 F
Southgate 21 K
Southgate 35 L
South Gluss 80 J
South Godstone 10 A
South Gorley 7 C
South Green 18 D
South-haa 80 H
South Hanningfield 18 E
South Harting 8 C
South Hayling 8 F
South Heath 17 A
South Heighton Denton 10 G
South Heighton Denton 9 J
South Hetton 49 M
South Hiendley 39 F
South Hill 4 F
South Hinksey 16 B
South Hole 12 H
South Holmwood 17 L
South Hornchurch 18 G
South-Horrington 14 J
South Hourat 51 B
South Hykeham 33 B
South Hylton 49 J
Southill 25 H
South Kesley 40 M
South Killingholme 41 G
South Kilvington 44 H
South Kilworth 24 C
South Kirkby 39 J
South Kirkton 67 D
South Kyme 33 F
South Lancing 9 E
Southleigh 6 A
South Leigh 16 A
South Leverton 40 L
South Littleton 23 F
South Lopham 27 D
South Luffenham 33 L
South Mains 51 H
South Malling 9 F
South Marston 15 C
South Middleton 54 K
South Milford 40 D
South Milton 5 L
South Mimms 17 B
Southminster 18 F
South Molton 13 G
South Moor 49 H
South Moreton 16 E
South Mundham 9 D
South-Muskham 33 A
South Newbald 40 F
South Newington 24 H
South Newton 15 L
South Normanton 32 C
South Norwood 17 J
South Nutfield 17 L
South Ockendon 18 G
Southoe 25 E
Southolt 27 G
South Ormsby 34 A
Southorpe 33 L
South Otterington 44 H
Southowram 39 E
South Oxhey 17 E
South Perrott 6 C
South Petherton 14 L
South Petherwin 4 C
South Pickenham 26 C
South Pool 5 L
Southport 38 A
Southpunds 81 H
South Radworthy 13 H
South Rauceby 33 E
South Raynham 34 M
Southrepps 35 L
South Reston 34 A
Southrey 33 C
Southrop 15 C
Southrope 16 L
South Runcton 26 B
South Scarle 33 B
Southsea 8 E
South Shian 64 K
South Shields 49 J
South Somercotes 41 L
South Stainley 44 K
South Stainmore 43 B
Southstoke 15 D
South Stoke 16 E
South Stoke 9 D
South Straiton 59 D
South Street 9 F
South Street 18 K
South Tawton 5 B
South Thoresby 34 A
South Tidworth 15 J
South Town 16 L
Southtown 79 H
South View 81 G
Southwaite 48 G
South Walsham 27 C
South Warnborough 16 L
Southwater 9 B
Southway 14 J
South Weald 18 D
Southwell 7 G
Southwell 33 D
South Weston 16 C
South Wheatley 4 C
Southwick 8 E
Southwick 9 F
Southwick 15 G
Southwick 25 B
Southwick 49 J
South Widcombe 14 F
South Wigston 32 M
South Willingham 41 K
South Wingfield 32 B
South Witham 33 H
Southwold 27 J
Southwood 14 M
Southwood 27 C
South Woodham Ferrers 18 E
South Wootton 34 L
South Wraxall 15 D
South Zeal 5 B
Sowerby 39 D
Sowerby 44 H
Sowerby Brigde 39 D
Sowerby Row 48 G
Sowton 5 C
Soyal 71 B
Spa Common 35 L
Spalding 33 J
Spaldington 40 E
Spaldwick 25 E
Spalford 33 B
Spanby 33 J
Sparham 35 K
Spark Bridge 42 F
Sparkford 14 M
Sparkwell 5 G
Sparrowpit 39 K
Sparsholt 16 D
Sparsholt 16 K
Spaunton 45 G
Spaxton 14 G
Spean Bridge 64 E
Speen 16 C
Speen 16 G
Speeton 45 L
Speke 38 G
Speldhurst 10 E
Spellbrook 18 A
Spelsbury 24 K
Spen Green 31 C
Spencers Wood 16 J
Spennithorne 44 D
Spennymoor 49 L
Sperrin 108 K
Spetchley 23 E
Spetisbury 7 B
Spexhall 27 E
Speybank 65 F
Spey Bay 72 J
Speybridge 66 A
Spilsby 34 A
Spindlestone 54 H
Spinkhill 39 M
Spinningdale 71 B
Spirthill 15 E
Spitewinter 32 B
Spithurst 9 F
Spithurst 10 G
Spittal 20 E
Spittal 46 E
Spittal 53 B
Spittal 78 H
Spittalfield 58 B
Spittal of Glenmuick 66 H
Spittal of Glenshee 66 K
Spixworth 27 B
Splatt 4 A
Spofforth 44 L
Spondon 32 E
Spooner Row 27 A
Sporle 26 C
Spott 53 C
Spratton 24 F
Spreakley 16 M
Spreyton 5 B
Spridlington 40 M
Springburn 57 L
Springfield 23 C
Springfield 48 D
Springfield 56 H
Springfield 58 J
Springfield 72 G
Springhill 103 E
Springholm 47 A
Springside 51 F
Springthorpe 40 L
Sproatley 41 B
Sproston Green 38 L
Sprotbrough 40 G
Sprouston 53 J
Sprowston 27 B
Sproxton 33 G
Sproxton 44 J
Spurstow 31 A
Srannda 74 M
Srònbdubh 70 A
Stabbing 18 B
Stabbing Green 18 B
Stackhouse 43 H
Stackpole 20 G
Stacksteads 38 F
Staddiscombe 5 G
Staddlethorpe 40 E
Staddon 12 M
Stadhampton 16 B
Stadhlaigearraidh 68 E
Staffield 48 H
Staffin 69 F
Stafford 31 F
Staffordstown 104 C
Stagsden 25 G
Stainburn 39 C
Stainburn 47 L
Stainby 33 H
Staincross 39 F
Staindrop 44 A
Staines 17 G
Stainfield 33 C
Stainfield 33 H
Stainforth 40 G
Stainforth 43 H
Staining 42 L
Stainland 39 D
Stainsacre 45 E
Stainton 40 G
Stainton 43 D
Stainton 44 A
Stainton 44 D
Stainton 48 K
Stainton by Langworth 33 C
Staintondale 45 H
Stainton Grove 44 A
Stainton le Vale 41 K
Stainton with Adgarley 42 H
Stair 47 M
Stair 51 F
Stairhaven 46 D
Staithes 45 A
Stakeford 49 F
Stake Pool 42 M
Stalbridge 7 A
Stalbridge Weston 7 A
Stalham 35 M
Stalham Green 35 M
Stalisfield Green 11 A
Stalland Common 27 A
Stalling Busk 43 F
Stallingborough 41 G
Stalmine 42 M
Stalybridge 39 G
Stambourne 26 L
Stambourne Green 26 L
Stamford 33 L
Stamford 54 M
Stamford Bridge 40 B
Stamfordham 49 E
Stanborough 17 B
Stanbridge 7 B
Stanbridge 25 K
Stanbury 39 A
Stand 57 M
Standburn 58 K
Standeford 31 J
Standen 10 F
Standford 9 A
Standish 38 E
Standlake 16 A
Standon 8 B
Standon 17 C
Standon 31 E
Standwell 32 B
Stane 52 B
Stanfield 35 K
Stanford 11 D
Stanford 25 H
Stanford Bishop 23 D
Stanford Bridge 23 A
Stanford Dingley 16 E
Stanford in the Vale 16 A
Stanford-le-Hope-Corringham 18 G
Stanford on Avon 24 C
Stanford on Soar 32 J
Stanford on Teme 23 A
Stanford Rivers 18 D
Stanghow 45 D
Stanhoe 34 J
Stanhope 49 K
Stanhope 52 J
Stanion 25 A
Stanley 31 C
Stanley 32 E
Stanley 49 H
Stanley 58 B
Stanley Common 32 E
Stanley Crook 49 L
Stanmer 9 F
Stanmore 16 D
Stanmore 17 E
Stanningfield 26 J
Stannington 49 E
Stannington 39 L
Stannington Station 49 E
Stansbatch 22 C
Stansfield 26 H
Stanstead 26 M
Stanstead Abbots 17 C
Stanstead Mountfitchet 18 A
Stansted 10 B
Stanton 22 H
Stanton 23 J
Stanton 26 J
Stanton 32 A
Stanton 32 G
Stanton 49 B
Stanton Prior 14 F
Stanton by Bridge 32 H
Stanton-by-Dale 32 F
Stanton Drew 14 F
Stanton Fitzwarren 15 C
Stanton Harcourt 16 A
Stanton Hill 32 C
Stanton in Peak 32 B
Stanton Long 31 K
Stanton Lucy 30 M
Stanton-on-the-Wolds 32 J
Stanton Saint Bernard 15 H
Stanton Saint John 16 B
Stanton Saint Quintin 15 E
Stanton Street 26 J
Stanton under Bardon 32 L
Stanton upon Hine Heath 31 D
Stanton Wick 14 F
Stanwardine in the Fields 30 F
Stanway 23 J
Stanway 18 C
Stanwell 17 G
Stanwick 25 E
Stanwick-Saint-John 44 A
Stanwix 48 D
Stanydale 81 G
Staoinebrig 68 H
Stape 45 G
Stapehill 7 F
Stapeley 31 B
Staple 11 B
Staple Fitzpaine 14 K
Staplecross 10 J
Staplefield 9 C
Stapleford 15 L
Stapleford 17 C
Stapleford 26 G
Stapleford 33 B
Stapleford 33 G
Stapleford Abbots 18 D
Stapleford and Beeston 32 F
Stapleford Tawney 18 D
Staplegrove 14 K
Staplehay 14 K
Staplehurst 10 F
Staplers 8 H
Stapleton 14 F
Stapleton 22 B
Stapleton 30 J
Stapleton 32 L
Stapleton 44 A
Stapleton 48 E
Stapleton Coat 14 L
Stapley 14 K
Staploe 25 H
Staplow 23 D
Star 20 F
Star 58 J
Stara 79 D
Starbotton 43 J
Starcross 5 F
Stareton 24 A
Starlings Green 26 K
Starston 27 E
Startforth 43 C
Startley 15 B
Stathe 14 L
Stathern 33 G
Station Town 49 M
Staughton Highway 25 E
Staunton 22 M
Staunton 23 G
Staunton in the Vale 33 D
Staunton on Arrow 22 C
Staunton on Wye 22 F
Staupes 44 K
Staveley 39 M
Staveley 43 A
Staveley 44 L
Staveley-in-Cartmel 42 F
Staverton 5 H
Staverton 15 D
Staverton 23 H
Staverton 24 E
Stavithie 59 G
Stawell 14 H
Staxigoe 78 J
Staxton 45 L
Staylittle 30 G
Staynall 42 M
Staythorpe 33 D
Ste Mary 9 M
Stean 43 J
Stearsby 44 M
Steart 14 G
Stedham 9 A
Steel Cross 10 D
Steele Road 48 B
Steen's Bridge 22 C
Steep 8 C
Steeple 7 H
Steeple 18 F
Steeple Ashton 15 H
Steeple Aston 24 L
Steeple Barton 24 L
Steeple Bumpstead 26 L
Steeple Claydon 24 M
Steeple Gidding 25 B
Steeple Langford 15 L
Steeple Morden 25 M
Steeton 39 A
Stein 69 D
Steinis 75 E
Steinmanhill 67 A
Stelling Minnis 11 D
Stembridge 14 L
Stemster 78 E
Stenhousemuir 58 K
Stenigot 34 A
Stenness 80 J
Stenscholl 69 C
Stenso 79 E
Stenton 53 C
Stepaside 4 D
Stepaside 20 H
Stepney 17 J
Steppingley 25 K
Sternfield 27 H
Stert 15 H
Stetchworth 26 H
Stettington 9 D
Stevenage 25 M
Steventon 16 A
Steventon 16 L
Steventon End 26 K
Stevington Weston 25 G
Stewartby 25 H
Stewarton 50 E
Stewarton 51 C
Stewartstown 104 A
Stewkley 25 K
Stewton 41 K
Steyning-Upper Beeding 9 E
Steynton 20 G
Stibb 12 L
Stibbard 35 K
Stibb Cross 12 M
Stibb Green 15 J
Stibbington 25 B
Stichill 53 J
Sticker 4 G
Stickford 34 D
Sticklepath 5 B
Sticklepath 13 G
Sticklesmere 26 J
Stickney 34 D
Stiffkey 35 G
Stifford's Bridge 23 D
Stillingfleet 40 A
Stillington 44 B
Stillington 44 M
Stilton 25 C
Stinchcombe 23 K
Stinsford 7 D
Stirchley 31 H
Stirling 57 J
Stirling 67 D
Stisted 18 B
Stithians 3 J
Stittenham 71 E
Stivichall 24 A
Stixwould 33 C
Stoak 38 K
Stobieside 52 D
Stobo 53 D
Stoborough 7 E
Stoborough Green 7 E
Stobshiel 53 B
Stobswood 49 C
Stock 18 D
Stockbridge 15 M
Stockbridge 39 B
Stockbriggs 52 E
Stockbury 10 C
Stockdalewath 48 G
Stockerstone 33 K
Stock Green 23 F
Stockingford 32 L
Stocking Pelham 26 K
Stockland 6 B
Stockland Bristol 14 G
Stockleigh English 13 L
Stockleigh Pomeroy 5 C
Stockley 15 E
Stocklinch 14 L
Stockport 38 J
Stockport 39 G
Stocksbridge 39 H
Stocksfield 49 G
Stockton 15 L
Stockton 22 C
Stockton 24 E
Stockton 27 F
Stockton 31 L
Stockton Heath-Thelwall 38 H
Stockton-on-Tees 44 B
Stockton on Teme 23 A
Stockton on the Forest 44 M
Stock Wood 23 F
Stodday 42 J
Stodmarsh 11 B
Stody 35 K
Stoer 76 H
Stoford 6 C
Stoford 15 L
Stogumber 13 J
Stogursey 14 G
Stoke 8 F
Stoke 12 H
Stoke 16 G
Stoke 18 H
Stoke 27 B
Stoke Abbott 6 C
Stoke Albany 25 A
Stoke Ash 27 G
Stoke Bardolph 32 F
Stoke Bliss 23 A
Stoke Bruerne 24 J
Stoke by Clare 26 L
Stoke-by-Nayland 26 M
Stoke Canon 5 C
Stoke Charity 16 K
Stoke Climsland 4 F
Stoke D'Abernon 17 K
Stoke Doyle 25 B
Stoke Dry 33 K
Stoke Ferry 26 B
Stoke Fleming 5 H
Stokeford 7 E
Stoke Gabriel 5 H
Stoke Gifford 14 C
Stoke Golding 32 L
Stoke Goldington 25 G
Stokeham 40 L
Stoke Hammond 25 K
Stoke Heath 31 E
Stokeinteignhead 5 F
Stoke Lacy 23 D
Stoke Lyne 24 L
Stoke Mandeville 16 C
Stokenchurch 16 C
Stoke Newingtonn 17 F
Stokenham 5 L
Stoke on Tern 31 D
Stoke-on-Trent 31 C
Stoke Orchard 23 H
Stoke Poges 17 D
Stoke Prior 22 C
Stoke-Prior 23 B
Stoke Rivers 13 G
Stoke Rochford 33 H
Stoke Row 16 E
Stoke Saint Gregory 14 L
Stoke Saint Mary 14 K
Stoke Saint Michael 14 J
Stoke Saint Milborough 31 K
Stokesay 30 M
Stokesby 27 C
Stokesley 44 F
Stoke sub Hamdon 14 L
Stoke Talmage 16 C
Stoke Trister 14 M
Stolford 14 G
Ston Easton 14 J
Stondon Massey 18 D
Stone 15 A
Stone 16 C
Stone 18 G
Stone 23 B
Stone 31 F
Stone-Allerton 14 H
Stonebridge 26 F
Stonebroom 32 B
Stone Cross 10 H
Stone-edge-Batch 14 E
Stonegate 10 E
Stonegrave 44 J
Stonehaugh 48 F
Stonehaven 67 G
Stonehouse 23 K
Stone House 43 E
Stonehouse 48 J
Stonehouse 52 E
Stone in Oxney 10 J
Stoneleigh 24 A
Stonely 25 E
Stoner Hill 8 C
Stonesby 33 G
Stonesfield 24 K
Stones Green 19 A
Stone Street 10 B
Stone Street 27 E
Stonethwaite 42 C
Stonethwaite 47 M
Stoneyburn 52 C
Stoney Cross 8 A
Stoneygate 67 C
Stoneygote 32 M
Stoneyhills 18 F
Stoneykirk 46 D
Stoney Middleton 39 L
Stoney Stanton 32 L
Stoney Stoke 14 M
Stoney Stratton 14 J
Stoney Stretton 30 J
Stoneywood 57 M
Stoneywood 67 E
Stonganess 80 E
Stonham Aspal 27 G
Stonnall 31 M
Stonor 16 F
Stonton Wyville 33 K
Stonybreck 81 C
Stonyfield 71 E
Stonyford 104 F
Stony Houghton 32 C
Stoodleigh 13 L
Stopham 9 A
Stopsley 25 L
Storeton 38 G
Stormont 105 D
Stormontfield 58 E
Stornoway/Steòrnabhagh 75 E
Storridge 23 D
Storrington 9 E
Storrs 42 F
Storth 42 F
Stotfold 25 L
Stoughton 8 F
Stoughton 17 K
Stoughton 32 M
Stoulton 23 E
Stourbridge 31 L
Stourport-on-Severn 23 B
Stour Provost 15 K
Stour Row 15 K
Stourton 15 K
Stourton 31 L
Stourton Caundle 7 A
Stove 79 F
Stove 81 H
Stoven 27 F
Stow 40 L
Stow 53 E
Stow Bardolph 26 B
Stow Bedon 26 C
Stowbridge 26 B
Stow cum Quy 26 G
Stowe 22 M
Stowe 30 L
Stowe-by-Chartley 31 F
Stowell 14 M
Stowey 14 F
Stowford 5 A
Stowlangtoft 26 J
Stow Longa 25 E
Stow Maries 18 E
Stowmarket 27 G
Stow-on-the-Wold 23 M
Stowting 11 D
Stowupland 27 G
Straad 56 L
Strabane 107 L
Strachan 67 G
Strachur 56 F
Stradbroke 27 H
Stradishall 26 H
Stradsett 26 B
Stragglethorpe 33 E
Straid 105 A
Straith 52 L
Straiton 51 H
Straiton 53 A
Straloch 65 M
Straloch 67 E
Stramshell 32 D
Stranagalwilly 107 M
Strang 37 B
Strangford 105 H
Stran-Millis 105 D
Stranocum 108 J
Stranraer 46 A
Stratfield Mortimer 16 H
Stratfield Saye 16 H
Stratfield Turgis 16 H
Stratford 17 J
Stratford 23 H
Stratford Saint Andrew 27 H
Stratford Saint Mary 18 C
Stratford Tony 15 L
Stratford-upon-Avon 24 D
Strath 70 A
Strathan 64 D
Strathan 76 H
Strathaven 52 D
Strathblane 57 L
Strathcanaird 76 L
Strathcarron 70 H
Strathcoil 63 L
Strathdon 66 E
Strathkinness 59 G
Strathmiglo 58 H
Strathmore 58 C
Strathmore 66 M
Strathpeffer 71 G
Strathrannoch 71 C
Strathtay 65 M
Strathwhillan 51 A
Strathy 77 F
Strathyre 57 E
Stratton 7 D
Stratton 12 L
Stratton 23 L
Stratton Audley 24 L
Stratton-on-the-Fosse 14 J
Stratton Saint Margaret 15 C
Stratton Saint Michael 27 E
Stratton Strawless 35 L
Straw 108 K
Streatham 17 H
Streatley 16 E
Streatley 25 L
Streat Westmeston 9 F
Street 14 H
Street 42 M
Street 45 D
Street Dinas 30 C
Street End 8 F
Streethay 32 G
Streetlam 44 E
Streetly 31 M
Strensall 44 M
Strensham 23 H
Stretcholt 14 G
Strete 5 H
Stretford 22 C
Stretford 38 J
Strethall 26 K
Stretham 26 D
Stretton 31 A
Stretton 31 J
Stretton 32 B
Stretton 32 G
Stretton 33 L
Stretton 38 H
Stretton en le Field 32 H
Stretton Grandison 23 D
Stretton Heath 30 J
Stretton-on-Dunsmore 24 B
Stretton-on-Fosse 24 G
Stretton Sugwas 22 F
Stretton under Fosse 24 B
Stretton Westwood 31 G
Strichen 73 L
Stringston 14 G
Strixton 25 D
Stroat 22 M
Stromeferry 70 G
Stromemore 70 G
Stromness 79 G
Stronaba 64 E
Stronachie 58 H
Stronachlachar 57 D
Stronchreggan 64 H
Stronchrubie 76 M
Strone 56 J
Strone 64 E
Strone 71 K
Stronmilchan 56 C
Stronord 46 C
Strontian 63 J
Strood 18 G
Stroud 8 C
Stroud 23 L
Stroud Green 23 K
Stroxton 33 H
Struan 69 H
Strubby 34 B
Strumpshaw 27 B
Strutherhill 52 B
Struthers 58 J
Struy 71 K
Stuartfield 67 B
Stubbington 8 E
Stubbins 38 F
Stubhampton 7 B
Stubshaw Cross 38 E
Stubton 33 E
Stuckgowan 57 D
Stuckton 7 C
Studfold 43 H

A B C D E F G H I J K L M N O P Q R S T U V W X Y Z

Studham 17 A
Studland 7 H
Studley 15 E
Studley 23 F
Studley Roger 44 G
Stuntney 26 D
Stunts Green 10 H
Sturbridge 31 E
Sturmer 26 L
Sturminster Marhall 7 E
Sturminster Newton 7 A
Sturry-Broad Oak 11 B
Sturton by Stow 40 L
Sturton le Steeple 40 L
Stuston 27 D
Stutton 19 A
Stutton 40 A
Styal 38 J
Styrrup 40 K
Suainebost 75 C
Succoth 66 C
Succoth 57 D
Suckley 23 D
Suckquoy 79 L
Sudborough 25 B
Sudbourne 27 L
Sudbrook 14 C
Sudbrook 33 E
Sudbrooke 33 C
Sudbury 26 M
Sudbury 32 D
Sudgrove 23 L
Suffield 35 L
Suffield 45 H
Sugnall 31 E
Suladale 69 E
Sulaisiadar 75 E
Sulby 37 B
Sulgrave 24 H
Sulham 16 E
Sulhamstead 16 H
Sulland 79 E
Sullington 9 E
Sullom 80 J
Sullom Voe 80 F
Sully 14 D
Sultigeo 79 G
Sumburgh 81 J
Summerbrigde 44 K
Summercourt 4 D
Summerfield 34 J
Summerhill 31 E
Summerleaze 14 B
Summerscales 43 M
Summerseat 38 F
Summit 39 D
Sunbigg 43 B
Sunbury 17 G
Sundaywell 47 A
Sunderland 47 J
Sunderland 49 J
Sunderland 53 H
Sunderland Bridge 49 L
Sundhope 53 G
Sundon Park 25 L
Sundridge 10 A
Sunk Island 41 G
Sunlight 38 G
Sunningdale-Ascot 17 G
Sunninghill 17 G
Sunningwell 16 B
Sunniside 49 H
Sunniside 49 L
Sunny Bank 42 F
Sunnylaw 57 J
Sunnyside 9 C
Sunnyside 10 D
Suntrap 53 A
Surbiton 17 H
Surfleet 33 J
Surfleet Seas End 33 J
Surlingham 27 B
Sustead 35 L
Sutcombe 12 M
Suton 27 A
Sutors of Cromarty 71 J
Sutterton 34 G
Sutton 9 D
Sutton 11 E
Sutton 14 M
Sutton 16 A
Sutton 17 H
Sutton 25 B
Sutton 25 J
Sutton 26 D
Sutton 27 L
Sutton 31 E
Sutton 31 E
Sutton 31 L
Sutton 33 D
Sutton 33 E
Sutton 35 M
Sutton 40 G
Sutton Abinger 17 K
Sutton-at-Hone 18 G
Sutton Bassett 25 A
Sutton Benger 15 E
Sutton Bonington 32 J
Sutton Bridge 34 K
Sutton Cheney 32 L
Sutton Coldfield 32 K
Sutton Courtenay 16 B
Sutton Crosses 34 K
Sutton cum Lound 40 K
Sutton Grange 44 G
Sutton Green 17 K
Sutton Heath Estate 27 L
Sutton Hill 31 H
Sutton Hohgrave 44 G
Sutton in Ashfield 32 C
Sutton-in-Craven 39 A
Sutton Lane Ends 38 M
Sutton Leach 38 H
Sutton Maddock 31 H
Sutton Mallet 14 H
Sutton Mandeville 15 L
Sutton Montis 14 M
Sutton-on-Hull 41 B
Sutton on Sea 34 B
Sutton-on-the-Forest 44 M
Sutton on the Hill 32 D
Sutton on Trent 33 A
Sutton Saint Edmund 34 K
Sutton Saint James 34 K
Sutton Saint Nicholas 22 F
Sutton Scarsdale 32 C
Sutton-under-Brailes 24 G
Sutton upon Derwent 40 B
Sutton-under-Whitestone-cliffe 44 H
Sutton Valence 10 C
Sutton Veny 15 G
Sutton Waldron 7 B
Swaby 34 A
Swadlincote 32 H
Swaffham 26 C
Swaffham Bulbeck 26 G
Swaffham Prior 26 G
Swafield 35 L
Swainby 44 E
Swainshill 22 F
Swainsthorpe 27 B
Swalcliffe 24 G
Swalecliffe 11 B
Swallow 41 G
Swallowcliffe 15 L
Swallowfield 16 J
Swanage 7 H
Swanbourne 24 M
Swanbridge 14 D
Swancole 31 L
Swan Green 38 L
Swanland 40 F
Swanley-Hextable 17 J
Swanmore 8 B
Swannington 32 H
Swannington 35 K
Swanscombe 18 G
Swansea/Abertawe 21 L
Swan Street 18 C
Swanton Abbot 35 L
Swanton Morley 35 K
Swanton Novers 35 K
Swanwick 8 E
Swanwick 32 B
Swarby 33 E
Swardeston 27 B
Swarister 80 E
Swarkestone 32 H
Swarland 49 B
Swarthmoor 42 E
Swartland 79 D
Swaton 33 J
Swatragh 108 L
Swavesey 25 F
Sway 8 D
Swayfield 33 H
Sweffling 27 H
Swell 14 L
Swepstone 32 H
Swerford 24 G
Swettenham 38 M
Swillbrook 38 B
Swillington 39 F
Swimbridge 13 G
Swinbrook 24 K
Swinderby 33 B
Swindon 15 F
Swindon 23 H
Swindon 31 L
Swine 41 B
Swinefleet 40 E
Swineshead 25 E
Swineshead 33 J
Swineshead Bridge 33 F
Swineside 43 J
Swiney 78 L
Swinford 16 A
Swinford 24 C
Swingfield Minnis 11 E
Swingfield Street 11 E
Swinhill 52 B
Swinhoe 54 M
Swinhope 41 K
Swining 80 F
Swinithwaite 43 F
Swinscoe 32 A
Swinside Hall 53 M
Swinstead 33 H
Swinton 38 J
Swinton 39 J
Swinton 44 G
Swinton 45 K
Swinton 54 D
Swintonmill 54 D
Swithland 32 J
Swordale 71 E
Swordland 63 F
Swordly 77 F
Sworton Heath 38 H
Swyddffynnon 29 L
Swynnerton 31 F
Swyre 6 F
Syde 23 L
Sydenham 16 C
Sydenham 17 J
Sydenham Damerel 4 F
Syderstone 34 J
Sydling Saint Nicholas 7 A
Sydmonton 16 G
Syerston 33 D
Syke 39 D
Sykehouse 40 D
Sykes 43 K
Syleham 27 E
Sylen 21 G
Symington 51 F
Symington 52 F
Symondsbury 6 F
Synod Inn 21 A
Syre 77 H
Syreford 23 M
Syresham 24 J
Syrmonds Yat 22 J
Syston 32 M
Syston 33 E
Sytchampton 23 B
Syunshin 103 E
Sywell 25 D

T

Taagan 70 E
Tabost 75 G
Tàbost 75 C
Tackley 24 L
Tacleit 75 D
Tacolneston 27 D
Tadcaster 40 A
Tadden 7 E
Taddington 39 K
Tadley 16 H
Tadlow 25 J
Tadmarton 24 G
Tadworth 17 L
Tafarnaubach 22 G
Tafarn-y-Gelyn 37 M
Taff's Well 14 A
Tafolwern 30 G
Tai'n Lôn 36 L
Taibach 21 L
Tai-bach 30 E
Tain 71 F
Tain 78 E
Tairgwaith 21 H
Tairlaw 51 J
Takeley 18 A
Takeley Street 18 A
Talachddu 22 D
Talacre 37 J
Talaton 6 A
Talbenny 20 D
Talbot Green 13 C
Talerddig 30 G
Talgarreg 21 A
Talgarth 22 D
Talisker 69 G
Talke 31 C
Talkin 48 H
Talladale 70 E
Talla Linnfoots 52 J
Tallarn Green 31 A
Tallentire 47 J
Talley 21 E
Tallington 33 L
Talmine 77 E
Talog 20 F
Tal-sarn 21 B
Talsarnau 29 C
Talskiddy 4 D
Talwrn 36 H
Tal-y-bont 29 E
Tal-y-bont 29 H
Tal-y-bont 36 J
Tal-y-Bont 37 G
Talybont-on-Usk 22 G
Tal-y-cafn 37 G
Tal-y-llyn 29 F
Talyllyn 22 G
Talysarn 36 L
Tal-y-Wern 29 J
Tamerton Foliot 5 D
Tamlaght 103 D
Tamlaght 108 L
Tamlaght O'Crilly 108 L
Tamnaherin Bridge 107 J
Tamnamore 104 D
Tamworth 32 K
Tanderagee 104 A
Tandragee 104 H
Tandridge 10 A
Tanfield 49 H
Tangasdal 68 K
Tangiers 20 D
Tangley 16 G
Tangmere-Boxgrove 9 D
Tangue End 33 M
Tangwick 80 J
Tankerness 79 H
Tankersley 39 J
Tannach 78 H
Tannachie 67 G
Tannadice 59 A
Tannadice 66 L
Tannington 27 H
Tansley 32 B
Tansor 25 B
Tantobie 49 H
Tanton 44 F
Tanworth-in-Arden 23 C
Tan-y-fron 37 L
Tanygrisiau 36 M
Tan-y-groes 20 C
Taobh a Deas Loch Aineort 68 H
Taobh a Tuath Loch Aineort 68 H
Taobh a' Ghlinne 75 G
Taobh Tuath 74 L
Taplow 17 D
Tappoch 57 M
Tara 105 H
Tarbert 55 J
Tarbert 55 M
Tarbert 56 L
Tarbert 63 C
Tarbert/Tairbeart 74 M
Tarbet 57 D
Tarbet 76 F
Tarbock Green 38 G
Tarbolton 51 F
Tarbrax 52 C
Tardebigge 23 C
Tarfside 66 J
Tarland 66 F
Tarleton 38 A
Tarlogie 71 F
Tarlscough 38 D
Tarlton 15 B
Tarnbrook 43 K
Tarporley 38 L
Tarr 13 J
Tarranat Rushton 7 B
Tarrant Crawford 7 B
Tarrant Gunville 7 B
Tarrant Hinton 7 B
Tarrant Keyneston 7 B
Tarrant Launceston 7 B
Tarrant Monkton 7 B
Tarrant Rawston 7 B
Tarrel 71 F
Tarring Neville 9 J
Tarring Neville 10 G
Tarrington 23 D
Tarsappie 58 E
Tarskavaig 69 M
Tarves 67 B
Tarvie 65 M
Tarvie 71 G
Tarvin 38 K
Tasley 31 L
Tassagh 104 G
Taston 24 K
Tatenhill 32 G
Tatham 43 G
Tathwell 34 A
Tatsfield 10 A
Tattenhall 38 K
Tatterford 34 M
Tattersett 34 M
Tattershall 33 F
Tattershall Bridge 33 F
Tattingstone 27 K
Tatworth 6 B
Taunton 14 K
Tavantaggart 50 B
Taverham 27 B
Tavernspite 20 J
Tavistock 5 D
Taw Green 5 B
Tawnawanny 103 A
Tawstock 13 G
Taxal 39 K
Tayinloan 50 B
Taynish 56 G
Taynton 23 G
Taynton 24 K
Taynuilt 56 C
Tayport 59 D
Tayvallich 56 G
Tealby 41 K
Tealing 59 A
Teangue 63 C
Teanna Mhachair 68 B
Tebay 43 A
Tebworth 25 K
Teconnaught 105 G
Tedburn Saint Mary 5 B
Teddington 17 H
Teddington 23 H
Tedstone Delamere 23 D
Tedstone Wafre 23 A
Teemore 103 G
Teeshan 108 M
Teeton 24 F
Teffont Evias 15 L
Teffont Magna 15 L
Tegryn 20 F
Teigh 33 K
Teigngrace 5 F
Teignmouth 5 F
Telford Dawley 31 H
Tellisford 15 G
Telscombe 9 J
Templand 47 C
Temple 4 E
Temple 11 E
Temple 53 A
Temple 57 L
Temple Bar 21 B
Temple Cloud-Clutton 14 F
Templecombe 14 M
Temple End 26 L
Temple Grafton 23 F
Temple Guiting 23 J
Temple Herdewyke 24 E
Temple Hirst 40 D
Temple Normanton 32 C
Templepatrick 104 C
Temple Sowerby 48 L
Templeton 13 L
Templeton 20 H
Templeton Bridge 13 L
Tempo 103 E
Tempsford 25 H
Ten Mile Bank 26 B
Tenbury Wells 23 A
Tenby/Dinbych-y-pysgod 20 H
Tenston 79 G
Tenterden 10 F
Terling 18 B
Ternhill 31 D
Terregles 47 B
Terrington 44 M
Terrington Saint Clement 34 L
Terrington Saint John 34 L
Terry's Green 23 C
Terrydremont 108 G
Terwick Common 8 C
Testwood 8 A
Tetbury 15 B
Tetbury Upton 15 B
Tetcott 4 C
Tetford 34 A
Tetney 41 K
Tetney Lock 41 K
Tettenhall 31 L
Teversal 32 C
Teversham 26 G
Teviothead 53 K
Tewel 67 G
Tewin 17 C
Tewkesbury 23 H
Teynham 11 A
Thakeham 9 E
Thame 16 C
Thames 17 G
Thames Haven 18 H
Thamesmead 17 J
Thanington 11 A
Thankerton 52 F
Tharston 27 E
Thatcham 16 H
Thatto Heat 38 H
Thaxted 26 K
The Aird 69 E
Theakston 44 G
Thealby 40 H
Theale 14 H
Theale 16 H
Thearne 40 F
The Bage 22 E
The Balloch 58 D
The Barony 79 D
Theberton 27 J
The Birks 67 G
The Bog 30 J
The Braes 69 H
The Bratch 31 L
The Bryn 22 L
The Burf 23 H
The Burn 66 M
The Bush 104 D
The Camp 23 L
The Chequer 31 A
The City 16 C
The Common 15 M
The Common 24 M
The Craigs 71 B
The Creagh 104 B
The Cronk 37 B
The Cross 107 J
The Cross Keys 104 G
Thedden Grange 16 L
Theddingworth 24 C
Theddlethorpe All Saints 41 L
Theddlethorpe Saint Helen 41 L
The Den 51 C
The Diamond 103 B
The Diamond 104 B
The Diamond 104 C
The Diamond 104 J
The Down 10 E
The Drones 108 J
The Drums 66 L
The Flatt 48 B
The Glen 108 G
The Grange 44 F
The Green 15 K
The Green 42 E
The Grove 35 K
The Hall 80 B
The Haughs 72 M
The Headland 49 M
The Heath 35 L
The Hermitage 17 L
The Hill 42 E
The Howe 37 D
The Howe 42 F
The Hundred 22 C
Thelbridge Barton 13 L
The Lee 17 A
The Leigh 23 H
The Lhen 37 B
The Lhen 46 L
Thelnetham 27 D
The Loup 104 B
The Marsh 30 J
Themelthorpe 35 K
The Middles 49 H
The Moor 10 E
The Mumbles 21 L
The Myte 23 H
The North 22 M
The Neuk 67 G
Thenford 24 H
The Pole of Itlaw 73 K
The Quarry 15 A
Therfield 25 M
Thetford 26 F
The Rhos 20 E
The Rock 104 A
The Sheddings 109 K
The Spa 105 G
The Stocks 10 J
The Temple 105 G
The Towans 3 H
The Town 3 A
The Vauld 22 F
Thevelton 27 D
The Village 31 L
The Wyke 31 H
Theydon Bois 17 F
Thick Hollins 39 D
Thickwood 15 D
Thimbleby 44 E
Thimbley Langton 34 A
Third Corgary 107 K
Thirlby 44 H
Thirlestane Whiteburn 53 F
Thirn 44 G
Thirsk 44 H
Thistleton 33 H
Thistley Green 26 E
Thixendale 45 K
Thockrington 49 D
Tholmair 68 E
Tholomas Drove 34 K
Tholthorpe 44 L
Thomas Chapel 20 H
Thomastown 66 C
Thompson 26 C
Thompsons Bridge 103 D
Thomshill 72 H
Thong 18 G
Thoralby 43 F
Thoresthorpe 34 B
Thoresway 41 K
Thorganby 40 B
Thorganby 41 K
Thorgill 45 D
Thorington 27 J
Thorington Street 26 M
Thorlby 43 M
Thorley Street 8 D
Thormanby 44 H
Thornaby-on-Tees 44 B
Thornage 35 G
Thornborough 24 M
Thornborough 44 G
Thornbury 12 M
Thornbury 14 C
Thornbury 23 A
Thornby 24 C
Thorncliffe 32 A
Thorncombe 6 B
Thorncombe 7 B
Thorncombe Street 17 K
Thorncote Green 25 H
Thorndon 27 G
Thorndon Cross 5 A
Thorne 40 G
Thorne Saint Margaret 13 M
Thorner 39 C
Thorney 33 B
Thorney 33 M
Thorney Hill 7 F
Thorney Toll 26 A
Thornfalcon 14 K
Thornford 6 C
Thorngumbald 41 B
Thornham 34 J
Thornham Magna 27 G
Thornham Parva 27 G
Thornhaugh 33 L
Thornhill 8 B
Thornhill 14 A
Thornhill 39 L
Thornhill 42 A
Thornhill 52 L
Thornhill 57 J
Thornhill Edge 39 E
Thornholme 45 L
Thornley 49 L
Thornley 49 M
Thornliebank 52 A
Thorns 26 H
Thornthwaite 44 K
Thornthwaite 47 M
Thornton 24 J
Thornton 32 L
Thornton 34 A
Thornton 38 D
Thornton 39 B
Thornton 40 B
Thornton 44 C
Thornton 54 D
Thornton 58 J
Thornton 59 A
Thornton-Cleveleys 42 L
Thornton Curtis 40 J
Thorntonhall 52 A
Thornton Hough 37 J
Thornton-le-Clay 44 M
Thornton-le-Dale 45 G
Thornton le Moor 40 M
Thornton-le-Moor 44 H
Thornton-le-Moors 38 G
Thornton-le-Street 44 H
Thorntonloch 54 A
Thornton Park 54 D
Thornton Rust 43 F
Thornton Steward 44 G
Thornton Watlass 44 G
Thornwood Common 17 F
Thoroton 33 D
Thorp Arch 39 C
Thorp Saint Peter 34 E
Thorpe 17 G
Thorpe 27 F
Thorpe 32 A
Thorpe 33 D
Thorpe 34 B
Thorpe 43 M
Thorpe 44 A
Thorpe Abbotts 27 D
Thorpe Acre 32 J
Thorpe Arnold 33 G
Thorpe Audlin 39 F
Thorpe Bassett 45 K
Thorpe Bay 18 H
Thorpe by Water 25 A
Thorpe Constantine 32 G
Thorpe Culvert 34 E
Thorpe End 27 B
Thorpe Fendykes 34 D
Thorpe Green 26 J
Thorpe Hesley 39 J
Thorpe in Balne 40 G
Thorpe Langton 25 A
Thorpe Larches 44 B
Thorpe le Fallows 40 L
Thorpe-le-Soken 19 A
Thorpe le Street Shiptonthorpe 40 C
Thorpe Malsor 25 A
Thorpe Mandeville 24 H
Thorpe Market 35 L
Thorpe Marriot 27 B
Thorpe Morieux 26 J
Thorpeness 27 M
Thorpe on the Hill 33 B
Thorpe Saint Andrew 27 B
Thorpe Salvin 39 M
Thorpe Satchville 33 K
Thorpe Tasburgh 27 E
Thorpe Thewles 44 B
Thorpe Underwood 44 L
Thorpe Waterville 25 B
Thorpe Willoughby 40 D
Thorrington 19 A
Thorton-in Craven 43 L
Thorton-le-Beans 44 H
Thorverton 5 C
Thrandeston 27 D
Thrapston 25 E
Threapland 43 M
Threapland 47 J
Threapwood 31 A
Three Bridges 9 C
Three Bridges 41 L
Three Chimneys 10 F
Three Cocked Hat 27 F
Three Cocks 22 E
Three Crosses 21 K
Three Cups Corner 10 H
Three Holes 26 A
Threekingham 33 J
Three Leg Cross 10 E
Three Legged Cross 7 C
Three Mile Cross 16 J
Threemilestone 3 J
Threlkeld 47 M
Threshers Bush 18 A
Threshfield 43 M
Threxton Hill 26 C
Thrigby 27 C
Thringarth 43 C
Thringstone 32 H
Thrintoft 44 E
Thriplow 26 G
Throckenholt 34 K
Throcking 25 M
Throckley 49 H
Throckmorton 23 F
Throop 7 F
Throphill 49 E
Thropton 49 B
Throsk 58 G
Througham 23 L
Throwleigh 5 B
Throwley 11 A
Thrumpton 32 J
Thrumster 78 H
Thrunton 54 L
Thrupp 23 L
Thrushelton 5 A
Thrushgill 43 G
Thrussington 32 J
Thruxton 15 M
Thruxton 22 J
Thrybergh 39 J
Thulston 32 E
Thundergay 50 C
Thundersley 18 H
Thurcaston 32 M
Thurcroft 39 M
Thurdon 12 L
Thurgarton 33 D
Thurgarton 35 L
Thurgoland 39 H
Thurlaston 24 B
Thurlaston 32 L
Thurlbear 14 K
Thurlby 33 B
Thurlby 33 L
Thurlby 34 B
Thurleigh 25 H
Thurlestone 5 G
Thurloxton 14 K
Thurlstone 39 H
Thurlton 27 F
Thurmaston 32 M
Thurnby 32 M
Thurne 27 C
Thurnham 10 C
Thurnham 42 M
Thurning 25 B
Thurning 35 K
Thurnscoe 39 J
Thurnscoe East 39 J
Thursby 48 G
Thursford 35 K
Thursford Green 35 G
Thursley 16 M
Thurso 78 D
Thurstaston 37 J
Thurston 26 J
Thurston End 26 H
Thurstonfield 48 D
Thurstonland 39 E
Thurton 27 B
Thurvaston 32 D
Thuxton 27 H
Thwaite 27 G

A B C D E F G H I J K L M N O P Q R S T U V W X Y Z

Thwaite 43 F
Thwaite Head 42 F
Thwaite Saint Mary 27 E
Thwing 45 L
Tibbermore 58 E
Tibberton 23 E
Tibberton 23 G
Tibberton 31 E
Tibenham 27 D
Tibshelf 32 C
Tibthorpe 40 C
Ticehurst 10 E
Tichborne 8 B
Tickencole 33 L
Tickenham 14 E
Ticklerton 30 M
Ticknall 32 H
Tickton 40 C
Tidcombe 15 J
Tiddington 16 B
Tiddington 24 D
Tidebrook 10 E
Tideford 4 F
Tidenham 14 C
Tideswell 39 L
Tidmarsh 16 E
Tidmington 24 G
Tidpit 7 C
Tidworth 15 J
Tidworth Camp 15 J
Tiers Cross 20 G
Tiffield 24 J
Tifty 67 A
Tigerton 66 M
Tigh a' Ghearraidh 68 B
Tigh-na-Blair 57 F
Tighnabruaich 56 L
Tighnafiline 70 B
Tigley 5 H
Tilbrook 25 E
Tilbury 18 G
Tilbury Juxta Clare 26 L
Tile Cross 32 K
Tile Hill 24 A
Tilehurst 16 E
Tilford 16 M
Tillathrowie 66 C
Tillers Green 23 G
Tillicoultry 58 G
Tillingham 18 F
Tillington 9 A
Tillington 22 F
Tillington Common 22 F
Tillyarblet 66 M
Tillybirloch 67 D
Tillydrine 66 J
Tillyfourie 67 D
Tillygarmond 66 J
Tillygreig 67 E
Tillykerri 67 E
Tillylodge 66 F
Tillytour 66 F
Tilmanstone 11 E
Tilney All Saints 34 L
Tilney cum Islington 34 L
Tilney Fen End 34 L
Tilney High End 34 L
Tilney Saint Lawrence 34 L
Tilshead 15 H
Tilstock 31 A
Tilston 31 A
Tilstone Fearnall 38 L
Tilsworth 25 K
Tilton on the Hill 33 K
Timberland 33 F
Timberscombe 13 J
Timble 44 K
Timperley 38 J
Timsbury 8 A
Timsbury 14 F
Timsgearraidh 74 F
Timworth Green 26 J
Tincleton 7 D
Tindale 48 H
Tingewick 24 M
Tingley 39 E
Tingrith 25 K
Tingwall 79 E
Tinhay 4 C
Tinshill 39 C
Tinsley 39 M
Tintagel 4 B
Tintern 22 M
Tintinhull 14 L
Tintwisle 39 G
Tinwald 47 B
Tinwell 33 L
Tipperty 67 E
Tipps End 26 A
Tiptoe 8 D
Tipton 31 M
Tipton Saint John 6 A
Tiptree 18 C
Tiptree Heath 18 C
Tirabad 21 F
Tirkane 108 L
Tirley 23 H
Tirphil 22 K
Tirril 48 K
Tirwinny 103 A
Tisbury 15 K
Tisley Green 9 C
Tisman's Common 9 B
Tissington 32 A
Titchberry 12 H
Titchmarsh 25 B
Titchwell 34 J
Tithby 33 D
Titley 22 B
Titlington 54 L
Titson 12 L
Tittensor 31 F
Tittleshall 34 M
Tiverton 13 M
Tivertone 38 K
Tivetshall Saint Margaret 27 D
Tivetshall Saint Mary 27 D
Tixall 31 J
Tixover 33 L
Toab 79 H
Toab 81 J
Tobermore 108 L
Tobermory 63 H
Toberonochy 56 D
Tobha Aisgeirnis 68 H
Tobha Beag 68 E
Tobha Mòr 68 E
Tobhtaral 75 D
Tobson 75 D
Tocher 67 A
Tockenham 15 E
Tockenham Wick 15 E
Tockholes 38 C
Tockington 14 C
Tockwith 44 L
Todber 15 K
Toddington 9 D
Toddington 23 J
Toddington 25 K
Todenham 24 G
Todhills 48 D
Todhills 59 A
Todlachie 67 D
Todmorden 39 A
Todwick 39 M
Toft 25 J
Toft 33 L
Toft Hill 49 L
Toft Monks 27 F
Toft next Newton 40 M
Toftrees 34 M
Tofts 78 F
Toftwood 27 A
Togston 49 C
Tokavaig 69 M
Tokers Green 16 F
Tolastadh a' Chaolais 75 D
Toldish 4 D
Toll 14 F
Toll 15 D
Toll 29 C
Toll 48 C
Tolland 13 J
Tollard Royal 7 B
Toll Bar 40 G
Toller Fratrum 6 C
Toller Porcorum 6 C
Tollerton 32 F
Tollerton 44 L
Toller Whelme 6 C
Tollesbury 18 F
Tolleshunt D'Arcy 18 F
Tolleshunt Knights 18 C
Tolleshunt Major 18 F
Toll of Birness 67 B
Tolm 75 E
Tolpuddle 7 D
Tolstadh bho Thuath 75 F
Tolworth 17 H
Tomatin 71 M
Tombreck 71 L
Tomchrasky 64 C
Tomdoun 64 B
Tomdow 72 K
Tomich 70 M
Tomich 71 E
Tomintoul 66 A
Tomintoul 66 G
Tom nan Ragh 56 J
Tomnaven 66 C
Tomnavoulin 66 A
Tomslèibhe 63 L
Tonbridge 10 B
Tonderghie 46 H
Tondu 13 C
Toneel 103 D
Tonfanau 29 E
Tong 31 H
Tonge 32 H
Tongham 16 M
Tongland 47 D
Tongue 77 E
Tongwynlais 14 A
Tonmawr 21 L
Tonna 21 L
Tonnaghmore Bridge 103 E
Ton-teg 14 A
Tonwell 17 C
Tonypandy 21 M
Tonyrefail 21 M
Toome 104 B
Toothill 8 A
Toot Hill 18 D
Topcliffe 44 H
Topcroft 27 E
Topcroft Street 27 E
Toppesfield 26 L
Toppings 38 F
Topsham 5 C
Torbay 5 J
Torbeg 50 F
Torbryan 5 E
Torcastle 64 E
Torcross 5 L
Tore 71 H
Torinturk 56 K
Torksey 40 L
Torlum 68 E
Torlundy 64 E
Tormarton 15 D
Tormisdale 55 K
Tormitchell 51 L
Tormore 50 C
Tormore 72 K
Tornagrain 71 J
Tornahaish 66 E
Tornapress 70 G
Tornaveen 66 F
Torness 71 L
Torpenhow 47 J
Torphichen 58 K
Torphins 66 F
Torpoint 4 J
Torquay 5 J
Torquhan 53 E
Torran 56 E
Torran 71 F
Torrance 57 L
Torrans 55 C
Torridon 70 D
Torrin 69 M
Torrisdale 77 E
Torrish 77 M
Torrisholme 42 J
Torrlaoighseach 70 K
Torroble 71 B
Torry 67 H
Torry 72 M
Torryburn 58 K
Torrylinn 51 D
Torsonce 53 E
Torterston 67 C
Torthorwald 47 B
Tortington 9 D
Tortworth 15 A
Torvaig 69 H
Torver 42 C
Torwood 57 M
Torworth 40 K
Tosberry 12 H
Toscaig 69 J
Toseland 25 F
Tosside 43 L
Tostock 26 J
Totaig 69 D
Totaig 70 K
Tote 69 E
Totegan 77 F
Tothill 34 A
Totland-Freshwater 8 G
Totley 39 L
Totnes 5 H
Toton 32 F
Totronald Acha 62 J
Totscore 69 B
Tottenham 17 F
Tottenhill 34 L
Totteridge 16 F
Totteridge 17 E
Totternhoe 25 K
Totterton 30 M
Tottington 38 F
Totton 8 A
Tournaig 70 B
Toux 72 M
Toux 73 M
Tovil 10 C
Toward 56 M
Toward Taynuilt 56 M
Towcester 24 J
Towednack 3 H
Tower Hill 38 D
Tower-of-Sark 48 D
Towersey 16 C
Towie 66 F
Towie 73 L
Towiemore 72 M
Tow Law 49 L
Town 43 K
Town End 26 A
Town End 42 F
Town Row 10 E
Town Yetholm 54 G
Townfield 49 G
Townhead 47 D
Townhead 48 L
Townhead of Greenlaw 47 D
Townhill 58 L
Townshend 3 H
Towthorpe 44 M
Towton 40 A
Towyn 29 A
Towyn 37 H
Toynton All Saints 34 D
Toynton Fen Side 34 D
Toynton Saint Peter 34 D
Trabboch 51 F
Trabbochburn 51 F
Traboe 3 M
Tradespark 79 H
Trallong 21 F
Tranch 22 L
Tranent 53 B
Trantlebeg 77 F
Trantlemore 77 F
Tranwell 49 E
Trapp 21 H
Traprain 53 C
Traquair 53 G
Trawden 39 A
Trawsfynydd 29 C
Tre Taliesin 29 H
Tre'r-ddol 29 H
Trealaw 21 M
Treales 38 B
Trearddur 36 D
Treaslane 69 E
Trebarrow 4 C
Trebartha 4 C
Trebarwith 4 B
Trebetherick 4 A
Treblary 4 B
Treborough 13 J
Trebudannon 4 D
Trebullett 4 C
Treburley 4 F
Trebyan 4 E
Trecastle 21 F
Trecwn 20 B
Trecynon 21 M
Tredavoe 3 G
Tredegar 22 K
Tredington 23 H
Tredington 24 G
Tredinnick 4 D
Tredinnick 4 E
Tredomen 22 D
Tredrizzick 4 A
Tredunnock 22 L
Treen 3 K
Treeton 39 M
Trefdraeth 36 H
Trefecca 22 D
Trefeglwys 30 G
Trefenter 29 L
Treffgarne 20 D
Treffynnon 20 D
Trefilan 21 B
Trefin 20 A
Trefnanney 30 E
Trefnant 37 H
Trefonen 30 F
Trefor 36 E
Trefor 36 L
Trefriw 37 K
Tregadillett 4 C
Tregaian 36 H
Tregare 22 M
Tregaron 21 B
Tregarth 36 J
Tregeare 4 C
Tregeiriog 30 B
Tregele 36 E
Tregeseal 3 G
Tregidden 3 M
Treglemais 20 D
Tregole 12 L
Tregonetha 4 D
Tregony 4 G
Tregoyd 22 E
Tregroes 21 A
Tregurrian 4 D
Tregynon 30 H
Trehafod 22 K
Treharris-Nelson 22 K
Treherbert 21 M
Treknow 4 B
Trelan 3 M
Trelash 4 B
Trelawnyd 37 H
Trelech 20 F
Treleddydfawr 20 D
Trelew 3 J
Trelewis 22 K
Treligga 4 B
Trelights 4 A
Trelill 4 B
Trelissick 3 J
Trellach 30 F
Trellech 22 M
Trelleck Grange 22 M
Trelogan 37 J
Trelystan 30 H
Tremadog 29 B
Tremail 4 B
Tremain 20 C
Tremaine 4 C
Tremar 4 F
Trematon 4 F
Tremeirchion 37 H
Tremethick Cross 3 G
Trenance 4 D
Trenarren 4 G
Trench 31 H
Trenear 3 H
Treneglos 4 B
Trenewan 4 H
Trent 14 M
Trentham 31 F
Trentishoe 13 D
Treoes 13 C
Treorchy 21 M
Trerulrfoot 4 F
Tresaith 20 C
Trescott 31 L
Trescowe 3 H
Tresean 3 F
Tresham 15 A
Tresillian 4 G
Tresillian 3 J
Tresinney 4 B
Tresinwen 20 A
Treskinnick Cross 12 L
Tresmeer 4 C
Tresparrett 4 B
Tressait 65 L
Tresta 80 B
Tresta 81 G
Treswell 40 L
Trethewey 3 G
Trethomas 14 A
Trethowel 4 D
Trethurgy 4 D
Tretio 20 D
Tretire 22 J
Tretower 22 G
Treuddyn 37 M
Trevalga 4 B
Trevanson 4 A
Trevarrian 4 D
Trevarrick 4 G
Trevaughan 20 F
Trevellas 3 F
Treverva 3 J
Trevethin 22 L
Trevigro 4 F
Treviscoe 4 D
Trevone 4 A
Trewalder 4 B
Trewarmett 4 B
Trewartenick 4 G
Trewassa 4 B
Trewellard 3 G
Trewen 4 C
Trewidland 4 F
Trewint 12 L
Trewithian 4 G
Trewoon 4 D
Treyarnon 4 A
Treyford 8 C
Triangle 39 D
Trickestt's Cross 7 F
Trillick 103 E
Trimbley 23 B
Trimdon 49 M
Trimdon Colliery 49 M
Trimdon Grange 49 M
Trimingham 35 L
Trimley 27 L
Trimley Saint Martin 19 B
Trimley Saint Mary 19 B
Trimsaran 21 G
Trimstone 13 D
Trinafour 65 L
Trinant 22 K
Tring 17 A
Trinity 9 M
Trinity 66 M
Trislaig 64 H
Trispen 3 F
Tritlington 49 B
Trochry 58 A
Troedyraur 20 C
Trofarth 37 G
Trondavoe 80 J
Troon 3 H
Troon 51 E
Trory 103 D
Troston 26 J
Troswell 4 C
Trottiscliffe 10 B
Trotton 9 A
Troutbeck 42 C
Troutbeck 48 K
Troutbeck Bridge 42 C
Trow Green 22 M
Trowbridge 15 G
Trowell 32 F
Trowle Common 15 G
Trowley Bottom 17 B
Trows 53 J
Trowse Newton 27 B
Trudoxhill 15 G
Trull 14 K
Trumaisgearraidh 68 C
Trumpan 69 D
Trumpet 23 D
Trumpington 26 G
Trunch 35 L
Truro 3 J
Trusham 5 F
Trusley 32 E
Trusthorpe 34 B
Truthan 3 F
Trysull 31 L
Tuckenhay 5 H
Tuckhill 31 L
Tuddenham 26 E
Tuddenham Saint Martin 27 K
Tudhoe 49 L
Tudweiliog 29 A
Tuffley 23 L
Tufton 20 E
Tugby 33 K
Tugford 31 K
Tullamurry Bridge 105 K
Tullanaguiggy 103 A
Tullibody 58 G
Tullich 56 F
Tullich Muir 71 F
Tulliemet 65 M
Tullintrain 107 J
Tulloch 67 K
Tulloch 72 G
Tullochgorm 56 E
Tulloes 59 A
Tullyallen 104 D
Tullyard 104 K
Tullybanocher 57 F
Tullycorker 103 F
Tullyhogue 104 A
Tullykin 105 G
Tullymacreeve 104 L
Tullymore 104 D
Tullymore Lo. 108 M
Tullymurdoch 58 C
Tullynessle 66 F
Tullynewy 108 M
Tullyroan 104 D
Tully South 103 H
Tullywill 104 G
Tulnacross 104 A
Tumble 21 G
Tumby 33 F
Tumby Woodside 34 D
Tummel Bridge 65 L
Tummery 103 B
Tunga 75 E
Tunnel Hill 23 H
Tunstall 10 C
Tunstall 27 C
Tunstall 27 L
Tunstall 41 E
Tunstall 43 G
Tunstall 44 D
Tunstall 31 C
Tunstead 35 L
Tunworth 16 L
Tupsley 22 F
Tupton 32 B
Tur Langton 24 C
Tur Langton 32 M
Turbiskill 56 G
Turgis Green 16 H
Turin 59 A
Turkdean 23 M
Turmoyra 104 E
Turnastone 22 E
Turnberry 51 H
Turnchapel 5 G
Turnditch 32 E
Turner's Green 24 A
Turners Hill 9 C
Turners Puddle 7 D
Turnhouse 58 L
Turnworth 7 A
Turriff 73 K
Turton Bottoms 38 F
Turves 25 C
Turvey 25 G
Turville 16 F
Turville Heath 16 F
Turweston 24 H
Tutbury-Hatton 32 D
Tutnall 23 C
Tutshill-Sedbury 14 C
Tuttington 35 L
Tuxford 33 A
Twatt 79 D
Twatt 81 G
Twechar 57 M
Tweedmouth Spittal 54 E
Tweedsmuir 52 J
Twelveheads 3 J
Twemloe Green 38 M
Twenty 33 M
Twerton 15 D
Twickenham 17 H
Twigworth 23 H
Twineham 9 F
Twinhoe 15 D
Twinstead 26 M
Twitchen 13 H
Twitchen 30 M
Two Bridges 5 D
Two Dales 32 B
Two Gates 32 K
Twycross 32 L
Twyford 7 B
Twyford 8 B
Twyford 16 F
Twyford 24 M
Twyford 32 H
Twyford 33 K
Twyford 35 K
Twyford Common 22 J
Twynholm 47 D
Twyning 23 H
Twynllanan 21 E
Twyn-y-odyn 14 A
Twyn-y-Sheriff 22 L
Twywell 25 A
Ty Rhiw 14 A
Ty Mawr Cwm 37 K
Ty'n-y-groes 37 G
Tyberton 22 F
Tyburn 31 M
Tycroes 21 H
Tycrwyn 30 E
Tydd Gote 34 K
Tydd Saint Giles 34 K
Tydd Saint Mary 34 K
Tye Green 18 B
Ty-hen 28 C
Tyldesley 38 F
Tyler Hill 11 B
Tylers's Green 18 A
Tylorstown 21 M
Tylwch 30 K
Tynan 104 G
Ty-nant 21 A
Ty-nant 30 A
Ty-nant 30 D
Tyndrum 57 A
Tyneham 7 H
Tynehead 53 B
Tynemouth 49 J
Tynewydd 21 M
Tyninghame 53 C
Tynron 52 K
Tyn-y-ffridd 30 B
Tynygongl 36 F
Tynygraig 29 L
Tyn-y-graig 22 A
Tyrella 105 K
Tyrie 73 L
Tyringham 25 G
Tythegston 13 C
Tytherington 15 A
Tytherington 15 G
Tytherington 15 L
Tytherington 38 M
Tytherleigh 6 B
Tytherton Lucas 15 E
Tywardreath 4 E
Tywardreath Highway 4 E
Tywyn 29 H
Tywyn 37 G

U

Uachdar 68 B
Uagbeach 30 J
Ubbeston 27 H
Ubbeston Green 27 H
Ubley 14 F
Uckerby 44 D
Uckfield 10 G
Uckington 23 H
Uddingston 52 A
Uddington 52 E
Udimore 10 J
Udny Green 67 B
Udny Station 67 E
Udstonhead 52 A
Uest Cliffle 11 E
Uest Hythe 11 D
Uest Street 10 C
Uffcott 15 F
Uffculme 13 M
Uffington 16 A
Uffington 31 G
Uffinton 33 L
Ufford 27 L
Ufford 33 L
Ufton 24 E
Ufton Nervet 16 H
Ugadale 50 F
Ugborough 5 H
Uggeshall 27 J
Ugglebarnby 45 D
Ugley 26 K
Ugley Green 26 K
Ugthorpe 45 D
Uig 56 J
Uig 62 J
Uig 69 D
Uig 69 E
Uiginish 69 D
Uigshader 69 E
Uilinish 69 H
Ulbster 78 H
Ulceby 34 A
Ulceby 40 J
Ulceby Cross 34 A
Ulcombe 10 C
Uldale 47 J
Uley 15 A
Ulgham 49 C
Ullapool 70 C
Ullenhall 23 C
Ullenwood 23 L
Ulleskelf 40 A
Ullesthorpe 24 B
Ulley 39 M
Ullingswick 23 D
Ullock 47 L
Ulpha 42 B
Ulrome 41 A
Ulsta 80 F
Ulting 18 E
Ulzieside 52 G
Umberleigh 13 G
Unapool 76 J
Underbarrow 42 F
Underhoull 80 A
Underriver 10 B
Underwood 14 B
Undy 14 B
Unifirth 81 G
Union Mills 37 B
Unstone 39 M
Unstone Green 39 M
Unthank 48 K
Unthank End 48 K
Upavon 15 J
Up Cerne 7 A
Upchurch 10 C
Upcott 22 E
Upend Kirtling 26 H
Up Exe 5 C
Uphall 58 K
Upham 8 B
Upham 13 L
Uphampton 23 B
Up Hatherley 23 L
Uphill 14 E
Up Holland 38 E
Uplawmoor 51 C
Upleadon 23 G
Upleatham 44 C
Uplees 11 A
Uploders 6 F
Uplowman 13 M
Uplyme 6 B
Upminster 18 G
Up Nately 16 L
Upottery 6 A
Upper Affcot 30 M
Upper Ardchronie 71 B
Upper Ardroscadale 56 L
Upper Arley 31 L
Upper Arncott 24 L
Upper Aston 31 L
Upper Astrop 24 H
Upper Badcall 76 F
Upper Ballinderry 104 F
Upper Basildon 16 E
Upper Benefield 25 B
Upper Bighouse 77 F
Upper Boddington 24 E
Upper Borth 29 H
Upper-Brailes 24 G
Upper Breinton 22 F
Upper Broughton 33 G
Upper Bucklebury 16 H
Upper Burnhaugh 67 G
Upper Caldecote 25 H
Upper Camster 78 H
Upper Catesby 24 E
Upper Chapel 22 D
Upper-Chute 15 J
Upper Coberley 23 L
Upper Cragabus 55 L
Upper Dallachy 72 J
Upper Dean 25 E

A B C D E F G H I J K L M N O P Q R S T U V W X Y Z

Upper Denby 39 H
Upper Derraid 72 K
Upper Dicker 10 G
Upper Dunsforth 44 L
Upper Eathie 71 J
Upper Elkstone 32 A
Upper End 39 K
Upper Farringdon 16 L
Upper Framilode 23 K
Upper Froyle 16 M
Upper Gillock 78 H
Upper Gills 78 E
Upper Glenfintaig 64 F
Upper Godney 14 H
Upper Gravenhurst 25 L
Upper Green 16 G
Upper Hackney 32 B
Upper Halling 10 B
Upper Hambleton 33 K
Upper Hardres Court 11 E
Upper Hartfield 10 D
Upper Haugh 39 J
Upper Heath 31 K
Upper Helmsley 44 M
Upper Hergest 22 B
Upper Heyford 24 F
Upper Heyford 24 L
Upper Hill 22 F
Upper Hindhope 53 M
Upper Hopton 39 E
Upper Hulme 32 A
Upper Inglesham 15 C
Upper Killay 21 K
Upper Knockando 72 L
Upper Lambourn 16 D
Upperlands 108 L
Upper Lochton 67 G
Upper Longdon 31 J
Upper Longwood 31 G
Upper Ludstone 31 L
Upper Maes-coed 22 E
Upper Midhope 39 H
Uppermill 39 D
Upper Milovaig 69 D
Upper Minety 15 B
Upper North Dean 16 C
Upper Obney 58 B
Upper Oddington 24 K
Upper Ollach 69 H
Upper Poppleton 44 L
Upper Quinton 23 F
Upper-Rissington 23 M
Upper Rochford 23 A
Upper Sanday 79 H
Upper Seagry 15 E
Upper Shelton 25 G
Upper Sheringham 35 H
Upper Skelmorlie 56 M
Upper-Slaughter 23 M
Upper Soudley 23 K
Upper Stoke 27 B
Upper Stondon 25 L
Upper Stowe 24 F
Upper Street 7 C
Upper Street 27 C
Upper Street 27 D
Upper Street 35 L
Upper Sundon 25 L
Upper Swainswick 15 D
Upper-Swell 23 J
Upper Tean 31 F
Upperthird 107 L
Upperthong 39 E
Upper Tillyrie 58 H
Upperton 9 A
Upper Tooting 17 H
Upper Tote 69 F
Uppertown 79 K
Upper Tysoe 24 G
Upper Upham 15 F
Upper Upnor 18 H
Upper Wardington 24 H
Upper Weald 24 J
Upper Wheedon 24 F
Upper Wield 16 L
Upper Winchendon 16 C
Upper Winchendon 24 M
Upper Woodford 15 L
Upper Woolhampton 16 H
Upper Wootton 16 H
Uppingham 33 K
Uppington 31 G
Upsall 44 H
Upsettlington 54 D
Upsher Green 26 M
Upshire 17 F
Up Somborne 16 K
Upstreet 11 B
Up Sydling 7 A
Upthorpe 26 J
Upton 4 F
Upton 7 E
Upton 8 A
Upton 13 J
Upton 16 C
Upton 16 E
Upton 16 G
Upton 24 F
Upton 25 B
Upton 25 F
Upton 27 C
Upton 32 L
Upton 33 D
Upton 33 L
Upton 37 J
Upton 38 K
Upton 39 F
Upton 40 K
Upton 40 L
Upton 17 D
Upton Bishop 23 G
Upton Cheyney 15 D
Upton Cressett 31 K
Upton Cross 4 F
Upton Grey 16 L
Upton Hellions 5 C
Upton Lovell 15 L
Upton Magna 31 G
Upton Noble 14 J
Upton Pyne 5 C
Upton Saint Leonards 23 L
Upton Scudamore 15 G
Upton Snodsbury 23 E
Upton upon Severn 23 H
Upwaltham 9 D
Upware 26 D
Upwell 26 A
Upwey 7 D
Upwood 25 C
Uradale 81 H
Uragaig 55 E
Urchfont 15 H
Urdimarsh 22 F
Ure 80 H
Urgha 74 M
Urlay Nook 44 B
Urmston 38 J
Urquhart 71 H
Urquhart 72 H
Urra 44 F
Urray 71 G
Urswick 42 E
Usan 59 B
Ushaw Moor 49 L
Usk 22 L
Usselby 40 M
Utkinton 38 L
Utley 39 B
Uton 5 C
Utterby 41 K
Uttoxeter 32 D
Uwchmynydd 28 C
Uxbridge 17 D
Uyeasound 80 B
Uzmaston 20 E

V

Valley Truckle 4 B
Valley/Y Fali 36 E
Valleyfield 58 K
Valsgarth 80 A
Valtos 69 F
Vange 18 H
Varteg 22 L
Vatten 69 G
Vaul 62 A
Vaynol Hall 36 J
Vaynor 22 G
Veensgarth 81 G
Velindre 22 E
Vellow 13 J
Veness 79 E
Venn 5 H
Vennington 30 J
Venn Ottery 6 A
Venny Tedburn 5 C
Ventnor 8 H
Verham Dean 16 G
Verham Street 16 G
Vernolds Common 30 M
Verwood 7 C
Veryan 4 G
Veryan Green 4 G
Vicarage 6 D
Vicarscross 38 K
Vickerstown 42 H
Victoria 4 D
Victoria Bridge 107 L
Vidlin 80 F
Viewpark 52 A
Vigo Village 10 B
Vinehall Street 10 H
Vines Cross 10 H
Virginia Water 17 G
Virginstow 4 C
Vobster 15 G
Voe 80 F
Voe 80 H
Vow 108 H
Vowchurch 22 E
Voxter 80 J
Voy 79 G

W

Waberthwaite 42 B
Wackerfield 44 A
Wacton 27 E
Wadbister 81 D
Wadborough 23 E
Wadcrag 47 M
Waddesdon 24 M
Waddingham 40 M
Waddington 33 B
Waddington Bashall 43 K
Wadebridge 4 A
Wadeford 6 B
Wadenhoe 25 B
Wadesmill 17 C
Wadhurst 10 E
Wadshelf 39 L
Wadworth 40 G
Waen 37 L
Waen-fâch 30 E
Wag 78 K
Wainfleet All Saints 34 E
Wainfleet Bank 34 E
Wainfleet Saint Mary 34 E
Wainhouse Corner 12 L
Wainstalls 39 A
Waitby 43 B
Wakefield 39 F
Wakerley 33 L
Wakes Colne 18 C
Walberswick 27 J
Walberton 9 D
Walcot 15 F
Walcot 23 F
Walcot 30 M
Walcot 31 G
Walcot 33 H
Walcote 24 C
Walcott 33 F
Walcott 35 M
Walden 43 J
Walden Head 43 J
Walden Stubbs 40 D
Walderslade 10 C
Walderton 8 F
Walditch 6 F
Waldley 32 D
Waldridge 49 H
Waldringfield 27 L
Waldron 10 G
Wales 39 M
Walesby 33 A
Walesby 40 M
Walford 22 C
Walford 22 J
Walford 30 F
Walgherton 31 B
Walgrave 25 D
Walkden 38 F
Walker 49 J
Walker Fold 43 K
Walker's Green 22 F
Walkerburn 53 D
Walkeringham 40 L
Walkerith 40 L
Walkern 25 M
Walkerville 44 D
Walkhampton 5 D
Walkington 40 F
Walk Mill 39 A
Wall 32 G
Wall 49 D
Wallaceton 47 B
Wallacetown 51 H
Wallacetown 51 E
Wallasey 37 J
Wallbottle 49 H
Wallingford 16 E
Wallington 8 E
Wallington 17 H
Wallington 25 M
Wallis 20 E
Walliswood 9 B
Wallridge 49 E
Walls 81 G
Wallsend 49 J
Wall under Heywood 31 K
Wallyford 53 B
Walmer 11 F
Walmer Bridge 38 B
Walmersley 38 F
Walmley 32 K
Walpole 27 H
Walpole Cross Kays 34 L
Walpole Highway 34 K
Walpole Marsh 34 K
Walpole Saint Andrew 34 K
Walpole Saint Peter 34 K
Walsall 31 M
Walsall Wood 31 M
Walsden 39 D
Walsgrave on Sowe 24 B
Walsham Le Willows 27 G
Walshford 44 L
Walsoken 34 K
Walston 52 F
Walter's 16 C
Walterstone 22 H
Waltham 11 D
Waltham 41 K
Waltham Abbey 17 F
Waltham Chase 8 B
Waltham Cross 17 F
Waltham on the Wolds 33 G
Waltham Saint Lawrence 16 F
Walthamstow 17 F
Walton 14 H
Walton 19 B
Walton 22 B
Walton 24 D
Walton 24 C
Walton 25 K
Walton 31 D
Walton 32 B
Walton 33 M
Walton 39 C
Walton 39 F
Walton 48 E
Walton-and-Weybridge 17 G
Walton Cardiff 23 H
Walton East 20 E
Walton Highway 34 K
Walton in Gordano 14 E
Walton-le-Dale 38 B
Walton on the Hill 17 L
Walton-on-the-Hill 31 J
Walton-on-the-Naze 19 A
Walton on the Wolds 32 J
Walton-on-Trent 32 G
Walton West 20 D
Walwen 37 J
Walwick 49 D
Walworth 44 A
Walwyn's Castle 20 D
Wambrook 6 B
Wanborough 15 F
Wandsworth 17 H
Wangford 26 E
Wangford 27 J
Wanlip 32 M
Wanlockhead 52 H
Wansford 25 B
Wansford 41 A
Wanstead 17 F
Wanstrow 14 J
Wanswell 23 K
Wantage-Grove 16 A
Wapley 15 A
Wappenbury 24 B
Wappenham 24 J
Warbleton 10 H
Warborough 16 B
Warboys 25 F
Warbstow 4 C
Warburton 38 H
Warcop 43 B
Warden 18 M
Warden 49 D
Ward Green 27 G
Wardington 24 H
Wardlaw 53 G
Wardle 39 D
Wardle Barbridge 31 B
Wardley 33 K
Wardlow 39 L
Wardses 43 E
Wardy Hill 26 D
Ware 11 B
Ware 17 C
Wareham 7 E
Warehorne 11 D
Warenford 54 H
Warenton 54 H
Waresley 25 J
Warfield 16 J
Wargrave 16 F
Warham 35 G
Waringsford 104 J
Wark 49 D
Wark 54 G
Warkleigh 13 G
Warkton 25 A
Warkworth 49 C
Warlaby 44 E
Warland 39 D
Warleggan 4 E
Warmfield 39 F
Warmingham 38 L
Warmington 24 H
Warmington 25 B
Warminster 15 G
Warmlake 10 C
Warmsworth 40 G
Warmwell 7 D
Warndon 23 E
Warnford 8 C
Warnham 9 B
Warningcamp 9 D
Warninglid 9 C
Warningstown 104 E
Warren 20 G
Warren 38 M
Warren Mill 54 H
Warrenpoint 104 L
Warren Row 16 F
Warren Street 10 C
Warrington 25 G
Warrington 38 H
Warsash 8 E
Warse 78 E
Warslow 32 A
Warter 40 C
Warthill 44 M
Wartle 66 F
Wartling 10 H
Wartnaby 33 G
Warton 32 K
Warton 42 J
Warton 49 B
Warwick 24 D
Warwick Bridge 48 H
Warwick-on-Eden 48 G
Wasbister 79 E
Wasdale Head 42 B
Washaway 4 E
Washbourne 5 H
Washbrook 27 K
Washfield 13 L
Washfold 43 F
Washford 13 J
Washford Pyne 13 L
Washington 9 E
Washington 49 J
Wasing 16 H
Waskerley 49 K
Wasperton 24 D
Wass 44 J
Watchet 13 J
Watchfield 14 H
Watchfield 15 C
Watchgate 43 A
Watendlath 47 M
Water 38 C
Waterbeach 26 G
Waterbeck 47 C
Waterden 34 J
Water End 17 A
Water End 17 B
Waterfall 32 A
Waterfoot 38 F
Waterfoot 52 A
Waterford 17 C
Waterhead 42 C
Waterhead 51 J
Waterheads 53 D
Waterhill of Bruxie 73 L
Waterhouses 32 A
Waterhouses 49 L
Wateringbury 10 B
Waterlip 14 J
Waterloo 4 E
Waterloo 7 E
Waterloo 35 L
Waterloo 38 D
Waterloo 52 B
Waterloo 58 B
Waterlooville 8 F
Watermeetings 52 H
Watermillock 48 K
Water Newton Chesterton 25 B
Water Orton 32 K
Waterperry 16 B
Waterrow 13 M
Watersfield 9 D
Waterside 51 C
Waterside 51 J
Waterside 57 M
Waterside 66 E
Waterside 67 E
Waterstock 16 B
Waterston 20 G
Water Stratford 24 J
Waters Upton 31 D
Waterthorpe 39 M
Waterworks 104 A
Water Yeat 42 F
Watford 17 E
Watford 24 F
Watford Gap 32 K
Wath 44 G
Wath 44 H
Wath upon Dearne 39 J
Watlington 16 C
Watlington 34 L
Watnall 32 F
Watten 78 H
Wattisfield 27 D
Wattisham 26 M
Wattle Bridge 103 H
Wattlesborough Heath 30 J
Watton 26 C
Watton 40 C
Watton at Stone 17 C
Wattston 57 M
Wattstown 21 M
Wattsville 22 K
Waughs Cross Road 104 H
Waunarlwydd 21 K
Waunfawr 36 L
Wavendon 25 G
Waverbridge 47 J
Waverton 38 K
Waverton 47 J
Wawne 41 B
Waxham 35 M
Waxholme 41 E
Wayford 6 B
Waytown 6 C
Way Village 13 L
Weachyburn 73 K
Weald 16 A
Wealdstone 17 E
Weare 14 H
Weare Giffard 12 J
Wearhead 48 M
Wearne 14 L
Weasdale 43 B
Weasenham All Saints 34 M
Weasenham Saint Peter 34 M
Weatheroak Hill 23 C
Weaverham 38 L
Weaverthorpe 45 L
Webheath 23 C
Wedderlairs 67 B
Weddington 32 L
Wedhampton 15 H
Wedmore 14 H
Wednesbury 31 M
Wednesfield 31 M
Weecar 33 B
Weedon 24 M
Weedon Lois 24 J
Weeford 32 K
Week 13 L
Weekley 25 A
Week Saint'Mary 12 L
Weel 40 F
Weeley 19 A
Weeley Heath 19 A
Weem 65 L
Weeping Cross 31 J
Weeting 26 F
Weeton 38 A
Weeton 39 C
Weeton 41 H
Weir 39 A
Weirbrook 30 F
Welbeck Abbey 39 M
Welborne 27 A
Welbourn 33 E
Welburn 44 M
Welbury 44 E
Welby 33 H
Welches Dam 26 A
Welcombe 12 H
Weldon 25 A
Welford 16 D
Welford 24 C
Welford-on-Avon 23 F
Welham 25 A
Welham 40 K
Welham Green 17 B
Well 16 M
Well 34 B
Well 44 G
Well Hill 17 M
Well Town 13 L
Welland 23 H
Wellbank 59 D
Wellesbourne 24 D
Welling 17 J
Wellingborough 25 D
Wellingham 34 M
Wellingore 33 E
Wellington 13 M
Wellington 22 F
Wellington 31 G
Wellington Heath 23 D
Wellow 8 G
Wellow 15 G
Wellow 33 A
Wellpond Green 17 C
Wells 14 J
Wellsborough 32 L
Wells-Next-the-Sea 35 G
Wellwood 58 L
Welney 26 A
Welshampton 31 D
Welsh Bicknor 22 J
Welsh End 31 D
Welsh Hook 20 D
Welsh Newton 22 J
Welsh Newton Common 22 J
Welshpool/Y Trallwng 30 H
Welsh Saint Donats 13 C
Welton 24 F
Welton 40 K
Welton 48 G
Welton-Dunholme 33 C
Welton le Marsh 34 B
Welton le Wold 41 K
Welwick 41 H
Welwyn Garden City 17 B
Welwyn-Codicote 17 B
Wem 31 D
Wembley 17 E
Wembury 5 G
Wembworthy 13 K
Wemyss Bay 56 M
Wenallt 30 A
Wendens Ambo 26 K
Wendlebury 24 L
Wendling 26 C
Wendover 17 A
Wendron 3 H
Wendy 25 J
Wenlli 37 K
Wennington 18 G
Wennington 25 F
Wennington 43 G
Wensley 32 B
Wensley 47 F
Wentbridge 39 F
Wentnor 30 M
Wentworth 17 G
Wentworth 26 D
Wentworth 39 J
Wenvoe 14 A
Weobley 22 F
Weobley Marsh 22 F
Wepre 37 M
Wereham 26 B
Wergs 31 L
Wernrheolydd 22 L
Werrington 4 C
Werrington 31 C
Wervin 38 K
Wesham 38 A
Wessington 32 B
West Aberthaw 13 F
Westacott 13 G
West Acre 34 M
West Allerdean 54 D
West Alvington 5 H
West Anstey 13 H
West Ashby 34 A
West Ashling 8 F
West Ashton 15 G
West Auckland 44 A
West Bagborough 14 G
West Barkwith 33 C
West Barns 53 C
West Barny 45 D
West Barsham 34 J
West Bay 6 F
West Beckham 35 H
West Bennan 51 D
West Bergholt 18 C
West Bexington 6 F
West Bilney 34 L
West Blatchington 9 F
West Boldon 49 J
Westborough 33 E
Westbourne 8 F
Westbourne 7 F
West Bradford 43 K
West Bradley 14 J
West Bretton 39 E
West Bridgford 32 F
West Bromwich 31 M
West Buckland 13 G
West Buckland 14 K
West Burrafirth 81 G
West Burton 9 D
West Burton 43 F
Westbury 15 G
Westbury 24 J
Westbury 30 J
Westbury Leigh 15 G
Westbury-on-Severn 23 K
Westbury-sub-Mendip 14 H
West Butterwick 40 H
Westby 33 H
Westby 38 A
West Byfleet 17 G
West Caister 27 C
West Calder 52 C
West Camel 14 M
West Challow 16 A
West Charleton 5 L
West Chelborough 6 C
West Chevington 49 C
West Chiltington Common 9 E
West Chinnock 6 C
Westcliff-on-Sea 18 H
West Clyne 72 A
West Coker 6 C
Westcombe 14 J
West Compton 6 F
West Compton 14 J
Westcott 6 A
Westcott 17 K
Westcott 24 M
Westcott Barton 24 K
West Cross 21 K
West Curry 4 C
West Curthwaite 48 G
West Dean 9 D
West Dean 15 M
West Deeping 33 L
West Derby 38 G
West Dereham 26 B
West Ditchburn 54 L
West Down 13 D
Westdown Camp 15 H
West Drayton 33 A
West Drayton 17 D
West Edington 49 E
West End 16 A
West End 17 G
West End 8 B
West End 14 E
West End 15 L
West End 25 G
West End 27 C
West End 40 F
West End 43 M
West End 52 F
West End Green 16 H
Wester Aberchalder 65 A
Wester Balgedie 58 H
Westerdale 44 F
Westerdale 78 G
Wester Dechmont 52 C
Wester Dechmont 58 K
Wester Denoon 58 C
Wester Ellister 55 K
Westerfield 27 K
Westerfield 81 G
Wester Fintray 67 D
Wester Fodderletter 66 A
Westergate-Barnham-Yapton 9 D
Wester Gruinards 71 B
Westerham 10 A
Wester Lealty 71 E
Westerleigh 15 A
Wester Main 71 K
Wester Newburn 59 G
Wester Ord 67 D
Wester Quarff 81 H
Wester Skeld 81 G
Westerton 59 B
Wester Watten 78 H
Westerwick 81 G
West Farleigh 10 B
West Felton 30 F
Westfield 10 J
Westfield 17 H
Westfield 23 D
Westfield 27 A
Westfield 58 K
Westfield 78 D
West Fleetham 54 L
Westgate 35 G
Westgate 40 H
Westgate 49 G
Westgate on Sea 11 C
West Ginge 16 D
West Grafton 15 J
West Green 16 J
West Grimstead 15 M
West Grinstead 9 B
West Haddlesey 40 D
West Haddon 24 F
West Hagbourne 16 E
West Hagley 23 B
Westhall 27 J
West Hall 48 E
Westhall 67 A
West Hallam 32 E
West Halton 40 F
Westham 10 H
Westham 14 H
West Ham 17 J
Westhampnett 9 D
West Hanningfield 18 E
West-Harptree 14 F
West Hatch 14 K
Westhay 14 H
Westhead 38 D
West Heath 16 H
West Heath 16 J
West Helmsdale 77 M
West Helmsdale 78 K
West Hendred 16 D
West Heslerton 45 K
Westhide 23 D
West Hill 6 A
Westhill 67 D
Westhill 71 L

West Hoathly 9 C
West Holme 7 E
Westhope 22 F
Westhope 30 M
West Hope 43 C
West Horndonn 18 D
Westhorpe 27 G
Westhorpe 33 J
West-Horrington 14 J
West Horsley 17 K
West Hougham 11 E
Westhoughton 38 E
West Houlland 81 G
Westhouse 43 G
Westhouses 32 B
Westhumble 17 L
West Hyde 17 D
West Ilsley 16 D
Westing 80 A
West Itchenor 8 F
West Keal 34 D
West Kennett 15 F
West Kilbride 51 B
West Kingsdown 10 B
West Kington 15 D
West Kirkby-Hoylake 37 J
West Knapton 45 K
West Knighton 7 D
West Knowle 15 K
West Kyloe 54 H
Westlake 5 G
West Lambrook 14 L
West Langdon 11 E
West Langwell 77 L
West Lavington 9 A
West Lavington 15 H
West Leake 32 J
West Learmouth 54 G
Westleigh 12 J
Westleigh 13 M
Westleton 27 J
West Lexham 34 M
Westley 26 J
Westley 30 J
Westley Waterless 26 H
West Lilling 44 M
Westlinton 48 D
West Linton 53 D
West Littleton 15 D
West Looe 4 H
West Luccombe 13 F
West Lulworth 7 D
West Lutton 45 K
West Lydford 14 M
West Lyn 13 E
West Lynn 34 L
West Mains 52 C
West-Mains 54 H
West Malling 10 B
West Malvern 23 D
West Marden 8 F
West Markham 33 A
Westmarsh 11 B
West Marton 43 L
West Mersea 18 F
West Milton 6 C
West-Minster 17 H
West Monkton 14 K
West Moors 7 F
West Mostard 43 E
Westmuir 59 A
West Muir 66 M
West Ness 44 J
Westness 79 E
West Newton 14 K
West Newton 34 L
West Newton 41 B
Westnewton 47 J
Westnewton 54 G
West Norwood 17 H
West Ogwell 5 E
Weston 8 C
Weston 16 D
Weston 24 H
Weston 25 M
Weston 27 F
Weston 31 B
Weston 31 D
Weston 31 F
Weston 31 K
Weston 33 A
Weston 33 J
Weston 38 G
Weston 39 B
Weston 52 F
Weston Bampfylde 14 M
Weston Beggard 23 D
Weston by Welland 25 A
Westonbirt 15 B
Weston Colville 26 H
Weston-Easton 7 G
Weston Green 26 H
Weston Green 27 A
Weston Heath 31 H
Weston Hills 33 M
Westoning 25 L
Weston in Gordano 14 E
Weston Jones 31 E
Weston Longville 27 A
Weston Lullingfields 30 F
Weston-on-the-Green 24 L
Weston-on-Trent 32 H
Weston Patrick 16 L
Weston Rhyn 30 C
Weston-Sub-Edge 23 J
Weston-super-Mare 14 E
Weston Turville 17 A
Weston-under-Lizard 31 H
Weston under Penyard 23 G
Weston under Wetherley 24 B
Weston Underwood 25 G
Weston Underwood 32 E
Westonzoyland 14 H
West Orchard 7 B
West Overton 15 F
Westow 45 K
West Park 67 G
West Parley 7 F
West Peckham 10 B
West Pennard 14 J
West Pentire 3 F
West Porlock 13 E
Westport 14 L
Westport 50 E
West Putford 12 M
West Quantoxhead 14 G
West Rainton 49 M
West Rasen 40 M
West Raynham 34 M
Westrigg 52 B
West Rounton 44 E
West Row 26 E
West Rudham 34 M
West Runton 35 H
Westruther 53 F
Westry 26 A
West Saltoun 53 B
West Sandwick 80 E
West Scrafton 43 J
West Side 22 K
West Side 79 E
West Somerton 27 C
West Stafford 7 D
West Stockwith 40 L
West Stoke 8 F
West Stonesdale 43 F
West Stoughton 14 H
West Stour 15 K
West Stourmouth 11 B
West Stow 26 J
West Stowell 15 J
West Tanfield 44 G
West Tarbert 56 K
West Thorney 8 F
West Thurrock 18 G
West Tilbury 18 G
West Tisted 8 C
West Tofts 26 C
West Tofts 58 B
West Torrington 33 C
West Torrington 40 M
West Town 14 F
West Tullyfergus 58 C
West Tytherley 15 M
West Walton 34 K
Westward 47 J
Westward 48 G
Westward Ho 12 J
Westwell 11 D
Westwell 23 M
West Wellow 8 A
West Wemyss 58 L
West Wick 14 E
Westwick 26 D
Westwick 35 L
West Wickham 26 G
West Wickham 17 J
West Williamston 20 H
West Wilton 43 F
West Winch 34 L
West Winterslow 15 M
West Wittering 8 F
Westwood 6 A
Westwood 15 G
West Woodburn 49 A
West Woodhay 16 G
Westwood Heath 24 A
West Woodlands 15 G
Westwoodside 40 H
West Worldham 16 L
West-Worlington 13 L
West Wratting 26 G
West Wycombe 16 C
West Yell 80 E
Wetheral 48 G
Wetherby 39 C
Wetherden 26 J
Wetheringsett 27 G
Wethersta 80 J
Wetherup Street 27 G
Wetley Rocks 31 C
Wettenhall 38 L
Wetton 32 A
Wetwang 45 K
Wetwood 31 E
Wexcombe 15 J
Wexham Street 17 D
Weybourne 35 H
Weybread 27 E
Weydale 78 E
Weyhill 15 M
Weymouth 7 D
Whaddon 15 M
Whaddon 23 L
Whaddon 24 M
Whaddon 25 J
Whale 48 L
Whaley 32 C
Whaley Bridge 39 K
Whaley Thorns 32 C
Whaligoe 78 H
Whalley 38 C
Whalton 49 E
Wham 43 H
Whaplode 34 G
Whaplode Drove 34 K
Whaplode Saint Catherine 34 K
Wharfe 43 H
Wharles 38 B
Wharles 42 M
Wharley End 25 G
Wharncliffe Side 39 H
Wharram le Street 45 K
Wharton 22 F
Wharton 38 L
Whashton 44 D
Whatcombe 7 A
Whatcote 24 G
Whatfield 26 M
Whatley 15 G
Whatlington 10 H
Whatton 33 D
Whauphill 46 E
Whaw 43 F
Wheatacre 27 F
Wheathampstead 17 B
Wheathill 31 K
Wheathill 103 D
Wheatley 16 B
Wheatley 16 M
Wheatley Hill 49 M
Wheatley Lane 38 C
Wheaton Aston 31 H
Wheddon Cross 13 J
Wheedlemont 66 C
Wheedon Bec 24 F
Wheelerstreet 16 M
Wheelock 31 B
Wheelock Heath 31 B
Wheelton 38 B
Wheen 66 L
Wheldrake 40 B
Whelford 15 C
Whelpley Hill 17 A
Whelston 37 J
Whempstead 17 C
Whenby 44 M
Wherstead 27 K
Wherwell 16 K
Wheston 39 K
Whetersfield 26 L
Whetsted 10 B
Whetstone 32 M
Whicham 42 E
Whichford 24 G
Whigstreet 59 A
Whillington 43 G
Whilton 24 F
Whimble 12 M
Whimple 6 A
Whimpwell Green 35 M
Whinburgh 27 A
Whin Lane End 42 M
Whinnieliggate 47 D
Whinnyfold 67 C
Whippingham 8 E
Whipsnade 17 A
Whipton 5 C
Whissendine 33 K
Whissonsett 34 M
Whistley Green 16 F
Whiston 25 D
Whiston 31 J
Whiston 32 A
Whiston 38 G
Whiston 39 M
Whitacre Heath 32 K
Whitbeck 42 E
Whitbourne 23 D
Whitburn 49 J
Whitburn 52 C
Whitby 38 G
Whitby 45 E
Whitchurch 5 D
Whitchurch 6 B
Whitchurch 14 A
Whitchurch 14 F
Whitchurch 16 K
Whitchurch 20 D
Whitchurch 22 J
Whitchurch 31 A
Whitchurch Hill 16 E
Whitchurch-on-Thames 16 E
Whitcombe 7 D
Whitcott Keysett 30 L
Whiteabbey 105 A
Whiteacen 72 L
Whiteash Green 26 L
Whitebridge 65 A
Whitebrook 22 M
Whitecairn 46 A
Whitecairns 67 E
Whitecastle 52 F
Whitechapel 43 K
White Colne 18 C
White Coppice 38 B
Whitecraig 53 B
Whitecroft 22 M
White Cross 4 D
Whitecross 31 F
Whitecross 58 K
Whitecross 104 L
Whiteface 71 C
Whitefield 38 F
Whitefield 67 A
Whitefield 71 K
Whiteford 67 A
Whitegate 38 L
Whitehall 11 A
Whitehall Village 79 F
Whitehaven 47 L
Whitehead 105 B
Whitehill 8 C
Whitehill 20 H
Whitehill 67 C
Whitehill 103 D
Whitehills 73 G
Whitehouse 56 K
Whitehouse 66 F
Whitekirk 59 K
White Kirkley 49 K
White Lackington 7 D
Whitelackington 14 L
White Ladies Aston 23 E
Whiteleaf 16 C
Whiteley Bank 8 H
Whiteley Village 17 G
Whiteleys 46 A
Whitelock's End 23 C
Whitemans Green 9 C
Whitemire 72 G
Whitemoor 4 D
White Ness 81 G
White Notley 18 B
Whiteparish 8 A
White Pit 34 A
Whiterashes 67 E
White Rocks 22 J
White Roothing or White Roding 18 A
Whiterow 78 H
Whiteshill 23 L
Whiteside 48 F
Whiteside 52 C
Whitesmith 10 G
Whitestaunton 6 B
Whitestone 5 C
White Waltham 16 F
Whiteway 23 L
Whitewell 43 K
Whitewell 73 L
Whiteworks 5 D
Whitewreath 72 H
Whitfield 11 E
Whitfield 15 A
Whitfield 24 J
Whitfield 48 J
Whitford 6 B
Whitford 37 J
Whitgift 40 E
Whitgreave 31 F
Whithorn 46 H
Whiting Bay 51 D
Whitland 20 F
Whitletts 51 F
Whitley 15 D
Whitley 16 J
Whitley 38 H
Whitley 40 D
Whitley Bay 49 F
Whitley Chapel 49 G
Whitley Lower 39 E
Whitley Row 10 A
Whitminster 23 K
Whitmore 31 E
Whitnage 13 M
Whitnash 24 D
Whitney-on-Wye 22 E
Whitrigg 47 F
Whitrigg 47 J
Whitsbury 7 C
Whitsome 54 D
Whitson 14 B
Whitstable-Herne Bay 11 A
Whitstone 12 L
Whittingham 54 L
Whittingslow 30 M
Whittington 23 E
Whittington 23 M
Whittington 26 B
Whittington 30 F
Whittington 31 L
Whittington 32 G
Whittington 39 M
Whittlebury 24 J
Whittle-le-Woods 38 B
Whittlesey 25 C
Whittlesford 26 G
Whitton 22 B
Whitton 23 A
Whitton 27 K
Whitton 40 F
Whitton 44 B
Whitton 49 B
Whitton 53 J
Whittonstall 49 G
Whitway 16 G
Whitwell 8 H
Whitwell 17 B
Whitwell 33 L
Whitwell 39 M
Whitwell 44 D
Whitwell Street 35 K
Whitwell-on-the-Hill 44 M
Whitwick 32 H
Whitwood 39 F
Whitworth 39 D
Whixall 31 D
Whixley 44 L
Whome 79 G
Whorlton 44 A
Whorlton 44 E
Whygate 48 F
Whyle 23 A
Whyteleafe 10 A
Wibdon 22 M
Wibtoft 24 B
Wichenford 23 B
Wichford 26 D
Wichling 10 C
Wick 7 C
Wick 7 F
Wick 9 D
Wick 13 C
Wick 15 D
Wick 23 E
Wick 78 H
Wick 81 H
Wick Saint Lawrence 14 E
Wicken 24 J
Wicken 26 D
Wicken Bonhunt 26 K
Wickenby 40 M
Wicken Green Village 34 J
Wickersley 39 M
Wickford-Ramsden Bellhouse 18 E
Wickham 8 E
Wickham 16 D
Wickham 49 H
Wickhambreaux 11 B
Wickhambrook 26 H
Wickhamford 23 J
Wickham Market 27 L
Wickhampton 27 C
Wickham Saint Paul 26 L
Wickham Skeith 27 G
Wickham Street 26 H
Wickham Street 27 G
Wicklewood 27 A
Wickmere 35 L
Wickwar 15 A
Widdington 26 K
Widdon Down 5 B
Widdrington 49 C
Widdrington Station 49 C
Widecombe in the Moor 5 E
Widegates 4 F
Widemouth Bay 12 L
Wide Open 49 E
Widewall 79 L
Widford 17 C
Widford 18 D
Widmerpool 32 J
Widnes 38 H
Widworthy 6 A
Wigan 38 E
Wiggaton 6 A
Wiggenhall Saint Germans 34 L
Wiggenhall Saint Mary Magdalen 34
Wiggenhall Saint Mary the Virgin 34 L
Wiggenhall Saint Peter 34 L
Wigginton 17 A
Wigginton 24 G
Wigginton 44 M
Wigglesworth 43 L
Wiggonby 48 G
Wiggonholt 9 E
Wighill 40 A
Wighton 35 G
Wigmore 10 C
Wigmore 22 C
Wigsley 33 B
Wigsthorpe 25 B
Wigston 32 M
Wigthorpe 40 K
Wigtoft 33 J
Wigton 47 J
Wigtown 46 E
Wigtwizzle 39 H
Wilbarston 25 A
Wilberfoss 40 B
Wilburton 26 D
Wilby 25 D
Wilby 27 D
Wilby 27 H
Wilcot Woodborough 15 J
Wilcott 30 F
Wilcove 4 J
Wilcrick 14 B
Wildboarclough 39 K
Wilden 23 B
Wilden 25 H
Wildhern 16 G
Wildhill 17 B
Wildsworth 40 H
Wilford 32 F
Wilkesley 31 B
Wilkhaven 72 D
Wilkieston 53 A
Willand 13 M
Willaston 31 B
Willaston 38 G
Willen 25 B
Willenhall 31 M
Willerby 45 L
Willerby 40 F
Willersey 23 J
Willersley 22 B
Willesden 17 E
Willett 13 J
Willey 24 B
Willey 31 G
Williamscot 24 H
Willian 25 L
Willingale 18 D
Willingdon 10 K
Willingham 26 D
Willingham by Stow 40 L
Willington 24 G
Willington 25 H
Willington 32 H
Willington 49 L
Willington 49 J
Willington Corner 38 K
Willisham 27 K
Willisham Tye 27 K
Willitoft 40 E
Williton 13 J
Willoughby 24 E
Willoughby 34 B
Willoughby-on-the-Wolds 32 J
Willoughby Waterleys 24 C
Willoughby Waterleys 32 M
Willoughton 40 L
Willsborough Lees 11 D
Wilmcote 24 D
Wilmington 10 G
Wilmington 6 A
Wilmington 17 J
Wilmslow-Alderley Edge 38 M
Wilnecote 32 K
Wilpshire 38 C
Wilsden 39 B
Wilsford 15 H
Wilsford 15 L
Wilsford 33 E
Wilsill 44 K
Wilson 32 H
Wilsontown 52 C
Wilstead 25 H
Wilsthorpe 33 L
Wilstone 17 A
Wilton 15 J
Wilton 15 L
Wilton 44 C
Wilton 45 G
Wimbish 26 K
Wimbish Green 26 K
Wimbledon 17 H
Wimborne Minster 7 E
Wimborne Saint Giles 7 C
Wimbotsham 26 B
Wimpole 25 J
Wimpstone 24 D
Wincanton 14 M
Wincham 38 L
Winchburgh 58 L
Winchcombe 23 J
Winchelsea 10 J
Winchelsea Beach 10 J
Winchester 8 B
Winchfield 16 M
Winchmore Hill 17 D
Winchmore Hill 17 F
Wincle 38 M
Windermere 42 C
Winderton 24 G
Windhill 71 G
Windlesham 16 J
Windley 32 E
Windmill Hill 10 H
Windmill Hill 14 K
Windrush 23 M
Windsor 17 G
Windsor 105 D
Windygates 58 J
Windyridge 32 J
Windywalls 79 B
Windy-Yett 51 C
Wineham 9 E
Winestead 41 G
Winfarthing 27 D
Winford 8 H
Winford 14 F
Winforton 22 E
Winfrith Newburgh 7 D
Wing 25 K
Wing 33 K
Wingate 49 M
Wingates 38 E
Wingates 49 B
Wingerworth 32 B
Wingfield 15 G
Wingfield 25 K
Wingfield 27 H
Wingham 11 B
Wingmore 11 E
Wingrave 25 K
Winkburn 33 A
Winkfield 16 J
Winkfield Row 16 J
Winkhill 32 A
Winkleigh 13 K
Winksley 44 G
Winkton 7 F
Winless 78 H
Winmarleigh 42 M
Winnersh 16 J
Winscales 47 L
Winscombe 14 E
Winsford 13 H
Winsford 38 L
Winsham 6 B
Winshill/Stapenhill 32 G
Winskill 48 L
Winslade 16 L
Winsley 15 D
Winslow 24 M
Winson 23 M
Winsor 8 A
Winster 32 B
Winster 42 F
Winston 27 G
Winston 44 A
Winston Green 27 G
Winstone 23 L
Winswell 12 M
Winterborne Clenston 7 B
Winterborne Herrington 7 D
Winterborne Houghton 7 A
Winterborne Kingston 7 E
Winterborne Monkton 7 D
Winterborne Stickland 7 B
Winterborne Whitechurch 7 B
Winterborne Zelston 7 E
Winterbourne 15 A
Winterbourne Abbas 6 F
Winterbourne Bassett 15 F
Winterbourne Curridge 16 D
Winterbourne Dauntsey 15 M
Winterbourne Earls 15 M
Winterbourne Gunner 15 M
Winterbourne Monkton 15 F
Winterbourne Steepleton 6 F
Winterbourne Stoke 15 L
Winterburn 43 L
Winteringham 40 F
Winterley 31 B
Wintersett 39 F
Winterton 40 J
Winterton-on-Sea 27 C
Winthorpe 33 A
Winthorpe 34 E
Winton 7 F
Winton 43 B
Wintringham 45 K
Winwick 24 C
Winwick 25 B
Winwick 38 H
Winyates 23 C
Wirksworth 32 B
Wirswall 31 A
Wisbech 34 K
Wisbech Saint Mary 34 K
Wisborough Green 9 B
Wiseton 40 K
Wishaw 32 K
Wishaw 52 B
Wisley 17 G
Wispington 33 C
Wissett 27 H
Wissington 26 M
Wistanstow 30 M
Wistanswick 31 E
Wistaston 31 B
Wistaston Green 31 B
Wiston 9 E
Wiston 20 E
Wiston 52 E
Wistow 25 F
Wistow 40 A
Wiswell 38 C
Witcham 26 D
Witchampton 7 B
Witcombe 14 L
Witham 18 B
Witham Friary 15 G
Witham on the Hill 33 L
Witham Saint Hugh's 33 B
Withcall 34 A
Witherenden Hill 10 E
Witheridge 13 L
Witherley 32 L
Withern 34 B
Withernsea 41 E
Withernwick 41 B
Withersdale Street 27 E
Withersfield 26 L
Witherslack 42 F
Withiel 4 D
Withiel Florey 13 J
Withington 22 F
Withington 23 M
Withington 31 F
Withington 31 G
Withington 38 J
Withington Green 38 M
Withleigh 13 L
Withnell 38 B
Withybrook 24 B
Withycombe 13 J
Withyham 10 D
Withypool 13 H
Witley Court 23 B
Witnesham 27 K
Witney 24 K
Wittering 33 L
Wittersham 10 J
Witton 66 M
Witton Bridge 35 M
Witton Gilbert 49 L
Witton-le-Wear 49 L
Witton Park 49 L
Wiveliscombe 13 M
Wivelsfield 9 F
Wivelsfield Green 9 F
Wiveton 35 G
Wix 19 A
Wixford 23 F
Wixoe 26 L
Woburn 25 K
Woburn Sands 25 K
Woking-Byfleet 17 K
Wokingham 16 J
Wold Newton 41 K
Wold Newton 45 L
Woldingham 10 A
Woldingham Garden Village 10 A
Wolf's Castle 20 D
Wolfclyde 52 F
Wolferlow 23 A
Wolferton 34 L
Wolfhill 58 B
Wolfsdale 20 D
Woll 53 H
Wollaston 25 D
Wollaston 30 J
Wollerton 31 D
Wolsingham 49 K
Wolston 24 B
Wolvercote 16 B
Wolverhampton 31 L
Wolverley 23 B
Wolverley 31 D
Wolver-Stonyton-Stratford 25 G
Wolverton 16 H
Wolverton 24 D
Wolvesnewton 22 M
Wolvey 24 B
Wolvey Heath 24 B
Wolviston 44 B
Wombell 39 J
Wombleton 44 J
Wombourne 31 L
Womenswold 11 E
Womersley 40 D

Y

Z

Ireland 1:301,000

A

Abbert 95 F
Abbeville 84 E
Abbey 95 M
Abbeydorney 89 G
Abbeyfeale 89 J
Abbeylara 97 A
Abbeyleix 92 D
Abbeyshrule 96 F
Abbeyside 85 E
Abington 90 J
Accony 100 H
Achill 100 F
Achill Sound 100 H
Achonry 102 G
Ackle Back 106 L
Aclare 101 J
Adamstown 86 J
Adare 90 H
Addergoole 101 L
Addragool 95 D
Adrigole 82 J
Agaharroo 102 B
Agall 96 M
Aghaboe 91 F
Aghabullogue 84 D
Aghacashel 97 B
Aghaconny 97 A
Aghada 84 J
Aghade 86 C
Aghadiffin 101 M
Aghadoe 83 A
Aghadoon 100 A
Aghadoon 100 C
Aghadreenagh 103 L
Aghafore 83 M
Aghagower 101 K
Aghalan 103 G
Aghaloory 97 A
Aghamore 101 M
Aghamore 102 M
Aghamuck 96 B
Aghancon 91 C
Agharra 96 F
Aghaterry 92 H
Aghavannagh 93 G
Aghavas 102 M
Aghaville 83 H
Aghaward 101 H
Agher Cross Roads 97 M
Aghern 84 F
Aghnacliff 97 A
Aghnagar Bridge 82 B
Aghnalaly 92 D
Aghnamullen 103 M
Aghowle 87 A
Aglish 85 D
Aglish 91 B
Aglish 95 K
Ahadallane Cross Roads 84 D
Ahafona 89 E
Ahakista 83 G
Ahascragh 96 G
Ahaunboy 83 M
Ahenny 85 C
Aherla 84 G
Aighe 106 H
Aillebrack 94 A
Alkill 104 G
Allen 92 C
Allenwood 97 L
Allihies 82 H
Alloon Cross Roads 95 J
Alt Upper 107 L
Altadush 107 G
Altagowlan 102 H
Altashane 107 C
Altateskin 102 J
Altnapaste 107 G
Ambrosetown 86 J
America 96 G
Anablaha 83 B
Analog Cross 98 D
Anascaul 88 M
Anbally 95 E
An Geata 100 B
Anglesey Bridge 91 G
Anlore 103 H
Annacarriga 90 F
Annacarty 91 G
Annacotty 90 J
Annacurragh 93 G
Annadale 102 J
Annagary 106 F
Annagassan 98 E
Annagh 95 J
Annagh 96 A
Annagh Castle 91 A
Annagh Cross 89 C
Annaghdown 95 D
Annaghmore West 95 F
Annagleve 104 K
Annamoe 93 E
Annayalla 104 K
Annesbrook or Loughhanmore 98 G
Annestown 85 F
Annfield 91 H
Annie Brady Bridge 101 A
Annis Grove 97 A
Aphort 106 E
Ara 101 L
Araglin 84 C
Archerstown 97 E
Ard 94 E
Ardacluggin 82 H
Ardagh 83 K
Ardagh 90 G
Ardagh 96 F
Ardagh 97 C
Ardagh 98 D
Ardagh 100 L
Ardagh 107 H
Ardaghy 103 J
Ardan 96 M
Ardanary 87 C
Ardanew 97 H
Ardara 106 H
Ardattin 86 C
Ardbooly 90 B
Ardcanny Rectory 90 E
Ardcath 98 G
Ardcorky 101 L
Ardcrony 91 A
Ardea 82 F
Ardee 98 D
Ardenagh 86 J
Ardfert 89 G
Ardfield 83 M
Ardfinnan 85 A
Ardgehane 83 M
Ardglass 84 F
Ardgroom 82 F
Ardhoom 101 H
Ardled 92 D
Ardlougher 103 K
Ardloy 102 G
Ardmaghbreague 97 F
Ardmeen 106 F
Ardmore 85 G
Ardmore 94 E
Ardmorney 97 G
Ardmoy 102 K
Ardnacrany 96 J
Ardnagreevagh 100 L
Ardnagrena 83 K
Ardnaree 101 E
Ardnaree 107 E
Ardnasodan 95 E
Ardonagh Cross Roads 97 G
Ardoughter 89 H
Ardpatrick 90 L
Ardra 84 J
Ardrah 83 G
Ardrah 83 H
Ardrahan 89 G
Ardrahan 95 L
Ardrumkilla 95 E
Ardscull 92 E
Ardsoreen 102 K
Arigna 102 H
Arinagh 101 J
Arklow/An tInbhear Mór 87 B
Arless 92 E
Arranagh 90 K
Arryheernabin 107 B
Artane 98 L
Arthurstown 86 H
Arvagh 103 K
Ashbourne/Cill Dhéagláin 98 K
Ashfield 92 E
Ash Field 97 C
Ashford 90 K
Ashford 93 E
Ashgrove 91 A
Ashhill 91 L
Ashline 90 A
Ashton 83 F
Ashton 87 E
Askamore 87 A
Askanagap 93 G
Askeaton 90 G
Askill 102 C
Askillaun 100 H
Askingarran 87 E
Askintinny 87 B
Ass Bridge 101 G
Astee 89 E
Athavallie 101 L
Athboy 97 J
Athea 89 J
Athenry 95 H
Athgarvan 92 C
Athgreany 92 F
Athlacca 90 L
Athleague 96 D
Athlone/Baile Átha Luain 96 H
Athnaleenta 84 E
Athnid 91 H
Athy/Baile Átha j 92 E
Attanagh 92 D
Attavally 100 C
Attinkee 96 L
Attiregan 95 J
Attymass 101 H
Attymon 95 J
Aubawn 103 K
Auburn 96 H
Aucloggeen 95 E
Aughabrack 82 H
Aughacasla 88 M
Aughagault 107 H
Aughanloge Bridge 89 F
Aughatubbrid 92 D
Aughils 89 K
Aughinish 95 G
Aughnasheelan 102 J
Aughness 100 F
Aughrim 93 G
Aughrim 96 G
Aughrim 102 F
Aughris 102 D
Aughrus More 100 K
Aughvaneen 85 C
Avoca 93 G
Avoncore 84 J

B

Baconstown 97 M
Badgerisland 91 F
Bailieborough 97 C
Bailyhaght 90 L
Balbriggan/Baile Brigín 98 H
Balbyruin 92 D
Baldongan 98 L
Baldoyle 98 L
Baldwinstown 98 G
Balla 101 L
Ballaba 95 L
Balladrihid 102 D
Ballafa 95 J
Ballagh 86 J
Ballagh 89 M
Ballagh 91 G
Ballagh 95 C
Ballagh 96 B
Ballagh 96 E
Ballaghaderreen 102 K
Ballaghbehy 89 J
Ballaghkeen 87 D
Ballaghlea 96 D
Ballaghmore 91 F
Ballaghnatrillick 102 B
Ballaghnatrillick Bridge 102 B
Ballahulk 97 F
Ballally 97 F
Ballardiggan 95 L
Balleen 91 J
Balleese 93 H
Ballesbridge 93 B
Ballickmoyler 92 H
Ballina 87 G
Ballina 90 F
Ballina 95 B
Ballina 95 E
Ballina 97 G
Ballina/Béal an Átha 101 E
Ballinaboy 94 A
Ballinabrackey 97 L
Ballinabranagh 92 H
Ballinaclash 93 G
Ballinacor 93 H
Ballinacostello 101 M
Ballinadee 84 K
Ballinadrum 86 C
Ballinafad 94 B
Ballinafad 102 H
Ballinagar 97 K
Ballinagleragh 102 J
Ballinakill 92 D
Ballinalack 97 D
Ballinalee 96 C
Ballinamara Cross Roads 86 A
Ballinameen 102 K
Ballinamona 87 D
Ballinamore 102 M
Ballinamore Bridge 96 D
Ballinamuck 96 C
Ballinanima 90 L
Ballinapark 101 A
Ballinard Cross 90 M
Ballinascarty 83 M
Ballinasloe/Béal Átha na Sluaighe 96 G
Ballinaspig 84 H
Ballinattin 86 K
Ballinclashet 84 L
Ballinclay 86 J
Ballinclea 92 F
Ballincloher 89 H
Ballincollig 84 G
Ballincor 96 K
Ballincrea 86 H
Ballincrick 106 J
Ballincurra 90 G
Ballincurrig 84 F
Ballincurry 91 M
Ballindaggan 86 F
Ballindangan 84 C
Ballinderreen 95 H
Ballinderry 91 A
Ballinderry 93 G
Ballindine 95 B
Ballindoney 86 F
Ballindooly 95 G
Ballindrait 107 H
Ballindrehid 101 M
Ballineen 83 J
Ballingarrane 90 G
Ballingarry 90 G
Ballingarry 90 M
Ballingarry 91 B
Ballingarry 91 M
Ballingeary 83 E
Ballinglanna 83 M
Ballinglin 87 B
Ballingurteen 83 J
Ballinhassig 84 H
Ballinira 106 E
Balliniska 90 K
Ballinkilin 86 B
Ballinla 90 K
Ballinleeny 90 L
Ballinloghig 88 L
Ballin Lough 85 F
Ballinlough 91 E
Ballinlough 95 C
Ballinlough 97 E
Ballinluggaun 94 J
Ballinluska 84 H
Ballinphonta 89 C
Ballinrea Cross 84 H
Ballinrobe 95 A
Ballinrooaun 95 F
Ballinrostig 84 J
Ballinruan 90 B
Ballinruan Cross Roads 86 L
Ballinskelligs 82 E
Ballinspittle 84 K
Ballintaggart 86 A
Ballintantassig 84 C
Ballintaw 90 H
Ballinteer 93 B
Ballintemple 84 H
Ballinter Bridge 97 J
Ballintlea 85 E
Ballintober 96 A
Ballintober 101 K
Ballintogher 102 E
Ballintombay 87 B
Ballintra 106 M
Ballintroohan 108 D
Ballintubbert 92 E
Ballinunty 91 L
Ballinure 91 L
Ballinurra 85 C
Ballinvarry 86 E
Ballinveny 91 E
Ballinvoher 83 J
Ballinwillin 85 D
Ballitore 92 F
Ballivor 97 H
Ballon 86 C
Balloo 107 C
Balloor 102 B
Ballure 102 C
Ballvengland 90 G
Ballyagran 90 K
Ballyargadaun 95 A
Ballybanoge 87 D
Ballybaun 96 G
Ballybay 103 M
Ballybay 104 K
Ballybeg 85 B
Ballybeg 86 F
Ballyboe 107 A
Ballybofey 107 G
Ballyboggan 97 L
Ballyboghil 98 L
Ballyboodin 91 F
Ballybornia 96 H
Ballyboro 86 F
Ballyboy 91 G
Ballyboy 96 L
Ballyboyle 106 M
Ballybrack 82 E
Ballybrack 82 M
Ballybrack 83 A
Ballybrack 97 M
Ballybricken 90 J
Ballybritt 91 C
Ballybrittan 97 L
Ballybrittas 92 B
Ballybrommell 86 C
Ballybrood 90 J
Ballybrophy 91 F
Ballybunnion 89 E
Ballybyran 97 K
Ballycahane 90 F
Ballycahill 91 E
Ballycahill 91 H
Ballycallan 86 A
Ballycally 90 D
Ballycanew 87 D
Ballycarney 87 D
Ballycarney 92 H
Ballycarra 101 K
Ballycashin 86 F
Ballycastle 101 B
Ballyclare 96 B
Ballyclogh 84 A
Ballycolgan 95 E
Ballycolla 91 F
Ballycollin 97 K
Ballycomclone 87 B
Ballycommon 91 D
Ballycomoyle 97 D
Ballycomy 92 G
Ballyconlought 95 D
Ballyconneely 94 A
Ballyconnell 92 J
Ballyconnell 102 A
Ballyconnell 103 G
Ballyconway 89 J
Ballycorick 90 D
Ballycorney 90 F
Ballycotton 84 J
Ballycraddock 85 F
Ballycrossaun 96 K
Ballycroy 100 F
Ballyculhane 90 E
Ballycullane 85 E
Ballycullane 86 H
Ballycullane 92 E
Ballycullen 93 E
Ballycumber 96 M
Ballycurrane 85 G
Ballycurrin 86 E
Ballydangan 96 G
Ballydavid 88 H
Ballydavid 95 M
Ballydavis 92 A
Ballydehob 83 K
Ballydeloughy 84 C
Ballydesmond 83 C
Ballydine Cross Roads 85 C
Ballydonegan 82 H
Ballydoogan 96 J
Ballydooley 96 A
Ballydotia 95 E
Ballydowane 85 F
Ballydowling 93 H
Ballyduff 85 D
Ballyduff 85 F
Ballyduff 87 D
Ballyduff 88 M
Ballyduff 89 H
Ballyduff 89 L
Ballyduff 92 J
Ballydurn Cross Roads 85 F
Ballyduvane 83 M
Ballyeafy 85 A
Ballyederlan 106 L
Ballyedmond 87 D
Ballyeighan 91 B
Ballyeighter 95 M
Ballyerony 86 E
Ballyfad 87 B
Ballyfair 92 C
Ballyfarnagh 101 L
Ballyfarnan 102 H
Ballyfasy 86 H
Ballyfeard 84 L
Ballyferriter 88 L
Ballyfin 92 A
Ballyfolan 93 A
Ballyforan 96 D
Ballyfore 97 K
Ballyfore 97 L
Ballyfoyle 84 L
Ballyfoyle 92 G
Ballygaddy Cross Roads 91 C
Ballygalvert 86 F
Ballygamboon Upper 89 K
Ballygar 96 D
Ballygarden 96 B
Ballygarrett 87 A
Ballygarrett 87 E
Ballygarries 101 K
Ballygarry 101 K
Ballygarvan 84 H
Ballygawley 102 D
Ballyglass 95 A
Ballyglass 95 J
Ballyglass 95 L
Ballyglass 101 L
Ballyglass 101 M
Ballyglass West 101 M
Ballygorey 85 F
Ballygorman 107 C
Ballygrady 84 A
Ballygriffin 91 K
Ballyguin 101 H
Ballygup 86 E
Ballyhack 86 H
Ballyhade 92 H
Ballyhagan 97 L
Ballyhahill 89 J
Ballyhaise 103 L
Ballyhale 86 D
Ballyhale 95 D
Ballyhall 86 D
Ballyhander 84 K
Ballyhar 83 B
Ballyhaunis 101 M
Ballyheadon 85 F
Ballyhean 101 K
Ballyhear 95 B
Ballyheashill 97 L
Ballyheelan 97 A
Ballyheen 84 A
Ballyheerin 107 B
Ballyheige 89 G
Ballyhenry 91 E
Ballyhenry 95 A
Ballyhillin 107 C
Ballyhilloe 83 L
Ballyhisky 91 D
Ballyhooly 84 B
Ballyhorgan East 89 H
Ballyhoura 84 B
Ballyhuppahane 92 A
Ballyillaun 90 A
Ballyjamesduff 97 B
Ballykeating 84 C
Ballykeefe Cross Roads 86 A
Ballykeeran 96 H
Ballykeroge 85 E
Ballykett 89 F
Ballykett Fair Green 89 F
Ballykillageer 87 B
Ballykilleen 97 L
Ballykilty 85 G
Ballykinsella 86 F
Ballyknockan 93 D
Ballylacy 87 B
Ballylaghnan 90 C
Ballylanders 90 M
Ballylaneen 85 F
Ballylawn 107 H
Ballyleaan 90 D
Ballyleague 96 B
Ballylegan 85 B
Ballyleigh 84 G
Ballylennan 107 H
Ballylevin 97 K
Ballylickey 83 G
Ballyliffin 107 C
Ballyline 86 A
Ballylongane 84 J
Ballylongford 89 E
Ballylooby 85 A
Ballylucas 87 G
Ballyluoge 96 G
Ballylusk 87 A
Ballylusk 93 E
Ballylusky Cross Roads 91 L
Ballylynan 92 E
Ballymacadam 85 A
Ballymacallen 96 J
Ballymacar 86 H
Ballymacarbry 85 B
Ballymacaw 86 K
Ballymachugh 97 B
Ballymackey 91 D
Ballymackney 98 A
Ballymacoda 85 G
Ballymacoolaghan 96 K
Ballymacormick Cross Roads 96 C
Ballymacquin 89 G
Ballymacurly 96 A
Ballymacward 95 J
Ballymadog 85 G
Ballymagan 107 F
Ballymagaraghy 108 A
Ballymahon 96 F
Ballymakeery 83 F
Ballymakenny 98 E
Ballymaquiff 95 L
Ballymartle 84 H
Ballymeeny 101 F
Ballymoe 96 A
Ballymoney 107 E
Ballymoon 86 C
Ballymore 84 J
Ballymore 88 L
Ballymore 92 C
Ballymore 96 J
Ballymore 107 A
Ballymorris 85 F
Ballymorris 92 E
Ballymote 102 G
Ballymount 92 F
Ballymoylin 96 B
Ballymullavill 96 H
Ballymun 98 K
Ballymurn 87 G
Ballymurphy 86 F
Ballymurphy 95 B
Ballymurray 96 E
Ballymurry 95 J
Ballynabarna 96 J
Ballynabola 86 H
Ballynacallagh 82 H
Ballynacally 90 D
Ballynacarrick 106 J
Ballynacarriga 83 J
Ballynacarrigy 97 D
Ballynacarrow 102 D
Ballynaclogh 85 F
Ballynaclogh 91 D
Ballynacole 84 J
Ballynacorra 84 J
Ballynacorra 96 D
Ballynacorra 96 J
Ballynacourty 85 E
Ballynacree 97 E
Ballynadrideen 90 J
Ballynadrumny 97 L
Ballynafid 97 D
Ballynagall 88 H
Ballynagaragh 84 K
Ballynagarde 90 H
Ballynagaul 85 H
Ballynagoraher 101 G
Ballynagore 97 G
Ballynagreanagh 90 M
Ballynagree 83 F
Ballynaguilkee 85 E
Ballynaguilla 90 K
Ballynahaia 103 M
Ballynahallia 89 L
Ballynahattina 95 F
Ballynahinch 90 F
Ballynahinch 91 K
Ballynahow 82 A
Ballynahown 94 J
Ballynahown 96 H
Ballynakill 85 E
Ballynakill 86 C
Ballynakill 95 M
Ballynakill 96 H
Ballynakill 96 K
Ballynakill 97 K
Ballynakilla 82 J
Ballynakilla 84 F
Ballynakilla 95 E
Ballynakilly Upper 82 C
Ballynalty 95 A
Ballynamona 84 C
Ballynamona 84 H
Ballynamona 85 H
Ballynamona 86 J
Ballynamrossagh 90 M
Ballynamult 85 E
Ballynare Cross Roads 97 M
Ballynarry 97 A
Ballynasaggart 96 E
Ballynasare 89 G
Ballynaskreena 89 G
Ballynastangford 101 L
Ballynastuckaun 95 E
Ballynavar Bridge 83 M
Ballyneety 85 E
Ballyneety 90 J
Ballyneill 85 C
Ballynellard 87 G
Ballyness 107 A
Ballynew 100 K
Ballynoe 83 M
Ballynoe 84 F
Ballynoe Bridge 90 G
Ballynora 84 G
Ballynultagh 87 A
Ballyorril 87 D
Ballyoskill 92 D
Ballyoughter 87 D
Ballyoughtera 83 L
Ballypatrick 85 C
Ballyphilip 85 D
Ballyphilip 86 C
Ballyphilip 91 F
Ballypickas 92 D
Ballyporeen 85 A
Ballyquin 85 G
Ballyquin 88 J
Ballyquirk 86 B
Ballyragget 92 G
Ballyre 84 J
Ballyregan 84 G
Ballyregan 90 H
Ballyriggin 90 M
Ballyroan 92 D
Ballyroddy 102 L
Ballyroe 91 J
Ballyroe 92 E
Ballyroe Cross Roads 92 E
Ballyroebuck 87 A
Ballyroon 82 J
Ballyrub 84 K
Ballysadare 102 D
Ballyshakikin 90 L
Ballyshannon 92 F
Ballyshannon 102 C
Ballysloe 91 J
Ballysmuttan 93 A
Ballysteen 90 D
Ballytarsna 86 D
Ballythomas 92 E
Ballytoole 92 F
Ballyvaghan 95 K
Ballyvaldon 87 G
Ballyvalloo 87 G
Ballyvalode 90 J
Ballyvaloon 84 E
Ballyvaltron 93 H
Ballyvergin 86 J
Ballyvirane 91 K
Ballyvirrane 89 K
Ballyvoge 82 M
Ballyvoige 83 J
Ballyvoneen 96 D
Ballyvonnavaun 90 B
Ballyvourney 83 F
Ballyvoyle Cross Roads 85 E
Ballywalter 91 M
Ballywalter 95 A
Ballywilliam 86 E
Balrath 97 F
Balrath 98 G
Balrothery 98 H
Balscaddan 98 H
Balteen 82 M
Baltimore 83 K
Baltinglass 92 F
Baltray 98 E
Balynana 88 L
Banada 101 J
Banagher 96 L
Bandon 84 G
Bangor 100 F
Banna 89 G
Bannow 86 L
Bansha 91 K
Banteer 84 A
Bantry 83 G
Bard Inch 83 E
Barefield 90 B
Barleymount 83 A
Barna 90 J
Barna 91 E
Barna 95 G
Barnacawley 102 K
Barnacohoge 101 J
Barnaderg 95 F
Barnagowlane 83 H
Barnalisheen 91 H
Barnalyra 101 J
Barnawheel 87 K
Barnesmore 106 M
Barnhill Cross 98 E
Barnycarroll 101 L
Barrack 84 E
Barracuragh 91 H
Barraderry 91 G
Barraduff 83 B
Barraduff 89 E
Barrahaurin 84 D
Barranny 95 D
Barrigone 90 D
Barrbosky 101 A
Barringtonsbridge 90 J
Barroughter 95 M
Barry 96 F
Barry Beg 96 H
Barryroe 84 K

Batterstown 98 K
Baughna 97 G
Baunogemeely 92 D
Baunogephlure 92 J
Baunreagh 83 F
Baunreagh 86 B
Baunskeha 86 E
Baunta Commons 86 A
Bauntlieve 90 A
Bauragoogeen 89 J
Bauraneag 89 J
Bauravilla 83 L
Bauteogue 92 D
Bauvin 95 J
Bawn 91 D
Bawnboy 103 G
Bawnbrack 91 K
Bawndunhill 85 C
Bay Bridge 92 A
Beagh 95 B
Beagh 102 E
Beal 89 E
Bealaclugga 95 K
Bealadangan 94 F
Bealad Cross Roads 83 M
Bealaha 89 B
Bealin 96 H
Bealnablath 83 J
Bealnablath 84 G
Bealnamorive 84 D
Beaufort 83 A
Bective 97 J
Beenalaght 84 D
Beenbane 88 L
Beennamweel 84 D
Beennaskehy 84 B
Bekan 101 M
Belalt 103 A
Belan Cottage 92 F
Belclare 95 E
Beldaragh 98 H
Belderg 101 A
Belfarsad 100 H
Belgooly 84 L
Bellacorrick 101 D
Bellagarvaun 100 F
Bellahillan Bridge 103 K
Bellahy 101 J
Bellanaboy Bridge 100 C
Bellanacargy 103 L
Bellanagare 102 K
Bellanaman 104 G
Bellanamore 107 G
Bellanamullia 96 H
Bellananagh 97 A
Bellaneeny 96 G
Bellanode 103 J
Bellavary 101 H
Bellaveeny Lower 100 F
Belleville 95 H
Bellewstown 98 G
Bellia 89 E
Bellinvreena 90 M
Bellmount 96 L
Belmullet 100 C
Belrea 96 H
Beltra 101 G
Beltra 102 D
Belturbet 103 K
Belvelly 84 H
Belville 101 E
Bennettsbridge 86 B
Berrillstown 98 G
Berrings 84 D
Bettystown/Baile an
Bhiataigh 98 H
Bilboa 92 H
Binalt 107 E
Binvoran 89 F
Birdhill 90 F
Birr 91 B
Bishop's Quarter 95 G
Black Bull 98 K
Black Lion 96 M
Blackburn Bridge 107 G
Blacklion 86 C
Blacklion 102 F
Blackpool 90 L
Blackrath Gate 92 F
Blackrock 84 H
Blackrock 93 B
Blackrock 98 B
Blackwater 87 G
Blackwater Bridge 83 D
Blackwater Bridge 97 L
Blackwood 97 L
Blanchardstown/Baile
Bhalainséir 98 K
Blane Bridge 89 J
Blarney 84 E
Blennerville 89 K
Blessington 93 A
Blind Key 97 D
Blue Ball 96 M
Bluebell 84 F
Blueford 83 C
Bodenstown 92 C
Bodyke 90 C
Bofiekil 82 J
Bofin 100 K
Bogay 107 J
Boggan 86 A
Boggan 97 C
Bogganstown 97 M
Boggaun 91 E
Boggaun 102 J
Bogtown 101 B
Bohagh 96 A
Boharboy 98 C
Bohateh 90 C
Bohaun 101 K
Boheeshil 82 C
Boher 90 J
Boher 96 J
Boheraphuca 91 C
Boheratreem Cross Roads
91 K
Boherboy 83 C
Boherlahan 91 L
Bohermeen 97 F
Bohernamona 91 H
Boherquill 97 D
Bohola 101 H
Bohoona 94 J
Bohullion 107 E
Boladurragh 86 F
Boley 92 E
Boley 92 E
Boleyard 101 L
Boleybeg 95 M
Boley Cross Roads 87 A
Boleythomas 96 D
Bolinarra 96 H
Bolinglanna 100 H
Bolinrush 87 A
Boola 85 G
Boolacullane 89 L
Boolakennedy 85 A
Boolanlisheen 90 M
Boolard 90 K
Booleenshare 89 G
Boolteens 89 K
Boolyduff 90 A
Borna 90 M
Borris 86 B
Borris in Ossory 91 F
Borrisokane 91 A
Borrisoleigh 91 H
Boston 95 K
Bottomstown 90 L
Bouladuff 91 H
Boyerstown 97 J
Boyle 102 L
Bracket Gate 98 K
Bracklin 97 H
Brackloney 97 B
Brackloon 101 M
Brackloon Cross Roads
102 K
Bracknagh 92 B
Bracknagh 96 E
Brackwanshag 101 H
Braddocks 103 J
Brahalish 83 G
Bramblestown 86 B
Brandon 88 J
Brannockstown 92 C
Bray/Bré 93 B
Breaghna 83 J
Breaghva 89 E
Breaghwy 101 E
Breaghwy 101 K
Breaghwy 102 A
Breanloughaun 95 H
Bredagh 96 D
Bree 86 J
Breeda 85 D
Breedoge 102 K
Breenagh 107 G
Brideswell 87 A
Brideswell 96 H
Bridge 89 H
Bridge 95 J
Bridge 101 G
Bridge 107 E
Bridgeacrin 98 B
Bridge End 107 E
Bridge End 107 F
Bridgefoot 97 D
Bridgeland 92 J
Bridgetown 86 M
Bridgetown 90 F
Bridgetown 106 M
Brierfield 96 A
Brinlack 106 C
Brinny 84 G
Briska 85 E
Brittas 90 J
Brittas 93 A
Britway 84 F
Broadford 90 F
Broadford 90 K
Broadway 87 K
Brockeragh 101 G
Brocklagh 96 C
Broken Bridge 90 K
Brookfield 84 G
Brookloage 84 H
Brook's Cross Roads 91 B
Broomfield 104 K
Brosna 89 M
Brosna 91 B
Brosna 101 M
Brough Cross Roads 84 B
Broughal 96 L
Broughane Cross Roads
89 L
Browne's Cross Roads 97 A
Brownstown 86 B
Brownstown 86 K
Brownstown Cross Roads
92 C
Bruff 90 L
Bruree 90 L
Bryanlitter 104 G
Buckode 102 B
Buffer's Alley Cross Roads
87 D
Buggaeen Cross Roads
84 A
Bulgaden 90 L
Bullaun 95 J
Bulldun 95 E
Bullyhandy 97 G
Bunacurry 100 E
Bunaw 82 F
Bunbeg 106 F
Bunbrosna 97 D
Bunclody 86 C
Buncrana 107 F
Bundoran 102 B
Bundorragha 100 M
Bunduff Bridge 102 B
Bunglass 97 L
Bungosteen Bridge 106 L
Bunlahy 97 A
Bunlin Bridge 107 E
Bunmahon 85 F
Bunnaglass 95 L
Bunnahowen 100 C
Bunnahowen 94 B
Bunnanaddan 102 G
Bunnyconnellan 101 E
Bunowen Beg 94 A
Bunratty 90 E
Bunree 101 E
Burnchurch 86 A
Burncourt 85 A
Burnfoot 107 F
Burnfort 84 E
Burren 95 G
Burren 101 G
Burrenfadda 90 D
Burt 107 F
Burtonport 106 E
Bushfield 90 F
Butlers Bridge 103 L
Butlerstown 84 K
Buttevant 84 B

C

Cabra 98 K
Cabragh 101 C
Cackanode 83 F
Cadamstown 91 C
Cadamstown 97 L
Cagagh Lake 83 A
Caher 82 J
Caher 85 A
Caher 90 C
Caher 94 J
Caher 95 A
Caheradrine 95 H
Caherakillen 95 J
Caherbarnagh 82 E
Caherbarnagh 83 C
Caherconlish 90 J
Caherconnell 95 K
Caherdaniel 82 E
Caherdowney 83 F
Caherea 90 A
Caherlea 95 H
Caherlistrane 95 E
Caherlough 90 B
Cahermore 82 H
Cahermore 95 L
Cahermuckee 83 H
Cahermurphy 89 C
Cahernarry 90 H
Caherogan 89 C
Cahersherkin 94 M
Cahersiveen 82 B
Caldragh 96 B
Caldragh Cross Roads
102 L
Calhame 106 L
Caliernacaha 83 E
Callaghansmills 90 B
Callan 86 A
Callanafersy 89 K
Callow 94 A
Callow 101 H
Callow 102 K
Calry 102 E
Caltra 95 F
Caltragh 96 E
Caltraghlea 96 G
Calverstown 92 F
Camira 91 D
Camolin 87 D
Camp 89 K
Campile 86 H
Camross 91 C
Cangullia 89 L
Canningstown 97 C
Canonstown 98 E
Capira 96 K
Cappa Old 91 K
Cappagh 84 F
Cappagh 85 E
Cappagh 90 G
Cappagh 93 G
Cappagh White 91 G
Cappaghmore 95 K
Cappagowlan 96 M
Cappalinnan 91 F
Cappamore 90 J
Cappanacreha 94 C
Cappanaloha 83 G
Cappanargid 92 C
Cappanrush 97 K
Cappataggle 95 J
Cappeen 83 J
Cappoquin 85 D
Cappry 107 G
Carboggy 97 C
Carbury 97 L
Cargagh 97 B
Carhoomeengar 83 D
Carhoon 95 M
Carickkallen 103 L
Cark 107 G
Carker 83 B
Carlanstown 97 F
Carlingford 98 B
Carlough 102 J
Carlow/Ceatharlach 92 H
Carn 96 J
Carn 103 A
Carna 94 E
Carnagh 97 A
Carnaross 97 F
Carndonagh 107 C
Carnew 87 A
Carney 91 A
Carney 102 A
Carnley 101 M
Carnoneen 95 E
Carnowen 107 H
Carntullagh 106 L
Carownisky 100 L
Carracastle 101 J
Carradownan 103 K
Carraduffy 106 M
Carragh 92 C
Carraghs 95 C
Carraholly 100 J
Carran 86 B
Carran 95 K
Carrane Cross Roads 90 L
Carraroe 94 E
Carras 95 B
Carraun 101 E
Carrick 86 M
Carrick 94 C
Carrick 106 C
Carrick 106 K
Carrickabaoy 97 B
Carrickart 107 B
Carrickashedoge 98 A
Carrickboy 96 F
Carrickinare 103 M
Carrickmacross 98 A
Carrickmaguirk 97 A
Carrickmore 107 H
Carricknamaddoo 97 B
Carrick-on-Shannon 102 L
Carrick-on-Suir/Carraig na
Siúire 85 C
Carrickroe 103 F
Carrig 84 B
Carrig 91 B
Carrig 93 A
Carrig Beg 86 C
Carrigadrohid 84 D
Carrigagowen 91 A
Carrigagulla 84 D
Carrigaholt 89 E
Carrigahorig 91 A
Carrigaline/Carraig Uí
Leighin 84 H
Carrigallen 103 K
Carrigan 97 A
Carriganimmy 83 F
Carrigans 107 J
Carrigatogher 91 D
Carrigeen 84 G
Carrigeen 84 K
Carrigeen Cross Roads 92 J
Carriggower 93 E
Carrigkerry 89 J
Carrigmore 93 H
Carrignavar 84 E
Carrigrohane 84 H
Carrigtohill 84 J
Carrow 84 C
Carrowbaun 101 M
Carrowbehy 101 M
Carrowcrory 102 G
Carrowduff 96 A
Carrowkeel 95 C
Carrowkeel 95 M
Carrowkeel 107 E
Carrowkeel 108 D
Carrowkeelanahglass 95 C
Carrowkennedy 100 M
Carrowleagh 101 F
Carrowmenagh 108 A
Carrowmore 95 A
Carrowmore 101 B
Carrowmore 101 H
Carrowmore 101 L
Carrowmore 102 D
Carrowmoreknock 95 D
Carrownacon 101 K
Carrownaglogh 101 F
Carrowncully 102 L
Carrowneden 102 D
Carrowntawy 102 D
Carrowntober 95 F
Carrowntreila 101 E
Carrowphadeen Cross
Roads 96 E
Carrowreagh 96 G
Carrowreagh 97 C
Carrowreagh 102 D
Carrowreagh 107 E
Carrowroe 95 D
Carrowroe 95 C
Carrowrory 96 E
Carrowteige
Carrowteige 100 C
Carstown Cross Roads 86 A
Carton 97 M
Cartron 95 F
Cartron 95 L
Cartron 96 A
Cartronnagilta 102 J
Casagh 86 H
Cashel 91 L
Cashel 92 D
Cashel 94 B
Cashel 95 C
Cashel 100 E
Cashel 102 C
Cashel 106 K
Cashelgarran 102 A
Cashelmore 107 A
Cashelshanaghan 107 E
Cashla 95 H
Castelcooly 107 F
Castlebaldwin 102 G
Castlebar/Caisleán an
Bharraigh 101 G
Castlebellingham 98 B
Castleblakeney 95 F
Castleblayney 104 K
Castlebridge 87 G
Castlecary 108 D
Castlecomer 92 G
Castleconnell 90 F
Castleconor 101 E
Castlecoote 96 D
Castlecor 84 A
Castlecor 97 E
Castle Cove 82 E
Castlecuffe 91 C
Castledermot 92 E
Castledockrell 86 F
Castleellis 87 D
Castlefinn 107 L
Castlefore 102 M
Castlefreke 83 M
Castlegal 102 B
Castlegar 95 G
Castlegregory 88 J
Castlehill 100 F
Castlehill 101 D
Castleisland 89 L
Castlejordan 97 L
Castleleiny 91 E
Castlelyons 84 F
Castlemaine 89 K
Castlemartyr 84 J
Castlemoyle 95 F
Castleplunket 96 A
Castlepollard 97 D
Castlequarter 107 F
Castlequater 95 E
Castlerahan 97 B
Castlerea 96 A
Castleshane 103 J
Castletown 83 J
Castletown 87 B
Castletown 90 K
Castletown 91 F
Castletown 95 K
Castletown 97 D
Castletown 97 F
Castletown 97 G
Castletown Bearhaven 82 J
Castletown Manor 101 E
Castletownroche 84 B
Castletownshend 83 L
Castlewarren 86 B
Castlewhite 87 A
Castlewray 107 H
Cathaganstown 91 L
Causeway 89 G
Cavan 103 L
Cavanagarvan 103 J
Cavangarden 102 C
Cavetown 102 L
Cecilstown 84 A
Celbridge/Cill Droichid 97 M
Chanonrock 98 A
Chapel 86 F
Chapelmidway 98 K
Chapeltown 82 B
Chapeltown 89 G
Charlestown 96 M
Charlestown 98 A
Charlestown 101 J
Cheekpoint 86 H
Cherry Grove 90 H
Cherryville 92 B
Chimneyfield 84 E
Church Cross 83 K
Church Hill 89 G
Church Hill 107 D
Church Town 107 F
Church Town 107 H
Church Village 101 H
Churchfield 90 E
Churchfield 95 A
Churchstreet 102 K
Churchtown 83 A
Churchtown 84 J
Churchtown 86 L
Churchtown 87 K
Churchtown 89 F
Churchtown 92 E
Claddagh 95 F
Claddagh 101 J
Claddaghduff 100 K
Claggan 94 C
Claggan 100 F
Claggan 107 A
Claggan South 107 D
Clamper Cross 89 M
Clanco Bridge 91 A
Clane 92 C
Clara 93 G
Clara 96 M
Clarahill 92 A
Clare 96 J
Clare 97 B
Clarecastle 90 A
Clareen 91 C
Clareen 95 B
Claregalway 95 E
Claremorris 101 L
Clarina 90 H
Clarinbridge 95 H
Clash 91 E
Clashanahy 85 G
Clashbeg 86 A
Clashmore 85 G
Clash North 89 J
Clashwilliam 86 B
Cleady 83 D
Cleanderry 82 F
Cleary's Cross Roads 85 G
Cleggan 100 K
Clenagh 90 D
Cleraun 96 E
Cleristown 86 J
Clerragh 102 K
Clifden 94 A
Cliff 102 C
Clifferna 97 B
Cliffony 102 B
Clogagh 83 M
Clogga 87 B
Clogh 87 D
Clogh 91 F
Clogh 92 G
Cloghan 95 E
Cloghan 96 F
Cloghan 96 L
Cloghan 97 G
Cloghan 107 G
Cloghane 82 M
Cloghane 88 J
Cloghans Hill 95 B
Cloghatanny 96 M
Cloghaun Cross Roads
102 K
Cloghboley 102 A
Cloghboola 83 F
Cloghboy 106 H
Cloghbrack 94 C
Cloghbrack 97 H
Cloghchurnel 97 A
Cloghdonnell 83 K
Clogheen 85 A
Clogheen 85 B
Clogher 88 L
Clogher 89 L
Clogher 101 G
Clogher 101 K
Clogher 102 K
Clogher 102 L
Cloghera 90 F
Clogherеen 83 B
Clohergoole 97 B
Clogherhead 98 E
Cloghfin 107 H
Cloghjordan 91 B
Cloghmacoo 97 C
Cloghmore 100 H
Cloghmore 103 J
Cloghna 92 H
Cloghpook 92 G
Cloghran 98 L
Cloghroe 84 D
Cloghroe 107 G
Clohamon 87 A
Cloheden 86 F
Clohernagh 86 K
Clologe 87 D
Clomantagh 91 J
Clonadacasey 92 D
Clonaddadoran 92 D
Clonaghadoo 92 A
Clonakenny 91 E
Clonakilty 83 M
Clonalea 91 D
Clonard 97 H
Clonard Little 87 G
Clonaslee 92 A
Clonavoe 97 K
Clonbane 92 D
Clonbern 95 F
Clonbrick 90 E
Clonbroney Cross Roads
96 C
Clonbulloge 97 L
Clonbur 95 A
Cloncrave 97 H
Cloncullen 96 F
Cloncurry 97 M
Clondalever 97 E
Clondalkin/Cluain Dolcain
93 A
Clondaw 87 D
Clondelara 96 L
Clondouglas 89 H
Clondulane 84 F
Clone West 87 D
Clonea 85 C
Clonee 98 K
Cloneen 91 L
Clonegall 86 C
Cloneraff or Bloomhill 96 H
Clones 103 H
Cloney 92 B
Clonfert 96 K
Clonfert Cross Roads 96 K
Clongarran 86 C
Clongeen 86 J
Clonglll 97 F
Clonincurragh 91 F
Clonjordan 86 F
Clonlearne Cross Roads
97 H
Clonlost 97 H
Clonmany 107 C
Clonmeen 91 F
Clonmel/Cluain Meala 85 B
Clonmellon 97 E
Clonmore 91 E
Clonmore 92 J
Clonmore 97 K
Clonmore 98 E
Clonmult 84 F
Clonony 96 L
Clonoulty 91 G
Clonroche 86 F
Clontibret 104 G
Clontrain 97 C
Clontumpher 96 C
Clonwhelan 97 D
Clonycavan 97 H
Clonygowan 92 A
Clonyhague 97 G
Cloolough 102 K
Cloonacool 101 J
Cloonaddra 96 B
Cloonageeher 96 C
Cloonagh 97 A
Cloonagh 102 A
Cloonaghgarve 95 B
Cloonaquin 102 E
Cloonart 96 C
Cloonascragh 95 F
Cloonatleva 95 J
Cloonback 97 A
Cloonbannin 83 C
Cloonbard 102 K
Cloonbrone 94 C
Clooncallaga 95 F
Coonconeen 89 E
Clooncoose 95 K
Clooncrim 101 M
Cloondacarra 96 A
Cloondaff 101 G
Cloondara 96 C
Cloonderreen 84 K
Cloondrinagh 89 F
Cloone 102 M
Clooneagh 96 C
Clooneagh 102 G
Clooneen 97 A
Cloone Grange 102 M
Clooney 106 H
Cloonfad 95 C
Cloonfad 102 K
Cloonfallagh 101 L
Cloonfinish 101 J
Cloonfower 101 M
Cloonkeen 96 A
Cloonkeen 101 K
Cloonkeevy 102 G
Cloonken 83 E
Cloonkirgeen 83 J
Cloonlara 90 F
Cloonliffen 95 A
Cloonmackon 89 H
Cloonmagunnaun 102 K
Cloonminda 95 C
Cloonmore 96 E
Cloonmore 101 L
Cloonmore Cross Roads
101 J
Cloonmoylan 91 A
Cloonnaglasha 95 B
Cloonnamaskry 96 K
Cloonoon 91 A
Cloonprohus 89 J
Cloonsellan 96 E
Cloonsreane 96 B
Cloonteen 90 J
Cloontia 102 G
Cloontooa 95 E
Cloontowart 101 M
Cloonusker 90 C
Cloonygorman 83 H
Cloonymorris 95 J
Cloonyquin 96 B
Cloran 97 E
Closh 91 C
Clountane 89 L
Cloverhill 103 L
Cloyne 84 J
Cluddaun 101 A
Cluidrevagh 95 E
Clurreeny 91 D
Clyard 95 A
Clydagh Bridge 89 M
Clynacantan 82 A
Clynch 97 F
Cnocnagur 95 B
Coachford 84 D
Coalbrook 91 M
Coan 92 G
Cobh/An Cóbh 84 H
Coggalkeenagh 96 B
Colbinstown 92 F
Colciste 87 B
Coldwells 92 F
Coldwood 95 H
Colehill 96 F
Collegeland 97 J
Collin 107 C
Collinstown 97 E
Collon 98 D
Collooney 102 D
Collops 97 C
Collorus 82 F
Colmanstown 95 F
Colp 98 H
Commeen 106 F
Commeen 107 G
Common 86 M
Common Bridge 106 H
Commons 91 L
Commons 91 M
Cong 95 A
Conna 84 F
Connagh 91 A
Connahill 87 A
Connolly 90 A
Convamore 84 B
Convent 85 F
Convoy 107 H
Cooga 90 J
Coogue 101 M

A B C D E F G H I J K L M N O P Q R S T U V W X Y Z

Ireland 1:301,000 181

Kirwans Cross 98 D
Kishkeam 83 C
Kishyquirk 90 J
Knappagh 100 M
Knight's Town 82 B
Knock 89 F
Knock 91 F
Knock 94 E
Knock 101 L
Knockacappul 83 B
Knockacarhanduff Commons 91 G
Knockadalteen 102 G
Knockaderry 90 G
Knockagraffy 101 L
Knockainy 90 M
Knockaiooan 89 M
Knockalafalla 85 C
Knockalough 89 F
Knockalougha 89 H
Knockanacullin 85 E
Knockanaddoge 92 G
Knockanaffrin 85 B
Knockananna 93 G
Knockaneden Cross 82 C
Knockanevin 84 C
Knockanillaun 101 E
Knockanure 89 J
Knockarasser 95 G
Knockaroe 91 F
Knockatober 101 L
Knockaunagloon 85 E
Knockaunalour 84 E
Knockaunaneagh 90 C
Knockaunavoher 90 M
Knockaunbrack 89 H
Knockaunglass 82 C
Knockavannia 85 B
Knockavaud 82 J
Knockavoher 83 L
Knockawaddra 89 K
Knockboy 85 E
Knockbrack 107 H
Knockbride 97 C
Knockbridge 98 A
Knockbrit 91 L
Knockburden 84 G
Knockcroghery 96 E
Knockdrin 97 G
Knockeenadallane 83 C
Knockeencreen 89 L
Knockeens 83 E
Knockeor 103 J
Knockferry 95 D
Knockglass 95 A
Knockgraffon 91 K
Knockhall 96 B
Knockletteragh 106 J
Knocklofty 85 B
Knocklong 90 M
Knocklough Cross Roads 97 E
Knockmanagh 83 B
Knockmannon Cross Roads 91 J
Knockmeal 85 E
Knockmonalea 85 G
Knockmore 91 D
Knockmore 101 H
Knockmourne 84 F
Knockmoyle 95 M
Knockmoyle 101 G
Knocknaboley 93 G
Knocknabooly 89 F
Knocknabool Cross 83 C
Knocknacree 92 J
Knocknagashel 89 L
Knocknagilky 93 G
Knocknagillagh 97 B
Knocknagree 83 C
Knocknahila 89 C
Knocknahilan 84 G
Knocknakillew 95 A
Knocknalina 100 C
Knocknalower 100 C
Knocknanagh 83 C
Knocknew 86 B
Knockraha 84 E
Knockroe 84 G
Knockroe 95 A
Knockrower East 83 B
Knocks 83 J
Knocks 92 A
Knockskagh 83 M
Knockstown 86 F
Knocktoosh 90 K
Knocktopher 86 D
Knockundervaul 89 H
Knockviear Bridge 102 L
Knockyhena 83 C
Knoppoge 84 B
Knoppoge 84 E
Knoppoge 89 M
Knottown 87 G
Knuttery 84 E
Krockastoller 106 F
Kylaiwreashy 85 C
Kylebrack 95 M
Kylegarrif 95 M
Kylemore Bridge 96 K
Kylesalia 94 E
Kyletalesha 92 A

L

Laban 95 L
Labasheeda 89 F
Lackabaun 83 E
Lackagh 92 B
Lackagh Bridge 107 E
Lackamore 89 G
Lackamore 90 J
Lackan 93 A
Lackan 97 D
Lackan Cross 96 D
Lackareagh 83 J
Lackaroe Cross Roads 91 C
Lacken 87 G
Lackey 91 F
Laconnell 106 H
Ladysbridge 84 J
Lag 107 C
Lagganstown 91 K
Laghtane 90 J
Laghy 106 M
Lahard 103 K
Lahardaun 101 G
Laheratanvally 83 K
Lahinch 94 M
Lake Village 91 B
Lakyle 89 F
Lamoge 85 C
Lanesborough 96 B
Lankill 100 M
Laracor 97 J
Laragh 93 D
Laragh 97 M
Laragh 104 K
Larah 103 L
Largan 96 B
Largan 101 D
Larganboy 101 M
Largy 106 L
Largydonnell 102 B
Lattacrom 103 M
Lattin 90 M
Latton 103 M
Lauragh 82 F
Laurencetown 96 K
Lavagh 102 G
Laytown/An Inse 98 H
Leabeg 96 L
Leabgarrow 106 E
Leagh 92 H
Leaha 96 D
Leamlara 84 F
Leamnaguila 83 B
Leamyglissane 83 B
Leanamore 89 F
Leap 83 L
Lecarrow 95 M
Lecarrow 96 E
Lecarrow 102 D
Lecarrow 102 H
Leckanarainey 102 E
Leckanvy 100 M
Leckaun 102 E
Leckemy 108 D
Legan or Lenamore 96 F
Leggah 97 A
Lehardan 107 E
Leighlinbridge 86 B
Leitrim 89 C
Leitrim 96 C
Leitrim 102 L
Leitrim Middle 89 J
Leixlip/Léim an Bhradáin 98 K
Lemanaghan 96 L
Lemybrien 85 E
Lennaght 103 J
Leperstown 86 L
Lergynasearhagh 106 H
Lerrig 89 G
Letter 83 E
Letter Beg 100 L
Lettera 95 C
Letterbarra 106 M
Lettercallow 94 E
Letterdunane 83 D
Letterfinish 82 F
Letterilly House 106 J
Letterkelly 89 C
Letterkenny/Leitir Ceanainn 107 H
Letterleague 107 G
Lettermacaward 106 J
Lettermakenny 107 G
Lettermore 94 E
Lettermore 94 F
Lettermullan 94 E
Levally 95 F
Levallyroe 95 B
Lewagh 91 H
Liberty Hall 83 D
Lifford 107 H
Limerick Junction 90 M
Limerick/Luimneach 90 E
Limestone Brook Bridge 106 M
Linsford 107 F
Lisacul 101 M
Lisbabe 83 B
Liscannor 94 M
Liscarney 100 M
Liscarrigane 83 F
Lisclogher Cross Roads 97 H
Liscooly 107 L
Lisdoonvarna 94 M
Lisdowney 92 G
Lisdrumneill Cross Roads 102 K
Lisduff 91 C
Lisduff 95 C
Lisduff 95 J
Lisduff 97 E
Lisduff 102 M
Lisduff 103 L
Lisgall 98 A
Lisgoold 84 F
Lisheen 83 K
Lisheenaclara 95 M
Lisheenaguile 96 K
Lisheencrony 89 E
Lisheennacreagh 83 K
Lisheennapingina 83 L
Lismacaffry 97 D
Lismore 85 D
Lismullane 90 J
Lisnageer 103 L
Lisnageeragh 96 A
Lisnageeragh 97 D
Lisnagry 90 F
Lisnalanniv 84 C
Lisnamuck 85 B
Lispatrick 84 K
Lispole 88 M
Lisreagh 103 L
Lisrevagh 96 E
Lisroe 90 A
Lisronagh 85 B
Lisryan 97 D
Lissaclarig 83 K
Lissacresig 83 F
Lissadorn 102 L
Lissalway 96 A
Lissamona 83 K
Lissanisky 95 A
Lissaphooca Cross Roads 84 G
Lissard 97 E
Lissatava 95 B
Lissatinning Bridge 82 C
Lissavaird 83 M
Lisselton 89 H
Lissinagroagh 102 F
Lissiniska 102 C
Lissycasey 90 D
Lissyconnor 83 C
Listellick 89 K
Listerlin 86 E
Listowel 89 H
Listry Bridge 83 A
Lisvarrinane 90 M
Littleton 91 H
Lixnaw 89 H
Lobinstown 98 D
Loch Gowna 97 A
Lodge Park 97 J
Loghill 89 F
Loher 82 E
Lomanagh 83 E
Lombardstown 84 A
Longfield 98 A
Longford 91 C
Longford 92 A
Longford/An Longfort 96 C
Longstorie 90 J
Longwood 97 H
Lorrha 91 B
Lorum 86 C
Loskeran 85 H
Losset 97 A
Loughaclerybeg 95 J
Loughan 97 F
Loughanaphuca 100 H
Loughanavally 96 J
Loughanboy 101 M
Loughane 84 J
Loughanure 106 F
Lougher 88 M
Loughglinn 102 K
Loughlass 92 E
Loughmoe 91 H
Loughmorne 103 M
Loughrea 95 M
Loughshinny 98 L
Louisburgh 100 M
Loumanagh 83 C
Louth 98 A
Lower 101 L
Lower 106 M
Lower Ballycotteen 94 M
Lowertown 83 K
Lowtown 92 F
Lucan 98 K
Luddan 107 F
Lugdoon 101 F
Luggacurren 92 E
Lugganammer 102 M
Lukeswell 86 D
Lullymore 97 L
Lumclean Cross Roads 96 L
Lung Cut 102 K
Lurga Bridge 102 M
Lurgan 102 K
Lurganboy 102 E
Lurganboy 107 E
Lurganearly 104 K
Lusk 98 L
Lyracrumpane 89 H
Lyre 84 A
Lyre 89 L
Lyredaowen 83 C
Lyrenamon 84 E

M

M'Gann's Cross 95 F
Maam Cross 94 C
Maas 106 J
Mace 101 K
Macroom 83 F
Maddockstown 86 B
Madore 83 L
Maganey 92 E
Maghera 90 A
Maghera 106 H
Magherabeg 93 H
Magheraboy 107 C
Magheraclone 97 C
Magheracloy 107 H
Magheradrumman 107 B
Magheraveen 96 E
Magherdrumman 108 D
Maghery 106 E
Mahanagh 95 F
Mahanagh 101 K
Mahoonagh 90 G
Mainham 97 M
Mainistir 102 L
Malahide/Mullach Íde 98 L
Malin 108 A
Malin Beg 106 G
Malin More 106 G
Mall 88 M
Mallow/Mala 84 B
Manger 102 C
Manning 84 C
Mannion's Cross Roads 96 H
Manorcunningham 107 H
Manorhamilton 102 E
Manselstown 91 H
Mansfieldstown 98 A
Mantlehill 90 D
Mantua 102 L
Manulla 101 L
Marble Hill 107 A
Mardyke 91 L
Marlfield 85 B
Marlfield 93 A
Marshalstown 84 C
Marshalstown 86 F
Marsh South 98 B
Martinstown 97 F
Massbrook 101 H
Masshill 101 F
Mastergeehy 82 B
Masterstown 91 K
Matehy 84 D
Maudlin 92 G
Maulane 84 F
Maulanimirish 83 H
Maulatrahane 83 L
Maulykeavane 83 B
Maulyneill 83 D
Maum 94 C
Maum 100 H
Mauricesmills 90 A
Mayfield 84 H
Mayfield 101 L
Mayglass 86 M
Maynooth/Maigh Nuad 97 M
Mayo 101 L
Meallalaghta 107 C
Meanus 83 A
Meanus 90 H
Meelaherragh 84 A
Meelick 96 K
Meelin 89 M
Meeltran 101 M
Meenachallow 106 J
Meenacladdy 106 C
Meenacross 106 F
Meenacross 106 H
Meenadeeny 106 J
Meenahaw 107 C
Meenahony 84 D
Meenaneary 106 H
Meenasrona 107 G
Meenasrona 107 K
Meenataggart 106 M
Meenatotan 106 F
Meenavean 106 G
Meen Bridge 83 K
Meendurragha 89 M
Meenkilly 89 M
Meenlaragh 107 A
Meennaraha 102 C
Meenreagh 107 E
Meens 83 C
Meenskeha 83 C
Meentullynagarn 106 L
Meenybraddan 106 J
Melkagh 96 C
Menlough 95 F
Menlough 95 G
Middle 107 A
Middle Town 107 C
Middletown 106 F
Midfield 101 M
Midleton 84 J
Milehouse 86 F
Milemill 92 C
Milestone 91 G
Milford 90 K
Milford 92 H
Milk 102 B
Millbrook 97 E
Mill Cove 82 J
Milleen 89 M
Millford 107 E
Millheld 84 H
Millquarter 86 H
Millroad 86 M
Millstreet 83 C
Millstreet 85 E
Milltown 86 C
Milltown 86 D
Milltown 87 D
Milltown 88 L
Milltown 89 K
Milltown 91 H
Milltown 92 C
Milltown 92 J
Milltown 93 A
Milltown 95 B
Milltown 95 F
Milltown 96 J
Milltown 97 A
Milltown 97 C
Milltown 103 K
Mill Town 104 K
Milltown 106 L
Milltown 106 M
Milltown Cross Roads 86 B
Milltown Malbay 89 C
Milltownpass 97 G
Minane Bridge 84 L
Minard East 88 M
Mitchelstown 84 C
Mitchelstown 97 E
Moanabricka 90 K
Moanflugh 83 F
Moanmore 90 M
Moat Bridge 96 K
Moate 96 J
Mocklershill 91 L
Modelligo 85 E
Modreeny 91 B
Mogeely 84 J
Mogh 91 K
Moglass 91 L
Mohill 102 M
Moig 90 D
Molly 97 A
Monacahee 86 H
Monaghan/Muineachán 103 J
Monalahy 84 D
Monamolin 87 D
Monard 84 E
Monard 90 M
Monargan Glebe 106 H
Monaseed 87 A
Monaster 90 H
Monasteraden 102 K
Monasterevin 92 B
Monatore 92 F
Monavanshere 84 D
Monee Cross Roads 84 E
Moneen 89 D
Moneenbog 96 C
Money 106 F
Moneyboy 96 B
Moneygall 91 E
Moneygold 102 A
Moneyhaughly 107 H
Moneylahan 102 B
Moneyteige Middle 87 B
Mongagh 96 B
Monilea 97 G
Monintown 97 D
Monivea 95 H
Monkstown 84 H
Monkstown 93 B
Monnagh 91 F
Monroe 85 A
Monroe 91 D
Monroe 95 E
Monroe 97 G
Montpelier 90 F
Mooncoin 85 F
Moone 92 F
Moonroe 90 K
Moor 102 K
Moore Park House 84 C
Moorfield Cross Roads 96 K
Mór 100 B
Morenane 90 H
Morley's Bridge 83 E
Mornington 98 H
Moroe 90 J
Mosney 98 H
Mothel 85 C
Mount Bellew Bridge 95 F
Mountbolus 96 M
Mountcharles 106 M
Mountcollins 89 M
Mounthenry 95 D
Mountkelly 92 J
Mountmellick 92 A
Mountnagle 84 B
Mount Nugent 97 B
Mountrath 92 A
Mount Rivers 83 A
Mountrivers Bridge 89 C
Mountshannon 90 C
Mount Talbot 96 D
Mount Temple 96 J
Mounttrasna 94 C
Mount Uniacke 85 G
Moveen 89 E
Moville 108 D
Moyadda 89 F
Moyasta 89 E
Moycarky 91 H
Moycullen 95 D
Moydow 96 F
Moyglass 95 M
Moyhora 92 G
Moylaw 101 D
Moyle 92 H
Moylough 95 F
Moylough 101 J
Moymore 90 B
Moynagh 97 A
Moynalty 97 F
Moynalvy 97 M
Moyne 91 H
Moyne 93 G
Moyne 102 K
Moyne 103 K
Moynehall 103 L
Moyrene 89 J
Moyrus 94 E
Moyvally 97 L
Moyvoon 95 D
Moyvore 96 J
Moyvoughly 96 J
Muckanagh 96 E
Muckanaghederdauhaulia 94 F
Mucklon 97 M
Muff 96 D
Muff 97 C
Muff 107 F
Muine Bheag/Bagenalstown 86 B
Muineagh 107 C
Muingingaun 100 C
Muingvautia 89 L
Muingwee 89 H
Muingwore 101 F
Muingyroogeen 84 A
Mullabohy Cross Roads 98 A
Mullacrew 98 A
Mullafarry 101 E
Mullagh 89 C
Mullagh 95 M
Mullagh 96 M
Mullagh 97 F
Mullagh 97 M
Mullagh 100 M
Mullaghard 97 F
Mullaghattin 98 B
Mullaghboy 97 A
Mullaghboy 102 M
Mullaghmacormick 96 B
Mullaghmore 95 F
Mullaghmore 102 B
Mullaghroe 102 G
Mullan 103 J
Mullanasole 106 M
Mullanmore 106 J
Mullanour 86 J
Mullany's Cross 101 J
Mullary Cross Roads 98 D
Mullaun 102 H
Mullawornia 96 F
Mullen 102 K
Mullennakill 86 E
Mullinacuff 87 A
Mullinahone 91 M
Mullinavat 86 D
Mullingar/An Muileann g Cearr 97 G
Mully 102 J
Mullymagowan 97 B
Mullymucks 96 B
Mulrany 100 J
Multyfarnham 97 D
Mungan 86 E
Mungret 90 H
Murlas Bridge 106 M
Murntown 86 J
Murragh 83 J
Murrays Cross 98 E
Murreagh 88 L
Murrens 97 E
Murrisk 100 M
Murroogh 94 J
Murvey 94 A
Mutton Bridge 83 H
Myshall 86 C
Myslerstown Cross Roads 92 C

N

Na Gorta 88 L
Naas/An Nás 92 C
Nad 84 A
Naran 106 H
Narraghmore 92 F
Naul 98 H
Navan 97 J
Neale 95 A
Nealstown 91 C
Nedanohe 82 F
Neigham 86 B
Nenagh/An t-Aonach 91 D
Newbawn 86 J
New Birmingham 91 M
Newbliss 103 J
Newbridge 90 G
Newbridge 96 D
Newcastle 85 B
Newcastle 93 A
Newcastle 93 E
Newcastle 95 J
Newcastle West 90 G
Newcestown 83 J
Newchapel 85 B
Newell's Bridge 97 G
Newinn 91 K
New Inn 95 J
New Inn 97 B
New Inn Cross Roads 92 B
Newkarket on Fergus 90 E
New Kildimo 90 H
Newmarket 84 A
Newmarket 86 D
New Mills 92 A
Newmills 107 G
Newpark 96 E
Newport 90 F
Newport 101 G
New Ross 86 E
Newton 90 M
Newtown 85 E
Newtown 85 F
Newtown 86 L
Newtown 89 E
Newtown 90 L
Newtown 90 M
Newtown 91 F
Newtown 92 H
Newtown 93 E
Newtown 95 L
Newtown 95 M
Newtown 96 A
Newtown 96 D
Newtown 96 E
Newtown 96 G
Newtown 96 J
Newtown 96 K
Newtown 97 M
Newtown 98 D
Newtown 98 G
Newtown 101 K
Newtown Cloghans 101 E
Newtown Cunningham 107 H
Newtown Forbes 96 C
Newtown Girley 97 F
Newtown Gore 103 K
Newtown Lodge 84 F
Newtownlow 97 K
Newtownlynch 95 G
Newtown Monasterboice 98 D
Newtown Sandes 89 J
Newtownshandrum 90 K
New Twopothouse 84 B
Nicker 90 J
Nobber 97 F
Nohaval 84 L
Nolagh 97 C
Nore Bridge 91 F
Northgrove 91 C
Northlands 97 C
North Ring 83 M
Noughaval 94 M
Nurney 86 C
Nurney 92 B

O

O'Briensbridge 90 F
Oaghley 89 H
Oakstown 97 J
Oatfield 90 E
Oatlands 97 F
Oatquater 94 H
Oghermong 82 B
Oghil 94 H
Oghil 96 K
Oghill Cross Roads 102 M
Ogonnelloe 90 C
Oilgate 87 G
Old Bawn 87 E
Oldcastle 97 E
Oldcastletown 84 C
Oldcourt 93 A
Oldcourt 97 L
Oldgrange 86 E
Old Head 84 K
Old Kilcullen 92 C
Old Kildimo 90 H
Oldleighlin 86 B
Oldmill Bridge 90 G
Old Ross 86 J
Old Town 86 F
Oldtown 86 D
Oldtown 89 E
Old Town 92 D
Oldtown 92 G
Old Town 96 G
Oldtown 96 H
Oldtown 98 K
Oldtown 107 H
Old Twopothouse 84 B
Old Village 91 A
Omeath 98 B
Omeath 104 L
Onaght 94 H
Oola 90 M
Oranmore 95 H
Oristown 97 F
Oughterard 89 D
Oughterard 93 A
Oughterard 95 D
Oulart 87 D
Oultort 96 K
Ouvry Cross Roads 103 M
Ovens 84 G
Owenberg 101 F
Owenbristy 95 L
Owenduff 100 F
Owenerk 107 C
Owenmore Bridge 100 M
Ower 95 D
Owning 85 C
Owung 85 C
Oysterhaven 84 L

P

Paddock 89 G
Palace 86 F
Palatine 92 H
Pallas 83 M
Pallas 92 A
Pallas Cross 91 H

A B C D E F G H I J K L M N O P Q R S T U V W X Y Z

Turnpike 91 H
Turreen 96 E
Twomileborris 91 H
Tylas 98 G
Tynagh 95 M
Tyredagh Upper 90 B
Tyrrellspass 97 K

Woodville 96 H

Y

Yellow Furze 98 G
Youghal 91 D
Youghal/Eochaill 85 G

U

Uggoon 90 B
Umgall 107 C
Umlagh 107 B
Ummeraboy 83 C
Umrycam 107 B
Unionhall 83 L
Upperchurch 91 G
Upper Glanmire 84 E
Upton 84 G
Urglin 92 H
Urlaur 101 M
Urlingford 91 J

V

Valley 100 E
Valleymount 93 D
Ventry 88 L
Vicarstown 92 B
Villierstown 85 D
Virginia 97 B
Virginia Road 97 E

W

Waddingtown 86 J
Walkinstown 93 B
Wallslough 86 A
Walshestown 101 C
Walshisland 97 K
Walshtown 84 F
Walterstown 98 A
Walterstown 98 G
Ward 98 K
Warrington 86 B
Watch House Cross Roads
  92 C
Watch House Village 86 C
Waterfall 84 H
Waterfoot 103 A
Waterford/Port Láirge 86 G
Watergrasshill 84 E
Waterville 82 E
Weir Bridge 95 E
Welchtown 107 G
Wellingtonbridge 86 J
Westcove 82 E
West End 89 B
Westport 100 M
Westport Quay 100 M
Westtown 85 F
West Town 106 C
Wexford/Loch Garman 87 G
Whitebog 92 E
Whitechurch 84 E
Whitechurch 85 E
Whitechurch 86 H
Whiteford 91 B
Whitegate 84 J
White Gate 89 K
Whitegate 91 A
Whitehall 96 C
Whitehall 97 D
Whitehall 98 D
White Hill 106 L
Whitemount 86 D
White Quarry 97 F
Whiterath Cross Roads 98 B
White's Bridge 89 C
White's Cross 84 H
Whites Town 98 C
Wicklow/Cill Mhantáin 93 H
Wilkinstown 97 F
Willbrook 90 A
Willbrook 93 B
Williamstown 92 J
Williamstown 95 C
Williamstown 96 H
Williamstown 97 F
Williamsville 98 K
Willsborough 95 C
Wilton 90 G
Windgap 85 C
Windy Harbour 98 D
Wine Town 96 J
Winterhill 106 M
Wolfhill 92 E
Wooddown 97 G
Woodenbridge 87 B
Woodfield 95 C
Woodford 83 B
Woodford 91 A
Woodfort 84 C
Woodland 107 H
Woodstown 86 L
Woodtown 98 D
Woodville 89 L

A
B
C
D
E
F
G
H
I
J
K
L
M
N
O
P
Q
R
S
T
U
V
W
X
Y
Z

Europe

C

D

A B C D E F G H I J K L M N O P Q R S T U V W X Y Z

Hatvan (H) 144 L
Hauge (N) 130 D
Haugesund (N) 130 D
Hauho (FIN) 131 C
Haukeligrend (N) 130 A
Hausach (D) 134 M
Havelberg (D) 135 E
Haverfordwest (GB) 133 F
Havlíčkův Brod (CZ) 135 J
Havneby (DK) 130 K
Havnebyen (DK) 130 L
Havøysund (N) 129 B
Havsa (TR) 142 M
Hawick (GB) 132 L
Hayrabolu (TR) 142 M
Heby (S) 131 A
Hechtel (B) 134 F
Hede (S) 128 M
Hedemora (S) 131 A
Heerenveen (NL) 134 C
Heerlen (NL) 134 F
Hegyfalu (H) 144 K
Heide (D) 130 K
Heidelberg (D) 135 G
Heidenheim an der Brenz (D) 135 K
Heidenreichstein (A) 135 M
Heilbronn (D) 135 G
Heiligenblut (A) 140 B
Heiligenkreuz im Lafnitztal (A) 140 C
Heinola (FIN) 129 L
Helensburgh (GB) 132 F
Hella (IS) 128 D
Helleland (N) 130 D
Hellín (E) 139 G
Helmond (NL) 134 F
Helmsdale (GB) 132 C
Helmstett (D) 135 D
Helsingborg (S) 130 J
Helsingør (DK) 130 H
Helsinki/Helsingfors (FIN) 129 L
Heltermaa (EST) 131 F
Hemse (S) 131 G
Hengelo (NL) 134 F
Hennebont (F) 136 A
Heradsbygd (N) 130 B
Herceg-Novi (MNE) 140 M
Hereford (GB) 133 G
Herford (D) 135 D
Herisau (CH) 137 B
Hermagor (A) 140 B
Hermannstadt (Sibiu) (RO) 142 B
Herning (DK) 130 G
Herrenberg (D) 135 K
Herrera de Pisuerga (E) 138 C
Herreruela (E) 138 H
Herzberg (D) 135 E
Herzberg am Harz (D) 135 D
Herzogenburg (A) 135 M
Hesdin (F) 134 G
Hidasnémeti (H) 144 L
Hieflau (A) 135 M
High Wycombe (GB) 133 H
Híjar (E) 139 D
Hildesheim (D) 135 D
Hillerød (DK) 130 L
Hillesøy (N) 129 A
Hillswick (GB) 132 D
Hilversum (NL) 134 E
Himarë (AL) 143 A
Hindås (S) 130 J
Hinojosa del Duque (E) 138 H
Híos (GR) 143 H
Hirsilä (FIN) 129 L
Hirson (F) 134 H
Hirtshals (DK) 130 H
Hjeimeland (N) 130 D
Hjerkinn (N) 128 L
Hjo (S) 130 F
Hjørring (DK) 130 H
Hjortkvarn (S) 130 F
Hlohovec (SK) 144 K
Hobro (DK) 130 H
Hódmezővásárhely (H) 142 A
Hodonín (CZ) 135 M
Hof (D) 135 H
Hof (IS) 128 B
Hofgeismar (D) 135 D
Höfn (IS) 128 B
Hofors (S) 131 A
Höganäs (S) 130 H
Högsby (S) 131 G
Hohenau (A) 135 M
Hohenwestedt (D) 130 L
Hoisko (FIN) 129 H
Hokksund (N) 130 B
Hol (N) 130 A
Holbæk (DK) 130 L
Holice (CZ) 135 J
Hölick (S) 129 K
Hollabrunn (A) 135 M
Hollókő (H) 144 K
Hólmavík (IS) 128 A
Holmestrand (N) 130 E
Holmsund (S) 129 G
Holmudden (S) 131 E
Holstebro (DK) 130 G
Holsted (DK) 130 K
Holwerd (NL) 134 C
Holyhead (GB) 133 B
Holzminden (D) 135 D
Hønefoss (N) 128 L
Honfleur (F) 136 B
Honiton (GB) 133 G
Honkajoki (FIN) 129 L
Honningsvåg (N) 129 B
Hontianske Nemce (SK) 144 K
Hoogeveen (NL) 134 C
Höör (S) 130 M
Hoorn (NL) 134 C
Hoplandsjøen (N) 130 A
Horažďovice (CZ) 135 H
Hörby (S) 130 M
Horeftó (GR) 143 B
Horezu (RO) 142 B
Horn (A) 135 M
Horncastle (GB) 133 D
Horndal (S) 131 A
Horodok (UA) 144 J
Horokhiv (UA) 144 F
Horsens (DK) 130 L
Horten (N) 130 E
Hossegor (F) 136 H
Hoting (S) 129 G
Houdan (F) 136 C
Houeillès (F) 136 H
Houmnikó (GR) 143 C
Hov (DK) 130 L
Hovden (N) 130 D
Hovmantorp (S) 130 J
Höxter (D) 135 D
Høyanger (N) 128 L
Hoyerswerda (D) 135 F
Hoyos (E) 138 E
Hradec Králové (CZ) 135 J
Hranice (CZ) 144 G
Hrodna (BLR) 144 C
Hrubieszów (PL) 144 F
Hrvatska Kostajnica (HR) 140 H
Huben (A) 137 C
Huddersfield (GB) 133 C
Hudiksvall (S) 129 K
Huedin (RO) 142 B
Huelma (E) 138 M
Huelva (E) 138 L
Huércal Overa (E) 139 K
Huesca (E) 139 A
Huéscar (E) 139 K
Huete (E) 138 F
Huittinen/Lauttakylä (FIN) 129 L
Hultsfred (S) 131 G
Humenné (SK) 144 H
Humppila (FIN) 131 C
Hundested (DK) 130 L
Hunedoara (RO) 142 B
Hünfeld (D) 135 G
Hungen (D) 135 G
Hunstanton (GB) 133 D
Huntingdon (GB) 133 D
Huntly (GB) 132 G
Hurdal (N) 130 B
Hurezani (RO) 142 F
Húsavík (IS) 128 A
Huskvarna (S) 130 J
Husum (D) 130 K
Huy (B) 134 H
Hvalovo (RUS) 129 M
Hvalpsund (DK) 130 H
Hvammstangi (IS) 128 A
Hvar (HR) 140 M
Hveragerði (IS) 128 D
Hvide Sande (DK) 130 G
Hvittingfoss (N) 130 E
Hvolsvöllur (IS) 128 D
Hyères (F) 137 L
Hyltebruk (S) 130 J
Hyrynsalmi (FIN) 129 H
Hyvinkää (FIN) 129 L

I

Iaremcha (UA) 144 M
Iasinia (UA) 144 M
Iavoriv (UA) 144 J
Ibrice (TR) 143 D
Idar-Oberstein (D) 134 J
Idra (GR) 143 L
Idre (S) 128 M
Ieper (B) 134 E
Ierápetra (GR) 143 K
Ifjord (N) 129 B
Igal (H) 140 D
Iglésias (I) 141 J
Iğneada (TR) 142 M
Igoumenitsa (GR) 143 E
Igualada (E) 139 B
Ihtiman (BG) 142 L
Iieşti (RO) 142 D
Ilidža (BIH) 140 H
Iisalmi (FIN) 129 H
IJmuiden (NL) 134 E
Ikast (DK) 130 G
Iława (PL) 144 A
Ilchester (GB) 133 G
Ilfracombe (GB) 133 F
Ilia (RO) 142 B
I'lle Rousse (F) 137 M
Ilmenau (D) 135 G
Ilok (HR) 142 A
Ilomantsi (FIN) 129 J
Iłża (PL) 144 E
Imatra (FIN) 129 M
Immenstadt (D) 135 K
Imola (I) 140 F
Imotski (HR) 140 M
Impéria (I) 137 H
Imst (A) 137 C
Inari (FIN) 129 B
Inca (E) 139 F
Ineu (RO) 142 B
Infantado (P) 138 G
Ingolstadt (D) 135 L
Innertkirchen (CH) 137 E
Innsbruck (A) 137 C
Inowrocław (PL) 144 A
Însurăţei (RO) 142 D
Întorsura Buzăului (RO) 142 C
Inveran (IRL) 133 A
Inveraray (GB) 132 F
Inverbervie (GB) 132 G
Invergarry (GB) 132 F
Inverness (GB) 132 F
Inverurie (GB) 132 G
Ioánina (GR) 143 A
Ios (GR) 143 M
Ipsala (TR) 142 M
Ipswich (GB) 133 D
Iráklio (GR) 143 J
Ironbridge (GB) 133 C
Irun (E) 139 A
Irurzun (E) 139 A
Irvine (GB) 132 K
Isaba (E) 139 A
Isaccea (RO) 142 D
Ísafjörður (IS) 128 A
Isbister (GB) 132 D
Ischia (I) 141 B
Iseo (I) 140 A
Isérnia (I) 141 C
Iskra (BG) 142 L
Isle of Whithorn (GB) 132 K
Isola di Capo Rizzuto (I) 141 H
Isperih (BG) 142 H
Ispica (I) 141 L
Issoire (F) 136 F
Issoudun (F) 136 F
Istria (RO) 142 D
Istunmäki (FIN) 129 H
Itéa (GR) 143 F
Itháki (GR) 143 E
Itri (I) 141 B
Itzehoe (D) 135 A
Iu'e (BLR) 144 C
Ivacèvičy (BLR) 144 C
Ivajlovgrad (BG) 142 L
Ivalo (FIN) 129 B
Ivanava (BLR) 144 F
Ivanić Grad (HR) 140 D
Ivanjica (SRB) 142 E
Ivano-Frankivs'k (UA) 144 J
Ivano-Frankove (UA) 144 J
Ivrea (I) 137 E
Ivrindi (TR) 143 D
Izmajil (UA) 142 D
Izmir (TR) 143 H
Iznalloz (E) 138 M
Izsák (H) 142 A

J

Jaala (FIN) 129 L
Jablanac (HR) 140 G
Jablanica (BG) 142 G
Jablanica (BIH) 140 M
Jablonec nad Nisou (CZ) 135 J
Jablonica (SK) 144 K
Jabłonka (PL) 144 G
Jablonna (PL) 144 E
Jablunkov (CZ) 144 G
Jabugo (E) 138 H
Jaca (E) 139 A
Jadraque (E) 138 F
Jaén (E) 138 M
Jagoda (BG) 142 L
Jajce (BIH) 140 H
Jäkkvik (S) 129 D
Jakobstad/Pietarsaari (FIN) 129 G
Jambol (BG) 142 M
Jamena (HR) 142 E
Jämjö (S) 131 G
Jämsä (FIN) 129 L
Jánosháza (H) 144 K
Janów Lubelski (PL) 144 E
Janzé (F) 136 B
Jarandilla de la Vera (E) 138 E
Järna (S) 131 D
Jarocin (PL) 144 D
Jaroměř (CZ) 135 J
Jarosław (PL) 144 J
Järpen (S) 128 J
Järvenpää (FIN) 129 L
Jaša Tomić (SRB) 142 A
Jasło (PL) 144 H
Jászberény (H) 144 L
Jaunjelgava (LV) 131 J
Jawor (PL) 135 J
Jedburgh (GB) 132 L
Jędrzejów (PL) 144 H
Jelenia Góra (PL) 135 J
Jelgava (LV) 131 J
Jelsa (HR) 140 M
Jemnice (CZ) 135 M
Jena (D) 135 H
Jerez de la Frontera (E) 138 L
Jerez de los Caballeros (E) 138 H
Jesenice (SLO) 140 C
Jesi (I) 140 K
Jésolo (I) 140 F
Jessheim (N) 130 B
Jever (D) 134 C
Jevnaker (N) 130 B
Jezersko (SLO) 140 C
Jeżów (PL) 144 E
Jibou (RO) 144 M
Jičín (CZ) 135 J
Jieznas (LT) 131 M
Jihlava (CZ) 135 J
Jilemnice (CZ) 135 J
Jimbolia (RO) 142 A
Jimena de la Frontera (E) 138 L
Jindřichutov Hradec (CZ) 135 J
Jódar (E) 138 J
Joensuu (FIN) 129 J
Johno' Groats (GB) 132 C
Joigny (F) 136 C
Joinville (F) 137 A
Jokkmokk (S) 129 D
Jonava (LT) 131 M
Jondal (N) 128 L
Joniškis (LT) 131 J
Jönköping (S) 130 J
Jordanów (PL) 144 G
Jordet (N) 128 M
Jorgucat (AL) 143 A
Jørstad (N) 128 J
Josipdol (HR) 140 G
Josselin (F) 136 A
Joutsa (FIN) 129 L
Joutsijärvi (FIN) 129 E
Judenburg (A) 140 C
Juelsminde (DK) 130 L
Jule (N) 128 J
Juma (RUS) 129 F
Jumilla (E) 139 G
Junosuando (S) 129 D
Junsele (S) 129 G
Juodupė (LT) 131 J
Juratiški (BLR) 144 C
Jurbarkas (LT) 131 M
Jūrmala (LV) 131 J
Jüterbog (D) 135 E
Juuka (FIN) 129 J
Juva (FIN) 129 M
Jyderup (DK) 130 L
Jyväskylä (FIN) 129 L

K

Kaamanen (FIN) 129 B
Kaaresuvanto (FIN) 129 D
Kaïáfas (GR) 143 K
Käina (EST) 131 F
Kaiserslautern (D) 134 J
Kaišiadorys (LT) 131 M
Kajaani (FIN) 129 H
Kajnardža (BG) 142 H
Kalajoki (FIN) 129 H
Kalak (N) 129 B
Kalamáta (GR) 143 K
Kalambáka (GR) 143 B
Kalamítsi (GR) 143 C
Kalana (EST) 131 E
Kälarne (S) 129 K
Kalávrita (GR) 143 F
Kalce (SLO) 140 C
Kalevala (RUS) 129 J
Kálfafell (IS) 128 D
Kálfafellsstaður (IS) 128 E
Kálfshamarsvík (IS) 128 A
Kalí Liménes (GR) 143 J
Kálimnos (GR) 143 M
Kaliningrad (Königsberg) (RUS) 131 L
Kalinovik (BIH) 140 M
Kalisz (PL) 144 D
Kalithéa (GR) 143 B
Kalix (S) 129 H
Kalli (EST) 131 F
Kallsedet (S) 128 J
Kalmar (S) 131 G
Kalna (SRB) 142 F
Kálna nad Hronom (SK) 144 K
Kalnciems (LV) 131 J
Kalókastro (GR) 143 B
Kaloní (GR) 143 D
Kalpáki (GR) 143 A
Kalundborg (DK) 130 L
Kalush (UA) 144 J
Kalvåg (N) 128 L
Kalvarija (LT) 131 M
Kamáres (GR) 143 L
Kamariótissa (GR) 143 C
Kameno (BG) 142 M
Kamianka-Buz'ka (UA) 144 J
Kamień Pomorski (PL) 135 C
Kamin'-Kashyrs'kyi (UA) 144 F
Kamjanec (BLR) 144 F
Kampen (NL) 134 F
Kandalakša (RUS) 129 F
Kandava (LV) 131 J
Kandersteg (CH) 137 E
Kangasniemi (FIN) 129 L
Kankaanpää (FIN) 129 L
Kannus (FIN) 129 H
Kapfenberg (A) 135 M
Kaplice (CZ) 135 M
Kaposvár (H) 140 D
Kapp (N) 130 B
Kappel (D) 134 J
Kappeln (D) 130 L
Kappelshamn (S) 131 G
Kappelskär (S) 131 D
Kapustnoe (RUS) 129 F
Karabiga (TR) 143 D
Karaburun (TR) 143 H
Karacabey (TR) 143 D
Karacaköy (TR) 142 M
Karapelit (BG) 142 H
Karasjok (N) 129 B
Kårböle (S) 128 M
Karby (DK) 130 G
Karditsa (GR) 143 F
Kärdla (EST) 131 F
Kărdžali (BG) 142 L
Karesuando (S) 129 D
Kariani (GR) 143 C
Kariés (GR) 143 C
Karigasniemi (FIN) 129 B
Karis/ Karjaa (FIN) 131 C
Káristos (GR) 143 G
Karítena (GR) 143 K
Karkaloú (GR) 143 K
Karkkila (FIN) 129 L
Karksi-Nuia (EST) 131 F
Karlino (PL) 135 C
Karlobag (HR) 140 G
Karlovac (HR) 140 G
Karlovo (BG) 142 L
Karlovy Vary (CZ) 135 H
Karlsborg (S) 130 F
Karlshamn (S) 130 J
Karlskoga (S) 130 F
Karlskrona (S) 131 G
Karlsruhe (D) 134 M
Karlstad (S) 130 F
Karlstadt (D) 135 G
Karlstift (A) 135 M
Karnobat (BG) 142 H
Karow (D) 135 B
Kárpathos (GR) 143 M
Karpenissi (GR) 143 F
Karperó (GR) 143 B
Karsämäki (FIN) 129 H
Karstula (FIN) 129 H
Karttula (FIN) 129 H
Kartuzy (PL) 144 A
Karup (DK) 130 G
Karviná (CZ) 144 G
Kasala/Kasaböle (FIN) 129 K
Kaseberga (S) 130 M
Kaskinen/Kaskö (FIN) 129 K
Kassel (D) 135 D
Kastéli (GR) 143 J
Kastoriá (GR) 143 B
Katápola (GR) 143 M
Kateríni (GR) 143 B
Káto Ahaïa (GR) 143 F
Káto Nevrokópi (GR) 142 L
Katowice (PL) 144 G
Katrineholm (S) 131 D
Katthammarsvik (S) 131 H
Kaufbeuren (D) 135 K
Kauhajoki (FIN) 129 L
Kaunas (LT) 131 M
Kaupanger (N) 130 A
Kaustinen (FIN) 129 H
Kautokeino (N) 129 A
Kavadarci (MK) 142 K
Kavajë (AL) 143 A
Kavak (TR) 143 D
Kavála (GR) 143 C
Kavarna (BG) 142 H
Kávos (GR) 143 E
Kazanlăk (BG) 142 L
Kecel (H) 142 A
Kecskemét (H) 142 A
Kėdainiai (LT) 131 M
Kędzierzyn-Koźle (PL) 144 G
Keel (IRL) 133 A
Keflavík (IS) 128 D
Kehl (D) 134 M
Keila (EST) 131 F
Keipene (LV) 131 J
Keith (GB) 132 G
Këlcyrë (AL) 143 A
Kelloselkä (FIN) 129 E
Kells (IRL) 133 B
Kelmė (LT) 131 M
Kelso (GB) 132 L
Kem' (RUS) 129 J
Kemalpaşa (TR) 143 H
Kemer (TR) 143 D
Kemi (FIN) 129 H
Kemijärvi (FIN) 129 E
Kempten (D) 135 K
Kendal (GB) 132 L
Kenderes (H) 144 L
Kenilworth (GB) 133 C
Kenmare (IRL) 133 E
Kenmore (GB) 132 G
Kennacraig (GB) 132 K
Kepa (RUS) 129 F
Kępno (PL) 144 D
Kepsut (TR) 143 D
Keramotí (GR) 143 C
Kerava (FIN) 131 C
Keret' (RUS) 129 F
Kerí (GR) 143 J
Kérkira (GR) 143 E
Kermen (BG) 142 L
Kerteminde (DK) 130 L
Keşan (TR) 143 D
Keswick (GB) 132 L
Keszthely (H) 140 D
Kętrzyn (PL) 144 B
Kettering (GB) 133 D
Kęty (PL) 144 G
Keuruu (FIN) 129 L
Khemis Miliana (DZ) 139 L
Khodoriv (UA) 144 J
Khust (UA) 144 M
Khyriv (UA) 144 J
Kiáto (GR) 143 F
Kičevo (MK) 142 J
Kiel (D) 130 L
Kielce (PL) 144 E
Kifino Selo (BIH) 140 M
Kifissiá (GR) 143 G
Kihelkonna (EST) 131 E
Kiiminki (FIN) 129 H
Kiistala (FIN) 129 E
Kikinda (SRB) 142 A
Kil (S) 130 F
Kilbeggan (IRL) 133 A
Kilboghamn (N) 128 F
Kilchoan (GB) 132 F
Kildare (IRL) 133 B
Kilija (UA) 142 D
Kilingi-Nõmme (EST) 131 F
Kilíni (GR) 143 F
Kilkee (IRL) 133 A
Kilkeel (GB) 132 K
Kilkenny (IRL) 133 A
Kilkís (GR) 143 B
Killarney (IRL) 133 E
Killorglin (IRL) 133 E
Kilmarnock (GB) 132 K
Kilpisjärvi (FIN) 129 A
Kilronan (IRL) 133 A
Kilrush (IRL) 133 A
Kimito/Kemiö (FIN) 131 B
Kinbrace (GB) 132 C
Kindberg (A) 135 M
Kingsbridge (GB) 133 L
King's Lynn (GB) 133 D
Kingston upon Hull (GB) 133 D
Kingussie (GB) 132 F
Kinik (TR) 143 D
Kinna (S) 130 J
Kinnegad (IRL) 133 B
Kinross (GB) 132 G
Kinsale (IRL) 133 E
Kinsarvik (N) 128 L
Kinvarra (IRL) 133 A
Kiparissía (GR) 143 K
Kirchbach in Steiermark (A) 140 C
Kiriši (RUS) 129 M
Kirkby Lonsdale (GB) 132 L
Kirkcaldy (GB) 132 G
Kirkcudbright (GB) 132 L
Kirkenær (N) 130 C
Kirkenes (N) 129 B
Kirkjubæjarklaustur (IS) 128 D
Kirkkonummi/Kyrkslätt (FIN) 129 L
Kirklareli (TR) 142 M
Kirkwall (GB) 132 C
Kirovsk (RUS) 129 F
Kiruna (S) 129 D
Kirschlag (A) 135 M
Kisa (S) 131 D
Kisbér (H) 144 K
Kiskőrös (H) 142 A
Kiskunfélegyháza (H) 142 A
Kiskunhalas (H) 142 A
Kiskunlacháza (H) 144 K
Kisszállás (H) 142 A
Kisújszállás (H) 144 L
Kíthira (GR) 143 L
Kittilä (FIN) 129 E
Kitzingen (D) 135 G
Kivertsi (UA) 144 F
Kivik (S) 130 M
Kiyikoy (TR) 142 M
Kjøllefjord (N) 129 B
Kjustendil (BG) 142 K
Kladanj (BIH) 140 H
Kladno (CZ) 135 H
Kladovo (SRB) 142 F
Klagenfurt (A) 140 C
Klaipėda (Memel) (LT) 131 L
Klaksvík (DK) 130 K
Klašnice (BIH) 140 H
Klatovy (CZ) 135 H
Klaus (A) 135 L
Klausenburg (Cluj-Napoca) (RO) 142 B
Kleve (D) 134 F
Klingenthal (Sachsen) (D) 135 H
Klintehamn (S) 131 G
Klippan (S) 130 J
Ključ (BIH) 140 H
Kłodzko (PL) 144 G
Klokkarvik (N) 130 A
Klos (AL) 142 J
Kluczbork (PL) 144 D
Knaben (N) 130 D
Knarvik (N) 128 L
Kneža (BG) 142 G
Knidos (TR) 143 M
Knighton (GB) 133 C
Knin (HR) 140 H
Knittelfeld (A) 140 C
Knjaževac (SRB) 142 F
Knocktopher (IRL) 133 A
Knokke-Heist (B) 134 E
Knyszyn (PL) 144 B
Kobarid (SLO) 140 B
København (DK) 130 L
Koblenz (D) 134 J
Kobryn (BLR) 144 F
Kočani (MK) 142 K
Koçarli (TR) 143 H
Koceljevo (SRB) 142 E
Kočevje (SLO) 140 G
Kochel (D) 135 K
Kočkoma (RUS) 129 J
Köflach (A) 140 C
Køge (DK) 130 L
Kohila (EST) 131 F
Kokkola/Karleby (FIN) 129 H
Kola (RUS) 129 C
Kolari (FIN) 129 E
Kolašin (MNE) 142 J
Kolbeinsstaðir (IS) 128 A
Kolbuszowa (PL) 144 H
Kolding (DK) 130 L
Koležma (RUS) 129 J
Kolín (CZ) 135 J
Kolka (LV) 131 J
Kolky (UA) 144 F
Köln (D) 134 F
Kolno (PL) 144 B
Koło (PL) 144 D
Kołobrzeg (PL) 135 C
Kolomyia (UA) 144 M
Kolpino (RUS) 129 M
Komárno (SK) 144 K
Komárom (H) 144 K
Komotiní (GR) 142 L
Kondopoga (RUS) 129 J
Kongsberg (N) 130 B
Kongsvinger (N) 130 B
Königsberg (Kaliningrad) (RUS) 131 L
Königswiesen (A) 135 M
Königs-Wusterhausen (D) 135 E
Konin (PL) 144 D
Konispol (AL) 143 A
Kónitsa (GR) 143 A
Konjic (BIH) 140 M
Końskie (PL) 144 E
Konstanz (D) 135 K
Kópasker (IS) 128 B
Kópavogur (IS) 128 D
Koper (SLO) 140 F
Kopervik (N) 130 D
Köping (S) 131 D
Koplik (AL) 142 J
Koppang (N) 128 M
Kopparberg (S) 130 C
Koprivnica (HR) 140 D
Korbach (D) 135 D
Korçë (AL) 143 A
Korčula (HR) 140 M
Korenica (HR) 140 G
Korgen (N) 128 F
Koríni (GR) 143 F
Kórinthos (GR) 143 F
Korissía (GR) 143 G
Koríthi (GR) 143 J
Körmend (H) 140 D
Kórnik (PL) 144 D
Kornsjø (N) 130 E
Kornsjø (S) 130 E
Koróni (GR) 143 K
Koronowo (PL) 144 A
Koropí (GR) 143 G
Korpilombolo (S) 129 D
Korpo/Korppoo (FIN) 129 L
Korsør (DK) 130 L
Kortrijk (B) 134 E
Kos (GR) 143 M
Kościan (PL) 144 D
Kościerzyna (PL) 144 A
Kose (EST) 131 F
Košice (SK) 144 L
Kosiv (UA) 144 M
Koskullskulle (S) 129 D
Kosovska Mitrovica (KOS) 142 J
Kostenec (BG) 142 K
Kostinbrod (BG) 142 K
Kostomukša (RUS) 129 J
Kostrzyn (PL) 144 D
Kostrzyn (PL) 135 F
Koszalin (PL) 135 C
Kőszeg (H) 144 K
Koszyce (PL) 144 H
Kótas (GR) 143 A
Köthen (Anhalt) (D) 135 E
Kotka (FIN) 129 L
Kotor (MNE) 142 J
Kotor Varoš (BIH) 140 H
Kötschach (A) 140 B
Kouvola (FIN) 129 L
Kovdor (RUS) 129 F
Kovel' (UA) 144 F
Kovera (RUS) 129 M
Kovin (SRB) 142 E
Kowal (PL) 144 D
Kozáni (GR) 143 B
Koziegłowy (PL) 144 G
Kozienice (PL) 144 E
Kozina (SLO) 140 G
Kozloduj (BG) 142 F
Kragerø (N) 130 E
Kragujevac (SRB) 142 E
Krakau (Kraków) (PL) 144 H
Kraków (Krakau) (PL) 144 H
Kraljevica (HR) 140 G
Kraljevo (SRB) 142 E
Kralóvany (SK) 144 G
Kralovice (CZ) 135 H
Kramfors (S) 129 K
Kranj (SLO) 140 C
Kranjska Gora (SLO) 140 C
Kraśnik (PL) 144 E
Krasnystaw (PL) 144 F
Kratígos (GR) 143 H
Kratovo (MK) 142 K
Krefeld (D) 134 F
Krems an der Donau (A) 135 M
Kretinga (LT) 131 L
Kričim (BG) 142 L
Kristiansand (N) 130 D
Kristianstad (S) 130 M
Kristiansund (N) 128 H
Kristinehamn (S) 130 F
Kristinestad/Kristiinankaupunki (FIN) 129 K
Kriva Palanka (MK) 142 K
Krivodol (BG) 142 F
Križevci (HR) 140 D
Krk (HR) 140 G
Krokom (S) 128 J
Króksfjarðarnes (IS) 128 A
Kroměříž (CZ) 144 G
Kronach (D) 135 H
Kronstadt (Braşov) (RO) 142 C
Kronštadt (RUS) 129 M
Krośniewice (PL) 144 D
Krosno (PL) 144 H
Krosno Odrzańskie (PL) 135 F
Krotoszyn (PL) 144 D
Krško (SLO) 140 C
Krujë (AL) 142 J
Krumbach (Schwaben) (D) 135 K
Krumovgrad (BG) 142 L
Kruševac (SRB) 142 E
Kruševo (MK) 143 B
Krušovene (BG) 142 G
Krylovo (RUS) 131 L
Krynica (PL) 144 H
Krzeszyce (PL) 135 F
Ksar-el-Boukhari (DZ) 139 M
Ksar-es-Seghir (MA) 138 L
Küblis (CH) 137 C
Kubrat (BG) 142 G
Kučevo (SRB) 142 E
Kudirkos-Naumiestis (LT) 131 M
Kufstein (A) 137 C
Kuhmo (FIN) 129 J
Kuhmoinen (FIN) 129 L
Kuivastu (EST) 131 F
Kukës (AL) 142 J
Kula (BG) 142 F
Kula (SRB) 142 A
Kulata (BG) 142 K
Kuldīga (LV) 131 H
Kulmbach (D) 135 H
Kulmuksa (RUS) 129 J
Kumanovo (MK) 142 K
Kumkale (TR) 143 D
Kumla (S) 130 F
Kunes (N) 129 B
Kungälv (S) 130 E
Kungsbacka (S) 130 H
Kungshamn (S) 130 E
Kungsör (S) 131 D
Kunmadaras (H) 144 L
Kunszentmárton (H) 142 A
Kunžak (CZ) 135 M
Kuolajarvi (RUS) 129 E
Kuopio (FIN) 129 H
Kuortti (FIN) 129 L
Kupiškis (LT) 131 J
Kupres (BIH) 140 H
Kuressaare (EST) 131 F
Kurikka (FIN) 129 L
Kurów (PL) 144 E
Kuršėnai (LT) 131 J
Kuršumlija (SRB) 142 J
Kuru (FIN) 129 L
Kuşadasi (TR) 143 H
Küssnacht am Rigi (CH) 137 B
Kustavi (FIN) 129 K
Kutnà Hora (CZ) 135 J
Kutno (PL) 144 D
Kuusamo (FIN) 129 E
Kuusankoski (FIN) 129 L
Kuźnica (PL) 144 C
Kuzomen' (RUS) 129 F
Kvanndal (N) 128 L
Kværndrup (DK) 130 L

A B C D E F G H I J K L M N O P Q R S T U V W X Y Z

Särkisalmi (FIN) 129 M
Şarköy (TR) 143 D
Sărmaşu (RO) 142 B
Sarmingstein (A) 135 M
Särna (S) 128 M
Sarnen (CH) 137 B
Sárospatak (H) 144 L
Sarpsborg (N) 130 E
Sarrebourg (F) 137 A
Sarreguemines (F) 134 J
Sarria (E) 138 B
Sartène (F) 137 M
Saruhanli (TR) 143 H
Sárvár (H) 144 K
Sarzana (I) 140 E
Sásd (H) 140 D
Sássari (I) 141 J
Sassnitz (DK) 130 M
Säter (S) 131 A
Sátoraljaújhely (H) 144 L
Satu Mare (RO) 144 M
Sauda (N) 130 A
Sauðárkrókur (IS) 128 A
Saulieu (F) 137 A
Saulkrasti (LV) 131 J
Sault (F) 137 G
Saumur (F) 136 E
Saurbær (IS) 128 A
Sauve (F) 137 G
Savaştepe (TR) 143 D
Savelli (I) 141 H
Saverne (F) 137 B
Savigliano (I) 137 H
Šavnik (MNE) 142 J
Savona (I) 140 E
Savonlinna (FIN) 129 M
Sävsjö (S) 130 J
Savukoski (FIN) 129 E
Saxmundham (GB) 133 D
Saxnäs (S) 128 J
Scalasaig (GB) 132 F
Scalloway (GB) 132 D
Scanzano (I) 141 D
Scarborough (GB) 132 M
Scarinish (GB) 132 F
Schaffhausen (CH) 134 M
Scheibbs (A) 135 M
Schilpário (I) 140 A
Schio (I) 140 A
Schirmeck (F) 137 A
Schladming (A) 135 L
Schleiden (D) 134 J
Schleiz (D) 135 H
Schleswig (D) 130 L
Schleusingen (D) 135 G
Schlierbach (A) 135 L
Schönberg (D) 135 L
Schönebeck (Elbe) (D) 135 E
Schongau (D) 135 K
Schönthal (D) 135 H
Schrems (D) 135 M
Schrobenhausen (D) 135 K
Schwäbach (D) 135 G
Schwäbisch Gmünd (D) 135 K
Schwäbisch Hall (D) 135 G
Schwalmstadt (D) 135 G
Schwandorf (D) 135 H
Schwarzenbek (D) 135 A
Schwarzenburg (CH) 137 E
Schwaz (A) 137 C
Schwechat (A) 135 M
Schwedt (D) 135 C
Schweinfurt (D) 135 G
Schwerin (D) 135 B
Schwyz (CH) 137 B
Sciacca (I) 141 K
Scourie (GB) 132 B
Ščučyn (BLR) 144 C
Scunthorpe (GB) 133 D
Scuol (CH) 137 C
Sebeş (RO) 142 B
Seda (LT) 131 J
Sedan (F) 134 H
Sedbergh (GB) 132 L
Sedlčany (CZ) 135 H
Seduva (LT) 131 M
Seehausen (D) 135 E
Seelow (D) 135 F
Sées (F) 136 B
Seesen (D) 135 D
Seewiesen (A) 135 M
Segarcea (RO) 142 F
Segeža (RUS) 129 J
Segorbe (E) 139 D
Segovia (E) 138 F
Segré (F) 136 B
Segura (P) 138 E
Seiches-sur-le-Loir (F) 136 B
Seinäjoki (FIN) 129 L
Seini (RO) 144 M
Selb (D) 135 H
Selbu (N) 128 J
Selby (GB) 133 D
Sélestat (F) 137 B
Selfoss (IS) 128 D
Seljord (N) 130 E
Selles-sur-Cher (F) 136 F
Semizovac (BIH) 140 H
Senec (SK) 144 K
Senftenberg (D) 135 E
Senica (SK) 144 K
Senise (I) 141 G
Senj (HR) 140 G
Senlis (F) 136 C
Sennen (GB) 133 K
Sens (F) 136 C
Senta (SRB) 142 A
Sępólno Krajeńskie (PL) 144 A
Sepúlveda (E) 138 F
Seraing (B) 134 H
Sercaia (RO) 142 C
Sereď (SK) 144 K
Séres (GR) 143 C
Seroczyn (PL) 144 E
Serón (E) 139 K
Serpa (P) 138 G
Serra San Bruno (I) 141 H
Serres (F) 137 G
Sertã (P) 138 D
Sérvia (GR) 143 B
Sesimbra (P) 138 G
Sessa Aurunca (I) 141 B
Šestanovac (HR) 140 M
Sestriere (I) 137 H
Sestri Levante (I) 140 E
Sesvete (HR) 140 C
Sète (F) 137 G
Setermoen (N) 129 A
Settle (GB) 132 L
Setúbal (P) 138 G
Seurre (F) 137 D
Séverac-le-Château (F) 136 J
Severomorsk (RUS) 129 C
Sevilla (E) 138 L
Sevlievo (BG) 142 G
Seyðisfjörður (IS) 128 B
Sézanne (F) 136 C
Sfakiá (GR) 143 J
Sfântu Gheorghe (RO) 142 C
Sheerness (GB) 133 H
Sheffield (GB) 133 C
Shieldaig (GB) 132 F
Shkodër (AL) 142 J
Shrewsbury (GB) 133 C
Šiauliai (LT) 131 J
Šibari (I) 141 H
Šibenik (HR) 140 L
Sibiu (Hermannstadt) (RO) 142 B
Šid (SRB) 142 E
Sidi Aïssa (DZ) 139 M
Sidi Ladjel (DZ) 139 M
Sidi Lakhdar (DZ) 139 L
Sidirókastro (GR) 142 K
Siedlce (PL) 144 E
Siegen (D) 134 J
Siemiatycze (PL) 144 E
Siena (I) 140 K
Sieradz (PL) 144 D
Sierpc (PL) 144 A
Sierre (CH) 137 E
Sievi (FIN) 129 H
Sig (RUS) 129 F
Siğacik (TR) 143 H
Sighetu Marmaţiei (RO) 144 M
Sighişoara (RO) 142 C
Siğirci (TR) 143 D
Siglufjörður (IS) 128 A
Sigmaringen (D) 135 K
Sigüenza (E) 138 F
Sigüés (E) 139 A
Sigulda (LV) 131 J
Siilinjärvi (FIN) 129 H
Šilalė (LT) 131 M
Silistra (BG) 142 H
Silivri (TR) 142 M
Silkeborg (DK) 130 H
Silla (E) 139 G
Sillé-le-Guillàume (F) 136 B
Sillian (A) 137 C
Silloth (GB) 132 L
Sils im Engadin (CH) 137 F
Šilutė (LT) 131 L
Silves (P) 138 K
Simbach am Inn (D) 135 L
Simeria (RO) 142 B
Simitli (BG) 142 K
Şimleu-Silvaniei (RO) 144 M
Simo (FIN) 129 E
Simplon Dorf (CH) 137 E
Simrishamn (S) 130 M
Sinaia (RO) 142 C
Sindelfingen (D) 135 K
Sines (P) 138 G
Singen (D) 135 K
Siniscóla (I) 141 J
Sinj (HR) 140 M
Sinsheim (D) 135 G
Sintra (P) 138 G
Siófok (H) 140 D
Sion (CH) 137 E
Šipka (BG) 142 L
Siracusa (I) 141 L
Sirevåg (N) 130 D
Sirkka (FIN) 129 E
Široki Brijek (BIH) 140 M
Širvintos (LT) 131 M
Sisak (HR) 140 H
Sisteron (F) 137 G
Sitges (E) 139 E
Sitía (GR) 143 K
Sittard (NL) 134 F
Sjas'stroj (RUS) 129 M
Sjenica (SRB) 142 J
Sjöbo (S) 130 M
Skagastrond (IS) 128 A
Skagen (DK) 130 H
Skaidi (N) 129 B
Skaill (GB) 132 C
Skála (GR) 143 K
Skála Oropoú (GR) 143 G
Skálavik (DK) 130 K
Skalbmierz (PL) 144 H
Skalotí (GR) 142 L
Skælskør (DK) 130 L
Skanderborg (DK) 130 H
Skånevik (N) 130 A
Skänninge (S) 130 F
Skanörmed Falsterbo (S) 130 L
Skara (S) 130 F
Skærbæk (DK) 130 K
Skaréysko-Kamienna (PL) 144 E
Skarnes (N) 130 B
Skegness (GB) 133 D
Skei (N) 128 H
Skei (N) 128 L
Skellefteå (S) 129 G
Skelleftehamn (S) 129 G
Ski (N) 130 B
Skiathos (GR) 143 G
Skibbereen (IRL) 133 E
Skibotn (N) 129 A
Skidal' (BLR) 144 C
Skídra (GR) 143 B
Skien (N) 130 E
Skierniewice (PL) 144 E
Skillingaryd (S) 130 J
Skipton (GB) 133 C
Skíros (GR) 143 G
Skive (DK) 130 H
Skjern (DK) 130 G
Skjervøy (N) 129 A
Skjolden (N) 128 L
Skoczów (PL) 144 G
Skógar (IS) 128 D
Skole (UA) 144 J
Skópelos (GR) 143 G
Skopje (MK) 142 J
Skopun (DK) 130 K
Skórcz (PL) 144 A
Skotterud (N) 128 M
Skövde (S) 130 F
Skradin (HR) 140 G
Skrīveri (LV) 131 J
Skrunda (LV) 131 H
Skudeneshavn (N) 130 D
Skuodas (LT) 131 H
Skutvik (N) 128 F
Skwierzyna (PL) 135 F
Slagelse (DK) 130 L
Slagnäs (S) 129 G
Slaný (CZ) 135 H
Slatina (HR) 140 D
Slatina (RO) 142 G
Slavonski Brod (HR) 140 H
Sława (PL) 135 F
Sławatycze (PL) 144 F
Sławno (PL) 144 A
Sleaford (GB) 133 D
Sligo/Sligeach (IRL) 132 J
Šlissel'burg (RUS) 129 M
Slite (S) 131 G
Sliven (BG) 142 M
Slivnica (BG) 142 K
Slobozia (RO) 142 G
Slobozia (RO) 142 D
Slonim (BLR) 144 C
Slovenska Bistrica (SLO) 140 C
Słubice (PL) 135 F
Slunj (HR) 140 G
Słupsk (PL) 144 A
Smålandsstenar (S) 130 J
Smederevo (SRB) 142 E
Smjadovo (BG) 142 H
Smoljan (BG) 142 L
Smygehamn (S) 130 M
Sneek (NL) 134 C
Sobra (HR) 140 M
Sobrance (SK) 144 L
Sochaczew (PL) 144 D
Socuéllamos (E) 138 J
Sodankylä (FIN) 129 E
Soderfors (S) 131 A
Söderhamn (S) 129 K
Söderköping (S) 131 D
Södertälje (S) 131 D
Soest (D) 134 F
Sofija (BG) 142 K
Sofporog (RUS) 129 F
Sogndal (N) 130 A
Soini (FIN) 129 H
Soissons (F) 136 C
Sokal' (UA) 144 J
Söke (TR) 143 H
Soko Banja (SRB) 142 F
Sokółka (PL) 144 C
Sokolniki (PL) 144 D
Sokołów Podlaski (PL) 144 E
Solares (E) 138 C
Solenzara (F) 137 M
Solingen (D) 134 F
Sollebrunn (S) 130 F
Sollefteå (S) 129 G
Sóller (E) 139 E
Sollerön (S) 130 C
Solothurn (CH) 137 B
Solt (H) 140 D
Soltau (D) 135 A
Solund (N) 130 A
Sölvesborg (S) 130 M
Soma (TR) 143 D
Sombernon (F) 137 A
Sombor (SRB) 142 A
Somero (FIN) 129 L
Sommesous (F) 136 C
Soncino (I) 140 E
Sønderborg (DK) 130 L
Sondershausen (D) 135 D
Søndervig (DK) 130 G
Sóndrio (I) 140 A
Sonneberg (D) 135 G
Sonthofen (D) 135 K
Sopot (PL) 144 A
Şopotu Nou (RO) 142 F
Sopron (H) 144 K
Sora (I) 141 B
Soråker (S) 129 K
Sore (F) 136 H
Soria (E) 138 C
Sorø (DK) 130 L
Sørreisa (N) 129 A
Sorrento (I) 141 C
Sorsele (S) 129 G
Sortland (N) 128 F
Sørvågen (N) 128 F
Sørvágur (DK) 130 K
Sørvika (N) 128 M
Sosnovyj (RUS) 129 F
Sosnovyj Bor (RUS) 129 M
Sosnowiec (PL) 144 G
Sotillo de la Adrada (E) 138 F
Sotkamo (FIN) 129 H
Souflí (GR) 142 M
Souillac (F) 136 J
Soulac-sur-Mer (F) 136 H
Soúnio (GR) 143 G
Sour-el-Ghozlane (DZ) 139 M
Soúrpi (GR) 143 F
Southampton (GB) 133 G
Southend-on-Sea (GB) 133 H
Southport (GB) 133 C
South Shields (GB) 132 L
Søvaerøy (N) 128 F
Sovata (RO) 142 C
Soverato (I) 141 H
Soveria Mannelli (I) 141 H
Sovetsk (RUS) 131 L
Sozopol (BG) 142 M
Spa (B) 134 J
Spalding (GB) 133 D
Spárti (GR) 143 K
Spasskaja Guba (RUS) 129 J
Spétses (GR) 143 L
Speyer (D) 134 J
Spezzano Albanese (I) 141 G
Spilsby (GB) 133 D
Spinazzola (I) 141 C
Spišské Podhradie (SK) 144 H
Spittal an der Drau (A) 140 B
Split (HR) 140 M
Splügen (CH) 137 E
Spodsbjerg (DK) 130 L
Spoleto (I) 140 K
Spondigna/Spondinig (I) 140 A
Spotorno (I) 137 H
Srbica (KOS) 142 J
Srbobran (SRB) 142 A
Srebârna (BG) 142 H
Sredec (BG) 142 L
Sredec (BG) 142 M
Sremska Mitrovica (SRB) 142 E
Środa Śliska (PL) 135 F
Środa Wlkopolska (PL) 144 D
Staðarhólskirkja (IS) 128 A
Stade (D) 135 A
Stadskanaal (NL) 134 C
Stafford (GB) 133 C
Stainach (A) 135 L
Staines (GB) 133 H
Stalowa Wola (PL) 144 H
Stambolijski (BG) 142 L
Stamford (GB) 133 D
Stamsund (N) 128 F
Starachowice (PL) 144 E
Stará L'ubovňa (SK) 144 H
Stara Novalja (HR) 140 G
Stara Reka (BG) 142 G
Staravina (MK) 143 B
Stara Zagora (BG) 142 L
Stargard Szczeciński (PL) 135 C
Starigrad-Paklenica (HR) 140 G
Starnberg (D) 135 K
Starogard Gdański (PL) 144 A
Staro Orjahovo (BG) 142 H
Stary Dzierzgoń (PL) 144 A
Staryj Sambir (UA) 144 J
Staszów (PL) 144 H
Stavanger (N) 130 D
Stavenhagen (D) 135 B
Stavern (N) 130 E
Stavoren (NL) 134 C
Stavrós (GR) 143 C
Steenbergen (NL) 134 E
Steenwijk (NL) 134 C
Stege (DK) 130 L
Steinbukt (N) 129 B
Steinkjer (N) 128 J
Stenay (F) 134 H
Stenby (S) 130 F
Stendal (D) 135 E
Stení (GR) 143 G
Stenungsund (S) 130 E
Sternberg (D) 135 B
Stérnes (GR) 143 J
Stęszew (PL) 144 D
Stettin (Szczecin) (PL) 135 C
Steyr (A) 135 M
Stigliano (I) 141 D
Stilída (GR) 143 F
Štimlje (KOS) 142 J
Štip (MK) 142 K
Stíra (GR) 143 G
Stirling (GB) 132 F
Stjørdal (N) 128 J
Stockach (D) 135 K
Stockerau (A) 135 M
Stockholm (S) 131 D
Stockport (GB) 133 C
Stockton-on-Tees (GB) 132 L
Stöde (S) 129 K
Stoke-on-Trent (GB) 133 C
Stokite (BG) 142 L
Stokmarknes (N) 128 F
Stolac (BIH) 140 M
Stöllet (S) 128 M
Stómio (GR) 143 B
Ston (HR) 140 M
Stonehaven (GB) 132 G
Storå (S) 130 F
Storby (FIN) 129 K
Støren (N) 128 J
Storfors (S) 130 F
Storforshei (N) 128 G
Stórinúpur (IS) 128 D
Storlien (S) 128 J
Stornoway (GB) 132 B
Storslett (N) 129 A
Storuman (S) 129 G
Storvik (S) 131 A
Støvring (DK) 130 H
Strabane (GB) 132 J
Strakonice (CZ) 135 H
Straldža (BG) 142 M
Stralsund (D) 130 M
Stranda (N) 128 L
Strangford (GB) 132 K
Strängnäs (S) 131 D
Stranraer (GB) 132 K
Strasbourg (F) 137 B
Straßwalchen (A) 135 L
Stratford-upon-Avon (GB) 133 C
Stratóni (GR) 143 C
Straubing (D) 135 L
Street (GB) 133 G
Strehaia (RO) 142 F
Strenči (LV) 131 F
Stříbro (CZ) 135 H
Strimasund (S) 128 F
Strofiliá (GR) 143 G
Stromness (GB) 132 C
Strömstad (S) 130 E
Strömsund (S) 129 G
Strontian (GB) 132 F
Struer (DK) 130 G
Struga (AL) 143 A
Strumica (MK) 142 K
Stryi (UA) 144 J
Stryn (N) 128 L
Strzelno (PL) 144 D
Strzyżów (PL) 144 H
Stubbekøbing (DK) 130 L
Stuben (A) 137 C
Stuttgart (D) 135 K
Stugun (S) 129 G
Stykkishólmur (IS) 128 A
Subiaco (I) 141 B
Subotica (SRB) 142 A
Sučeviči (HR) 140 G
Sucha Beskidżka (PL) 144 G
Sućuraj (HR) 140 M
Sudbury (GB) 133 D
Şugag (RO) 142 B
Şuhl (D) 135 G
Suica (BIH) 140 H
Suippes (F) 137 A
Sukkozero (RUS) 129 J
Sulechów (PL) 135 F
Sulejów (PL) 144 D
Sulingen (D) 135 D
Sulitjelma (N) 129 D
Sulmona (I) 140 L
Sulzbach-Rosenberg (D) 135 H
Sumartin (HR) 140 M
Şümeg (H) 140 D
Şumen (BG) 142 H
Šumperk (CZ) 135 J
Sund (N) 128 F
Sundby (DK) 130 G
Sunde (N) 130 A
Sunderland (GB) 132 L
Sundsvall (S) 129 K
Sunndalsøra (N) 128 L
Sunne (S) 130 C
Suojarvi (RUS) 129 M
Suomussalmi (FIN) 129 H
Suonenjoki (FIN) 129 L
Supetar (HR) 140 M
Supurude Jos (RO) 144 M
Surdulica (SRB) 142 K
Surgères (F) 136 E
Sursee (CH) 137 B
Susa (I) 137 E
Susch (CH) 137 C
Sušica (BG) 142 G
Şuşteşti (RO) 142 D
Šusurluk (TR) 143 D
Sutme (S) 128 J
Sutomore (MNE) 142 J
Sutterton (GB) 133 D
Suwałki (PL) 144 B
Svaliava (UA) 144 M
Svanstein (S) 129 E
Svappavaara (S) 129 D
Svartnäs (S) 131 A
Svati Rok (HR) 140 G
Svédasai (LT) 131 M
Sveg (S) 128 M
Svelvik (N) 130 E
Svendborg (DK) 130 L
Svenes (N) 130 D
Svenljunga (S) 130 J
Svenstavik (S) 128 M
Sveštari (BG) 142 H
Svetlogorsk (RUS) 131 L
Svetogorsk (RUS) 129 M
Svetozarevo (SRB) 142 E
Svidnik (SK) 144 H
Svilengrad (BG) 142 L
Svinesund (S) 130 E
Svištov (BG) 142 G
Svitavy (CZ) 135 J
Svođe (SRB) 142 K
Svoge (BG) 142 K
Svolvær (N) 128 F
Swanage (GB) 133 G
Swansea (GB) 133 F
Świdnica (PL) 135 J
Świdnica (PL) 135 J
Świebodzin (PL) 135 F
Świecie (PL) 144 A
Swindon (GB) 133 G
Świnoujście (PL) 135 C
Swinoujscie (PL) 135 J
Syke (D) 135 A
Sysslebäck (S) 130 C
Szadek (PL) 144 D
Szarvas (H) 142 A
Szczecinek (PL) 144 A
Szczecin (Stettin) (PL) 135 C
Szczerców (PL) 144 D
Szczucin (PL) 144 H
Szczytno (PL) 144 B
Szécsény (H) 144 K
Szeged (H) 142 A
Szeghalom (H) 144 L
Székesfehérvár (H) 144 K
Szekszárd (H) 140 D
Szentes (H) 142 A
Szentlőrinc (H) 140 D
Szigetvár (H) 140 D
Szolnok (H) 144 L
Szombathely (H) 144 K
Szprotawa (PL) 135 F

T

Tábara (E) 138 B
Tabernas (E) 139 K
Tábor (CZ) 135 J
Tafalla (E) 139 A
Tain (GB) 132 B
Tain-l'Hermitage (F) 137 G
Taivalkoski (FIN) 129 E
Taivassalo (FIN) 129 K
Taizé (F) 137 D
Talamone (I) 140 J
Talavera de la Reina (E) 138 E
Tallinn (Reval) (EST) 131 F
Tălmaciu (RO) 142 C
Talmont-Saint-Hilaire (F) 136 E
Talpaki (RUS) 131 L
Talsi (LV) 131 J
Tamarite de Litera (E) 139 A
Tamási (H) 140 D
Tampere (FIN) 129 L
Tamsweg (A) 140 C
Tanabru (N) 129 B
Tăndărei (RO) 142 D
Tangen (N) 130 B
Tanger (Tanjah) (MA) 138 L
Tangermünde (D) 135 E
Tännäs (S) 128 M
Tannila (FIN) 129 H
Tanumshede (S) 130 E
Taormina (I) 141 L
Tapa (EST) 131 F
Tarancón (E) 138 F
Táranto (I) 141 D
Tarare (F) 137 D
Tarascon (F) 137 G
Tarascon (F) 136 M
Tarazona (E) 139 A
Tarbert (GB) 132 B
Tarbert (IRL) 133 A
Tarbes (F) 136 L
Tarbet (GB) 132 F
Tärendö (S) 129 D
Târgovište (BG) 142 G
Târgovişte (RO) 142 C
Târgu Jiu (RO) 142 B
Târgu Mureş (Neumarkt) (RO) 142 C
Târgu Ocna (RO) 142 C
Târgu Secuiesc (RO) 142 C
Tarifa (E) 138 L
Tärnaby (S) 128 J
Târnăveni (RO) 142 B
Tarnobrzeg (PL) 144 H
Tarnogród (PL) 144 H
Tarnów (PL) 144 H
Tarquinia (I) 140 K
Tarragona (E) 139 E
Tàrrega (E) 139 B
Tårs (DK) 130 L
Tartas (F) 136 H
Tărtăşeşti (RO) 142 G
Tarutyne (UA) 142 D
Tarvisio (I) 140 B
Tăşnad (RO) 144 M
Tata (H) 144 K
Tatabánya (H) 144 K
Tatarbunary (UA) 142 D
Tatranská-Lomnica (SK) 144 H
Tau (N) 130 D
Tauberbischofsheim (D) 135 G
Taunton (GB) 133 G
Tauragė (LT) 131 M
Tavannes (CH) 137 B
Tavernes (F) 137 H
Tavira (P) 138 K
Tavistock (GB) 133 F
Tczew (PL) 144 A
Tecuci (RO) 142 D
Teius (RO) 142 B
Tekirdağ (TR) 142 M
Telč (CZ) 135 M
Telford (GB) 133 C
Tels (A) 137 C
Telšiai (LT) 131 J
Tembleque (E) 138 F
Témpio Pausánia (I) 141 E
Tenala (Tenhola) (FIN) 131 C
Tende (F) 137 H
Ténès (DZ) 139 L
Tenterden (GB) 133 H
Tepelenë (AL) 143 A
Teplice (CZ) 135 H
Téramo (I) 140 K
Ter Apel (NL) 134 C
Teregova (RO) 142 B
Términi Imerese (I) 141 K
Térmoli (I) 141 C
Terneuzen (NL) 134 E
Terni (I) 140 K
Ternitz (A) 135 M
Terracina (I) 141 B
Terrassa/Tarrasa (E) 139 B
Teruel (E) 139 D
Tervel (BG) 142 H
Tervola (FIN) 129 E
Teslić (BIH) 140 H
Tetbury (GB) 133 G
Teterow (D) 135 B
Teteven (BG) 142 L
Tetovo (MK) 142 J
Teulada (I) 141 J
Thann (F) 137 B
Thássos (GR) 143 C
Thenia (DZ) 139 M
Theniet el-Had (DZ) 139 L
Thérmi (GR) 143 B
Thérmo (GR) 143 F
Thermopiles (GR) 143 F
Thessaloníki (GR) 143 B
Thetford (GB) 133 D
Theth (AL) 142 J
Thiene (I) 140 B
Thiers (F) 137 D
Thionville (F) 134 H
Thíra (GR) 143 M
Thirsk (GB) 133 D
Thisted (DK) 130 G
Thíva (GR) 143 G
Thomastown (IRL) 133 B
Thonon (F) 137 D
Thornhill (GB) 132 L
Thouars (F) 136 E
Thun (CH) 137 E
Thurles (IRL) 133 A
Thurso (GB) 132 C
Thusis (CH) 137 B
Thyborøn (DK) 130 G
Tiefencastel (CH) 137 C
Tielt (B) 134 E
Tierp (S) 129 K
Tigănaşi (RO) 142 F
Tihany (H) 140 D
Tihvin (RUS) 129 M
Tikša (RUS) 129 J
Tilburg (NL) 134 E
Tilbury (GB) 133 H
Til-Châtel (F) 137 A
Timau (I) 140 B
Timbáki (GR) 143 J
Timişoara (RO) 142 A
Timrå (S) 129 K
Tinca (RO) 142 B
Tineo (E) 138 B
Tinglev (DK) 130 K
Tingsryd (S) 130 J
Tínos (GR) 143 G
Tionedi Trento (I) 140 A
Tipperary (IRL) 133 A
Tiranë (AL) 143 A
Tirano (I) 140 A
Tire (TR) 143 H
Tîrgu Lăpuş (RO) 144 M
Tírnavos (GR) 143 B
Tirschenreuth (D) 135 H
Tissemsilt (DZ) 139 L
Tiszaföldvár (H) 142 A
Tiszafüred (H) 144 L
Titov Veles (MK) 142 K
Titran (N) 128 H
Titu (RO) 142 G
Tivat (MNE) 142 J
Tiverton (GB) 133 G
Tivoli (I) 141 B
Tizi Ouzou (DZ) 139 M
Tjåmotis (S) 129 D
Tjøme (N) 130 E
Tjong (N) 128 F
Tjøtta (N) 128 J
Tlumach (UA) 144 J
Tobarra (E) 139 G
Tobelbad (A) 140 C
Tobermory (GB) 132 F
Töcksfors (S) 130 E
Todi (I) 140 K
Toft (GB) 132 D
Tofta (S) 130 J
Toftlund (DK) 130 K
Toholampi (FIN) 129 H
Tokaj (H) 144 L
Tokari (RUS) 129 M
Toledo (E) 138 F
Tolmezzo (I) 140 B
Tolosa (E) 139 A
Tolvojarvi (RUS) 129 J
Tomar (P) 138 G
Tomaszów Lubelski (PL) 144 J
Tomaszów Mazowiecki (PL) 144 D
Tomelilla (S) 130 M
Tomelloso (E) 138 J
Tømmervåg (N) 128 H
Tonbridge (GB) 133 H
Tondela (P) 138 D
Tønder (DK) 130 K
Tongeren (B) 134 E
Tongue (GB) 132 B
Tonnerre (F) 137 A
Tønsberg (N) 130 E
Tonstad (N) 130 D
Topola (SRB) 142 E
Topol'čany (SK) 144 K
Topolog (RO) 142 D
Topolovgrad (BG) 142 M
Toral de los Vados (E) 138 B
Torbali (TR) 143 H
Torbay (GB) 133 G
Törberget (N) 130 B
Tordesillas (E) 138 E
Töre (S) 129 H
Töreboda (S) 130 F
Torgau (D) 135 E
Torhout (B) 134 E
Torino (I) 137 E
Tornal'a (SK) 144 L
Tornio (FIN) 129 E
Toro (E) 138 E
Törökszentmiklós (H) 144 L
Torpoint (GB) 133 K
Torralba (I) 141 J
Torrão (P) 138 G
Torre Annunziata (I) 141 C
Torre Baja (E) 139 D
Torreblanca (E) 139 E
Torre de la Higuera (E) 138 L
Torre del Campo (E) 138 J
Torre del Greco (I) 141 C
Torredembarra (E) 139 E
Torre de Moncorvo (P) 138 E
Torrejón el Rubio (E) 138 E
Torrelavega (E) 138 C
Torremolinos (E) 138 M
Torrent (E) 139 G
Torres Vedras (P) 138 G
Torrevieja (E) 139 G
Torrijos (E) 138 F
Torroella de Montgrí (E) 139 C
Torsby (S) 128 M
Tórshavn (Thorshavn) (DK) 130 K
Torsvåg (N) 129 A
Tórtoles de Esgueva (E) 138 C
Tortoli (I) 141 J
Tortona (I) 140 E
Tortosa (E) 139 E
Toruń (PL) 144 A
Tosno (RUS) 129 M
Tossa de Mar (E) 139 C
Tõstamaa (EST) 131 F
Tótes (F) 134 G
Tótkomlós (H) 142 A
Totnes (GB) 133 G
Toucy (F) 136 C
Toul (F) 137 A
Toulon (F) 137 G
Toulon-sur-Arroux (F) 137 D
Toulouse (F) 136 J
Tourcoing (B) 134 E